"With *Roots and Rhythm*, my fellow improviser Charlie Peacock is at it again—this time, depositing profoundly thoughtful, impactful words of beauty and insight into God's big heart for music and justice. By all means read this book."

—**Kirk Whalum**, Grammy Award–winning
jazz saxophonist and composer

"Working with Charlie Peacock in the studio and on stage changed the artistic trajectory of my life. . . . I'm excited that he's finally telling his story and I know it will inspire others."

—**Michael Roe**, singer-songwriter, cofounder of The 77s

"*Roots and Rhythm* is Exhibit A of a life well and fully lived."

—**Brent Bourgeois**, solo artist, member of Bourgeois Tagg and
cowriter of "I Don't Mind at All"

"Lyrically written and richly textured, *Roots and Rhythm* is the best sort of memoir: captivating, entertaining, and subtly coaxing readers to live their own lives more wholeheartedly."

—**Kristin Kobes Du Mez**, *New York Times* bestselling author of
Jesus and John Wayne

"*Roots and Rhythm* is the play of youth with the wisdom of age merging into a beautiful fireworks show. We all desperately need the sorts of honest, sage stories Charlie tells about the artful life—to see, in ourselves, the merging of the girl in the woman, the boy in the man, simultaneously growing more playful, imaginative, and wise."

—**Sara Groves**, recording artist and cofounder of Art House North

"With wit and transparency rooted in hard-won wisdom and insight, Peacock narrates the rhythms of his story and the artistry and anguish of his ancestors. Charlie's story as a musician, artist, author, and activist is that of a vibrant life interwoven with generations of hardship, beauty, and love."

—**Leah Payne**, author of *God Gave Rock and Roll to You:
A History of Contemporary Christian Music*

"Charlie Peacock's fluid, free-form narrative is infused with earnestness, poetic style, and heart. Most rewardingly, it reveals how his relationships, faith, and philosophical ideas have fundamentally shaped his unique and fascinating life in popular music."

—**Scott Derrickson**, director, producer, and screenwriter

"Charlie Peacock is a musician who defies labels, categories, and genres. . . . I love how we make music together—how he makes everyone feel welcome. But what I love most is his indomitable spirit and sparkle."

—**Jeff Coffin**, Grammy Award–winning saxophonist, solo artist, educator, and member of Dave Matthews Band

"Charlie rearranged all our lives musically when his Planet of Cyborgs vessel descended on ole Music City back in '89. . . . He is that rare class of musician who becomes the obsession of other musicians. And I'm not just referencing the novices; I'm speaking of musicians who are among the most skilled and decorated practitioners of the art, on this planet or any other."

—**Tommy Sims**, Grammy Award–winning songwriter, musician, and producer

"With rare understanding of the nexus of imagination and the marketplace, *Roots and Rhythm* offers philosophical and theological insight into Charlie's unique pilgrimage as an artist of unparalleled creativity and surprising generosity, nurturing the hearts and minds of a generation of singers and songwriters who long to learn from the master."

—**Steven Garber**, Senior Fellow for Vocation and the Common Good, M. J. Murdock Charitable Trust; author of *The Seamless Life: A Tapestry of Love and Learning, Worship and Work*

ROOTS & RHYTHM

A Life in Music

Charlie Peacock

William B. Eerdmans Publishing Company

Grand Rapids, Michigan

Wm. B. Eerdmans Publishing Co.
2006 44th Street SE, Grand Rapids, MI 49508
www.eerdmans.com

Book design by Lydia Hall

Printed in the United States of America

31 30 29 28 27 26 25   1 2 3 4 5 6 7

ISBN 978-0-8028-8437-4

Library of Congress Cataloging-in-Publication Data

Names: Peacock, Charlie, author.
Title: Roots and rhythm : a life in music / Charlie Peacock.
Description: Grand Rapids : Wm. B. Eerdmans Publishing Co., 2025. |
    Summary: "A musician reflects on the ways his art has been shaped by
    his family, the music industry, and a lifelong quest for creative expression
    that has led to deeper connections with God and the world"—Provided by
    publisher.
Identifiers: LCCN 2024018206 | ISBN 9780802884374 (hardcover) |
    ISBN 9781467468619 (epub)
Subjects: LCSH: Peacock, Charlie. | Peacock, Charlie—Religion. | Sound
    recording executives and producers—United States—Biography. | Musi-
    cians—United States—Biography. | LCGFT: Autobiographies.
Classification: LCC ML429.P343 A3 2025 | DDC 781.64092 [B]—
    dc23/eng/20240501
LC record available at https://lccn.loc.gov/2024018206

All photographs courtesy of the Charles and Andrea Ashworth Collection. Spe-
cial thanks to these talented photographer friends: Allister Ann, Jeremy Cowart,
Stephen Dean Holsapple, Kent Lacin, Jenae Medford, Joann Nazworthy, Ben
Pearson, David Roberts, and Michon Roberts.

CONTENTS

v

Contents

PRELUDE

I was gifted with a childhood defined by dirt.

I lived in a small white house on Whyler Road, next to the Yuba City livestock auction. Cattle grazed to the left of our home while peaches ripened across the road, their rootstock drinking deep the irrigation held tight by a patchwork of checks. Farther away, fertile clods gave way to varicose earth, hot and unfriendly. Everywhere a chicken—even today. Jackrabbits bounced like kick balls through the foxtail barley and star thistle. Three miles west as the crow flies, my grandma's house was surrounded by walnut and almond orchards.

The dirt stayed hopeful, even when the mud, wet from pump water, morphed into cracked crust and barley stubble, always one spark away from destruction. A mile farther west from Grandma's house was my great-grandparents' subsistence farm where the dirt did its earthy work of supporting banty chickens, turkeys, nervous goats, and watermelon vines.

All the way to the Sutter Buttes was field after field of dirt. Some of it chapped and sun-abused, the balance well loved. Every square foot farmed by a community of belief, a collective trust that the land would give food if they gave themselves to the land. And that's the way it was and is.

As a young child I only saw dirt. Then I saw the land and, eventually, place. A place of significance and meaning—a place that was in me as I was in it.

—

The land of my place on earth is filled with trees of extraordinary variety. A tree is the most potent physical symbol I can conjure to explain the serendipity, the interdependence and interconnectedness, that has been my life. So let's begin with roots, gnarly but spread wide, hidden deep in the soil of circumstance. These distribution networks, hosted by mother trees, are in the business of mutual flourishing, cosmic betterment, giving life to innumerable species for miles and miles. They converse in the unseen world. Unseen, that is, unless you're a grub, a mole, or an artist looking for something true: "I'm going down to Mystic, Louisiana, looking for the meaning in the dirt." A song I sang when I went looking for a place I'd never lived in, though it lived in me.

This book is about one artistic life rooted in America's soil, shame, and success. A life planted in the Northern California farm town of Yuba City and bent on surviving anywhere, including Nashville, Tennessee. Some roots were unpredictable and unverifiable before the advent of DNA access, but nevertheless they shaped the fruit of my life. In fact, the soil of soul, place, and past shaped me before I could offer permission, awareness, or appreciation at all.

This talk of trees and the land of my people is not a mere literary device. Trees my family planted, pruned, picked, logged, sawed, and revered—and in the case of my great-grandfather from Mystic, Louisiana, died for. They are part of who I am. Consider my roots. A dancing, gambling, Okie grandfather who liked to sing in that dust-bowl, reedy tone. The aforementioned great-grandparents, poor subsistence farmers, kindly feeding hungry hobos riding boxcars east and west just across the road from their patchwork house. I am the great-grandson of a cattle rancher in antebellum Texas, and fifty years later, a Louisiana piney-wood logger playing fiddle and a resonator guitar.

And so from those roots came the above-ground icon, the broad, firm trunk committed to holding the weight of the story past and yet to unfold. From the trunk skyward, artful branches grew, perfect in symmetry and randomness, embodying my hopes and dreams. My past—the roots—is evident in each tender, unique leaf in the now. The deep seeks the surface, seeks the sky, seeks transcendence.

Prelude

This book is about a journey to hold on to place and people with reverence, because before I made any music, those places and people made me—just as sure as roots make leaves. It's about sky-high dreams and transcendence too—about making my mark upon the earth and leaving a story for my children, grandchildren (Robert, Brinsley, Alfie, and Bridget), and those yet to come.

Though our lives are sure to be infinitely different, I hope you will find kinship in these stories, a love and care for people and planet, clues to an artful life, and maybe even a thing or two to learn from my prodigious mistakes. Because people and past are shaping you too, right? We're all swaying in the forest of family, place, and time. Conserving, pruning, protecting, and observing this forest for the trees is how we all breathe better now, and in the future. I hope that my journey of discovery and artistry will help you to examine your own life for its intricate wonder, its interconnectedness, and its inestimable value.

There's nothing neutral about place or the dirt under it. Put that theme in your pocket. There's a bit of it on every page.

—

From the outset, I had a structural/creative vision for the book based on my experience reading the stories of musicians (knowing what I liked and didn't). I determined that my chapters would not be chronological, and composition would blend jazz-like improvisation and tangential riffs. I've tried to build in handles so you can hang on for the ride. While my bent is literary, I've kept music fans who love anecdotes and minutiae in mind. And though it is more often associated with biography than memoir, I've included a robust discography for historians and self-professed music nerds. All in all, this book is a chapter-by-chapter remix of the music, places, and people that made me and the music I made.

This journey includes how an Ashworth became a Peacock; the origin story of my people and place, of the nature and nurture that caused my inevitable collision with ancestry and artistry, and the God of the Bible. The text is exposition and development, requiem and concerto, folk song and jazz. The early NorCal days, Exit Records, the CCM genre, pop hits, jazz, indie rock, and the Folk Americana boom early in the twenty-first century all make appearances. Three distinctly American places are featured: California, the Texas/Louisiana southern border region, and *Music City*, Nashville, Tennessee. Each one, a cradle of history. I name names and tell tales.

Throughout, I offer an artist's view of the rhythm, drama, and rewards of being a musician, songwriter, and music producer. It's a dream job, a calling, one that's allowed me to travel extensively and collaborate with incredible artists—but it's not for people who shy away from complexity or difficult decisions, or those eager to close up shop at 5:30 p.m. You can get the gig and prosper even if you're flawed and wounded (I am both), as long as you're even more resilient.

Returning to the tree metaphor, these are stories of trauma and resilience—trees scarred by lightning, severed branches, and names crudely carved in their skin. Yet, somehow, still bearing fruit. And that is the story of grace.

Threaded through this book is a name, *Andi*, a nickname for Andrea. While *Roots & Rhythm* tells the story of an artist's life and ancestry, there is no deeply rooted story without Andi. We have been writing a collective narrative, laboring side by side, for over half a century—since we were fifteen years old. In our economy, neither of us is making a contribution more important than the other. Marriage and meaningful life are a team sport. But if you must place someone forward as you read—a hero, a most valuable player—let it be her. This would please me to no end. For more on our mutual life, I would point you to *Why Everything That Doesn't Matter, Matters So Much: The Way of Love in a World of Hurt* (Harper Collins W, 2024).

Now, having offered some clues as to what this book is, I want to also be clear on what it isn't. This is not a celebrity musician book. I have many good ones in my library, but I am neither a proper celebrity nor interested in the literary conventions of that genre. I am an artist first, a writer, a concerned citizen, and a storyteller. I trust I've written the sort of hybrid memoir that only I could bring into the world. Isn't that the point of sitting down to write? And unlike truly famous musicians, I am "just well known"—an accurate description coined by my young daughter years ago.

Prelude

I am content with this station in life. It is all part of the outworking of a spiritual and artistic plot. One true to my roots and rhythm. Besides, fame is not all it's cracked up to be. Sure, if you're looking for an idea or a person to energize whatever it is you're selling or defending, fame has a form of power, a currency. Not every person or thing benefits from being scaled from one to a zillion, though. Now that I've worked for entertainment corporations for forty-plus years, I know I wouldn't have. Though my musical-artist career has never been more visible (thanks to streaming), most of my work has been quiet and behind the curtain, writing and producing music for the unknown and little-known, more well-known and, yes, the famous.

I've learned there are different economies at work. I enjoy a good wage and quantifiable success as much as the next person. But I find myself less interested in platform than in what poet-farmer Wendell Berry called *the Great Economy*. He wrote, "The Great Economy, like the Tao or the Kingdom of God, is both known and unknown, visible and invisible, comprehensible and mysterious." It is the "ultimate condition of our experience" on earth, where practical questions naturally arise from our experience. It is an economy of people, place, and things with more questions than answers.

Berry's poetic punch line? We are all implicated to give ourselves to the questions, and our consideration of those questions involves an "extremity of seriousness and an extremity of humility."[1] This book is documentation of me giving myself to the questions while incrementally living into the answers—all in the context of family, place, and art.

Emerging as a music artist, songwriter, and producer in the compact-disc era was a unique dispensation of good fortune—a sonic and technological landgrab. The first CD was a 1982 album by Swedish pop group Abba. And in the following years, everyone with the slightest bit of commercial success made money.

Yet, by 2004, Napster and file-sharing were eating the industry's lunch. The world had changed, and the music business with it. The golden ring had fallen from the carousel. I wondered if we'd ever see gold records again, let alone multiplatinum.

Gratefully, I've held that golden ring a few times. Perhaps just the right number of times. I've also suffered many disappointments building a lifetime career—some the result of my own doing, others foisted upon me by others. A few have absolutely wrecked me, created doubt in the wee hours of the morning, and put me in the ditch. All in all, my experiences are no worse than those of others—they're just mine.

I've learned to hold this music business thing lightly, to understand that opportunities are never as unique as I may think. Disappointments, never as bad as they feel. Accolades, meaningful but mostly vaporous.

—

In Texas and Louisiana, where some of my ancestors lived, there's a pine tree called loblolly. The word means "mire" or "mudhole." These trees grow in murky waters, but they're also excellent at reclaiming land that was cleared for farming. That's me: gaining clarity, reclaiming lost history, and growing from it.

Today I find myself embarking on a new time in life, one in which I'm allergic to power and done with empire building (thankfully), where I live with a years-long headache due to a neurological disorder, and where I find myself in the rusty buckle of the Bible Belt during one of the most contentious times in America's history. I have some thoughts and stories. And, as an editor friend assured me, I have the gray hair and the longer, deeper experience to tell those thoughts and stories. I hope she's right and that you'll grace me with a read and listen.

By reading and finding your own story within mine, we take the *me, me, me* out of memoir and replace it with the Great Economy's *we, we, we*. Good work if we can get it. I believe we can and will.

Charlie Peacock
Nashville, Tennessee

one

THE UNCIVIL WAR

On Tuesday, August 13, 2013, the mercurial Grammy-winning duo The Civil Wars debuted their second album atop the *Billboard* 200 chart. Having produced the record, I had bragging rights to the No. 1 album in the land. We bumped Robin Thicke's *Blurred Lines* out of the top spot and took our rightful place in pop music history. One more achievement irrefutably complete.

My dad, a gifted music teacher, had done his best to discourage me from trying to make it in pop music. It was too much of a long shot. Be a teacher, he said. Much more of a sure thing. For decades I worked to prove him wrong. I was the sure thing. I didn't need anything to fall back on. This latest trophy would remove any lingering doubts. Hard to know, though. Dad had been at rest in the Sutter Cemetery since Christmas of 1992.

I've been in the Top 40 of any music chart that counts many times in my serpentine career, but never No. 1 on the *Billboard* Top 200 album charts. This was rarefied air. Two decades earlier, I'd come close on the singles chart, which also ensures your tiny slice of pop music history. "Every Heartbeat" (cowritten with Amy Grant and Wayne Kirkpatrick) was a No. 2 pop single for Amy on the *Billboard* Top 100. Lamentably, Bryan Adams's soft-rock power ballad "(Everything I Do) I Do It for You" would not give up the No. 1 spot. Featured on the soundtrack album from the 1991 film *Robin Hood: Prince of*

Thieves, Bryan's song spent seven long weeks at No. 1. The album sold fifteen million copies worldwide. Fair enough. Amy's record would go on to sell a respectable five million.

That Tuesday at the top of the charts should've been filled with ecstatic celebrations. Imagine a party thrown by Columbia Records, famous friends present and accounted for, toasts all around, goodwill, and irrepressible optimism.

Never happened.

Later that evening, instead of a No. 1 party, we had a simple, somber celebration with Joy Williams, the female half of The Civil Wars, and her then-husband and manager, Nate Yetton. My encouraging wife, Andi, created a beautiful meal for us—fresh salmon we'd caught only weeks before on the Kenai River in Alaska, roasted okra and squash from our garden, and cherry tomato crostini.

We took our dessert of peach-blueberry crisp and sangria out to the screened-in porch. Over a chorus of cicadas and tree frogs, we pondered aloud what had brought us to such an anticlimactic moment.

At the pinnacle of pop music achievement, The Civil Wars were broken up. Not officially. But in every other way, yes.

Ten months earlier, using the language of divorce, the duo put out one of the more unusual press releases in pop music history. Per the Associated Press on November 7, 2012, "The folk-pop duo Joy Williams and John Paul White released a statement Tuesday announcing that because of 'internal discord and irreconcilable differences of ambition' they were unable to 'continue as a touring entity at this time.'"

The press release served to obfuscate more than clarify, and the fans weren't having any of it. The response ranged from sadness to anger.

Anyone with an up-close relationship with the duo was left reeling. Uncertain future. Vanishing fortune. Like Dean Kay and Kelly Gordon's classic song "That's Life" says: "You're riding high in April, shot down in May."

Even though I'd produced their first gold record, the auspicious *Barton Hollow*, there was no guarantee I'd helm the follow-up. After their successful debut, the world opened up to Joy and John Paul. I was happy for them. They were touring with Adele, featured with

Taylor Swift on the T Bone Burnett–produced hit "Safe and Sound" (for *The Hunger Games*), and sought after by other well-known producers. They'd already cut a few tracks with Rick Rubin at his studio, Shangri La in Malibu. Making the pilgrimage to Rubin's had become a trendy trip in recent years for one artist after another. The Civil Wars got in line.

Rick Rubin is a history-making producer and a thoughtful creator. He played a significant role in the mainstreaming of rap and the curation of Johnny Cash's poignant farewell, and those are just two of his star-bright achievements. Nonetheless, I doubted he'd add anything new to Joy and John Paul, or most importantly, steward the details of their performance at the level I did on their debut. By all accounts, Rick had become more of a guru, mic-dropping wisdom, than an all-in, let's-get-under-the-hood kind of record producer. And so it was. He left the duo with a meaningful trip to Malibu and some good demos.

I was in Tom Mackay's office at Universal Records in Santa Monica when he confidently informed me that T Bone Burnett would be producing the follow-up to *Barton Hollow*. This was the first time I'd met Tom; and he was all up in my business. Doubt draped across my shoulders. I wondered if Tom might be right. After all, T Bone did oversee *The Hunger Games* soundtrack. The song "Safe and Sound" had earned a Grammy, one more luminescent moment for the duo, T Bone, and *The Hunger Games* franchise.

I could feel my eyes burn and my cheeks redden. I pushed every feeling down to the basement of my belly. I learned a long time ago that the caprices of the music industry know no bounds. Only a panic-room mind and a Kevlar heart will do. With my guard up, I flew home to Nashville and turned my attention to the music I actually had some control over—my own.

Then I got the call.

I was asked to City House, a favorite restaurant in Nashville's Germantown neighborhood. I joined The Civil Wars and manager Nate at a table upstairs. Each took a turn explaining to me the particular path they took in choosing a producer for the follow-up to *Barton Hollow*. They had talked to UK producer Ethan Johns, checking his interest. Naturally, T Bone and Rick Rubin were also considered—all talented and decorated record producers. I hung in, listening, waiting for the bottom line.

Both Ethan and T Bone advised the duo to "go back to Charlie." In the view of these two esteemed producers, the artistic ethos wasn't broken, not by a long shot. Why change now?

Joy and John Paul asked if I'd go another round with them. Of course I would. I was audibly relieved.

Little did I know what I was signing up for.

—

Not long after a remarkable Bonnaroo performance, Joy gave birth to her first child. She did what all good mothers do: gave every bit of herself to her new son. When the time was right, we circled up the wagons and started the new record.

Though Joy and John Paul still possessed the gift, something had changed. The magic had been tinkered with. *Rolling Stone* magazine quoted me explaining what I'd sensed: "There was definitely a difference [in the personality dynamic]. I picked up on some sort of tension right from the start, but to me, it seemed like it was about fatigue. . . . I never saw them butt heads on the music."[1] And I didn't.

For *Barton Hollow*, my mission had been simple. Take an artistic, sonic Polaroid of Joy and John Paul doing their thing. Select the best of the performances. Edit and fix as needed. Then carefully overdub other instruments with the hand of a 1950s minimalist painter. Ad Reinhardt, your move.

Immediately, I knew the second record would be different than the first. Several songs were still being written. The fatigue of birth and nonstop touring sat in the room with us like an uninvited visitor. It was clear I'd have to be more hands-on this time out. I'd need to do some song-doctor-type cowriting. I'd have to amp up the positivity. And somehow, without being too invasive, move from a Polaroid aesthetic to something akin to a feature film.

Once under way, we worked hard but wisely, recording for nearly two weeks and never pushing too far into the evening, except to enjoy one of Andi's pleasurable feasts. Then the group and growing entourage prepared for their upcoming tour of the UK and Europe. They had already done some touring in the UK with superstar Adele. That exposure and positive reception, along with their enormous talent, ensured that the new tour would be the massive success we all hoped for.

With The Civil Wars overseas touring and my own American touring dates complete, Andi and I headed to our Northern California house in our hometown of Yuba City. That's where I got the call. The Civil Wars' UK and European victory lap had ended abruptly. Canceled.

Joy and John Paul weren't speaking to each other.

They were coming back to the States. This unexpected turn put the recording in limbo. I hoped it was only a postponement until things were patched up. The possibility that the record might be trashed and unreleased was left unspoken. There was enough hot confusion in the wind, no need to light a match and see the whole thing explode. At least not yet.

—

When I was twenty years old, I told my parents I would not work for their approval—more precisely, my father's approval. One summer, about to turn twenty-one, I camped out at my parents' condo while they were away. Upon their return, there was an argument, a variation on a consistent theme: I'd failed to make good on a responsibility Dad had given me. Upset and disappointed, he made his ultimate concern clear. It was time for me to grow up, take responsibility, be realistic, and quit screwing around.

My mother kept a note I wrote to her and Dad following the episode—one I found among her keepsakes after she passed away.

"As much as I want to show you both that I can succeed in the system, playing my music, caring for my family, this is self-centered greed and not the path of God. Don't push me to show you I'm somebody. I already am, simply by conception."

And yet, I have four decades of cyclical evidence that betrays me and my words in Shakespearean fashion. I feel like the protagonist in Bruce Cockburn's song "Pacing the Cage," having proven my identity so often that the magnetic strip on my ID is worn out. Don't push me? The push was then, and is now, in my blood, marrow, and skin. Genetic, socially constructed, generational, and more complex than my still-developing twenty-year-old brain could have ever conceived. I spent a lifetime captured and bound, pacing the cage, as if it were a long-foretold destiny written, as Bruce sings, in the *constitution of the age*.

Wasn't I at my best when I was pushed? Organizing the chaos, turning the swirl into creativity, order, and beauty? I liked analyzing and fixing problems. More to the point, I loved how I felt when my imagination and analysis were correct, my solutions fixed the problems, and loss was turned into art. I was Superman on a diet of hubris.

—

Sometime during the aftermath of the canceled tour and lingering bewilderment, it was decided that I would finish the record. By myself. No more arting from the artists. The collective Elvis had left the building. Was I asked to do this or did I offer? It wouldn't have mattered. I felt I had to do it and wanted to. The Civil Wars' second album needed a producer, so hypervigilant that no detail would go unnoticed, no problem unidentified. Someone so resilient he wouldn't stop until it was right. Sounded like my kind of gig. More like my kind of lifestyle.

Most artists need a little reminder now and again not to get stuck by minor and temporary conflict. I've played the role of therapist many times in the studio. Identifying and encouraging productive disagreements and squelching the opposite. What brought The Civil Wars to acute enmity was something altogether different. As the *New York Times* reported: "These are the moments when you perhaps regret naming your band The Civil Wars."[2]

This level of conflict was new territory for me. I wondered, how do I create under a weighty, soul-sucking mess and actually succeed at what I hope to accomplish? I would find out.

I'd taken notes during our songwriting and recording sessions. From these scribbles, I created a comment/opinion chart in Excel for every song. This included overdub notes from the duo and manager, Nate Yetton. Joy committed to dropping by our studio, the Art House, to listen now and again, check progress, and offer her thoughts. She remained artful and helpful. Armed with my war-room chart and the trusty, basic aesthetic from *Barton Hollow*, I mapped a way forward.

The mission was clear. Finish well for the fans. Finish well for the several families dependent on the success of the second record—including mine. I'd never produced a record that didn't come out, and I wasn't about to start now.

Joy and John Paul agreed to a few hours in the studio, separately, to make minor vocal fixes. These sessions didn't add up to more than half a day's work. I was now the creative go-between amid the conflict. Joy called me "their Switzerland."

Neutral nation or diplomat was one thing, but I knew better than to become an artist's ambition. Ever. Yet, there I was, doing just that, again. I was overfunctioning, giving 110 percent, stretching my body and mind thin with responsibilities not entirely mine.

I can see myself beginning each day, sitting in front of the computer screen, dependent, asking God for help. I didn't have to have it all figured out. A plan was good. I could work it faithfully and still keep in mind the sage advice not to be anxious, but instead, stay thankful and prayerful.

Help, I whispered.

—

I compiled the best of Joy's and John Paul's performances and began to overdub additional instrumentation. A steady crew of Nashville's A-team musicians joined me in the effort: Barry Bales (upright bass), Sam Ashworth (percussion), Jerry Douglas (dobro), Dan Dugmore (pedal and lap steel), Mark Hill (bass), Andy Leftwich (fiddle and mandolin), Jerry McPherson (electric guitar), Gabe Scott (hammer dulcimer), Aaron Sterling (drums), and Jeff Taylor (harmonium, accordion, pump organ). Richie Biggs, my longtime engineer, and assistant James Sweeting were also there to help.

Even with the occasional extra hand stopping by the studio, I couldn't ignore the obvious. I was mostly alone and lonely, suffering from too little sleep and scary tinnitus and hearing dropouts. One positive remained constant, though. The music. Nothing diminished my enthusiasm for the music. Even dimmed by conflict, the sound of the duo still shone brightly.

There was one problem, though, for which there might not be a remedy. We were a few songs short of a full-length album.

Undaunted, Nate Yetton presented a plan. I'd finish the work of producing one or more of the tracks the duo had recorded with Rick Rubin. There was also an excellent iPhone voice memo of the song "D'Arline"—one recorded at the end of a songwriting session. Richie Biggs cleaned up the recording with some noise reduction and equalization. It was added to the record. Simple enough.

The Rubin collaboration wasn't as easy. As Rick reportedly said via his attorney, "I've never co-produced anything, ever." Our respective managers had a little dustup over credits. Eventually, we agreed to a full producer credit for any of the songs in question. Rubin would be credited with the duo's vocal performance, while credit for instrumentation and mix would go to me. I took the vocal and acoustic guitar demos from Shangri La and developed "I Had Me a Girl" into the full version heard on the record.

Still, *Rolling Stone*'s review of the record appeared to give Rubin credit for my work on "I Had Me a Girl": "Co-produced by country-rock doctor Rick Rubin, it's the pair's most aggressive track to date, heartsick electric guitar searing while tom-tom beats whomp like cardiac thunder. The record could use more tracks like this, where the instrumental drama matches the lush, scenery-eating vocals."[3] I was miffed.

When it was time to mix, I headed up to New York City with Nate, Joy, and Andi. We camped out for a few days with mix engineer Tom Elmhurst at the storied Electric Lady Studios in Greenwich Village. All songs but two were mixed by Tom. Richie Biggs delivered on "Tell Mama" and "Sacred Heart." The final touch was Bob Ludwig's mastering.

We had rescued the project and lived to tell. Nate Yetton shopped it to labels, and Columbia Records won out. The album was released with a black-and-white cover image of billowing clouds of smoke and dust—the fruit of calamity.

I knew the music was a solid follow-up to *Barton Hollow*, even if it was a record in search of its artists. The recording sold 116,000 copies the first week and is gold-certified. It was No. 1 in the US, Canada, and the UK. Also, it was No. 1 Top Digital, Top Folk, Top Tastemaker, and Top Rock albums on the *Billboard* charts. Even without the artists, it won another Grammy, Country Duo/Group Performance, for the track "From This Valley," written by Joy, John Paul, and Phil Madeira. The Civil Wars had also caught the attention of the rich and famous. Reading their glowing tweets was an end-of-day ritual.

T Bone Burnett honored me with a kind note regarding my production. Alluding to Dylan and more, he wrote: "Just heard eleven songs. Killer. Man, did I have it right about who should produce it. *Blood on the Tracks* territory. They have broken through some sound barrier. Post Coltrane Rockabilly Acid Chamber Music. Thanks for taking such good care of those kids—those monster artists. You have unleashed something totally new on the world."

Such was the hope. My need to create something entirely new was as strong as my need for air, food, and water. For better or worse, I am the spawn of individualism. Originality as religion. Art as exploration. All my life, I've heard people say there's nothing new; everything has been done before. The Old Testament book of Ecclesiastes has something to say about the subject too: there is nothing new under the sun, wrote Israel's King Solomon.

Ironically, the folk-rock group The Byrds came to international prominence by singing ancient lyrics straight out of Solomon's text. It was a folk song written by social activist Pete Seeger, who was famous for many things, including the credo scripted on his banjo: "This machine surrounds hate and forces it to surrender."

In October 1965, The Byrds took Pete's song "Turn! Turn! Turn!" to the No. 1 spot on the *Billboard* singles chart. "To everything (turn, turn, turn)," they sang. "There is a season (turn, turn, turn), and a time to every purpose, under heaven." Within three years, The Byrds were effectively broken up; all but one of the original members had quit, or in the case of David Crosby, been fired. As Ecclesiastes 3:20 asserts, "All go to the same place; all come from dust, and to dust all return."

Chapter One

On October 7, 2013, Columbia Records released a third and final single from *The Civil Wars*, "Dust to Dust."

—

Before The Civil Wars, I thought my days of significant commercial success had passed. It's always great to win big, though, and who wouldn't want to? It winds up the ego and boosts the bank account. Opportunities, once out of reach, are paraded to your doorstep. You're a winner.

Then it's over, and you're back to the sort of ebb and flow the average person experiences. Most people will never do the kind of work that can alter all of life so quickly, for better or worse. Wonder and whiplash.

No matter how many hits an artist has or how ubiquitous his or her star becomes, an artist's time in the white-hot spotlight will pass. The same can be said of music producers and songwriters. The ability to show the businesspeople the business will naturally taper off (unless you're Stan Lee, who died at ninety-five at the zenith of his career).

Through it all, in times of bluster or blubbering tears, humility or whoring, a few things have remained constant. I'm still a small, needy man. A tape-making boy, wounded, yet occasionally full of wonder. Any good that has ever come my way is all of grace—a long string of undeserved incidents where God took a tiny speck of creative appropriation and made it into something beyond my dreams. And he did it knowing full well I would take credit for it.

Certainty can be slippery—a puddle of pondering fit for Descartes and the ancient Greeks. Not love, though. You know when you've been loved, cared for, watched over. With confidence, I hold to the belief that God has loved me and Andi, our whole family, with an imaginative affection that still surprises me, surprises us.

But just because I'm loved doesn't mean I'm lovely. And just because there's first aid, I'm not without my wounds and scars.

For most of my life, I've embodied the little engine that could. Inching up the mountain one railroad tie at a time, huffing and puffing, "I think I can, I think I can, I think I can." With a drop of above-average talent and a thousand gallons of the need to prove myself, I beat unassailable odds. No question. But I got in the music game at just the right time.

—

In the early 1990s, I had the opportunity to spend twenty minutes alone in conversation with esteemed writer Frederick Buechner. I learned a lesson that day about the influence pop music has on our ability to live meaningful lives. Buechner, a Presbyterian minister, graduate of Princeton and Yale, author of thirty-plus books, spent a lifetime of reflection, imagining good, and creating award-winning literature. He has the good kind of fame—no bathroom mirror selfies or dance challenges, just insight and wisdom.

Buechner generously asked about my music and what I was up to of late. "Well," I told him, "I co-wrote the song that's No. 2 on the pop charts in America right now, a song sung by Amy Grant."

"Amy Grant?" he puzzled. "Never heard of her."

Millions of albums sold, culturally ubiquitous, well beyond Amy's previous Christian audience, five singles on Top 40 radio, on every talk show in the land, graced magazine covers, won Grammys, and sold-out world tours. *Shall I go on, Mr. Buechner?*

What rock did a Presbyterian have to live under to have not heard of Amy Grant? At first, I thought this was an amusing story about a great man of letters and faith wisely avoiding media. Then, years later, in an overwhelmed season of life, I understood. I needed to find Buechner's rock—and quick. Pop music had lost all power to rescue. It's not that it isn't a meaning-maker. It's that the meaning it makes is not enough.

Eventually, every successful person in the music business must find a new path forward—a reinvention—a commitment to the most sustainable income stream or meaningful direction he or she still has. If not, you're on your way out. Bursts of sudden or returning fame are not enough. Faithful, daily work more often is.

There is some evidence of commercial success in our home. Records on the wall, trophies here and there. I imagine this is what sparked the question we overheard a visiting friend ask our daughter

Molly many years ago: "Is your dad famous?" Already perspicacious, Molly answered, "No. Just well-known."

Sadly, many once-famous artists (or well-known, for that matter) fail to survive for a simple reason. They don't know how not to be famous or even just well-known. Or how to scale down the lifestyle their peak earning years once afforded them. Even Paul McCartney, arguably the greatest living songwriter of the twentieth century, could not make a living from the sales of only *Egypt Station*, his No. 1 *Billboard* album from 2018, or only *McCartney III* from 2020. Lucky for him, his older songs and recordings still earn at a brisk pace, to put it mildly. McCartney, perhaps the wealthiest musician in the world, is still busy creating. Not only has he survived the extreme edge of fame, but he has thrived as an artist and a businessperson. His name is not on the tip of every fourteen-year-old's tongue, but he's at work, still showing up. For reasons that I imagine are deeply personal to him, Paul McCartney keeps on coming.

I had a few producer managers interested in me when the first Civil Wars album, *Barton Hollow*, was gold-certified.

One said, "You know why I want to work with you?"

"Why?" I asked.

"Because you're a survivor."

And at fifty-six years old, I guess I was. Famous or not.

I attended a memorial service for Andi's stepfather in our hometown—long after many career milestones. My mother was there with us. After the service, people ate Costco hors d'oeuvres and homemade cookies and visited with one another. A very elderly, silver-haired woman approached Mom. Apparently, they'd known each other well in the past. I didn't recognize her, but she remembered me as a teenager. She asked, "Chuckie, are you still making your tapes?"

I don't use magnetic recording tape anymore. It's more like I'm making my ones and zeros on a computer. But the answer is yes, I'm still making my tapes. I am the boy who made tape after tape until someone in the music business took notice. I'm a teenager who left high school at sixteen, who at eighteen married his best friend, Andi. Together, we're the couple that left the farm town they grew up in for the big city and the wide-open world where it made perfect sense to dream as big as the planet. I'm the son who did what the father didn't think could be done and what the father, not for lack of talent, couldn't do himself.

Weeks before the breakup of The Civil Wars, right before they launched their world tour, I left Nashville, touring in support of *No Man's Land*, my first vocal record in a decade. Unlike The Civil Wars, my tour was spartan and scheduled to be short. Passenger van, Hampton Inns, and singer-songwriter clubs like Rockwood Music Hall in New York City and The Red Room in Boston, where rock legend Al Kooper dropped by for sound check and conversation.

I'd read and enjoyed Al's book *Backstage Passes and Backstabbing Bastards: Memoirs of a Rock 'n' Roll Survivor*. As the title intimates, Al has seen and done it all—a survivor. He wrote a teenybopper hit from the early 1960s titled "This Diamond Ring," played on Dylan's "Like a Rolling Stone," then turned around and played on the Rolling Stones' "You Can't Always Get What You Want." He also produced that bit of sonic ubiquity known as "Freebird." The Civil Wars was our connection. Al was a fan.

East Coast or West, if I drew a hundred people at that point in my artist career (at age fifty-six), I'd have been happy. As a young man, numbers-wise, I was never more than an underachieving college-level act; a club headliner in California, the UK, and Europe; and perhaps a more significant main-stage headliner at Christian music festivals in the States and beyond in the '80s and '90s. By the era of The Civil Wars duo, my time as a touring artist had long since passed. Unlike that road dog Willie Nelson, I didn't take to living on a tour bus. I always liked being on the road again, as in returning to it, but the novelty would wear off within a week. Then, instantly, I was too tired, too lonely, too hungry—a situation no obsessive, compulsive man ought to ever be in. It is a fate that comes with a warning label: Crossbones, do not enter, water unsafe to drink, excessive use of adverbs.

I wanted another go-around though, even if it would be modest. I was proud of my new record and committed to promoting it with a tour. The explosion of rootsy Americana music had opened the mind of musicians and audiences to take a second look at old forms with new eyes, ears, and curiosity. Yes, some of the Americana revival was questionable, as if stomps and claps a song doth make.

For me, no pretension was required. This was my family story, lush branches on my family tree. As noted earlier: *Louisiana piney-wood loggers playing fiddles and resonator guitars; a dancing, gambling, Okie grandfather singing like Woody Guthrie and Hank Williams; great-grandparents, poor subsistence farmers; me, the great-grandson of a Texas cattle rancher.* All that and more made me a legit purveyor of Americana, and not just some musical tourist.

Inspired by my family, I made a record about going down to Mystic, Louisiana, looking for the meaning in the dirt. I heeded the warning I sang: "The blue sky you seek might be muddy water deep, might be an old door locked for a reason." In Cali-For-Ni-A, I heard Great-grandpa Miller say to me, "Go out back little one to the tool shed where you found that kitty cat stone cold dead. Guard your mind from the memory; turn your head if need be." That's right. *Do whatcha gotta do, boy, but get it done.*

My team did just that. They worked hard and put together the best possible bookings for me, including one date in the UK, at Shepherd's Bush Club in London. After that bit of fun, Andi and I planned to join The Civil Wars at their concert in Dublin. I'd introduced Joy to Bono in 2011 at the Nashville stop on the 360° Tour. I imagined the Hewsons taking in the duo's Dublin show. Then, refusing the night its end, we'd all collect at the pub, Finnegan's of Dalkey, where Paddy Moloney of The Chieftans (a Civil Wars collaborator) would wish the celebrated pair well, and Bono would entertain us with arcane stories, part beautiful, part bluster. In one's rock fantasy camp thought-bubble, it could have easily gone that way.

Through no fault of the imagination, it didn't.

—

If my dad were alive today, I'd invite him to go bait fishing—that was our thing together. All we'd need is a lake or river where we could cast once and sit back in a boat, or cheap canvas chairs onshore, with a Coors Light and have a lifetime-deferred talk. I'd tell him, "Dad, pop music wasn't the long shot you thought it was. But it's been a long, switchback, potholed road. It has been an odyssey. More reversals of fortune than I could possibly keep track of."

It's this reality that my young and overly confident self didn't see coming. In my immature naïveté, I suppose I thought you reached the top, and all would be, and always would be, well. I'd scratch and crawl my way up the ladder, then there'd be an elevated, mostly straight, only slightly bumpy at most, stroll into the sunset.

Another thing I didn't know then is how generative life is. In spite of breakups and shake-ups, life keeps coming back for more, and often the more is good and right. And sometimes it even sustains this righteous rhythm and rhyme for days, weeks, months, and years. The resilience of good is the comeback kid.

Speaking of comeback kids, I know two.

Both John Paul White and Joy Williams are comeback kids. The long arc of the redemptive and generative 180 is on their side. My side. Your side. We are all coming back from something toward something new. Maybe even something we never wanted but yet needed. I can't speak for John Paul and Joy, but I watch from a distance. They look like two crazy-talented solo artists, one in Alabama, the other in Tennessee, staying faithful to the craft of music making and being present as spouses, parents, and citizens. It's a full-time job civil-engineering the soulful, artful world you hope to inhabit and leave to your children and neighbors. And they're on it.

Bottom-line, closing remarks, cymbal crash and cadenza: the view from the oxygen-deprived but glorious pop music summit may have been far too brief, but JP and Joy did not skimp on the music, ever, and the music lives on. Te Deum. No brag, just fact.

Also a fact, the collapse of The Civil Wars at the height of their success reanimated old stories, existential questions, and undefined anger and pain in my life. Having a No. 1 record with a nonexistent band was unprecedented. And it was a visceral experience that took its pound of flesh. Like Dante's *Divine Comedy*, midway through life's journey (well, okay, more than midway there), I was "in a dark wood." Again. Therapy ensued.

A studio visit from a few years earlier came to mind. T Bone had invited me to the Sound Emporium studio in Nashville for the making of his much-lauded soundtrack for *O Brother, Where Art Thou?*—a story based on Homer's *Odyssey*. I watched and listened as Gillian Welch and David Rawlings deftly shaped music for the Baby Face Nelson getaway scene. The three chain-gang escapees were about to come into some money.

What is an odyssey? Nothing short of an eventful journey marked by many changes of fortune. Something, it turns out, my deep ancestry knows well.

two

ODYSSEY, MIGRATION, AND MYSTERY

A favorite odyssey story of mine is from my mother's roots, the paternal Williamsons and maternal Millers (other great-grandparent surnames are Phillips, Bryan, Bond, and Finley). All their birth origins are southern: Arkansas, Kentucky, Georgia, Texas, Tennessee, Louisiana, and Mississippi. Deeper ancestral origins are northwestern Europe: England, Wales, Ireland, Scotland, and Sweden.

Except for a favorite great aunt, Edgule Miller from the Choctaw Nation, Indian Territory, Oklahoma, last stop on the Choctaw "trail of tears."

By the turn of the twentieth century, those ancestors not down for the count in a southern grave somewhere had made their way to Durant in Bryan County, Oklahoma—where my mother, Alice, was born in 1936. I've yet to discover why Durant.

I like to imagine they had a few good years in Oklahoma before the inspiration to skedaddle again: the Great Depression and the Dust Bowl era. When asked, my grandfather Marvin General Williamson played down the dust, saying it was more about finding work.

My great-grandparents Bob and Maggie Miller pioneered the move. Theirs was a classic *Grapes of Wrath* migration story, landing in Sutter County, California, in the 1930s. They worked in the fruit, alongside other American migrants and immigrants from Greece, Japan, Mexico, and Punjab, India—eventually creating their own subsistence farm next to a Mexican family enclave on Jefferson Road in Yuba City—a dead-end road that ran adjacent to the Colusa branch of the Sacramento Northern railroad tracks (later Western Pacific).

The married children followed soon after in 1939. Grandpa Williamson secured a gig delivering a car from Durant to Los Angeles. From there, four hundred miles north by bus and train reunited the family with the Miller elders. The Williamsons had arrived in the land of opportunity, the agricultural bowl that is Sutter County—predominantly wheat, rice, corn, almonds, walnuts, tomatoes, grapes, peaches, and plums (prunes) ripe for the picking. My mother's first residence in California was farm labor housing provided by the Harter Cannery.

Marvin and his brother-in-law Steve Miller didn't take to the migrant laborer life and schemed an ingenious, entrepreneurial exit.

When the yield from legacy walnut and almond orchards dwindled, trees had to be pulled. The spent trees could be piled and torched or cut into firewood. Wood from the larger, thicker walnut trees might be salvaged for furniture or cabinetry.

Marvin and Steve bartered with a farmer to remove his trees in exchange for the valuable wood. Having no proper equipment, they first pulled the trees with a chain and truck. Then they jacked up the truck till the rear wheels hovered above ground. After scrounging an extra wheel hub, they welded a sprocket to it. With the sprocket hub attached to the back axle of the pickup, they ran chain to another sprocket that turned a saw blade. Their pop-up sawmill in place, the two men proceeded to cut the trees into marketable pieces and sell them off for a significant profit. They had their stake and never looked back. Reversal of fortune.

This positive story is important to my music career because it is a sign and symbol of the problem-solving ingenuity I was born into. I didn't appreciate this fully until later in life, but my Miller great-grandparents' subsistence farm and my Williamson grandparents' property were imagination labs. They never bought anything they could instead create with imagination and existing, seemingly random materials within reach. Every problem was an opportunity to ponder a creative solution. It was here that I first learned that incongruent elements, imagined well for, could be shaped into something new and usable—even enjoyable.

This required a way of seeing. No one thing had a single identity inapplicable outside its primary purpose or use. Quite the opposite. A piece of tire rubber became a rubber washer between bolt and nut stopping a water leak. Hay-bale wire cinched up a sagging gate. Manure fertilized vegetables. A rusted, bent nail could be brought back to life when hammered straight against the carbon steel of a Ford Model A detached leaf spring. New bedding and clothing were artfully crafted from material scraps.

This ancestry trained me to see into things and to extrapolate new possibilities. All of this found its way into artistry and music production. It wasn't just seeing. It was hearing too. Is there really a great distance between straightening a bent nail and a bent musical note? There isn't. One requires a strong foundation of carbon steel, the other a foundation of tuning to A-440 Hz. Having a standard for what is straight or in tune also gives the curious a point of departure for creating elasticity and tinkering with notions of straight and in tune. It is a way of seeing, hearing, and ultimately being in the world. Eyes to see, ears to hear, hands to craft. All that and more.

An equally important artistic influence from this ancestral branch is language. Certainly, dialect, accent, and the words used. But the melody of conversation, dynamics, and silence too. This was a very lively, often irreverent crowd. In contrast to the general quiet of my dad's parents, this crew knew how to have a good time. They danced, drank, and chewed. Played a lot of cards and 42 (a domino game). Grandpa Marvin burst into song often. What I reckon were both improvised songs and tunes from the Okie/Texan canon (think Woody Guthrie and Bob Wills and the Texas Playboys).

Several family members used volume and modulated pitch as their principal devices for being heard over the din. All-in, though, there was such musicality to their South-meets-Okie vernacular, laughter, and tone.

The family did on occasion experience the word "Okie" as pejorative, and the young were eager to transcend any negative association and assimilate as Californians.

19

Within the family circle of trust, though, "Okie" represented grit, an accent, and gut-busting humor and goodness. Aunt Edgule could turn "Good God, kid" into a three-note hook as sticky as could any Nashville songwriter. Grandpa Marvin did the same with "Well, better get a move on" or "That's the damndest thing I ever seen." To this day, I like to think I can flex a spot-on imitation of these two at will. In contrast, Ol' Bob Miller, my great-grandfather, barely said a word. He may have been satisfied with the verbosity of his progeny and relations.

The legendary country artist Clint Black and I once discussed our grandparents. Clint had been on the PBS show *Finding Your Roots*, and that got us talking ancestry at a mutual friend's birthday party. Clint shared a story about two of his old-timers who talked on the phone often but left long episodes of silence neither felt compelled to fill. A practice that baffled younger family members. Wasn't silence a gap to be closed?

Like negative space in painting, silence plays an important role in music. The musician Robert Fripp, best known as a founding guitarist in the British band King Crimson, once had a side project called the League of Crafty Guitarists—twelve in all. When asked why one of the guitarists wasn't playing, Fripp's legendary reply was: *Someone must provide the silence.*

On my mother's side of the family, her grandfather Robert Dallas Miller provided the silence.

Another key element to the musicality of this side of the family was—actually still is—hyperdynamics. For example, imagine my grandfather Marvin in the living room, leaning out of his chair, gesticulating toward my dad and yelling, "Now, Bill, you know damn well that ain't true!" Then came Dad's rebuttal, equal parts country and college with likely some vocab Marvin didn't know (like "copacetic"). Does Marvin come back with more volume? No. He regains authority by reaching for his spit can, leaning back in his chair, and saying under his breath, "Still don't make no damn sense." Then he spits tobacco into the can, and so ends the perfect verse and chorus.

At the height of The Civil Wars' trip to the top of the pops, someone asked me what I thought the secret to their success was. I answered without hesitation: "Hyperdynamics. Loud louds and soft softs. They suck you in. You can't help but listen."

—

My father's family have their own odyssey. A story I can trace much further back than that of my mother. Like the Millers and Williamsons, they were migrant workers and survivors with lyrical refrains and surprising beats. They too came from the South and serendipitously ended up in Yuba City, California.

I wasn't always a Peacock. It's a stage name, a pseudonym, a PKA, "professionally known as." I borrowed it from the jazz bassist Gary Peacock in 1978, when punk gave way to new wave, and you could see that The Police and Elvis Costello were going to amount to something. As stage names go, it's proved reliable and memorable.

I was born Charles William Ashworth to Calvin Willard Ashworth and Alice Margaret Williamson in Yuba City, California, on August 10, 1956. While Mom's parents were the Okie farming migrants of the 1930s, Dad's parents were logging and sawmill migrants. They left Louisiana for California in the 1920s in hopes of a new and better life.

My paternal grandfather, Lee Jackson Ashworth, was born in 1898 in Starks, Louisiana—thirty miles north of Lake Charles and five miles from the Sabine River and Texas border. Lake Charles is Zydeco music territory, the birthplace of the Queen of Zydeco herself, Ida Lewis Guillory. A bona fide Louisiana Creole.

Dad, on occasion, would suggest with a wink and a smile, "I might be a Louisiana Creole, you never know."

Neither he nor his grade-school children were sophisticated enough to parse Creole identity and culture.

My sister Terri and I had another option in mind.

I have this vivid memory of us in the living room. It's summer, the mid-1960s. We're smiling, gripping the armrests of our dad's recliner, leaning in bright-eyed and sincerely asking:

"Dad, are you a Negro?"

For many at that moment in history, the word "Negro" was pejorative and racist. But in our early childhood, the word was a simple descriptor for persons of African heritage. A term Dr. Martin Luther King Jr. and the potent intellectual James Baldwin used to describe their race. Not that we had any faithful familiarity with this history apart from television newscasts. The impulse to differentiate, to *other* at all times, was insidiously normalized.

Under the bright California summer sun, Dad quickly turned from his copper-brown shade to a deep shade of brown. Terri and I looked like someone else's children. Neither of us had Dad's black hair and dark brown skin. We were white, like Mom, with her blonde hair and alabaster skin. And we were white because the whole world told us so. And even more to the point, we were white because we occupied white spaces with white citizens, more than not. Even while living in Sutter County, an unusually diverse, multiracial, and multicultural place.

Thanks to Mom's family background and openheartedness, there was never any hint of racist avoidance. Our neighbors, best friends, and playmates were of Greek, Japanese, Mexican, and Punjab ancestry. We were in and out of their lives and homes, as they were ours.

Still, I would be nineteen years old before I visited the home of a Black friend—Nathan Owens, a musician I greatly admired from the local Owens Brothers band.

While Terri and I were too young in the mid-1960s to grasp concepts of race, ethnicity, ancestry, or the science of melanin and skin pigmentation, Dad was not. His jokey, uneducated allusions to Louisiana Creoles masked a deep desire to understand himself and to know the family's Louisiana past—whatever the story might be. I try not to attach feelings to him that he never expressed. Still, he spoke of Louisiana often. I can't help but tie this to a fundamental human need: to know and to be known and to understand the places your people have occupied.

Grandpa Ashworth was secretive and rigidly silent. He offered Dad nothing, and by all accounts, answered no questions. This was not the musical, useful silence of Fripp, Black, and Miller. This silence bellowed, shrieked. No amount of attenuation or equalization could excise its shrill and puzzling presence. It was silence as triangle (the orchestral percussion instrument). If like me you've recorded a triangle, then you know what I mean. No matter how much you turn it down in a mix, it can always be heard.

There was a reckoning coming, though. A no-triangle remix. An incremental reveal. A doing away with secrets.

Thirty years would pass before the people and stories Dad sought were uncovered by his sister Connie. As substantive and helpful as her initial genealogy work was, it was mostly family trees. She handed off to me, and I concentrated on narrative.

I discovered the entire Ashworth story had been hiding in plain sight for hundreds of years, documented by writers and historians, including the legendary scholar Carter G. Woodson, founder of the Association for the Study of African American Life and History, and Frederick Law Olmstead, the designer of Central Park in New York City (writing as a reporter for the *New York Times*). The Ashworths, Olmstead noted, "were a rich Mulatto family, settled in Texas during the earliest days of the Republic."[1] This historical nugget noted, what I found was an unjust and tragic reversal of fortune. Collectively, the stories are, to borrow from essayist Ross Gay, *a potluck of sorrows*.

Unbeknownst to Dad, his family has been a four-hundred-year American case study in enslavement, the history of free Blacks during chattel slavery, pioneer Black ranchers, mixed-race families during Reconstruction, and white-passing.

Slavery and Freedom in Texas (Gillmer),[2] *Black Cowboys in the American West* (Glasrud and Searles),[3] and *In Search of the Racial Frontier* (Taylor)[4] are a few of the books I've collected that feature the Ashworths—in particular, my third great-grandfather, Tapley Ashworth, and his brothers William and Aaron. Journalist Tim Hashaw, in his book *The Birth of Black America*,[5] maintains that a direct lineage exists between enslaved Angolans taken to Jamestown (or Point Comfort) in the 1620s and our ancestors.

Dad died before learning any of this or knowing his ancestral DNA. He is, in fact, rooted in West Africa, indigenous America, the United Kingdom, and northern Europe. As am I.

—

Grandpa Ashworth was fifty-eight years old when I was born and still working as a sawyer. Lumber was his trade. The Louisiana of his youth was flush with forests full of southern yellow pines, and logging was steady work; there was an insatiable demand for short, longleaf, and slash pines for construction lumber, pulpwood, and turpentine. In sawmill work, the sawyer's responsibility is to read the incoming logs, square them up, and make quick and accurate decisions about how many and what thickness of boards can be sawed from the log.

At the time of Reconstruction, following the Civil War, nearly all of Louisiana was forested with virgin cypress trees and longleaf yellow pines. There were millions of the latter, tall, straight, and alluring to the enterprising mind. Following the repeal of the Homestead Act, between 1880 and 1920, industrial lumber companies clear-cut the entire state, leaving a stump-scape of over four million acres. At its peak in 1910, 63,000 lumberjacks and sawmill hands were employed.

This was dangerous work with little to no safety standards. Tens of thousands were injured, and hundreds died, including my musical progenitor and great-grandfather George Reilly Baggett Sr., in 1904. He was just thirty-nine, a handsome fiddler, and husband to Alzenith Ellanora Hodges, whom he married on her fourteenth birthday, July 21, 1887. Along with Alzenith, Great-grandpa George left behind six children, including my grandmother, Ella Nora.

We have no record of fiddle songs he might've played or out of what tradition. Only a tintype photo of him holding his instrument. This tiny artifact of photography is our one link to the musician to which all musicians in our family are indebted. It is a sacred touchstone.

Though the Ashworth surname has made contributions to popular music and music education, the roots of the music are the Baggett name and the genetics of Grandma Ella.

In a similar way, but related to ancestry, the Ashworths are not the genesis of our African and indigenous genetics. They've simply received the most press, the most entries in history and sociology books. The attribution belongs to a great-grandmother, the first woman of African ancestry to marry an Ashworth man who immigrated to English America.

—

The profitable Louisiana lumber boom ended in 1920, leaving the small sawmills to cut up the detritus left by the corporate opportunists. This set the stage for migration.

By 1923, my grandfather Lee Jackson Ashworth was rid of Louisiana and working a booming sawmill circuit in northern and central California. These were grand forests of diverse trees for the cutting—Leviathan, compared to the piney woods of Louisiana. He traveled to California by train with his brother-in-law in 1922. Once the men found work, my grandma Ella and Eloise, their first child, followed. Alzenith arrived shortly thereafter. California's golden motto of Eureka, *I Have Found It*, fits the scenario well. In my grandparent's case, the treasure was plentiful work and a new start.

Like many migrants to the West, my grandfather broke with his past. He felt no obligation to keep the memory of his Louisiana and Texas people and place alive. There were no soliloquies of reminiscence. The ethos of the American West promotes leaving it all behind. Separation and survival are dominant values. You're too busy scouting your next move and creating what's new to stay rooted to the past. Growing up as a native, rural Californian, I saw breaking with the past as admirable, nearly a moral imperative. It wasn't until I moved to the American South that I learned to let the dead speak to the living. To allow roots to affect the fruit.

Whether it be the arrival of the Irish at Ellis Island, the Great Migration of African Americans out of the South, or 300,000 Tom Joads leaving the Dust Bowl of Oklahoma for Cali-For-Ni-A, all migrations have commonalities.

When Pulitzer Prize–winning author Isabel Wilkerson was writing *The Warmth of Other Suns*, she discovered the work of E. G. Ravenstein, a nineteenth-century geographer who promulgated migration laws. One such rule was that people (immigrants) go no further than is necessary to achieve their goals. This rings true to my own experience, and I see it applying to the migrations on my mother's side and to this grandfather as well.

I have documentation that shows my Grandpa Ashworth, at twenty years old, working a job in Kansas City—a straight shot north by train from DeRidder, Louisiana—740 miles. He made it that far. I imagine it was an audition of sorts. He came back to Louisiana, married my grandmother, and they went as far as they needed to go. Which was California, with its vibrant logging industry.

Isabel Wilkerson, speaking on NPR's *TED Radio Hour* in 2021, makes several good arguments for why people on the whole don't like to talk about where they migrated from. "Every migration," she says, "is a referendum on the place that people are leaving, and it's a vote of confidence and a leap of faith in—and hopefulness about the place that they are going to."[6]

The referendum declares, in no uncertain terms, this is a place you leave. Too much sharing of history can feel like going backward. This is particularly true when poverty, suffering, persecution, and trauma are why a family migrates. Everything is invested in the new life—it has to work. Wilkerson also points out that our migrant family members, like my grandfather, might have been suffering from PTSD (posttraumatic stress disorder), a disorder that will work overtime to hide the stories your brain is determined to keep secret. As it is said, you're only as sick as your secrets.

PTSD wasn't identified and named a disorder with a wide range of effects until the late 1970s. The only remedy for anyone before then was to do what people have always done: suppress thoughts and emotions, medicate, and, for a man in 1920, follow the masculine code of the time. Sentimentality and oversharing were not on the menu. The patriarch, a man's man, was strong, aggressive, in control, having power and demonstrating courage and resilience. Anything less was weakness. And weakness could get you killed.

I see my paternal grandfather as one small actor in a centuries-old American saga about our free multiracial family, who were coerced by caste, moving in time through the nation's ever-shifting categories of race; along the way, experiencing ostracism, racism, and violence; constantly having to fight for and prove themselves worthy of the most basic human dignities.

As with my dad, I try not to attach feelings to my grandfather he did not express. Still, based on the stories I've collected over the years, I don't think it's a stretch to believe he knew something of the *potluck of sorrows* his ancestors endured—perhaps he endured.

I've walked the ground where he grew up in Louisiana. I would've left too.

Grandpa shared a middle name, Jackson, with his paternal grandfather. Sadly, he never met the man. Andrew Jackson Ashworth was murdered on June 29, 1897, just ten months before my grandpa was born. Andrew Jackson Ashworth (my second great-grandfather) died from a gunshot wound inflicted by his nephew Archie Ashworth, son of his brother, Isaiah Ashworth.

My dad never knew this fact about his great-grandfather. No one in the family did until Aunt Connie shared her research and I dug deeper.

Great-grandfather Andrew suspected that his nephew Archie, a "young, robust fellow" said to be of "bad reputation," was stealing his sheep. On Tuesday, June 29, while running his dogs, Andrew caught his nephew red-handed, skinning a stolen sheep.

The New Orleans paper reported that "The evidence went to show that the young Ashworth drove some sheep out of his Uncle's pasture near Mystic, Louisiana," and "Mr. Ashworth caught up with him in the road."

A double-barreled shotgun was brandished, and Archie "shot his old uncle in the road and left him where he fell." It was six hours before Andrew was found.

As he was a man of good reputation, Andrew's neighbors "clamored for revenge." A lynch mob formed, and seventy-plus men "scoured the country," itching to capture Archie and his two alleged accomplices, Bloodworth and Buxton.

The deputy sheriff and constable cornered the fugitives first. Archie knew lynching was a credible threat and pleaded with the officers to give him a way out: "Shoot me down right here. I don't want to be killed at the hands of a mob composed mainly of my own people."

The authorities arrested the accused and quelled the bloodthirsty lynch mob. Another sheriff and his deputy traveled up from Lake Charles to Mystic, taking custody of the trio for arraignment the following day in Lake Charles.[7]

Six months later, on February 26, 1898, Archie Ashworth was convicted of murder and sentenced to life imprisonment.

Unrelated to the murder, two of Archie's first cousins were sentenced the same day: Owen, for burglary; Dempsey, forgery. Three years each. Both convicts were sons of Thompson Ashworth, the younger brother of Andrew and Isaiah.

Three Ashworth brothers. Three Ashworth sons. Three sentences handed down on one day.

The sons were incarcerated at the Louisiana State Penitentiary, the very prison that folk music icon Lead Belly would sing his way out of a few decades later. Folklorist John A. Lomax, most famous as the curator of Archive of American Folk Song of the Library of Congress, asked Louisiana governor O. K. Allen to release the musician. His services were needed elsewhere.

The prison was and still is known as Angola, named after the former plantation on which it resides—which was named after the home country of its slave labor. During the American colonial period, at least 25 percent of enslaved Africans came from the Angola-Congo region. *All three Ashworth convicts had Angolan ancestry. Whether they knew this fact is lost to history.*

Once inside Angola prison, the Ashworth sons were thoroughly inspected and inventoried. Dempsey, with his heavy eyebrows and considerable scars. Archie, with short teeth, a small mouth, and tiny ears. Owen's disfigured first toe. Each one described as swarthy. Archie couldn't read or write.

Within a year, the annotator of the public record noted all three convicts as dead. Like dominos, they fell in succession. Archie was taken by epileptic hysteria; Owen, morbus cholera; and Dempsey, influenza.[8]

While several newspapers had covered the murder, and Archie's trial and appeals to the Louisiana Supreme Court, it was the *Times-Democrat* in New Orleans (September, 28, 1897) that printed a folksy memoriam of my second great-grandfather.

Andrew Jackson Ashworth, the copy opined, "was one of the most respected 'red bones' in Calcasieu Parish."

A step up from the racist half-handed compliment their competition, the *Times-Picayune*, printed just after the murder on July 3: "Andrew Ashworth was a Red Bone, but was considered a good, law-abiding citizen."

—

I first heard the word "redbone" in the early 1970s. A television show called *Don Kirshner's Rock Concert* featured an eclectic mix of recording artists. I don't think I ever missed an episode. It was like oxygen to a teenage musician. I remember Redbone, a band from Los Angeles fronted by the Vegas brothers of Mexican and indigenous American descent. They scored a Top 5 hit on the *Billboard* Hot 100 with their single "Come and Get Your Love." It was a penetrating earworm for its time. The song returned for an encore in the opening credits of the blockbuster Marvel film *Guardians of the Galaxy* in 2014.

Next, I heard an anachronistic artist named Leon Redbone. His act in the '70s would have fit perfectly in the Americana music boom of the 2010s, with all the stomping, claps, and old-timey instrumentation and vocal affectations. I might have been solicited to produce the sharply suited, bluesy Mr. Redbone. I'll give him this, he created a memorable American character for an Armenian fellow born on the island of Cyprus. That's a long way off from Robert Johnson's deal with the devil at a crossroads in Mississippi. And no points for appropriating the word "Redbone." Still, no less a vaudeville man than Bob Dylan gave Leon his imprimatur, inspiring *Rolling Stone* magazine to introduce Leon to the Woodstock generation, a full three years before his debut recording.

I wondered, what did this curious word, "redbone," signify?

As my own musical story got under way, interest and circumstances were such that I played and wrote jazz and soul/R&B/funk music—essential items on the menu of American musical styles invented by Black Americans. This put me in the company of young Black musicians who shared a passion for this music and more. I made lifetime friends like Henry Robinett (guitarist and Charles Mingus's nephew),

Aaron Smith (former Motown drummer), Alphonza Kee (bassist, The Staple Singers), and Roger Smith (organist, Tower of Power).

We shared the stories of our past and created new ones together surrounding music and family—still do, forty-five years later. Among our generation in Northern California, it was more common than not for our bands to be multiracial. Respect for the music and for one another's skill gave birth to diversity. NorCal 1970s heroes like Tower of Power, Santana, War, Malo, Sly and the Family Stone, Herbie Hancock, and Azteca bore witness to this way of being in the world. A pattern that still defines us today.

We celebrate diversity of thought, experience, and creativity. All these friends and their families have unique origins and odysseys, all worthy of curiosity, attention, and respect. As we do with our music, so with friendship. Listen, learn, and love. We are committed mutual caretakers of the music and one another.

I've known my brother-in-law Boomer Williams since I was fifteen. Raised by his grandparents, he hails from a large Black family in Yuba City. Boomer and Andi's sister Paula were high school sweethearts, married for fifty-plus years. As unique as the language of the Okie/Texan Williamsons and Millers was to my youth, Boomer could give as good or better with his own inherited dialect, style, and verbal reactions. As a lifelong writer, reader, and people-watcher/listener, I love to hear people play with the English language—to make words uniquely their own. Like jazz, it delights me.

For example, through Boomer and musician friends, I learned that a "kitchen" isn't just where you cook. Backstage, minutes before curtain, if Vince Ebo asked singing partner Clarice Jones, "How's my kitchen?" he was looking for an assessment of his coiffure. Specifically his neckline. If she answered, "Oh baby, you better clean that kitchen!" then Vince, with hair pick in hand, made quick work of the nape of his beautiful black crown. For Vince and Clarice, messy kitchens were unacceptable.

Through family and friendships I also learned the meanings and uses of "redbone."

It is a multifunctional word denoting ethnicity, ancestry, *and* skin color. It can be pejorative, complimentary, and descriptive of a people group.

When the word "redbone" is used positively, as in "That is one fine redbone," I know a light-skinned Black person is being admired. See rapper Lil' Wayne channeling the Song of Solomon with "Yeah, that's Tunechi right there. . . . Redbone mangos right there." When used pejoratively, "redbone" relates to caste and colorism, the gradation of skin color, as in "You know nothing about being Black in America. You're redbone."

When I uncovered the newspaper story describing my second great-grandfather as a "Redbone," I knew there was still more to learn—a personal story. I had to find out what this meant to me, to our family. How would the past, even a single word like "Redbone," inform the present and future? Was I, a white man, also a Redbone?

According to celebrated academic Henry Louis Gates Jr., by definition, yes.

Gates is the director of the Hutchins Center for African & African American Research at Harvard University and host of *Finding Your Roots*, his hugely popular genealogy series with PBS Television (the one that Clint Black appeared on). In an online column from August 11, 2017, entitled "Tracing Your Roots: Untangle My Redbone Heritage," Professor Gates defines the word "redbone" as "a term referring to people of mixed African, European and Native American ancestry."

This is my exact makeup, as per Y-DNA, mtDNA, and autosomal DNA testing. All three tests locate my dominant non-African ancestry where I would expect: northwestern Europe, Ireland, Scotland, and England (Ashworth being an English surname), with no more than 1 percent going to indigenous American (which fits with the commonly held belief that a fifth great-grandmother is indigenous). Autosomal and mtDNA testing trace my African ancestry to Angola, Cameroon, Congo, Nigeria, and western Bantu peoples in general.

This confirmation did not make me Black. It added a significant missing piece to our family ancestry. It answered the naïve, curious question that my sister and I asked of Dad so long ago. And as a son, it took care of unfinished business for the father.

Early in my research I encountered historians, genealogists, and writers perpetuating the notion of a Louisiana Redbone. Was this even a legit ethnicity or people group to which I belonged?

After twenty-five years of research, I'm still not confident I have a clear, unambiguous answer. To lift a well-used line from Winston Churchill, "It is a riddle wrapped in a mystery inside an enigma." The Louis Gates definition is clear. It's everything else that isn't.

What's important today is that I know the roots of my tree, and that's no small thing. I know sufficiently, not exhaustively. With enough dangling mystery to keep my eyes and heart open for the trustworthy.

It all comes down to rhythm now. Shaking the tree. Harvesting the good fruit, leaving the culls to feed the soil and return to dust.

three

MUSIC CITY, NASHVILLE, TENNESSEE

A unique camaraderie exists among musicians. The bond begins when you are young and full of promise and undiluted enthusiasm. We, strange creatures that we are, learn to love music, and we learn to love talking about music with the zeal of a new religious convert. In few words: we are obsessed. Somehow we all find each other. And what a relief it is to meet our doppelgangers: the unwavering fellow devotees who love music with the same passion that we do.

As with professional sports, succeeding at music as a real job takes skill and ability, obsessive love and not a little luck. Without diminishing anyone for whom music is an avocation, or one gig among others, it is a very tiny club of musicians around the world who make a living at music for a lifetime. It is, in a sense, a survivor's club. We share a deep history. First, with the very idea of becoming a working musician, then some stretch of success, followed by the astonishment—and hopefully gratitude—that we are still getting paid to make music well past what the world may think is our shelf life.

Going the distance is not something anyone can adequately train you for. This business is too mercurial. You have to figure it out as you go. Even though my father was a musician, he could not prepare me for the music industry I entered. Though there was overlap, his experiences as a bandleader, educator, and instrumentalist were unlike mine. Yet, because the obsessed do eventually find each other, we create for ourselves something like a communally constructed library of myth, humor, heroes, nomenclature, pop music history, gear-talk, teachers, industry contacts, and stories—lots of stories—each one filled with the rise and fall common to all captivating stories. In my freshman year of high school, I found a few of the obsessed, and they found me.

My first paying gig was playing trumpet with Blind Horse, an organ-driven horn band led by Warren Panico and the best musicians at Yuba City High. Our name was taken from the Faces album, *A Nod Is as Good as a Wink to a Blind Horse*. Now, I wasn't going to be a musician. I was one.

When I was sixteen, I had a Datsun pickup equipped with JBL instrument speakers and an 8-track player (just like my friend Rick the DJ). No 8-track cartridge garnered more airtime than Neil Young's *Harvest*, an iconic record tracked at Quad Studios in Nashville, February 6–8, 1971. Andi loved this record, as did I. The single "Heart of Gold" featured guest artists James Taylor and Linda Ronstadt, who recorded with Young while both were in Nashville to appear on Johnny Cash's television show.

Fast-forward eighteen years to the fall of 1989. I'm thirty-three years old and recording with producer Brown Bannister at the very same Quad Studios in Music City, USA. Our family was freshly relocated from Sacramento to Nashville, having arrived late in the evening of July 15. Classic, middle-class, modern migration. Two thousand miles by U-Haul truck, pulling a car trailer. Family of four and one dog, aptly named Porter Waggoner, after the country music star.

I was at Quad to record my first album for Sparrow Records, *The Secret of Time*, with a cohort of gifted instrumentalists. The memory of the people who turned the album into reality is as palpable to me as ever. Apart from Jerry McPherson on guitar, I had only recently met the bassist, Tommy Sims, and drummer, Chris McHugh. They were in a rock band called White Heart, popular in Christian music and known for a revolving door of musicians, including the session guitarist and producer, Dann Huff. Brown had produced the band's most recent album, *Freedom*. Impressed with Tommy, Chris, and band guitarist Gordon Kennedy, Brown was using the three musicians on his sessions.

Jimmy Abegg, acoustic guitarist and my closest musical ally, filled out the band of five musicians tracking at Quad. Jeff Balding was engineering with Steve Bishir in the second engineer spot. At this point in life I'd logged thousands of hours in the studio as a session player, artist, and producer. But this was distinct from any experience up to that point. Jeff and Brown were taking me to school (though I didn't let on that this was the case).

Sometimes moving to a different place requires you to grow up and stretch out. You live in a place for years, creating comfort, learning from your peers and mentors, but one day your elbows hit the walls. Someone or something calls you toward a roomier unknown. I can imagine that's what my grandfather Ashworth felt—at some point, Singer, Louisiana, got too snug (and dangerous) to hold the future of his young family. In this way, place itself can be a producer/creator; our family, contemporaries, and environment hampering or honing us.

> Time is a gift of love and grace,
> Without time there'd be no time to change,
> Time to be tried, humbled and broken,
> Time to hear the word of love spoken.[1]

I had progressed through all the circles available to me living in Sacramento. It was time to migrate to a world-respected music city, one where the creativity and business of popular music were a priority. That's not to say Sacramento hadn't served an essential purpose in my musical life. It had. It was in Sacramento that I learned to become a working songwriter, a studio musician, a record producer, and a recording and touring artist. I performed and recorded with the very best musicians, worked weekly playing my own music in Northern California music venues, and signed my first management, publishing, agent, and record company contracts while living in Sacramento.

Far from hindering my development, Northern California and Sacramento was the exact place I needed to be to start my music career. It's where I met the visual artist and songwriter Stephen Holsapple. Steve opened up a world of art and creative people to me I otherwise would not have known. Including percussionist Bongo Bob Smith (who was always in my court as a collaborator and introduced me to Bill Graham Management) and singer-songwriter Bob Cheevers (who employed me often to play on song demos and generously loaned me gear for years). Singer-songwriter Brent Bourgeois was a true peer. While neither of us were overtly competitive toward the other, we alternately raised the proverbial bar, grew together, and remain close friends and coworkers today. And there was the intuitive Jimmy Abegg, who introduced me to Mary Neely, who put my music in front of A&M and Island Records. Yet, Sacramento had a musical ceiling, and not only had I hit it, I was broke. Just like my Ashworth, Williamson, and Miller grandparents going west for available, well-paid work, Andi and I were compelled to head east for the same.

Like Louisiana and Oklahoma decades earlier, California had become a place you leave.

When we arrived in Nashville, I'd already met or corresponded with a handful of Nashvillians. I'd met the session drummer Steve Brewster in Germany in 1988 on a shared concert bill. Peter York, A&R (artists and repertoire) director at Sparrow Records, had hired me in the fall of 1988 to produce a record for Margaret Becker (*Immigrant's Daughter*). I'd spent a week at Peter's Nashville home in the early spring of '89 while I cut vocals on Margaret at the Gold Mine with engineer Bill Deaton.

Publishing executive Jimmy Gilmer I knew from CBS Songs, my music publisher at the time. Jimmy, apart from running the Nashville office, was known for singing a classic pop smash from the 1960s, "Sugar Shack," by Jimmy Gilmer and the Fireballs. Nashville music executive Mike Blanton had befriended me over the phone in 1988, and it wasn't long before I bumped into Mike's number-one artist, Amy Grant, and her crew of musicians. One of her crew in particular would go on to play a significant role in my production career: guitarist Jerry McPherson. Jerry and I first met outside Boston, at

Dan Russell's NewSound music festival on June 25 of 1988. We reconnected six weeks later at the Greenbelt Music Festival at Castle Ashby in Northhampton, England. We've been friends and collaborators ever since.

I'm still amazed at the pace this new Nashville musical world opened up to me, like puzzle pieces magically moving into place, completing the picture I might have hoped for but couldn't predict.

—

When I led the commercial music program at Lipscomb University, I taught students my theory concerning *circles of affirmation*. Peel back the veneer on the career of every gifted and successful musician, and you'll find a set of circles. The circle is a community of people that the musician must dwell in, be affirmed by, and pass through before moving on to the next. The collection of circles is the sequence of people and events that confirms that the musician is on the right path; that the musician's music dream is not only possible but probable.

Take the recording artist Billie Eilish. On the surface, it might appear that the teenager jumped from a bedroom studio to international fame overnight. That's the trope. Not true. She is the daughter of two actor/musicians and the sister of Finneas, also a musician/producer (the first circle). Billie competed in talent shows, sang with the Los Angeles Children's Choir, and worked on the film *Diary of a Wimpy Kid*. Each of these represented a circle to pass through and generally required some amount of affirmation, encouragement, and support by one community of influence after another. Even her Grammy wins are symbols of affirmation from the American music industry, yet another circle.

Sadly, musicians can also measure their ascent toward music as a vocation by all the fellow musicians they leave behind. It's a cold, hard fact that not everyone travels with you to the next circle. You could play with hundreds of musicians over the course of twenty years and be the last one standing.

Meeting and working with all the other last ones standing are when music makes good on its imaginative, creative promise. Experience, virtuosity, and a childlike, giddy curiosity liberate, beckoning you to imagine, to experiment, and to truly create in ways even your wildest dreams can't approximate.

—

Summer 1989, Nashville, Tennessee. The sound of the Mid-South was in my ears, but the Brown Bannister session at the fabled Quad Studios had yet to occur. We had just landed in Nashville, and I was busy writing new songs in my makeshift studio, the living room of our small Shadowood apartment in Bellevue. Concert lighting tech Keith Rintala called. He was in Nashville for the night with Edie Brickell and the New Bohemians—*did I want to go for Mexican food with him and the singer-songwriter Steve Forbert*?

Steve had moved to Nashville from NYC in 1985, on the tail of "Romeo's Tune," his charming hit single from 1980. Driving back after lunch, Steve stopped in Green Hills and introduced me to Amy Kurland at the Bluebird Café, her tiny club with an incalculable, international influence. The Bluebird is where you go to hear songwriters perform songs they just wrote that morning or ones popularized by recording artists heard around the world. On June 6, 1987, a twenty-something songwriter from Oklahoma named Garth Brooks auditioned and was booked to play a writers' night a month later. Today, Garth has sold a massive 157 million albums in the US and is the top American recording artist of all time—bigger than even Elvis. Similarly, a fourteen-year-old named Taylor Swift was discovered by music exec Scott Borchetta at the Bluebird. One hundred twenty million albums later, she is *the* Taylor Swift. The Bluebird is a definite circle of affirmation.

Thanks to Steve, I performed at the Bluebird shortly after meeting Amy and have done so many times since. It is the site of my first in-town gig, and the place I sang my first hit song, "Every Heartbeat," cowritten with Amy Grant and Wayne Kirkpatrick. You can see my Grammy-nominated daughter-in-law Ruby Amanfu in the documentary *Bluebird: An Accidental Landmark That Changed Music History*. And today I live around the corner from the Bluebird Café, where it sits nestled in between a barber shop and a hair salon at 4104 Hillsboro Pike. My Nashville life come full circle.

Once on Tennessee soil, no single event ushered me into a new circle of musicianship and production more than recording my third solo album, *The Secret of Time*. In the spring of 1989, right before moving to Nashville, I had signed a new recording agreement with Sparrow Records. Label executives Peter York and Bill Hearn had driven up from Los Angeles to Fresno to hear me and my band. We were playing a five-hour set at a club called the Wild Blue, and their trip north was one last bit of due diligence before making an offer. At the same time, back in Nashville, Michael Blanton was preparing his own offer.

I love and admire Michael, but Bill and Peter were prepared to move beyond enthusiasm to straight talk. A single declarative statement clinched the deal: "If you sign with us and move to Nashville, you will never stop working." And they were right. I didn't. All I wanted was to create music and have it provide for my family of four. Thanks to the help of many, I'd been doing just that. I was sure that moving to Music City would keep me pointed in a positive direction.

Peter, now my new A&R person, had coaxed Brown Bannister into producing me, and I was all for it. I knew nothing about Brown, except that he was Amy Grant's producer. He'd made a great record with Amy in 1988 for A&M Records, titled *Lead Me On*. Mike Blanton had sent me a copy, and I thought it was a stellar piece of pop music work: especially thoughtful songs, a high-level of musicianship, and immaculately recorded and mixed.

I met Brown at a restaurant in Nashville and immediately felt at ease with him. I had worked with the late British producer Nigel Gray on my second solo album on Island Records. I was a fan of the early records he'd produced for The Police. We worked well together, but it had not been the mind-blowing producer-as-mentor experience I longed for. Even so, working with Nigel did lead to a conviction that's guided my own production career: if I cannot help an artist make a significantly better and more successful record than the artist would on his or her own, I'm not the best choice.

—

Jeff Balding and Brown, together, modeled a level of engineering and production I'd yet to achieve—honestly, I didn't even know it existed. I'd worked with Jeff Balding once before in Los Angeles in 1988, mixing Margaret Becker's *Immigrant's Daughter*—my very first Grammy nomination as a producer in the rock gospel category. I'd been impressed with Jeff then, but this was next level twice over. It wasn't that Jeff and Brown spent hours getting sounds (we were all doing that in those days). Their genius was in the sculpting of those sounds as wholly unique creations per song and doggedly pursuing excellence without any eye on the clock. Nothing was signed off on until it was thought to be perfectly designed for the song and per-formance. If that goal wasn't attained, they weren't afraid to scrap it all and begin again. I got the ethos of all that, but prior to this, all my recording experiences had faced some limitation, whether it be budget, skill, gear, or time.

Jeff and Brown were recording like they had all the gear and skill they would ever need (their own and that of the musicians), and all the time and money in the world, too. Talk about a better and more successful record than I could have made on my own. For one thing, I had never seen so much world-class gear in my life. In Northern California, I hadn't known any engineers or producers that brought their own racked gear to a session. I'm not talking about a single piece of recording gear tucked under your arm—no, this was a display of riches in audio form. Between Jeff and Brown, they'd brought five four-foot-tall racks filled with the very best of new and old preamps, EQ, compressors, and effects. Actually, they did not bring them; cart-age did. And to sweeten the deal, they owned the cartage company. This was an important lesson in the music business: as you have op-portunity, cultivate multiple income streams. Even smarter, get the record companies to pay you for the ancillary business you create (like cartage and rental gear).

Cartage is the musician's best friend. No more trucking your own instruments and recording gear; you make enough money doing your job to employ cartage experts to store, care for, and transport your stuff. And Jeff and Brown had the best stuff; the newest George Mas-senburg equipment racked right alongside the vintage gear of sonic pioneers like Rupert Neve and Bill Putnam. They even had their own custom speakers—Tannoy Super Gold Monitors with Mastering Lab crossovers. I was all eyes and ears, taking notes and seeing how high the bar had been raised.

It wasn't only the outboard gear. It was instruments too. Around Jerry's station out on the tracking-room floor, he had a Bradshaw custom switching board, racks of amplifiers and outboard pedals and effects, and a guitar for every need. This was a huge education. In the history of pop music, each electric guitar had made some unique contribution, and out of that contribution, innovations in sound are continually created. If the sound you were hunting for required a 1958 Stratocaster, you didn't play your Chet Atkins, Gretsch Country Gentleman. Apples and oranges. And here I thought you got by on what you could afford. Yes and no.

In order to play in this league, to be among the best in the world, I quickly learned you don't compromise by not having the right tool for the job. How I would ever afford to join this elite club was beyond me. I was still trying to keep our Dodge station wagon running, satiating the oil leak with daily quarts of cheap motor oil and propping up the broken front seat with a two-foot piece of 2×4. Maybe someday I'd even be able to find a lowercase letter *g* to complete the Dodge logo on the tailgate.

Despite these game-changing instruments and gear, Brown met one obstacle he could not overcome—the Nashville Police Department.

After taking a whole day to rewire the studio with their own Mogami cables, then trying the drum kit in the usual spot in the studio, Brown and Jeff agreed it still wasn't the right sound. They wanted more natural ambience with longer, yet controllable reflections. They explored the studio complex, and after some experimentation determined that the lobby near the back door was perfect. The drum kit was moved, more cable run, and mics placed to capture this new and better sound. The room was small, reflective, and loud—and I might add that the drummer, Chris McHugh, was a heavy hitter. So much so, that my California musician friends Vince Ebo and Roger Smith would nickname him "Bamm-Bamm," child drummer from the '60s Flintstones cartoon.

Even with the sound finally dialed in, Brown and Jeff's commitment to excellence had pushed our actual band tracking late into the evening. By the time we were going for performance takes on the songs, it was past 10 p.m. That's when the first complaints were delivered by a law student living just across the parking lot. Maybe it was Chris who alerted us in the control room: "Hey, man, the police are outside."

Quad Studios was sound-proofed, but their lobby, facing the law student's apartment complex, wasn't. Brown, a diplomat if there ever was one, assured the police we would be done soon and the banging snare drum and crashing cymbals would cease.

Not so. You cannot rush the world's greatest drum sound. We were caught between three realms of moral seriousness: doing right by the music, by the law, and by the neighbors. The police returned. There's a sequence to these things: warning, citation, arrest. Mild-mannered Brown pushed it right up to the handcuffs.

Stand down, Brown. You've showed me how far you're willing to go to make a record better than I could possibly make on my own. I will follow you anywhere.

Brown, channeling singer Bobby Fuller, fought the law and the law won (thankfully, no arrests). We packed up the entire contents of the studio, days of setup and tweaking, and followed Brown and Jeff out to the Bennett House studio in Franklin. More accurately, sometime past midnight we all went home, and second engineer Steve Bishir and the cartage crew from Underground Sound took our gear to the new studio and set up through the night. When we arrived the next morning, everything was just as it had been at Quad, sans police.

After the basic tracks were finished at the Bennett House, Brown and I moved our operation out to Castle Recording Studios, where we cut overdubs and vocals (helped out by a young Byron House on occasion, who went on to play bass with Robert Plant, Nickel Creek, and more). This daily time together with Brown cemented our friendship and mutual respect. Without any sort of formal invitation, I became the newest member of Brown's growing production ensemble made up of musicians and engineers, most of us, a decade or so younger than him. The core group included Wayne Kirkpatrick, Tommy Sims, Jimmie Lee Sloas, Chris McHugh, Jerry McPherson, Eric Darken, Gordon Kennedy, and engineers Jeff Balding, Bill Deaton, Rick Will, and Steve Bishir. (Brown was still using his first-call keyboard greats, Shane Keister and Robbie Buchanan, too, though less so.) Kim Keyes, Chris Rodriguez, Bonnie Keen, Chris Eaton, Kim Fleming, and Vicki Hampton were a few of the first-call background vocalists during this era.

Another musician joined the crew under unusual circumstances. I was aware of a music software company in the Northwest that was creating third-party samples for all the major digital samplers and keyboards on the market, but especially related to E-MU Systems. E-MU gave me an artist endorsement in 1985, and I was using the SP-12 drum machine and the Emulator sampler keyboard. Brown and I, looking for new sounds not on the market yet, reached out to the company in the Northwest. They just so happened to have someone in Nashville in possession of their newest unreleased sounds and samples: a student at Belmont University, keyboardist Blair Masters.

I called Blair and asked how quickly he could get himself—gear and sounds—out to the Castle. First, he had to finish his classes, and then he was booked at the Benson Music studio to join other students in recording song demos for the publishing company. Benson had given him the opportunity once or twice before.

"Blair, are you getting paid for this?" I asked.

"Well, sort of. Last time they paid us in Baskin-Robbins coupons."

I choked back laughter and told him, "Blair, finish your classes, find a sub, and get out here ASAP. We're paying in US dollars."

Blair has had a remarkable career, playing on hundreds of albums, and he continues to tour as keyboardist with Garth Brooks.

Prior to the recording sessions for *The Secret of Time*, while I was putting the finishing touches on my new songs, I was also attempting to write a pop song for Amy Grant. Both Brown (her producer) and Michael Blanton (A&R executive) had thrown open the door of opportunity, and I was determined to rush through it with a smash hit under my arm.

After signing to Island Records in 1985, I was asked to take a shot at writing something more pop-radio-friendly to add to the release in late 1986. While in Leatherhead, England, working on the record with Nigel Gray, I'd come up with a song idea that emerged as "Message

Boy," a 12/8 shuffle leaning toward pop. A great R&B example of this rhythm is the 1964 Holland-Dozier-Holland classic, "How Sweet It Is (to Be Loved by You)." In the '80s, Tears for Fears used a tighter, drum-machine version of the beat for their ubiquitous hit "Everybody Wants to Rule the World."

My "Message Boy" had the shape of a hit, but it was the wrong time, wrong label, and dare I say, wrong artist. It was a fail. My belief in the 12/8 rhythm and the way I'd put it all together never faltered, though. This, I was convinced, was the right rhythmic direction for Amy. It especially lent itself to my jazzy, percussive, syncopated singing style. I figured they wouldn't have asked me to pitch something if they didn't want a little of my thing on it. A title came to me: "Every Heartbeat."

I finished the track, sang the "Every Heartbeat" chorus, put nonsense lyric melodies on the verses, made a cassette, and drove the Dodge out to Amy's farm. I brought along two other songs I had in progress, "Dear Friend" and "Drowning Man." I was nothing if not confident. That is, until I reached the intimidating, oversized-brick entry and iron gate that required a code. Once inside the gate, I pointed my beater of a station wagon down the long gravel lane lined with trees toward the house.

I had entered a world not my own. There were lakes, an airplane, horses, barns, multiple houses, outbuildings, and several employees busying themselves. It was a serene, beautiful setting. But I was way out of my league and knew it. Yet, once I was greeted outside by a pregnant Amy Grant with no airs or pretension, my self-doubt faded to the shadows. Nope. I was right where I was supposed to be. After a sweet and memorable time with Amy getting to know each other and listening to the songs I brought, she chose "Every Heartbeat" and "Dear Friend" to keep for consideration. No promises, but the music was in front of her.

Days later, Amy misplaced the cassette. I replaced it. There were hints from Brown and A&R that "Every Heartbeat" might be in the running for the next album. Great. Weeks passed, and I received a call from Michael Blanton (functioning as manager and A&R): "Brown and I are out at Amy's. What are you doing right now? We are choosing songs for the album and Amy has lost the cassette again."

Mike wanted me to come right out, bring a new cassette, and, as he requested, "Sing along to the cassette, bring some good energy, and dance around the living room."

"I think if you'll do that," he said, "it's as good as done."

I did just that. Mike was right. Amy and Wayne Kirkpatrick finished the song with flair, and it was confirmed as one of the songs Brown would produce for what would become a No. 2 *Billboard* Pop smash single in the summer of 1991 on *Heart in Motion*, and a five-time platinum, Grammy-nominated pop Album of the Year in 1991.

> I see the mission up ahead of me and I tremble as
>   one shaken;
> But if I have the eyes of faith, the eyes to see,
> I will leave the outcome in the hands of the one who
>   called me.
> And over and over I must learn and relearn
> That whether I decrease or whether I increase is not my
>   concern.[2]

After my initiation into Brown's musical world with *The Secret of Time* (which received a Grammy nomination for Rock Gospel Album of the Year in 1991), the recording crew dove right into creating the Twila Paris album *Cry for the Desert*. Brown enlisted me to arrange a few of the songs and play keyboards. First, I needed to meet with Twila at her home, check keys and tempo, and leave with some piano/vocal Sony Walkman cassette demos. He provided me with the time and address, and I was on my way.

Only problem was, Brown failed to mention to Twila that I'd be working on her album and was on my way to her house.

Imagine: I pull the Dodge into the stone driveway of her classic Nashville brick manse, park, and ring the doorbell. No answer. Try again. I see a shadow fade across a window. Minutes later, the door cracks open. Now the fun begins. She thinks I'm a gardener reporting for duty and begins to direct me to the backyard where my botanical assignment awaits.

"Uh, no, I'm Charlie Peacock, the arranger. Brown sent me." Blank look, puzzlement, phone call to Brown, and warm greeting, in that order. Lovely person and a great songwriter. Gardening is a noble vocation, but not why I came to Nashville. We made a tape, and I headed off to do my job.

Next up on the production schedule was a Reunion Records project titled *Our Christmas*, where Brown was committed to producing both Al Green and a Phil Keaggy/Kim Hill duet. He was so busy at the time that I was enlisted to coproduce. For Al, I arranged "The First Noel" to start minimal with a string quartet and build to an Al Green–worthy gospel music climax. After enlisting Bob Bailey, Kim Fleming, Ullanda McCullough, Vicki Hampton, and my own bandmember Vince Ebo for the big choir finish, I played the role of the absent Al and sang a temporary lead vocal (what we used to call a "scratch vocal").

Brown and I drove to Memphis to record Al at Kiva Studios, owned by Gary Belz and guitarist Joe Walsh. It was eventful. I had sent Al the work tape to learn the arrangement. Obviously, he hadn't studied it. I was a tight coil of nerves and trying my best not to show it.

This was Al Green—along with Smokey Robinson and Gladys Knight, my top soul and R&B vocal influence. I had a moral obligation to get this right.

I joined Al out in the tracking room around the microphone, put on some headphones, and had Brown roll the tape with my scratch vocal in the mix. I nervously explained to Al that it was me singing the lead vocal and that we were only listening to it to pick up the idiosyncrasies of the arrangement. In short order, the arrangement made sense, and I left the room for Al to do his thing without my interference. Five or so takes into recording we were almost there.

Though only a one-off track for a multiartist holiday record, it was no less fun, or rewarding, to hear Al transform my arrangement into his undeniable, iconic sound. As electric as Al sounds, though, neither Brown nor I were willing to compromise on quality because a legend was behind the microphone.

Drama ensued. There was a technical problem with a few of the tracks we'd recorded. This, combined with our opinion that Al had yet to fix a few pitch issues, meant we needed more vocal takes. He had a friendly, positive attitude and conceded to sing two more. Oops. I still wasn't convinced we were getting the absolute best, the best in the world had to give.

"Al, we're so close," I told him, amping my voice up to maximum positive. "The performance is amazing. Could we grab another take of the first verse, maybe? I promise, one more and we'll be done." Brown backed me up with his own encouragement.

It was then that the man who gave the world "Let's Stay Together" and "Love and Happiness" smiled, removed his headphones, and spoke these words into the microphone: "If you wanna hear it again, you're gonna have to get the boy on the tape to sing it."

The boy on the tape smiled. Al was the last one standing that day.

four

WAITING FOR GOD
TO SHOW HIS FACE

My parents raised me for fourteen years. No more, no less.

Imperfect and wounded, as all parents are, Mom and Dad had their hits and misses. When needed, Grandma Lois, my mom's mother, would keep me and provide serenity, love, and kindness. Her house on El Margarita Road was my safe place, a second home and first-choice shelter. My dad's parents put themselves in charge of taking me to Sunday school, where felt board characters represented the Bible's A-listers, fools, and villains. Several of my aunts pitched in too, and all in all, the bulk of the raising got done. Karoly, my mom's youngest sister, cared for me often and introduced me to The Beatles and The Beach Boys. Dad's sister Connie was always an encourager, letting me practice and record all night in her combo pool house–game room.

Then Jack Kerouac took over.

Mom and Dad were bright, and either the first, or among the first, in their families with college degrees. My parents would be the generation to make good on the American Dream in a contemporary fashion, the fruit of migration. Everything was new, and the promise was unfolding before them. It was all going to turn out great. No reason to think otherwise.

There was a problem, though, as old as dirt: their collective humanity. That is, all the stories each one brought to the marriage and those they embodied together over time. My folks loved each other till death did part. But it was never, ever easy for them. Instead, it was like they had a spring-loaded marriage; a deranged jack-in-the-box waiting to jump out and scare the hell out of them—and my sister Terri and me too. It was like we had a peace thief stalking us, breaking and entering into windows of heart and mind to steal shalom. Though small in number, those days were weighty in effect.

In truth, harmful enough to alter my brain, my life.

To leave it there would be dishonest, unfair, and simply inaccurate. The overwhelming majority of our childhood days are ones to remember and be thankful for. Terri and I were loved, doted on, and championed by our parents for a good, long while. My mom was attentive and present: a room mother for Cub Scouts, all of that, even while working outside the home for several years. She was on it, until she wasn't. And writing-wise, she was the wordsmith that inspired my poetry, essay, and lyric writing.

Dad was busy working out one long trajectory of achievement and overwork: Air Force band, telephone lineman, and weekend music gigs. Then back to college, more weekend gigs, and working for the California Peach Advisory Board fourteen to sixteen hours a day during the summer. Then he began teaching and running a high school music department. All this, while still playing what were called "dance jobs" and working the peaches for the state (for fifteen years or so), June through August.

Too busy for us or not, both my sister and I would say that our dad was fun, and funny, and loving. Until he wasn't.

Mom endured various illnesses—known and unknown—and what I now understand as recurring, untreated depression. I also know she brought a hurt into her marriage too painful to speak of, yet it likely influenced her person and marriage more than she could ever know. I love her more now in death than I ever could in life. Sad but true. If I could just wake her and tell her I finally understand.

For Dad, it was a different kind of hurt. Like me, he was born into a family with lots of loving women. "Little Willie" they called him. I suspect that for all of them he was a child of promise. Where might he go with all of this musical talent?

His father, Lee Jackson Ashworth, the sawyer from Louisiana's piney woods, gave him no encouragement. Grandpa knew nothing of what a gifted kid might do in music to make a life. His father-in-law had been an amateur musician, so was his wife's nephew, Tommy. Music didn't do either of them much good. One died from a logging accident. The other broke his back while logging, his body bent permanently parallel to the ground.

Dad showed his father what he could do. He became a hard worker in all things music, and a much-loved teacher. But like his father before him, he abused alcohol for a time. The alcohol had its way with him, and consequently with those he professed to love. There was no place for the shame to go but inward. He didn't have a highly skilled therapist on call as his son has had in various seasons of life. He had the man thing of his era going against him, too. *Men don't crack. They don't give up. They push through, and they certainly don't talk about their feelings to a stranger.* Dad never found a safe space to process. Just like with Mom, what I would give to wake Dad up from the grave and tell him I understand. He did the best with what he had.

—

When I retrace my history through the lens of age and experience, all I see is the intertwining of art and ad hoc spirituality—even my seeking Jesus—or if seeking is too strong, then simply holding open space for his presence and teaching. It's clear now that I'd been trying to answer lifesaving, cosmic questions since I've had the capacity to ponder such things.

In his *Letters to a Young Poet*, Rainer Maria Rilke writes, "Be patient towards all that is unsolved in your heart and try to love the questions themselves." He warns to avoid searching for answers you're not yet ready to live. "Live the questions now," he wrote. "Perhaps then, someday far in the future, you will gradually, without even noticing it, live your way into the answer."[1]

Before I'd read a word of Rilke, somehow I understood this counsel. Must've heard it on the wind.

As a teenager and young adult, I studied the writer-poets Jack Kerouac, Gary Snyder, and LeRoi Jones (and the constellation of Beat writers surrounding them) with the same verve I gave to memorizing the monthly contents of *Rolling Stone* magazine. This opened up the world to me physically, intellectually, and imaginatively and set me on a strict nonconformist, question-loving path. Through LeRoi Jones (Amiri Baraka) and his seminal book *Blues People: Negro Music in White America* (1963) I read a Black man trace Black music from slavery to contemporary jazz. Though too insulated and immature to feel the full weight of American history, I got my first look at the long Black story behind my culturally truncated view of the music I loved so much. It was a start.

British journalist Steve Turner has been writing about rock music since 1969, when his first article was published in *Beatles Monthly*. He's written definitive *New York Times* best sellers on Johnny Cash and The Beatles: *The Man Called Cash: The Life, Love, and Faith of an American Legend* and *Beatles '66: The Revolutionary Year*. I've seen some of his private photo collection of interview subjects—they're raw and right in the moment—and I've also heard audio from two fascinating interviews about Christian spirituality, one with John Lennon in 1971, the other with the Killer himself, rock pioneer Jerry Lee Lewis. Epic rock history and journalism.

My favorite book of Steve's, though, is *Jack Kerouac: Angelheaded Hipster*. According to Steve, "Jack Kerouac was essentially a writer with spiritual preoccupations: Waiting for God to show his face."

Kerouac's buddy Allen Ginsberg told Steve, "I think that spirituality was our primary thing . . . we all had some kind of visionary experience that pushed us out of the notion of art as just some career or commerce."[2]

Spiritual preoccupations. Visionary experiences. Art as more than just a career or commerce. Check. This bit here says so much of how I learned to define artistry. It has evolved and matured. But certainly, this is the foundation.

By the age of fifteen, home and family had become a bit of a rickety roller coaster ride. Unstable. Might have a good day or week. Could be tap dancing in a minefield, or "crawling across cut glass," like Dylan sang. I was too young to accurately discern and articulate the surrounding narrative, yet too old not to respond. I counted on not counting on anything. Unknowingly, I'd spent most of my brief life rehearsing for a role that would shape and define me for decades. Enter stage left. Hit your mark, Chronic Hypervigilant, Over Self-Reliant Child. Meet your audience.

Throughout my three-year stint in high school (I graduated as a junior), my parents' loneliness and longings, pain and anger oozed or detonated in plain sight more often than not. The gaps of time between "incidents and accidents," an apt phrase of Paul Simon's, was narrowing. By then, I'd added my own incidents of skin and mind to the drama.

For a blip of a moment, I auditioned the angsty, irresponsible behavior common to teens in the early 1970s. Generally, though, I behaved well. Especially where what came natural to me, or made sense to me, was rewarded. I left eighth grade as class president, having given a commencement address (just as my mother had two decades earlier) and slipped right into success in high school, especially in the music program, where I was named Freshman Bandsman of the Year. I was on my own achievement track, not a screw-your-life-up track.

I did have one abnormal, unspoken, and unshakable shadow shame—it wasn't mine to carry, but I lived with its weight. My parents never found out, and I never told them: a second cousin seven years older than me sexually abused me when I was five. He swore me to secrecy. Thankfully, it's a secret I no longer keep.

All of this unstable, ping-pong living was a setup. A trauma trap. A tricky foundation laid. A predisposition to receive Kerouac's writing as gospel. As providence would have it, I met one of his disciples.

David Parker was a music student of my dad's at Marysville High School. He was three years older and played the trumpet and the electric guitar. People emphasized the electric guitar back then, as if someone like Thomas Edison had recently brought it out of the workshop. David was smart, quiet, with a thin, stark shadow. I liked him. David and I, along with other students, would occasionally play music together. They were all from Marysville High. I was from the rival, Yuba City High, just across the Feather River.

Dad allowed our "rock group" to practice in the band room. The only thing remotely rock about our quintet was the slight overdrive of David's Fender amp. I didn't learn to hear the subtleties and beauty of distortion until I was a young record producer.

I lived in a peach orchard suburb in the farm country of Northern California. This location didn't allow for much contact with the more sophisticated outside world. Haight-Ashbury, with its hippies and musical soundtrack was only 125 miles due south of me. Didn't matter then. Could have been a thousand miles. Still, there were proxies, ways to draw near, enough to give light to the imagination.

Rolling Stone magazine and KPFA in Berkeley were two such helps. They were as close to the counterculture as I was going to get for a while. I must have said something to David Parker about a "far-out" article in *Rolling Stone.* Something triggered his generosity. He knew a cosmic secret, known by the dharma tribe and the principalities and powers of the air. David let go his grip, and the secret became mine.

He said, "Read *On the Road,* a novel by Jack Kerouac. Next, read *The Dharma Bums,* another novel by Jack Kerouac." And that's how Jack Kerouac ultimately raised me from age fourteen to eighteen.

Kerouac was a lousy parent. Yet, as suburban shamans go, a kid could do no better or worse. Kerouac, a writer and former football star, was a game-changer for me. (Kerouac is still getting traction today. It seems like every new, curious generation since the 1950s let Jack have a go at their right cerebral hemisphere.) Jack Kerouac's characters deconstructed social obligation and blind obedience. They replaced them with unwavering individualism and a robust distrust of all institutions and authority. Indeed. I could no longer trust my parents to make good decisions. Check. I was already morphing into something of an epiphyte. My parents and my house were the eternal wood of the bald cypress: strong yet ornamental with roots obscured in murky volatility, but I was Spanish moss—I needed a place to live. I was in the house, but not of it.

Kerouac also had the mad vision to suggest that if you didn't want to do something, then don't—a notion I loved as much as I'd ever loved anything. Heightened by an opening and freeing of the mind, even a teenager like me could possess world-changing awareness. As the 1970 Funkadelic song says, "Free your mind and your ass will follow."

"Freedom" was loosely defined as liberty to reject traditional ideas about education, marriage, work, sexuality, material possessions, and identity in general. Kerouac made it clear that the whitewashed world of predictable, rote behavior was a death trap void of the necessary and far better ecstatic life. I couldn't have agreed more.

Through stories in *Rolling Stone* and the lives of older kids around me, I saw a new breed of imaginative, creative people changing the world and having a whole lot of fun doing it. I wanted to be in that number. A son of laughter. A beatific Zen saint humanist in search of transcendence, yes, and also a boy who longed to be pulled out of the pain that too often came from the words and deeds of loved ones.

There was a nonconformist artist gestating inside my teenage self, and Kerouac put language to it. But that wasn't all. Kerouac revealed a God-hauntedness that far exceeded my own. Steve Turner writes, "After taking LSD with Allen Ginsberg and Timothy Leary—during the trip Jack was shouting to Leary: 'Can your drugs absolve the mortal and venial sins which our beloved Savior Jesus Christ, the only Son of God, came down and sacrificed his life upon the cross to wash away?'"[3]

It was Kerouac's novel *The Dharma Bums* that drummed my soul most. If *On the Road* set me free willy-nilly, *The Dharma Bums* gave my newly gained freedom its first true shapes. Risk, adventure, a storied life, spiritual transcendence, and the role of religion in grooming dynamic, imaginative global citizens.

All of this described the Dharma bum himself, the mountaineer, Zen poet, Gary Snyder, or as Kerouac named him in his novel, Japhy Ryder. Steve Turner posits that Jack saw Gary as the "spiritually consistent person" he would never be.

By the time I read *On the Road*, I was an easy mark. I'd been sucking up the ethos of antimaterialism, unimpressed with the American Dream. I was listening for clues, hoping to find the path to an adventurous, spontaneous human destiny. Implicitly, explicitly, I heard, I saw, and was changed. Almost overnight I became one kind of person in the world and not another.

The Zen poet Gary Snyder offered more than jazzy, intellectual rebellion.

Snyder was a person integrated with the land, in search of enlightenment, artistic, and a steward of words. He found a way to bridge post–WWII ideas about manhood with a new mind-set of openness and generosity to people and place.

I imagined him good with an axe and a better dream, one cosmic, not simply American.

I wanted to be someone who was good with words, music, and the better dream that Gary Snyder hinted at.

Seventeen and attending junior college, I had the idea of bringing Gary Snyder to the school. I wrote a letter, and he came. He brought along a small tribe of Nevada City hippie-looking folks.

It's been decades since my first exposure to Kerouac and Snyder. I can still call to mind much of the ad hoc beat doctrine, partly accurate, some imagined. Kerouac and Snyder awakened me to both the futility and connectedness of life, and offered me a vocabulary to describe my restlessness.

When I'm producing a record and artists refuse to risk, rip themselves wide open, and rebel against the status quo, I hurt for them. I think, *why aren't you trying to go somewhere no one else is going? Why is your reach so limited? Where's your imagination? What keeps you from failing big in order to touch the diamond emerging from your rubble?* When I think like this, I know it's because of the influence of Kerouac, Snyder, Miles Davis, and Coltrane.

Coltrane's most popular recording, *A Love Supreme*, brought the full impact of his spiritual quest into the public square; a pursuit I signed up for decades ago.

It's remarkable that Coltrane had his greatest commercial success with his most explicitly spiritual recording. In the liner notes Coltrane announces, "Dear Listener: ALL PRAISE BE TO GOD TO WHOM ALL PRAISE IS DUE." The uppercase lettering was all Coltrane. Praising God was something he was very serious about. He closed the letter with "Seek Him every day. In all ways seek God every day. Let us sing all songs to God."

Coltrane was born in Hamlet, North Carolina, and raised in High Point. Both his grandfathers were African Methodist Episcopal Zion pastors. The inspiration for the AME Zion church was nothing less than spiritual, social, and economic emancipation. Abolitionist leaders Harriet Tubman, Frederick Douglass, and Sojourner Truth were all AME Zion members. Not bad company. Rather like what John Lewis called good trouble.

By his own admission, Coltrane had his first personal experiences of music making at church, in the Youth House outreach ministry of St. Stephens AME (where his grandfather had pastored). There, in the basement, a community worker and musician taught young men the basic fundamentals of music and how to play a few songs on their given instrument—which for Coltrane was the clarinet. Clarinet being the gateway woodwind to saxophone.

The church continued this helping and equipping role. When neighbors complained about Coltrane practicing at home, the minister gave John a key to the church. Now he could practice anytime he wanted.

The day the first US atomic bomb, "Little Boy," was dropped on Hiroshima, Japan, Coltrane enlisted in the navy. And like my own dad in the Air Force dance band, Coltrane served his time in the navy swing band. Once discharged, he headed back to Philadelphia, where he'd been since 1943, when first aware of what he called "the Muslim thing."[4]

At the risk of being reductive but desiring to be brief, the first pillar of Muslim faith is: "I bear witness that there is no god but God, and Muhammad is God's Messenger."[5] As in Judaism and Christianity, Muslims are monotheists. One God for all people.

Coltrane went on to encounter many religions and spiritual teachers, including gurus Krishnamurti and Paramhansa Yogananda. Coltrane became a religious syncretist—as did I for a good, long time. It was the zeitgeist of the era. I've heard it called "buffet spirituality."

Krishnamurti wrote, "To be serious, to be earnest, surely implies the capacity to find out what is true. Can I find out what is true if my mind is tethered to any particular point of view? If it is bound by knowledge, by belief, if it is caught in the conditioning influences that are constantly impinging upon it, can the mind discover anything new?"[6] Yogananda's name means "bliss through divine union." He was a big-name teacher of yoga, the author of *Autobiography of a Yogi*, and the founder of the Self-Realization Fellowship.

Coltrane also knew something of his West African ancestral roots, such as the Yoruba, a people group from Nigeria and Benin. Drumming and dancing are a part of Yoruban culture and religious festivals. Which might have been what Coltrane was reaching for with the rhythmic pulse of his compositions "Africa" and "Kulu Sé Mama."

I've made one record, *Love Press Ex-Curio*, with Coltrane's son Ravi on tenor saxophone. He was named after sitarist Ravi Shankar. Shankar's daughter Norah Jones is a bright talent. Serendipitously, my kids, son Sam Ashworth and his wife, Ruby Amanfu, have recorded with Norah on her Blue Note Records release *Pick Me Up Off the Floor*.

Coltrane's third son received a Yoruba name: Oranyan Olabisi. Oranyan of Oyo was one of the original founders of the Yoruba nation. The name Olabisi means "joy is multiplied." The Christians have a letter in their Bible, from the apostle Paul of Tarsus to the church at Philippi. In it are sixteen instances of the words "joy" and "rejoice" written by Paul, imprisoned and in chains. The multiplication of joy in the worst of circumstances.

Coltrane was a classic autodidact, and in no small part why I am the same. In the latter part of his life, he studied world music voraciously and was exposed again and again to the worldviews associated with various music, including traditional Negro spirituals, Vedic chants, Indian scales associated with Hinduism, and Buddhist temple worship.

Having studied Coltrane the seeker, I'm of the arguable opinion that his entire spiritual journey was an individualized attempt at syncretizing Christianity (the religion of his youth) with every religion and spiritual/philosophical idea he ever encountered. The only way Coltrane could make peace with all the differing views about religion and God was to create his own fusion of them. He wanted all paths to lead to the same God. Sticking to Christianity alone required one to interact with Jesus, the Christ. Jesus said about himself, "I am the way and the truth and the life. No one comes to the Father except through me" (John 14:6–7).[7] Something of an outrageous claim for a carpenter's son from Nazareth, North Israel.

In his own words, Coltrane summed up his spiritual influences best: "I believe in all religions."[8]

Coltrane told interviewer August Blume: "When I saw there were so many religions and kind of opposed somewhere to the next and so forth . . . it screwed up my head. I was kind of confused . . . and I just couldn't believe that just one guy could be right. Because if he's right somebody else got to be wrong, you know."[9]

Coltrane modeled the pursuit of musical innovation, individualism, spirituality, seeking, and questioning to me. In his last decade on earth, every time Coltrane picked up his instrument, he was seeking and praying to God. Like all seekers, he wanted to know and be known.

So did I.

These questions and more held me in their grip:

- How did I get here on this spinning ball of land and ocean?
- How am I me and not someone else?
- Is there a Creator or is evolution alone the explanation for the origin of life?
- If God does exist and is the maker of all things, what does he want for the sum of his creativity, specifically people; even more specifically, me?
- Am I supposed to be in relationship with God as some people say? If so, how?
- Where does music fit in among these questions?
- And why do some behaviors shame me and others make me feel more human and eager for life?

—

My Ashworth grandparents were members of the First Christian Church located at the corner of Eighth and H Streets in Marysville, California, just across the Feather River from Yuba City. My parents were married there. The attendance of our own family unit was spotty at best. We were waterskiing, fishing, Dad-needs-to-sleep attendees. If we weren't committed to one of those three on a Sunday, we might show up. Which is where my grandparents fit in. They were happy to take me and my little sister, even if sporadically.

That church is where I learned the hymns and songs common to American Christian faith of the era. Including "This Little Light of

Mine," "Onward, Christian Soldiers," and "Great Is Thy Faithfulness." Standing next to my grandpa Ashworth, I held my own worn hymnal and gained the first clues to the architecture of music. I could easily see that the pitch of our collective voices was meant to rise and fall in relationship to the notes and lyrics on the page. I kept my eye on the ups and downs.

In 1966, our family moved from town to the country and a township named Tierra Buena, "good earth," where my mother grew up. Three and a half miles. Our new home and subdivision had recently been carved out of an orchard, accurately named Tierra Del Sol, or land of the sun. My maternal grandparents, great and regular, both lived within walking distance, by road or by ditch.

Settled in by 1968, at not quite the two-year mark, my mom had a hysterectomy and appendectomy. Postsurgery she began reading the Bible in earnest, praying, and eventually, she became a steady churchgoer at First Christian. My sis and I accompanied, while Dad could opt out if he'd been up late on Saturday night playing a dance job.

In March of '69, Mom and I walked the chapel aisle together, hand in hand, to profess to minister Don Roberts that we desired to become Christians. A class for new believers preceded our baptism, on Sunday, the sixth of that April.

I became a regular attendee of youth group and various events, including a sleepover where I repeatedly and obsessively listened to Blood, Sweat & Tears, second album, the one riddled with hits.

Enthused with God and baseball, I gave a youth sermon conflating the two. Absent of grace, my preachment was a perfect example of what theologians call "works righteousness." Which is essentially, working my way to God, putting points on the majestic, spiritual scoreboard in heaven. There are religions that promote something like a point system. Christianity is not one of them, despite the persistent fiction to the contrary.

For a time, Dad was the choir director at First Christian. I, in turn, became one of its youngest members, reading music and singing alto and tenor parts. I also found the blues in that church. Alone one evening, while Dad sorted music in the back closet, I searched for the music embedded in the sanctuary piano. There it was: C E-flat F

G-flat G and B-flat. The blues scale. I'd been hearing this sound everywhere from my dad's jazz records, Uncle Walt's country albums, Aunt Karoly's rock and pop singles, and R&B and soul music on Top 40 radio. I checked that mystery off my list. Little did I know then that this scale, along with the pentatonic scale, are the foundational elements of my ancestral soundtrack.

One Sunday, Jim Jones brought a whole busload up to the church—followers of his from the People's Temple in San Francisco. Jim did some healing on one of our people, who coughed up what looked like a nasty hairball. Dad presciently pronounced the whole thing "bullshit." And in 1978, Jones was responsible for the mass suicide of those who had followed him down to Guyana to live at what was dubbed Jonestown. Late in the summer of 1971, days after turning fifteen, about to begin my sophomore year of high school, I got a real girlfriend. Andi Berrier and I were going steady. She was remarkably beautiful with her long red hair and sweet smile. I had hit the jackpot of girlfriends. We became inseparable best friends. She was smart, fashionable, and loved music. But to know her was to know her family, and their own incidents and accidents.

Due to circumstances in both of our families, it was fast becoming apparent I would need to take care of myself, and possibly Andi, too. Use your imagination here. Families unravel for a short list of reasons. I could name them, but I've got enough of the old recovery ethos in me not to. *Make amends and tell the truth, wherever possible, except when to do so would injure someone further.*

I plotted my emancipation—I wanted out, like the pit of a freestone peach. No clinging here. I needed more hours at work, STAT, and a car, or at least a motorcycle. Through deceit and hard work, I had all three in short order. I managed an early driver's permit for the motorcycle by purchasing a stolen pink slip for five dollars from a student. The pink slip was an official document to be signed by your drivers' ed instructor stating you'd completed the course, which I had not. I secured a copy of the instructor's signature, Melvin O. Good, and practiced tracing it for a week. Once confident, I boldly took the forged document to the DMV, paid the fee, passed the test, and was forever illegally legal.

For my entire junior year of high school, which would prove to be my last, I worked nearly full time at W. T. Grants and played gigs on the weekend. I was sixteen. *Men don't crack. They don't give up. They push through.* That year, at one point, I rented a dismal shack of a place on the edge of town and bought a small chrome dinette with a handful of spoons and forks. Within a week, the crisis that inspired this spending had passed. I got most of my money back. It was an audition for the leaving that was to come.

On those days and weeks when the light of our family was snuffed, when good and right took leave, I learned to leave the room. Sometimes physically, others by an odd survival trick of the brain—what I now know was disassociation. Again, an epiphyte; in it but not of it. If circumstances required that I hold the pose of anxiety, anger, and fear long enough, my legs would feel like they were crossing, or exchanging places, as if my left had switched to right and right to left. My vision would get stuck, like when you pause a video and the character on the screen appears to be seeing everything and nothing at the same time. It seemed as if a part of me was peeling off from my body, draping my frame like a gray, ghost overcoat.

It took me most of my adult life to realize it is neither normal nor healthy for a young teenage boy to feel the desperate need to plot an exit strategy from his family. With this truth acknowledged in my early sixties, I began to accept the life I had lived: five decades of festering anger, exhausting hypervigilance, a fierce survival instinct, and the unrelenting need to protect and provide for my family, no matter the cost.

five

SOME KIND OF VISIONARY EXPERIENCE

I was in Los Angeles in 1980, at the beginning of my musical artist career, meeting with record labels and playing the open-mic night at the Troubadour on Santa Monica in West Hollywood. Michael Stone, my manager, was employed by Warner Brothers Records in Burbank. He worked closely with an American solo artist named Gary Wright. Michael thought Gary might be the person to produce my debut album. I knew of Gary from his songs "Love Is Alive" and "Dream Weaver," two ubiquitous chart-topping hits in 1976. The latter was inspired by a book given to him by George Harrison of The Beatles.

And so it was that I found myself at Gary's home and studio for a surreal afternoon of sharing music and his spirituality (guru Paramhansa Yogananda), and admiring his collection of instruments, several given to him by George—his most frequent collaborator (and fellow follower of Yogananda). George had his own religion-inspired hit, "My Sweet Lord." A song I sang in the choir at First Christian Church, Marysville, California, in 1971. My dad, the choir director, edited the Krishna-centric lyrics to be exclusively Christian.

Time with the Dream Weaver was no one-off exception.

I had been to the Yogananda commune—the Self-Realization Fellowship founded by Swami Kriyananda outside Nevada City, California, near poet Gary Snyder's home. (When I first met drummer Aaron Smith, he, like Wright and Harrison, was a disciple of Yogananda. When I got him the gig playing drums on the 1983 Vector recording *Mannequin Virtue*, he still was.

For a time in the mid-1970s, the *Tao Te Ching* was my morning devotion, and I studied the popular Buddhism of Alan Watts and D. T. Suzuki. I also went to a Transcendental Meditation orientation to receive a mantra but had to punt. I didn't have money for the required flowers. No flowers, no mantra. The jazz bassist Marc Johnson introduced me to the writings of Krishnamurti. Rudolph Steiner and anthroposophy had been at the heart of a short-lived gig with the Sacramento funk band The Runners. I was becoming something like a walking comparative religion class, with the figure of Jesus always in the shadows.

During this same time frame of 1976–1980, four Irish high school students were beginning their own unique story of music and Jesus. Just after the summer of 1976, a fourteen-year-old musician named Larry Mullen posted a handwritten note on a bulletin board at Mount Temple School in Dublin, Ireland: "Drummer seeks musicians to form band." Paul Hewson showed up. And with very few fits and stutters as bands go, Paul had become Bono, and guitarist Dave Evans, the Edge. The other two band members, Larry Mullen and bassist Adam Clayton, both criminally handsome, kept their names. With the help of a manager, Paul McGuinness, the world would know the quartet as simply U2. They signed with Island Records in 1980 and released their first full-length album, *Boy*.

Bono tells this next story best in his memoir *Surrender*, so I'll get to the essential bits quickly and leave the Irish poetry to his account. Bono, Edge, and Larry attended a nondenominational Protestant Christian church known as Shalom Fellowship. Between *Boy* and their next release, *October*, it is widely reported that "a member of the Shalom Fellowship claimed to have had a prophetic vision from God about the band. God wanted the boys to give up the band as a sacrifice to Him and leave rock music altogether."[1]

This put the band in a quandary, each professing Christian dealing with it in his own way and time. Contextually, this was a time when a prophecy like this was taken quite seriously. Recipients might doubt or question; or be scared to death of its veracity with no faithful option but to surrender. People claiming to have such intimate knowledge of the will of God wielded a power differential. It was manager McGuinness that, in the end, brought the stronger, more convincing word to the young band. Honoring existing contracts, keeping your word, and caring for people were equally important ways of hearing from and being faithful to God. Some members of Shalom, like many other zealous prophecy-immersed groups of the time, set up a false dichotomy: *Choose rock music or Jesus.* You can't do both. They called U2's bluff and lost.

By 1982, Bono, Edge, and Larry had left Shalom behind. They kept following Jesus, but religion organized as they'd experienced it, no. Enter Jack Heaslip, former English teacher and guidance counselor at Mount Temple Secondary School, where U2 first met. Now an Anglican minister, Jack became chaplain to U2, the tour pastor, looking over the ever-growing flock of band, crew, and families until his death in 2015.

In a blessing offered to the band and crew the night before the 2001 Elevation Tour began, Jack prayed these words: "So we ask for that anointing to be poured out by the power of his Spirit. So we simply say: Come, Holy Spirit, and reign. Pour out your rule and anointing on this tour. Let nothing be an obstacle. Just melt away anything that is not of you, so that your power can flow without interruption. We claim your blessing and your anointing, because we ask it in the name of Jesus Christ. Amen."[2]

—

Though I observed the ubiquitous hippie Jesus Movement as a high schooler in the early 1970s, I had no interest in becoming what was called a Jesus freak. I had my childhood Christian church experience and took no issue with Jesus. My mix of spirituality and music reflected the times and musicians I admired, though. I already had ample direction for living the questions of art and God, going back to my early Christian experiences, as well as Kerouac, Snyder, and Coltrane—then, continuing on with new *spiritual* virtuoso musicians like Mahavishnu John McLaughlin (a disciple of guru Sri Chinmoy).

Though the American West Coast Jesus Movement of the 1970s is not something I know from deep experience, I eventually learned the story. And no musician epitomizes its nascence more than Larry Norman. Before there were any professing Christians, U2, The 77s, or myself recording for Chris Blackwell's Island Records, or any chart-topping pop hits from Amy Grant, Switchfoot, Sixpence None the Richer, Kirk Franklin, The Fray, Lauren Daigle, or Lecrae—there was Larry Norman, a Christian and recording artist for Capitol Records. He'd been in a psychedelic rock band on Capitol called People!, a one-hit assembly known for their 1968 cover of The Zombies' "I Love You."

Larry left the band just as the single peaked and the album was released. No hard feelings from Capitol Records, though. Under Mike Curb's direction, Capitol released Larry's first solo recording, *Upon This Rock* (1969), and made history. For over fifty years the idea has been promulgated that *Upon This Rock* was the first "Christian rock" record.[3] Larry described the album as "love songs to Jesus."[4] The set included a song titled "I Wish We'd All Been Ready."

Like my experience with recordings released by major labels A&M Records (1985) and Island Records (1986), Larry's solo outing with Capitol did not sell well. Still, Christian bookstores eventually took notice, and the record found an audience. Looking to recoup, Capitol leased the record to Heartwarming in 1972, a Nashville label started by John T. Benson of the southern gospel music family. Though Larry cooperated with the rerelease of *Upon This Rock*, years later he reflected: "I had very little interest in cultivating endorsements from the Church. I was out to create a dialogue. . . . I wanted to be on the battlefield, fighting a spiritual battle, trying to convince and convert the undecided. . . . Though I may have been in error in standing aside from the brethren by not performing for them, the established Church was simply immaterial to me."[5]

He never did find peace assimilating into the material church and playing nice with the Christian music industry that emerged from the Jesus Movement.

—

I walked into the last gasps of its energy in 1982 in Sacramento, California, at a church named Calvary Chapel Sacramento, then a year later, at Warehouse Ministries. The Warehouse (as it's known) was way out front on several ideas yet to reside in the average Christian mind, including naming your church a nonchurchy name like Elevate, Thrive, or Dream City. Admittedly, trailblazing as it was, the name Warehouse had aspirational limitations. But that was never an issue. The church's pastoral leadership, Mary and Louis Neely, had aspirations to spare, especially Mary.

I quickly picked up the Jesus Movement's history from this vantage of place and people. I formulated thoughts about all that went down socially, theologically, and musically. Calvary Chapel (Costa Mesa, California, as ground central), Vineyard, and Warehouse Ministries are my nexus of churches. Pastor Kenn Gulliksen, "sent out" by Calvary Chapel, started a church in West Los Angeles in 1974 and named it Vineyard. Within a year, another Vineyard was planted, with more to come, including the Anaheim Vineyard Christian Fellowship, pastored by John Wimber.

In 1982, the year I was introduced to Calvary Chapel Sacramento (pastored by John and Laura Cowan), the Association of Vineyard Churches (eight in all) was founded. Official ties to Calvary Chapel were severed. An inevitable outcome due to pastor John Wimber's theological influence on the Vineyard movement—an influence Calvary Chapel leadership was not fond of. With Kenn as the founder, John became the movement's natural leader.

Of all the musicians that collided with the Vineyard, none was more explosive than Robert Zimmerman, long since known as Bob Dylan. Bob tells the story of a visceral encounter with Jesus in 1978 at a hotel room in Tucson, Arizona: "Jesus put his hand on me. It was a physical thing. I felt it. I felt it all over me. I felt my whole body tremble. The glory of the Lord knocked me down and picked me up."[6]

Five of his band members at the time, singers Helena Springs and Mary Alice Artes, and musicians Steven Soles, David Mansfield, and T Bone Burnett, had all become followers of Jesus and attended gatherings at Pastor Kenn Gulliksen's Vineyard location in West Los Angeles. Mary Alice Artes is credited with enlisting Vineyard pastors Larry Myers and Paul Emond to visit Bob at home and minister to him there. Bob followed up his public profession by attending an in-depth Bible course at the Vineyard Christian Fellowship in Reseda,

California. What came next shocked Dylan's fans and rock music critics alike. He released a new album titled *Slow Train Coming*, produced by Muscle Shoals piano man Barry Beckett and the legendary Jerry Wexler. Guest guitarist Mark Knopfler summed it up in short order: "All these songs are about God."[7]

The Warehouse was also linked to Calvary Chapel and the founding pastor, Chuck Smith. Though that connection was never advertised as such or sufficiently explained. The allusion was that Pastor Louis, an ex-pat Assemblies of God missionary, was "sent out" and preached under the authority of Pastor Chuck (also formerly of the Assemblies of God denomination).

Along with teaching through books of the Bible, charismatic affectations and beliefs, altar-call evangelism, and ocean and river baptisms, it was music that tied Calvary, Vineyard, and Warehouse together. New music was created by musicians within the communities for musical worship (then called praise songs) and enjoyment. It was not long before there were weekly evangelism-centric concerts with "Jesus music" solo artists and bands. In-house recording studios were built, and publishing and record companies were founded and funded. Calvary Chapel had Maranatha! Music (as early as 1971); the Vineyard, Vineyard Music; the Warehouse, the *Rock & Religion* radio show, Sangre Productions, and Exit Records.

—

A key artist and musician in my Warehouse and Jesus travelogue is Jimmy Abegg, whom I met in 1982 at Maurice's American Bar in Sacramento at Fifteenth and Broadway. The bar was located across the street from the storied but defunct Tower Cut Rate Drug Store. Tower Records founder Russ Solomon got his start there selling used jukebox records.

Maurice's, curated by attorney Maurice Read, was a late 1970s restaurant and bar for Sacramento's artists, creative types, and left-of-center thinkers (later known as Melarkey's). I was a regular performer beginning in 1979. Andi bartended there for a time. Maurice's was where Sal Valentino of The Beau Brummels (a Top 40 pop band credited as early architects of the San Francisco sound) first heard me. As a result, Sal took me around to meet various record companies in Los Angeles. Sal and songwriter Stephen Holsapple lit the fuse on my career as a recording artist. Circles of affirmation.

Jimmy had come to the club to hear me perform. I was the odd curiosity and exception in Sacramento—a favorite local musician who had become a Christian yet headlined clubs playing his own music (which no one thought of as Christian music). As reported in the *Sacramento Bee*, "Charlie Peacock, the superlative keyboardist and bandleader who single-handedly pioneered 'original' rock music in Sacramento has undergone a religious conversion and is now a born-again Christian."[8] And so it was, hyperbole and all.

A few months later, in the same newspaper, local music critic David Barton wrote an article under the headline "ROCK 'N' ROLL IS BORN AGAIN." "Rock 'n' roll and Christianity are very much with us," opined Barton. "And there is a new generation of young Christians, raised on rock, who are attempting to blend their faith and their music. Name entertainers such as T Bone Burnett, Marvin Gaye, and Irish New-Wavers U2 have openly declared their Christian faith and are using their music to spread the Word."[9]

Barton quoted me as saying, "It's an opportunity for new listeners to view the socio-political landscape through the eyes of an artist who professes Jesus of Nazareth as the Christ." I was trying to sound more intelligent than I was. The depth of my sociopolitical knowledge was thin as glass and just as vulnerable.

I had my reasons for being wordy and nerdy.

At the time, American evangelical Christian theology aligned with a false assumption. It went something like this: Are you a Christian? Yes. Are you a musician? Yes. Then you are a Christian musician. Take your place serving the Christian church. When I renewed my confession of faith in Jesus in 1982, no Christian asked, "Will you continue playing nightclubs and theaters and developing as a pop recording artist?" Instead, the assumption was that I would be entering *music ministry*, becoming, in effect, a Christian artist, Christian musician, or music minister.

By definition, a musician or artist in music ministry was an accomplished itinerant vocalist, instrumentalist, and songwriter who traveled from church to church, providing special music and concerts in which an altar call was made. (An altar call is an invitation to accept Jesus as your personal Savior—which, for the recipient, often entailed leaving your seat and walking the aisle up to the altar or front of the church. This act became your public profession of faith in Christ alone.)

Eventually, this music-ministry function in the church was monetized, and contemporary Christian music (CCM) (as a genre and industry) was born.[10]

Three critical events put me on another course.

First was meeting Jimmy, who affirmed that I could, and perhaps should, remain doing what I'd been doing—playing nightclubs and developing as a pop recording artist.

Jimmy and I quickly became allies. He had traveled the faith-and-music road just a little longer than me. I considered him my elder and guide. I listened to what Jimmy had to say. He was passionate about Jesus without an ounce of religiosity. His favorite Bible verse was Jeremiah 29:11, "'For I know the plans I have for you,' declares the LORD, 'plans to prosper you and not to harm you, plans to give you hope and a future.'"

U2 were fans of Jeremiah as well. Years later, they put a coded version of Jeremiah 33:3 on the cover of *All That You Can't Leave Behind*: "Call to me and I will answer you and tell you great and unsearchable things you do not know." Bono referred to it as God's phone number.

Jimmy was no rock star yet. But he had lived outside under the stars and experimented with LSD, two distinctions I noted at the time. By way of a circuitous and mystical conversion, Jimmy quit trippin' to get "high on Jesus," just like the Kinky Friedman song says. All in all, Jimmy's combination of quirk and conviction was magnetic. I liked him very much.

Two, I read Francis Schaeffer's *Art and the Bible*. A few key ideas offered in the book were added to the foundation on which I built my house of music: art and artists need no pragmatic justification for existence; no single work of art could or should be required to detail the fullness of belief or conviction or be used as a litmus test for Christian profession; artists who do not profess Christ do good work, and it should be named as such; and God does not require realism over imagination. I added these to what I'd learned from Kerouac, Snyder, and Coltrane—especially art as more than career or commerce. Schaeffer's little pamphlet was invaluable because it was a marker on the trail of converging Jesus apprenticeship and authentic artistry. It pointed backward and forward to more teaching and clarity to come.

Three, I met Mary Neely of the Warehouse. She had envisioned a new spin on the music ministry model. Instead of the itinerant musical artist traveling from church to church, providing special music or a concert in which an altar call was made, what if the church was replaced by the nightclub, theater, or concert hall? What if the "altar call" of old was replaced by a new dependence on the Spirit to do the spiritual work of invitation vis-à-vis the artists, their music, and Spirit-inspired lyrics? What if?

At one point in my growing friendship with Jimmy, I became convinced I should set music aside and pursue a proper theological education. For three reasons, this was not unusual. First, the previously mentioned zeitgeist of the time; second, the musician who "led me to Christ," Michael Butera, was incrementally setting music aside and studying to be a pastor; and third, I'd had the inclination once before.

While a sophomore in high school, I hatched a short-lived plan to graduate early and attend Azusa Pacific, a Christian college in Southern California. On November 23, 1971, I wrote in my journal: "I've told some people that I'm going into religious study and missionary work. Some laughed. Others were shocked, and some were happy for me . . . my dad doesn't know my exact plans, and he still thinks I'm going to be a music major because he keeps saying, 'You'll never be a music major if you don't practice the trumpet more often.' I do know he thinks it's kind of strange that I'm reading the Bible so much."

With animated limbs, Jimmy's hands waving off the smoke from his cigarette, he argued against me attending the Calvary Chapel Bible School. According to Jimmy, my musical contribution to society would be sufficient.

Then Jimmy arranged for me to meet with the enigmatic Mary, the *Rock & Religion* radio show founder and budding auteur. It was Jimmy's sense that Mary should get to know me and that I should visit the Warehouse, where he and other musicians, such as the accomplished guitarist/songwriter Mike Roe, had found Christian fellowship, support, and a creative home.

Mary was cautious yet curious. After all, I was an unvetted outsider, with only Jimmy, a lovable but effusive artist, as my character witness. She greeted me with kindness and optimism. As our conversation revealed, I was doing what she and the other musicians aspired to: songwriting, performing, and recording for audiences beyond the church (though my reach was hardly broad—playing clubs in Sacramento, Tahoe, and the San Francisco Bay Area). Since I'd been steadily working as a session musician and producer for four years, my studio experience might've been slightly more than the other musicians in her orbit. She intimated this would be useful.

A dozen or so talented musicians were hanging around Warehouse Ministries then, names like Jimmy and Mike, Steve Griffith, Jan Volz, Mark Tootle, Steve Scott, and more, including those coming through playing concerts—Leon Patillo, Steven Soles, Maria Muldaur, Mylon LeFevre.[11] The idea was to build a recording studio, choose artists and bands from among the ranks, make records with them, and allow them to collectively do their part to create the musical world they wanted to live in.

So far, Mary had conceptualized a recording titled *Come Back Soon* (1978), recorded at Maranatha! Studio, and executive-produced two recordings, The Seventy Sevens' *Ping Pong over the Abyss* (1982) and Thomas Goodlunas and Panacea's *Take Me Away* (1983). The latter two were produced by Steven Soles (the Vineyard veteran with tenure in Bob Dylan's Rolling Thunder Revue, 1975–1976)[12] and released on the Warehouse's Exit imprint distributed by Word Records.

After my sit-down with Mary, I took a tour of the Warehouse concert space and the 24-track analog studio with its unusual broadcast-type recording console. I peeked at the smaller radio show studio, met some of the musicians, and heard the history. Which, I had to admit, was fascinating. Notably, the syndicated radio show *Rock & Religion* (1974–1977)—later rebranded as *Rockscope* (1977–1981).

The Brit journalist Steve Turner, a friend of Bono and Larry Norman, had been interviewed for the show early on and was also enlisted to conduct interviews. Along with founders Mary Neely and Mike Roe, other writers and announcers contributed to the show, including the aforementioned Englishman Steve Scott (once signed to Larry Norman's record label) and Davin Seay (coauthor of Al Green's memoir, *Take Me to the River*). The show was pressed on vinyl and aired Sunday morning when American radio stations met FCC (Federal Communications Commission) requirements with religious programming. Since *Rockscope* was about ferreting spiritual themes in rock music, it was a double bonus for rock and pop stations. Rock and religion—hence the original title. The show included music and interviews with Bonnie Bramlett, Arlo Guthrie, Pete Townsend of The Who, Roger McGuinn of The Byrds, T Bone Burnett and the Alpha Band, Richie Furay of the Buffalo Springfield, and many more. Much of this research later appeared in the book *Stairway to Heaven: The Spiritual Roots of Rock 'n' Roll*, written by Mary Neely and Davin Seay.

Steve Turner aggregated his ideas on the history of rock and religion in *Hungry for Heaven: Rock 'n' Roll and the Search for Redemption*. He had interviewed T Bone Burnett for *Rockscope*, and while staying with him in Los Angeles, Steve began to tease out the initial ideas for the book.

Decades after interacting with Mary and the Warehouse, I asked Steve to recap the experience. His take on Mary, the former Christian missionary, is insightful. "Mary wasn't in the USA for the whole '60s music revolution. She watched from a distance and viewed it as someone who'd experienced ritual music in Africa and Brazil up close and could see the similarities." At first, Steve thought Mary might be perpetuating a "Devil's Rock" origin story. He became convinced her take on the scene was genuine when she produced interviews with American musicians (such as Mickey Hart from the Grateful Dead) comparing themselves to shamans or boasting about putting listeners into trance states. It became clear to Steve that rock and religion had a common foe, what he poetically called the "horror of the mundane" and the "ambition to cause people to transcend that state."

This made me think of my young admiration for John Coltrane and his epic saxophone improvisations of prayer and search for transcendence. Or Steve's interview with poet Allen Ginsberg, where he claimed how Kerouac and the Beats "all had some kind of visionary experience."

Mike Roe, *Rockscope* cofounder, writer, and announcer, was on the other side of the microphone now. A walking encyclopedia of rock 'n' roll, Mike was the guitar-slinging frontman for the The 77s (previously the Scratch Band). In 1981–1982, the Scratch Band was one of many bands in Sacramento and San Francisco pitching themselves to me for gigs at the three clubs I played most (and conveniently was in charge of booking). I slotted the Scratch Band in a couple of times because I recognized their drummer, Mark Proctor, from Whitefire, a hometown band that played dances at Yuba City High School when I was a student.

As I'd done with Jimmy, Mike and I would join at the hip, along with recording engineer Daryl Zachman. We spent a concentrated six-year chunk of our lives together making music. But first, there had to be an understanding, an arrangement, a meeting of the minds with the church leadership.

Mary and her husband, Pastor Louis Neely, had invited me to become part of this unique experiment of a Christian church sponsoring pop recording artists—the kind committed to art-centric work and embodying the answers to my two unrelenting questions: What does it mean to be a disciple of Jesus? And what does it mean to be an artist?

As an idea? Sure, solid. Was it meant to be, though?

Andi and I had to pray and count the cost. We already had a supportive church fellowship in Calvary Chapel, Sacramento. We owned an 8-track recording studio in collaboration with a video production company that graciously funneled work to us. I performed somewhere in Northern California nearly every weekend. Of utmost concern, we were barely a year into following Jesus and had only two years of healthy family and financial stability to our credit. The first years of our teenage marriage had been anything but stable or safe.

We loved Jimmy and his wife, Michelle, but didn't know the Warehouse or the Neelys. This was jumping into the unknown just when the known was getting good. What made the decision complicated and arduous was that the musician who had *led me to the Lord* was very much against it. Thankfully, unlike U2, there were no prophecies of God's will to contend with—yet.

Though it trickled out over weeks, the offer from the Warehouse was complex: Jimmy and vocalist/bassist Steve Griffith were forming a band, Vector. They were up next on the recording schedule. I would join them as a keyboardist and singer/songwriter. If all went well with the collaboration and my "maturity in Christ," I would record my first solo album in the fall of '83. Less a promise, more a possibility. There was a good deal of what you might call Spirit-monitoring in those days, and people asking, "How's your walk?" The "with the Lord" part of that question was taken for granted. As church leaders, the Neelys reserved the right to discern what was what. To a contemporary reader, this is likely repugnant. I get it. Mary and Louis were a product of the Christian culture of the time common to nondenominational, charismatic churches with little to no church-government checks and balances. They were also extraordinarily generous people. Living with dramatic contradiction was the norm at the Warehouse.

Because I was a singer-songwriter, producer, and session musician who knew my way around a studio, more opportunities would also be possible. I might produce other artists, cowrite, play on recordings, etc. I would be given a monthly stipend to help with expenses, use of one of the church vans for out-of-town gigs, an American Express card that had to be paid off each month (which turned out to be great discipline), and most importantly, a key to Exit's 24-track recording studio. If it was empty, it was mine to use. A definite upgrade from my Tascam 8-track. Oh, and one more minor detail. I would lead musical worship at every Sunday evening service (something I'd never done). Yes, this was a Wednesday evening, Sunday morning, and Sunday evening kind of church—just like the Assemblies of God churches Mary and Louis grew up in.

I do not remember the moment when I said yes. I do remember the immediate discomfort of having done so. While my yes set in motion new life-altering possibilities, it naturally functioned as a no to others. I was already living in bifurcated community, trying to stay connected to my Sacramento arts crowd while gaining a whole new group of Christian friends at Calvary Chapel. People I loved and had loved and who had advocated for me for years were being pushed to the margins. Joining Mary and the Warehouse's music mission exacerbated this tenfold. There were only so many hours in a day, and I was already beginning to function like I had more than twenty-four.

I tried to keep old musical allies like Aaron Smith, Brent Bourgeois, Bongo Bob Smith, Steve Holsapple, Pat Minor, Larry Tagg, Henry Robinett, Bob Cheevers, Jim Caselli, and Erik Kleven close. The idea of following Jesus as an apprentice, artistically and spiritually, in the form of a seamlessly integrated life was still a ways off. Making everyone fit into this new Christian life was difficult. Mostly, I failed. No blueprint available. Unfortunately, I bought into numerous untrustworthy Christian cultural affectations at the time. The most egregious was seeing friends as "my old life." Or as evangelism projects instead of the loving, faithful friends they had always been. I was a product of "may the best argument win" school of apologetics and evangelism. In reality, few people were arguing with me at all. In most cases I created a chasm that didn't exist. That was on me.

Using the vernacular, when I was first *born again* (March 1982), I was in the single best band of my career, so far. Certainly the most original. I was clear-minded and the music was flowing. Our little family was prospering. In 1981, I'd formed the Charlie Peacock Group (CPG) with drummer Jim Caselli, guitarist Mark Herzig, bassist Erik Kleven, and tenor saxophonist Darius Babazadeh. Lindy Haber graciously managed us. Steve Holsapple produced and cowrote.

We played very difficult original material and a few covers, such as Talking Heads' "Cities" and an English Beat–inspired version of Smokey Robinson's "Mickey's Monkey." The calendar was full of our own bookings in San Francisco, Berkeley, Davis, Tahoe, and Sacramento. As well as opening slots with the quirky ensemble Oingo Boingo, Pablo Cruise, English organist Brian Auger, and bassist Jack Casady of Jefferson Airplane fame, fronting his new band, SVT. Bass players will recognize the letters SVT as the hallowed Ampeg SVT bass amplifier.

CPG recorded live at Moon Studios in Sacramento with Steve engineering. This led to seven finished songs and the 12-inch 45-rpm single "No Magazines" b/w "What They Like" (1982). Our friend Jeff

Viducich arranged for Tower Records to carry the single in the California stores and Japan. Seeing the single in the Japanese version of Tower literature was a thrill. Not exactly big in Japan, yet in Japan nonetheless. All seven songs are available now as *Last Vestiges of Honor (40th Anniversary Remastered)*.

Despite the likable covers, our music was decidedly the least commercial of any I'd ever attempted (apart from my jazz compositions). Imagine Ornette Coleman's Harmolodic period, mashed with '80s King Crimson, along with my new wave–ish vocals, and you'll have some sense of what we were up to. Many of the lyrics concerned my newly acquired commitment to sobriety and reinvigorated spiritual curiosity.

The skill and sound of this group of musicians were unprecedented. Fans rewarded us with loyalty and lines around the block. So, what else could I do but break up the band? I assign no blame to Jesus, but some part of the cultural "coming to the Lord" made me dumb as a rock.

It's difficult to remember how many people I've made amends to over the years, but if somehow I missed these brothers and sister Lindy, let it be said now in print. I am sorry. Please forgive me. You deserved better.

As planned, beginning in 1983, I played Moog synthesizer and sang with Vector (led by Steven Griffith and Jimmy), including the song "Running from the Light." Since the band had no permanent drummer, my friend Aaron Smith, then from the San Francisco band Romeo Void, filled in. That same year, Romeo Void peaked with their Top 40 hit "A Girl in Trouble (Is a Temporary Thing)," produced by David Kahne.

Steven Soles produced Vector, and Darryl Zachman engineered. I was familiar with modern recording consoles. The Exit console (a.k.a. board or desk) was shockingly old—like some product of an audio time machine. Instead of a modern board, Exit had an ancient tube console with big knobs the size of tennis balls. The sort you see in photographs of producer Phil Spector creating his wall of sound at Gold Star Studios in Hollywood. I was still in my *new technology is better* phase. I didn't have much confidence in the Exit console.

I was told that Buck Herring, once a Top 40 DJ turned recording engineer, had given the bygone console to the Warehouse. Buck had acquired it from Gold Star—the epicenter of West Coast pop history. Home to The Wrecking Crew (session musicians), "I Got You Babe," "You've Lost That Lovin' Feeling," The Beach Boys' *Pet Sounds*, and "Little Latin Lupe Lu," a song I knew from my childhood while watching *Shindig!* on television.

Gold Star gave the world a treasure chest of iconic pop recordings. Each one is a master class, forecasting the future of music, engineering, and production. It was an American counterpart to what George Martin and The Beatles were up to at Abbey Road in London.

What I remember most about working on the Vector record with Steve Soles is the sheer amount of used 2-inch reels of analog tape he brought from Los Angeles and his method of comping takes of the band's performance. The used tape, though erased, still had the names of the previous recording artists on the spine of their boxes. *Shall we use the Doobie Brothers next?*

Comping is a term to describe the assembly of various takes (performances) into one composite performance. You had to cut the 2-inch magnetic tape into sections with a razor blade to make a comp. An act of valor if there ever was one. Steven Soles would listen to each performance of a song and make detailed notes. Then the cutting would begin: "Let's use the intro from take three, then cut to the verse and chorus of take two." The sliced and removed pieces were hung and taped to the wall.

Next, the various lengths of tape were carefully reassembled with thin adhesive tape (on the MCI recorder) into one new comped version of the band's performance. While all this dangerous wizardry was going on, you'd have time to earn your law degree or cure cancer. Today, with digital workstations like Pro Tools and Logic, we do this in minutes, seconds. Digital recording had to be pioneered, too, though.

I first met Buddy and Julie Miller in 1986 in Berkeley, California. I played with my band at a showcase club on University Avenue called Berkeley Square, where Shalom Aberle was mixing (later of Eddie's Attic fame). Buddy and Julie were living in San Francisco then and wanted to come backstage to meet. I enjoyed them very much and would, years later, sing on one of Julie's albums. Buddy and I talked shop. I learned he was using a new digital recording platform, one

I lusted after, called Sound Designer, a precursor to Pro Tools (the music industry standard for digital audio recording).

Now, decades later, it's respectfully ironic that the dean of all things Americana and alt-country helped pioneer computer-based digital audio workstation recording. Buddy is one of those quietly humble, hugely talented musicians—a benchmark for grace through life and a guitar. And, like me, Buddy had a season of helping create what the Christian music industry called praise music or contemporary Christian music. His career has far too many seasons of diverse musical work, though, to associate him with a genre too small. Yet, if one is a connoisseur of the arcane, Buddy's work on *Bullfrogs & Butterflies* is the height of praise music esoterica.

Following my short stint with Vector, I did record my first solo album for Exit, *Lie Down in the Grass*, in the fall of '83—mixed in '84. I was allowed to produce myself but had lots of help from friends, old and new. Once the record came out, I was breathlessly sprinting with no finish line in sight. From 1983 to 1988, I produced nine records, signed with CBS Songs for music publishing, Bill Graham for management, and John Huie and Frontier Booking International for touring. There were distribution deals with A&M and Island Records. If I wasn't in the studio, I was playing local clubs, shooting videos, or touring with and supporting major acts of the time like The Fixx, General Public, Red Hot Chili Peppers, Missing Persons, Chris Isaak, and more.

Mary Neely and the Warehouse leadership were thrilled with these developments, even graciously giving me back my music publishing so I could make the deal with CBS Songs. Mary was always more comfortable with me (and all the Exit artists) being in the world of rock and pop music playing for everyone.

Of course, not every Christian who attended church at the Warehouse understood the mission. Had some been present for our opening slot with the Peppers and stayed for their encore with the band dressed in nothing but tube socks on their penises? That might've led to a classic church split. Maybe even a Reformation-era-type council and new creed: "We believe in one God, the Father, the Almighty, Maker of heaven and earth, of all that is seen and unseen. We believe that no recording artist, whether explicit or implicit in profession, sent out under the authority of a Christian church, shall perform before or following any act of nudity, even one deemed partial."

There was modest charting at album rock and college radio, and a couple of records were even spun on outlier Christian stations. I was never a star, but somehow the music was discovered by a small yet devoted and enthusiastic group of listeners. It set the tempo and direction for decades of my artistry, songwriting, and producing for other artists.

The friendship and help I received from Mary and the Warehouse over six years were invaluable. I am, with no exaggeration, eternally grateful. Our collaboration was never easy, though. I was never easy. Once, on a telephone call where disagreement reigned, Mary exclaimed, "You have a problem with authority!" Well, that and much more, Mary. After all, I was a hypervigilant, Kerouac-schooled nonconformist who left high school at sixteen as a junior to be a lifelong autodidact and entrepreneur.

Let's say I had some ideas beyond those Mary had for me.

What little cred I accrued while creating music at the Warehouse had opened up a world of opportunity. People came calling. I wanted the freedom to explore those possibilities and to formulate my own yes or no.

There was a long good-bye between the summers of '88 and '89 and our move to Nashville. The breaking away from the Warehouse might've begun with a phone call from music executive Tom Willett in November of 1986 to the church's Exit Records office. He was in Los Angeles sitting in a Grammy Award committee meeting. A contingent of folks associated with Christian music wanted to nominate my second solo album for Gospel Rock Album of the Year. Tom understood that associating with Christian music was off-mission for Exit and Island Records. He wanted to know if he should discourage the nomination. Exit said no gospel nominations for Charlie. I had no choice in the matter. This did not sit right with me.

In the end, the prohibition against associating with Christians outside the Warehouse is what broke me. U2 had built the model, closing the circle tight, having their own in-house pastor and insulated community. The Warehouse was similar but different since it was a church, and the pastoral leadership of Mary and Louis had autonomy.

All of us involved with Exit performed concerts at the Warehouse for Christians. Their well-known concert ministry booked many artists who would be considered mainstream contemporary Christian artists. However, I was strongly discouraged from performing at other churches or associating with anyone directly tied to gospel or contemporary Christian music (CCM)—this meant fans, journalists, record labels, executives, and artists. To do so would be mission drift. I stayed the course for many years before I swerved.

If Larry Norman had said, "I may have been in error in standing aside from the brethren by not performing for them," I was increasingly thinking and saying, "I am in error." I wanted the freedom to be God's musical person everywhere and in everything, living into the answer to what it meant to be (and here I'm going to say it) a Christian artist. *A genuine, nongenre, wholly imaginative, and free Christian and artist.* That's a definition I can live with. I just can't count on enough people to use it yet. So, I still don't.[13]

Ultimately, the Warehouse and I had a disagreement about what the will of God was. No different than U2 and their Shalom Fellowship. There are more ways to love God, people, and the planet than anyone could know or imagine. It only makes sense that sometimes your neighbor, or those you love most, just don't see the same way forward as you do—the same movement of love. One of the more freeing maxims I've ever received came from my friend Scotty Smith: "The will of God is often more a circle than a dot." Indeed. What matters most is what you do with your differences of opinion, your notions of what is real. How you treat the ones you disagree with.

Mary and I have long since made our peace. In her own words: "I was quite a preacher woman back in those days, starting a rock and roll record label! It was a mission for me, but I loved being around all of you amazing creative people." It was a calling, a mission from God for purposes Mary could not fully comprehend. In part, yes, but not in full. She was a visionary, and I've told her as much: "You saw and heard something new emerging long before others and found (received) the people whom God had chosen for the purpose, whether it be Steve Turner, Lou Maglia, Mike Roe, Jimmy Abegg, me or others." She had an eye and ear for inevitability.

I'm astonished at Mary's tenacity and achievement when I think of the stature of gatekeepers she put our music in front of. Especially now, knowing how tricky and capricious the music business is. To think she was able to coax the legendary Island Records founder Chris Blackwell to a nondescript warehouse alongside a freeway outside of Sacramento to hear her bands is a monumental, singular mic-drop. Walking down the hallway to the studio, the man who launched Bob Marley, Cat Stevens, and U2 might have asked in his British accent, "And what is this charming room used for?" *That would be the fifth-and-sixth-grade Sunday school room, Chris.*

In the big circle of destiny, Mary and I were right about some things and wrong about others. If I moved to Nashville to work with Christians, I'd become known as a Christian artist, and all our hard work would be undermined. One for Mary, sort of. If I moved to Nashville to work with Christians, plus eschew genres and accomplish a wide diversity of work, I would faithfully embody my mission: *A follower of Jesus and an artist—everywhere, in everything, for everyone.* One for me. Still in process.

If you compare U2 and Amy Grant, the contrast in outcome amplifies Mary's point. Amy began her career in CCM and signed to Word Records. U2, in rock music, signed to Island Records. My friend Dan Russell, who knows this terrain well, said many years ago, "You are where you are distributed." This means the genre identity imposed on you by others will result from the means of distribution by which they first come to know you. Even though both artists are pop music hit-makers of considerable success, U2 will go down in history as a rock band, not a Christian rock band. While Amy, no matter what she achieves or believes, will always be "the queen of Christian pop."[14]

Does this matter? Didn't they both end up at the 2022 Kennedy Center Honors on the same night? Am I making far too much of what some would say is a slight, innocuous differentiation?

I don't think so. The business of sorting out artistry and discipleship questions, shaping words and meaning, and making the world is all part of living into unfolding, trustworthy answers. It's my job. It's the work of the people for whom such things possess life-giving and life-taking seriousness.

Getting at and living out the most open and free definition of a student of Jesus and an artist has always been my God-haunted goal. Why? The alternative falls far short of truth and efficacy. Sometimes it's even a lie and a lingering failure affecting generations.

Consider the nuances of choice from some of the characters I've highlighted.

Dylan has stayed in the game for so long, reinventing himself so many times that he's like Picasso. Dylan's work is divided into periods. He's not a Christian artist. He's got his "born-again period," like Picasso and his "blue period." And, in case it needs to be said, he is Bob Dylan—a category of one.

After U2 decided they were most certainly not a Christian band and that Bono, the Edge, and Larry were finished with the traditional church as they knew it, Dylan was not far behind. After *Slow Train Coming*, Dylan put out two more "gospel" albums, *Saved* (1980) and *Shot of Love* (1981). It wasn't for everyone—generally loved or hated. As critic Ken Tucker said in 2017, reflecting on the short born-again period, "If you like your Dylan prickly and righteous and cunning, this is right up your alley."[15]

Dylan was learning on the public's dime what it meant to faithfully follow Jesus and continue to live into his own potential and acclaim as someone short-listed as the most celebrated solo artist of his generation, possibly of the twentieth century. He made his share of gaffes mimicking words and affectations that were less faithful to Jesus and more products of the time (such as leaning into author Hal Lindsey's end-times machinations). But Dylan eventually pivoted, which was and still is his way.

He'd been famous long enough before all the Christian brouhaha that he knew what it felt like to be co-opted by others for their pet agendas. Any musician with radar for this sort of thing will tell you how much this or that group loves its famous members. It could be a hometown, an AA group, a church, or a genre of music. The love of proximity to power and fame knows no boundary or shame. I think Dylan woke up to this afresh, saw that he believed his own lyric for "Gotta Serve Somebody," and returned to his former role as a mysterious minstrel—only wiser. And for this fan, the lyrics he wrote before and after this phase better reflect a seamless use of biblical story and imagery and following Jesus as a winsome student than most of the "gospel" songs.

I first met Larry Norman in the Netherlands, where we were headlining Flevo Festival. I did not know him. I did, however, observe that history had not been kind to him, or he'd not been kind to it. Likely both. This is often the fate of the inventor. The innovators that come after build on the inventor's work and understand its meaning and possible future function. Innovators have the benefit of new imagination and fresh wind at their back. Interestingly, when Bono came to speak to a group of musicians at our Art House home in Nashville in 2002, he asked if Larry would be in attendance.

Unlike Bob Dylan, U2 never needed a "born-again period." Amid all their reinventions and periods, the work of living into the answer of what it means to be a student of Jesus and an artist has been seamlessly integrated into life and music from the beginning, regardless of how proximate. It did seem to require keeping Christians at arm's length until the world tacitly agreed they would not predictably name U2 a Christian band. (The genre is too small, which would've limited their mobility, access, and fame—what I've heard Bono call *currency*.)

Perhaps a shift began early in the twenty-first century when Bono became vocal about the role of Christian commitment in caring for the African continent's HIV/AIDS emergency. Regardless of the date and circumstance, Bono warmed to partnering with his "brethren" in caring for people and the planet. (In a similar way to how I'd warmed to it before exiting the Warehouse.) And in the divine drama, the HIV/AIDS emergency is why he ended up on our doorstep in Nashville in 2002. And, if you'll allow for the possibility, it may be part of why the will of God in the shape of a circle nudged us two thousand miles east to Nashville in 1989. Once there, we would do many things, including meet Bono's friend Mark Rodgers. A friendship that led to a meeting of global consequences fronted by the world-wise Irish tenor.

Larry Norman, Bono, and Dylan—a trio of noncompliance if there ever was one. Couldn't square the circle and stay on mission. Even if the mission coordinates weren't precisely on the map. A genre too small. Clearly, getting too close to Christianity in the form of organized groups working a plan and having a plan for you can be an imagination-killer. Artists generally have a problem with this. Like, 99.9 percent of the time.

There were similar yet unique issues with the Warehouse and Exit Records. I had to leave. I'm grateful that love, reconciliation, and respect have had the last word, though.

—

Country-rock pioneer and Rock and Roll Hall of Fame inductee Richie Furay (Buffalo Springfield, Poco) was at the Warehouse's Exit studio once when the old Gold Star console was still in action. "Oh my gosh," he exclaimed. "Buffalo Springfield cut 'For What It's Worth' on this board!"

Of course, they did. Had I known this Hall of Fame history early on, my entire attitude while working on that console would have been changed. Sadly, I rarely understand the story I'm participating in until much later. I suspect this is a chronic human problem.

Even so, there is something happening here on earth, some unfolding drama. What it is, isn't exactly clear. We know in part but not in full. We see through tinted glass, cracked and splintered. It's time to stop. Time to pause and listen. Breathe and take a peek. What's that sound? You tell me. What's that sound? Can you hear it? What's that sound? Everybody look what's going down. Rock 'n' roll is born again, and again, and again.

Great-grandfather, George Reilly Baggett Sr. (1864–1904), Louisiana

Great-uncle, Tommy Baggett (1888–1971), Louisiana

Grandfather, Lee Jackson Ashworth (1898–1984), with first-born Eloise, Bon Ami, Louisiana, 1921

Great-grandparents, Robert Dallas Miller (1877–1964) and Margaret "Maggie" Miller (1884–1966)

Father, Bill Ashworth (1933–1992), 521st Air Force Band (circa 1954), trumpet, back row center

Parents, Alice and Bill Ashworth, wedding day, June 30, 1955

Father, Bill Ashworth, with me, my first birthday, August 10, 1957

Me, with mom, Alice Ashworth (1936–2017), grandmother, Lois Williamson (1912–1975), and her mother, my great-grandmother, "Maggie" Miller, four generations

Me in Dad's arms, grandmother Ella (1901–1985), and her mother, Alzenith Ellanora Baggett (1873–1959), four generations

Me, goat ridin' with Grandpa, Marvin Williamson (1904–1995), and Dad

Aunt Karoly, my generous guide to the music of the 1960s, and me in Tierra Buena

My beloved sister, Terri, and me—looks like we were an award-winning duo

The teenage songwriter at the beach, learning James Taylor songs

Andi and me, high school sweethearts, Yuba City High School, 1972

Here we are married at eighteen—Yuba-Sutter Fairgrounds, Yuba City,
California, May 18, 1975

Our young family in November 1981, blessed parents of daughter, Molly Nicole, and son, Samuel Brinsley

"Papa" and grandkids Robert, Brinsley, Bridget, and Alfie, 2018

Yes, I'm wearing a dashiki; with bassist Alphonza Kee (Staple Singers, Miroslav Vitous), big brother of gospel music legend John P. Kee (both students of Dad)

six

MUSIC IS HARD, PART ONE

In late January 2012, I sent music manager Cree Miller an email query: a hypothetical ask, similar to those I'd proposed to record labels and managers in the past. Would Jackson Browne like to be a guest vocalist on a record I'm producing? The artist is Holly Williams, daughter of Hank Jr. and granddaughter to the legendary Hank Williams. May I send Jackson the song?

While I was working on getting Jackson to a Los Angeles studio on February 15, Holly was checking with her friend, Gwyneth Paltrow. We'd have a condensed session with each guest vocalist, different songs, same day, back-to-back. In anticipation of it all coming together, I booked the B Room at Village Recorders from noon to 5 p.m.

We patiently waited to see if the singer-songwriter who defined my youth and the Oscar-winning actress and Goop guru—and sometimes singer—would say yes.

I had received a gracious affirmative from Jackson. Holly locked Gwyneth down. And with a snap, we were on for Wednesday. Andi, close to Holly, and seeing I needed a traveling companion, agreed to come along for the ride. Holly's husband, Chris Coleman, a touring member of Kings of Leon, also joined us. I'd met Chris several years earlier back when he was toiling for a company landscaping our studio property. At that time, he was also the drummer in the hope-deferred Luna Halo, a Nashville band signed to Rick Rubin's

American Recordings. They languished in limbo, waiting for the dust to settle after Rubin moved his operation from Warner Brothers to Columbia Records in 2007.

I had mad respect for Chris—especially after watching him do back-breaking work in the unforgiving sun. We had several conversations about the vicissitudes of the music business around a shovel and dirt. With Holly's record, Chris and I worked side by side. His talent was, and is, rich with intuition and soul. Not a bad visual artist either.

Like the busy people they are, both guest vocalists had somewhere to be immediately following the session. Time was incredibly tight. Each artist visited with Holly for far too long, and the time knot cinched even tighter. Jackson's song was "Gone Away from Me." A beautiful, moody bit of top-shelf songwriting from Holly. I had sent Jackson the song ahead of time. I had no idea if he'd listened or not.

We jumped into it, though. Pretty quickly, Jackson offered, "I hear a couple harmonies, but that's probably all." I thought everything and said nothing. Holly was looking for more of a duet with Jackson's classic voice prominent and recognizable. I let him meander through the song once, then stopped and pushed the talkback on the console.

Music can be a memory you haven't made yet. Like a roots-deep reminder that every spring provides the rain and milder air that coaxes buds to open, to begin their becoming. It happened before; it will happen again. It's natural—but still takes time and rhythm and a favorable environment.

"Jackson, what if you were to answer a couple lines such as . . ." I read him the lyrics.

"Alright, let's try it."

Uh oh, nothing like I was hoping for. Didn't have Jackson's personality, his special sauce.

"Let's try it again."

He asked me, "What are you hearing?"

In my head, I sang, "Jamaica say you will, help me find a way to fill, my lifeless sails and stay until, my ships have found the sea." Then I silently reshaped the essence of that melody to fit Holly's lyric and sang the idea back to him over the studio talkback. I imagine this took about three seconds.

"Okay, let's try it again."

He sang it and sounded just like Jackson Browne. Music memory, both reacquired and newly made.

As Bud Scoppa wrote in *Rolling Stone* back in March 1972, "('Jamaica Say You Will') perfectly embodies Browne's writing and performing approach."[1]

Apparently, I agree.

I was introduced to Bud Scoppa by Sal Valentino in 1980 when the '60s pop star invited me to Los Angeles to meet his music industry friends. When Atlantic Records was courting me as an artist in 1988, Bud wrote in *Music Connection* magazine, "Lots of sought-after acts were passed on for years before suddenly becoming hot properties. (Eight years ago, for example, I tried to get my boss at Arista [Clive Davis] to sign writer/singer Charlie Peacock—the current object of [Atlantic Records] Keith Cowan's desire)."[2] True story.

Right then, the object of my desire was recording enough of Jackson to create a viable part. The clock cut the session short. Jackson had to get over to KCRW for a radio show. Holly was disappointed that we didn't get more Jackson on the song. I tried to tell her there was no more Jackson to get.

Gwyneth's song didn't fare much better. First, she almost didn't make it to the session. President Obama was in town, and the roads were blocked. I had just come from Beverly Hills, though. I advised Holly, "Tell her to take West Olympic to Butler." Which she did, and traffic was fine. Once Gwyneth arrived, I was told she'd have to leave soon for Reese Witherspoon's house. As with Jackson, the prelude of visiting left little time for her vocal. She was there to sing a two-part harmony on Holly's seven-minute opus titled "Waiting on June." We had about thirty minutes left to get it. I did the math. This was a fail in progress.

As expected, we didn't come close to finishing. Gwyneth would return to the studio after Reese's party. That was the plan. At first, I thought we were all headed to the party. I misread the signs.

Instead, we gathered in the control room and waited—extra studio time purchased just to sit. I was annoyed. Thankfully, photographer friends Jeremy Cowart and Allister Ann kept us company. After three slow-motion hours, Holly checked in. It was impossible to leave Reese's party—it wouldn't be right. Gwyneth said she could finish up in the morning, at 8 a.m. *What?*

Gwyneth kept her word, sang well, and we finished with time to spare.

Acutely exhausted, Andi and I drove to LAX and boarded a plane. We were going in the right direction, the jetstream in our favor. Good-bye, Los Angeles. Hello, Nashville. Back to our beloved Music City, where life made more sense. And where most of the time, I didn't have to push the proverbial musical boulder up the hill.

Sense, however, would be deferred. Boulder descending.

Back in my home studio, Holly was struck with doubt about the recorded key of "Waiting on June." I wanted to get it right for her. We had a problem, though. Didn't we just spend two days, two thousand miles away, getting a vocal on Gwyneth (in what was now the wrong key)?

I told Holly to go home for the night and that I would see if I could change the pitch of the track and vocals. There's software that allows producers to change individual notes or bring the pitch of a whole song up or down. If the software is good (mine is), I can usually go up or down a whole step or more without detection. If it worked, Holly could still rerecord her vocal and play a new guitar part. Gwyneth's performance would have to be digitally altered—pitched up, as we say.

Along with Richie Biggs, I worked until the track and vocals were as good as they could possibly be. Holly told Gwyneth about the software trick. Her response was, oh, I don't know about that. When she asked to hear it, I groaned with dread and frustration. I knew what it meant. Chris Martin from Coldplay, Gwyneth's then-husband, listened and promptly vetoed it. I can hear the tuning, he said. Well, I could too, but once Gwyneth was tucked back underneath Holly's vocal, it would be unnoticeable. Honestly, what other option was there at this point? We couldn't recut the whole song and go back to LA just to record another vocal with Gwyneth.

It turns out we could. And we did.

Holly flew back out and took care of it. "Waiting on June" had become waiting on Gwyneth. I was done before the song was.

Session guitarist Jerry McPherson, an expert in guitar and sarcasm, has a jokester line he riffs on in the studio—at least one I credit him with.

"Music is hard," he says.

Yeah. It is.

—

The scene is the Lower East Side of Manhattan. Sheets of rain the size of grapes drench everything, including the band. They had rushed into the night at the storm's first sign. Shirts came off. Chests were joyously beaten. Dancing and whoops commenced. Band members lay prostrate on the cement, making rain angels with their windmilling arms and legs. They couldn't have been happier.

This burst of energy and ecstasy occurred on Allen Street on the sidewalk right outside Rockwood Music Hall. The band was Zach Williams and the Bellow, soon to be The Lone Bellow. I was the producer.

In July 2011, I flew to NYC to meet with Zach Williams and his then-manager, Kyle Griner, who'd had some success with Anberlin, an alt-rock band from Florida. Our goal was to finalize plans to record Zach's first commercially released album. Zach was exactly the kind of artist I was committed to working with. He needed little to no production props. His unbound, fully committed performances, combined with great songwriting, were more than enough.

Zach had a band. More a collective of Brooklyn friends than a band. They were known for their heroic, sold-out shows at the Rockwood Music Hall. This was their domain. They lit the room ablaze.

I was concerned that the essence of the band, and especially Zach's inspired, full-throttle approach, might not translate in a conventional studio setting.

I floated an idea: What if we recorded live at Rockwood? On the surface, it seemed impossible. The club was booked seven days a week. The only workable time frame might be between 3 a.m. and 11 a.m. If we worked fast and smart, I thought we could get basic tracks in three days, maybe two. Still, I didn't see how we could tear down all the recording gear each morning so the club could function in the evening.

We met with owner Ken Rockwood. He surprised us with a re-markable and generous solution. Ken agreed to let us record for two full days and a morning (if needed). He would shut the club down for two days. Amazing. He was living up to his reputation as a true artist advocate.

Ken could make it happen in September. We had two months to prepare. Zach and the band would make sure all the songs were record-ready. Engineer Richie Biggs and I would put together a mo-bile studio. We would fly some gear up from Nashville and rent the rest in NYC, including much-lauded Millennia microphone preamps from my friend John LaGrou.

Manager Kyle Griner and I put a deal together. The company Dave Kiersznowski and I formed, Twenty Ten Music (TTM), would fund the entire recording. In return, TTM would co-own the masters and half the music publishing. We planned on this being a short-term arrangement. I would be shopping the record to major labels and publishing companies. I wanted Zach to win big. In the end, all TTM needed was to be reimbursed for our investment. Then we'd give up any master or publishing rights. I'd get my usual producer fee when the label deal was secured.

Even with years of experience, I'd never made a record like this one. The club environment would become another instrument. Engineer Richie Biggs and I would be going for live performances of the songs us-ing a full array of microphones for recording, as well as mics run through the PA. This approach is common for live, remote recording.

This couldn't be just a live recording, though. My endgame was a little more complex. I wanted the record to sound like a studio recording with the essence of a live club performance. I also needed the performances we captured to have some flexibility. I planned to bring the record back to my studio in Nashville, where I'd give it some postproduction treatment. Most importantly, I wanted Zach to sound like himself with all his unique speedometer-pegging intensity.

Anticipating that Zach's voice might not last through thirteen or fourteen hours of live performance, I came up with a plan.

The method was to record a complete version of a song with the band and vocalists performing at peak level. While listening to each song as it was recorded, I made a note of any problem areas, such as a loose chorus or bridge.

Next, we rehearsed, tweaked, and recorded those problem areas—just those bits. I had to pay careful attention, making sure the new smaller sections matched the previous full-song versions. All the performances, large or small, had to match in tempo and intensity.

Finally, we recorded instrumental versions of the verses—any voice fatigue would be most noticeable in the verses. By recording instrumental sections (without the lead vocal), I'd have the option for Zach to sing verses back in Nashville.

This method produced two or three times the recorded material one would get from a recording-studio session. I was okay with it. With these contingencies in place, I was confident I'd be able to fix any problems that would reveal themselves in editing.

Zach and the band lived up to all expectations. Brian Elmquist and Kanene Doheny Pipkin were the perfect backing vocals to Zach's lead. The tracking band of Ben Mars, Brian Griffin, Matt Knapp, and Brian Murphy held nothing back.

We had our challenges, but they never did us in. We were having too much fun. The spirit and energy of our communion made it into the recordings. There was the rain party, special guests, and general mayhem—the latter stemmed mostly from the speed at which we were working. Our second engineer, James Sweeting, ran from the stage to the dressing room (our makeshift control room) hundreds of times. Creativity unleashes energy. It's an inherently generous force, propelling us forward.

The one-way glass windows facing the street were an endless source of entertainment. Hundreds of New Yorkers passed by every hour, checking themselves out in the mirror-like glass. Yes, you look hot. They couldn't see us recording, but we could see them preening.

One late evening we caught a group of people, cupping their faces, trying to see through the glass. I recognized sound engineer Eric Robinson and ran out to say hello. (We had worked together on a project with a Los Angeles artist named Lenachka.)

Eric was in the company of the producer, John Alagía, and some musicians. They'd been recording with Rachael Yamagata earlier that evening. That same night we recorded "Teach Me to Know" and asked Ken Rockwood to join the chorus of voices and claps.

After two days and a morning at Rockwood, we packed up and headed back to Nashville. I'd have to spend several days editing and compiling the final masters before any overdubs could be done. Once accomplished, Zach, Brian, Kanene, and her husband, Jason Pipkin, arrived in Nashville on September 20. It was time for overdubs and vocal fixes. Everything went as planned.

Richie Biggs mixed. Richard Dodd, of Tom Petty fame, mastered the record. We were ready to begin shopping the music to record labels, seeing where it took us. I was very confident that we had created a unique but right-on-time recording. Advocating for it was easy. We targeted some labels, and some came after us. Kyle Griner was out as manager.

Regardless of what happened in securing a deal with a major record label, Zach made it clear he wanted me to remain his advisor and confidant. Starting with our first meeting, we forged a bond of friendship and trust. I met with Zach in Nashville and in NYC, where he came to my hotel for a face-to-face meeting. He was a young man with a gigantic heart and a winsome smile. He wanted to go all-in with the music, but only if it could provide for his family and the friends who'd join him. Zach's iPhone lay on the table between us. The glass was shattered into ten thousand pieces. I told him, based on my experience developing artists, that he'd be just fine. Reaching for some humor, I added, "I think we'll at least do well enough to buy you a new phone."

He laughed. The journey was under way.

Not only did Ken Rockwood shut down his popular club so we could record there, but he also brought label executives to the bargaining table. He was kind, encouraging, and on it—sending me a note affirming, "The record is incredible. I would love to help any way I can." Immediately, Ian Ralfini, head of Manhattan/Blue Note, was interested, and Pete Ganbarg at Atlantic Records wanted to see Zach and the band live.

The heady combination of creative flow, innovation, and the desire to introduce record executives to this incredible music felt all too familiar. I have lived long enough to have been here before. Almost twenty-five years earlier, I had showcased for Atlantic Records at the Roxy in Los Angeles (the story Bud Scoppa had referenced). I had released one album for Island Records in 1986 and was offered another if I would trim my budget to something a little more indie-minded—A&R Kim Buie gently encouraging me to box in my weight class. More like $75K than $200K.

In his *San Francisco Chronicle* column of May 11, 1986, Joel Selvin reported, "Island Records president Chris Blackwell, a jet-set kind of guy who boasts residences in Nassau, Switzerland, Jamaica, Paris, London and elsewhere, is not the sort of person to go to Sacramento without a good reason. But there he was a couple of weeks back, checking out acts . . . including Bill Graham–managed Charlie Peacock." True enough. The newly appointed president of the label, Lou Maglia, had coaxed Chris into attending an afternoon showcase by me, The 77s, and others. Mary Neely of Exit Records had already negotiated a distribution deal with Island. Playing for Chris was the final step before the contract was signed.

I have very little memory of Chris, except that his energy was positive, he traveled light, and while sitting with me and listening to my newly recorded songs, he remarked that I could be the next Cat Stevens. Chris gave his stamp of approval, and that was the last I ever saw of him. As you can imagine, I did not become Cat Stevens, a spot still very much occupied.

Despite Lou Maglia's genuine enthusiasm for me, The 77s, and a band called Robert Vaughn & the Shadows, neither theirs nor my self-titled album sold well for Island. We entered the product pipeline via a distribution deal, and the full weight of the music distribution giant WEA's sales and promotion machine didn't naturally apply to us. The groovy, beach beatnik Chris Blackwell, and all the successful Island Records acts like Bob Marley, U2, and Steve Winwood, were spinning in a different orbit than us.

I wanted to work with heavyweight producer/engineer Elliot Scheiner on my second Island release. He did not come cheap, though—his domain was Steely Dan, Bruce Hornsby, and The Eagles. I'd been talking to Elliot for over a year. We were friendly enough that his wife, actress Diane Canova, asked if I'd be interested in a role on *Throb*, the sitcom she starred in. A thirty-something divorcee gets a job at an indie, new-wave record label named, that's right, Throb. I was just vain enough to consider it. Thankfully, Mary Neely voiced a strong no, and then in case I didn't hear, no again.

A&M Records had been a disappointing, lukewarm relationship, and now Island Records was looking far too similar. I needed a new label home, and Atlantic's West Coast A&R, Keith Cowan, was ready to make it happen. To sweeten the whole experience, even the great Atlantic Records founder, Ahmet Ertegun, came to a showcase and complimented me on my piano chops. It was as good as done.

In March 1988, Fabio Testa interviewed Keith, asked if he'd "seen anybody interesting lately."

"Yes," Keith replied. "Charlie Peacock. He played at the Roxy, and it was almost like an A&R convention—everybody was there. I was really moved, and after the first song I made a phone call to (VP/ General Manager) Paul Cooper, saying that we have to sign him—I was that excited. But even if we don't sign him, it was great to be there and to feel that."[3]

Despite the good vibes, I did not get to sign with Atlantic. Before the deal was done, my champion Keith Cowan had resigned or been fired—which one, I never knew. This scenario is a pre-Internet meme, a cliché of the music industry. Talk to a hundred baby-boomer recording artists, and a large number of them will tell a story about how they almost signed with a label, but the A&R rep got fired.

I didn't want Zach, or myself, near any crazy-making vignettes of this variety. I should've never wished for such a thing. Jinxed. Our art-on-art lovefest was about to get complicated. Cue the outsiders. It was time to play a Julius Caesar–inspired round of isolate and separate.

Zach was courted heavily by David Sonenberg's management firm by a junior manager named Beth Narducci. She was keen to be Zach's manager under David's watch, with his resources. I knew David and a former colleague of his, Scot McCracken. Because the music business is more like three degrees of separation, Scot and I were briefly entwined in a music start-up with attorney Jim Zumwalt, Full Sail University cofounder Jon Phelps, and Cincinnati billionaire Keith Lindner. One which bore little fruit, except that I was able to broker the temporary sale of *Paste* magazine to Jon and Keith—a move that saved the publication. It gave my friends Josh Jackson, Nick Purdy, Joe Kirk, and Tim Regan-Porter funding to continue publishing, and eventually transform the magazine into the media company it is today.

I had met with David Sonenberg only once before at his office in NYC. He proposed an idea for my consideration, one so lucrative we'd be "printing money." Between that visit and his reputation in general, I knew David Sonenberg was a smart guy adept at artist se-duction, gamesmanship, and hardballing—three things for which I had no interest or acumen.

If there were any reservations about David's style, Beth's presence in the mix had a calming effect. She would be the band's day-to-day manager. Beth was likable, ambitious, and ready to champion The Lone Bellow to the ends of the earth. The band signed with David, and Beth led the way. I would concentrate on the music and continue the search for the best record label partner.

Along with Manhattan and Atlantic Records, Warner Brothers entered the conversation, as did a new Sony start-up, Descendant Records, and Blue Note, now split off from Manhattan and helmed by producer Don Was.

EMI Christian Music Group CEO Bill Hearn was also an advocate for the band, sending me a note saying, "I've passed the new songs on to Don Was at Blue Note. He said he's a fan and met you recently in LA!" Correct. I cornered Don on a couch at Village Recorders. He was ready to listen to a song from The Lone Bellow when suddenly he popped up, saying, "Man, I'm so sorry, John Mayer needs me next door."

Don later told me in an email, "learning time management skills has been, by far, the most difficult aspect of having a record company gig!" I had nothing but empathy for him, especially because he was still producing records for artists like John Mayer, who wasn't even on his label. I'd run a very small label before and done that. Take over Blue Note and still produce? I wished him well. It was too early in his new gig. Blue Note would have to pass on The Lone Bellow.

Mike Elizondo and Lenny Waronker from Warner Brothers did take a good solid swing at it, though. Mike was eager to sign the band

and joined me in NYC for a showcase at Rockwood Music Hall. A few weeks later, the band came west and played for Lenny at the infamous Warner Brothers Records office in Burbank, a venerable spot affectionately dubbed the "ski lodge." Again, I'd been here before.

I'd first toured the building thirty-two years earlier when I was the artist, and Sal Valentino from The Beau Brummels was introducing me around. Lenny had produced The Beau Brummels album *Bradley's Barn* in Nashville, 1968. Norbert Putnam, Jerry Reed, and David Briggs were on the session. He kept a painting of the cover image in his office. The "Bradley" of the Barn is Owen Bradley. Along with Chet Atkins, Owen is considered the prime architect of the 1950s and '60s Nashville countrypolitan sound. He's also the grandfather of my friend Clay Bradley, with whom I have worked for years. It was Clay who came out to the house to see if I had any interest in producing Holly Williams. It wasn't lost on me that the grandson of the legendary Owen Bradley was asking me to produce the granddaughter of the legendary Hank Williams. That's what I call an *only in Nashville* moment. The Bradley name is country royalty in Nashville. Clay and I have worked on several projects, including the film I produced on legendary songwriter Hank Cochran. Bradley family stories are pretty high-rise as stories go. Almost as good as any Gordon Kennedy story about his dad, Jerry, who played on Roy Orbison's "Oh, Pretty Woman" and Dylan's *Blonde on Blonde*.

Mike Elizondo and Lenny Waronker are the good guys. I have nothing but high praise for their skill and integrity. They both have the same quality of character and true passion for music, and Mike is a world-class bassist and producer. Unfortunately, even these two honorable men couldn't stop a music business cliché from ruining The Lone Bellow's chances with Warner Brothers Records.

Warner Brothers, too, would have to pass. They had only so much money to spend on a folk/Americana act in that budget year. They wanted to take a shot at landing one of the genre's hottest indie bands; they were a frontrunner with Mumford & Sons and The Civil Wars. Several ho-heys later, they didn't land the band, and we'd already moved on.

Enter Jay Harren.

Jay had taken the post of VP of A&R at Descendant Records, the boutique label Terry Hemmings and Sony Entertainment were putting together. They wanted The Lone Bellow to be their maiden voyage act. Which might be the best option, especially if the desire to prove themselves meant the band would get all their attention and resources. I knew Terry well—he was and is a seasoned record executive—and I'd already had a million-selling hit record on Switchfoot with Sony's indie distribution company, RED.

I needed to meet Jay.

We met up in NYC, and I liked him immediately. Jay had started his music career at 99X in Atlanta with a friend of mine named Leslie Fram. Incidentally, 99X was also one of the stations that played Sarah Masen's song "All Fall Down" in 1996—Sarah was the first artist I signed to my re:think/EMI label prior to Switchfoot. Next, Jay was hired as an A&R manager for Columbia Records, working under Rick Rubin, where he signed Manchester Orchestra—a band that attended one of our nonprofit artist retreats in Nashville and was championed by my friend Joe Kirk, VP for *Paste*. These touchstones gave helpful familiarity to a new relationship.

The only issue with the Descendant/Sony option was that they offered the least amount of money. Which for me, and our company Twenty Ten Music, meant our start-up investment in the group would not be fully recouped. And I wouldn't receive my usual fees as a producer. Ultimately, the Descendant/Sony option for the record label and Sony/ATV for music publishing were the best choices for Zach and the band. Soon the folk/Americana music lovers would cast their votes, yea or nay. I had no reason to expect anything other than a wide-open embrace of this rousing, inspired trio.

I'm always open to mixing patronage and profit. When you first start out in the music business, this is all you do. You just don't know enough to call it that yet. I had a singular focus on setting Zach and the band up for success and backed up my resolve with my time and resources, happily.

Maybe that's why I didn't see the boulder rumbling downhill.

seven

MUSIC IS HARD, PART TWO

Before the Sony option came through, I stood in the office of one of America's oldest record labels, part of the Universal Music Group. At the A&R director's request, I was there to pitch The Lone Bellow record. We were right on the cusp of listening to a song. Imagine the executive's hand on the volume knob of a sleek Cambridge Audio CXA81 amplifier. He is about to turn it up when a question enters his mind, and he quickly rolls the knob back down to zero.

"Who's managing the band?"

I tell him. His response is immediate.

"Not interested."

That was a short meeting.

When you're a music producer developing future recording artists, you seldom get to choose the team who will come after you. There will be a booking agent, attorney, accountant, record label, publicist, and the managers: personal, social media, tour, and more. It's a bonus when your opinion is sought after. A strong, competitive recording handed off to a sketchy or incompetent team is doomed. Young, developing recording artists, YouTube influencers and Tik-Tok stars, (or whatever comes next) are at the mercy of all these folks—as are the music producers.

It's a cliché to say that the best artists don't have a mind for business. I've always bristled at the presumption. There's a seed of truth in it, though. Artists are often vulnerable, insecure, and uncomfortable with conflict and confrontation—especially so if someone on their team needs to be confronted about transgressing the artist's values and deepest cares. Taylor Swift is one of those artists who disproves the notion that a great artist can't possibly be good at business. You can be both, but it takes work and staying power.

The gap in experience and knowledge between a veteran music executive with thirty years of experience and a twenty-four-year-old novice recording artist is huge. There's no comparison. On any subject or level of conflict, it is not a fair fight. Anyone can throw a punch, but it takes years of practice to make subtle, hidden moves that are unseen and efficacious.

—

Like Lenny and Mike from Warner Brothers, Zach Williams is one of the good guys. I wanted him and his family to win. The most important thing to me was that The Lone Bellow get a strong start. If they did, it would result in a lasting career, one filled with meaningful and steady contributions to culture. From the outset, I made it clear I wouldn't stand in the way of any opportunities that would benefit his career or family.

Unfortunately, with management and an attorney at work on Zach's behalf, his isolation and our separation became more pronounced, and for me, actually painful. The last attorney in the loop was especially disrespectful to me and dismissive of what I'd helped the band accomplish. David Sonenberg and I had agreed to the basic terms: reimbursement of the expenses our company, Twenty Ten Music, had paid for; our partial relinquishing of publishing rights; my producer advance and royalty points.

Strangely, Zach's attorney viewed these negotiated terms as if they were arbitrary—a mere starting place for him to scratch and snarl his way to victory for his client. This went on for six months. I had to remove myself from the back-and-forth; my friend and attorney Lynn Morrow would have to tell me when the nightmare on Old Harding Road (our studio address) was over.

It didn't take long for legal fees to accrue to the point that my producer fee was solely a means to pay the bill. This reminded me of the time the virtuoso banjoist Béla Fleck played on a record for me—one that required both of us to sign a short form contract—for superfluous reasons. He was paid a fee, which was essentially the same amount paid to his attorney for negotiating the fee. This sort of vexing music business zero-sum math is all too common.

I reached out to Zach, asking him—maybe begging—to intercede with his attorney on my behalf. More accurately, our behalf. It was too late. The damage had been done. I don't think he knew who to believe.

And so it was that an attorney who had nothing to do with me or the music I'd funded and helped create was running The Lone Bellow show. Disrespected, accused, and wronged, Ashworth ancestral history and my own temper raged through me like a storm-engorged river. If it'd been in a Louisiana sawmill in 1890, oh, man, there'd have been a fight.

Of the manipulative schemes, memes, and themes that music businesspeople perpetuate, none is simpler than planting doubt in an artist's mind. All you need to do is pose a question and offer your professional opinion. Here's a hypothetical example:

"Did you agree that Charlie would be reimbursed for his out-of-pocket expenses?"

"Yes. Why do you ask?"

"I think it's unfair, that's all. If I'd been involved from the beginning, I would have positioned you as working on spec as well, with your own unique expenses. You're the artist. He needs you! How many months did you work on the record? Four? You had to take care of your monthly nut, plus extra food and transportation costs. That's at least $30K right there. What's Charlie asking for expenses? Twenty-thousand dollars in cash outlay plus in-kind services for his studio? Why should you pay for a producer's home studio? That doesn't make sense. By my math, you're $30K in, and he's $20K in. Sounds like you're the one who ought to be reimbursed."

That is how it's done; doubt created in the one previously most trusted. The oldest trick in the book— and I mean the Book literally, as in the Hebrew Torah, Genesis, chapter 3, verse 1.

All in all, the postcreativity part of The Lone Bellow story is not the sort that I'd willingly subject myself to again. Emphasis on willingly—sometimes you see the crazy coming, sometimes it slips past you.

—

Like the executive at Universal, music business survivors usually arrive at a common motto sooner or later: Life's too short to work with people I neither like nor trust. They have, at this point in their career, thinned the herd and will keep thinning. No matter their love and respect for artists, the experienced do not suffer fools gladly, except when the fool stirs the sound of mass applause and rings the bell of the great digital cash register in the cloud. Cease that activity? You're gone.

In contrast, budding artists are new on the scene, too often scared people-pleasers, not wanting to appear as inexperienced as they are, hoping to God they don't trash this first (and at present, only) opportunity to do the thing they love for life. Like I said, it's not a fair fight.

I know this from experience. I was that budding artist at twenty-four.

If I roll my own film back, the flickering images remind me I have no room to judge the inexperienced young artist. I know the territory well. I've been the insecure one trying to choose what's best for my ego, music, and family, getting the order all mixed up, and ever so conveniently forgetting to love my neighbor as I would love myself.

Beginning in 1984, I was moved along by a serendipitous nexus of people and events all within a two-year period. It seemed everything I ever dreamed of for my music and its success was coming to pass.

In the fall of that year, I received a call from a young booking agent in NYC named John Huie, with Frontier Booking International (FBI), a talent agency he founded with Ian Copeland and Buck Williams, two agents he'd worked with at the Paragon Agency in Macon, Georgia. At Paragon, they'd booked southern rock pioneers the Charlie Daniels Band and a high school favorite of mine, the Allman Brothers. With FBI, they were booking the emerging stars of the present and future, bands like The Police, REM, The Bangles, The

Fixx, and The English Beat spinoff, General Public. They were the "it" agency, the place to be.

Ian, and his brothers Miles and Stewart, were an unbeatable juggernaut of punky, new wave/alternative music success. Stewart, as the drummer with The Police; Miles as manager and the impresario behind IRS Records.

I was thrilled to get a call from FBI, let alone be offered the support slot in front of current hit-makers The Fixx. They were on top of the pop world with Top 40 US radio hits "Saved by Zero" and "One Thing Leads to Another."

John wanted to know if I had a band and would I be able to join The Fixx in Phoenix on the final leg of a US tour. Yes, of course, and thank you. This was the call I'd been waiting for, hoping for.

This was the year that Exit Records, the small independent label in Northern California, had released my debut album, *Lie Down in the Grass*. It was picked up by A&M Records for a rerelease. I knew little to nothing about music distribution. Word Records in Waco, Texas, had distributed the first pressing, and it was obvious something had gone wrong—something I was yet to learn. The record stores that mattered to me, my hometown Tower Records and Rick Deprato's Esoteric Records, didn't even carry *Lie Down in the Grass*. I was confused and more than a little embarrassed. Now, with A&M, I was told it would be rereleased and available everywhere.

Lynn Arthur Nichols, an A&R executive and future guitarist with the MCA act Chagall Guevara, was instrumental in the A&M deal. Lynn and Mary Neely played Gil Friesen, and Herb Alpert and Jerry Moss (the *A* and the *M*), my record and made a deal. Along with taking on distribution of the entire Word catalog, A&M would give special marketing and promotion attention to me, Amy Grant, Russ Taff, and a phenomenal guitarist named Phil Keaggy (artists I would go on to work with in years to come). It would be Amy, though, that exceeded all expectations—a pop star was born.

The Copelands were doing business with Herb and Jerry too. The Police were signed to the label in the US, and Miles distributed IRS through A&M.

In June of 1983, I was contacted by a former KSAN DJ named Bonnie Simmons (now a Rock Radio Hall of Fame inductee). Bonnie was working for Bill Graham, the legendary Bay Area rock promoter and manager. My friend and collaborator Bongo Bob Smith had slipped Bonnie some of my new music. She liked it and invited me to Bill's office in San Francisco for a meeting regarding their management client, Carlos Santana.

Joining us in the meeting were managers Mick Brigden and Arnie Pustilnik. With no hits to my credit, they wanted me to write a few for Carlos. They explained that Carlos always began a new project by creating out of his ethnic background and the plentiful well of reverence for his heroes, like John Coltrane. They agreed this was as it should be, resulting in generally great music. Santana music. Still, they added, there's always the question of songs for radio once we begin interfacing with the Columbia Records A&R and promotional teams. I nodded like I knew something about such things.

After an hour of positivity and encouragement, I drove back to Sacramento and began writing some song-starts for the famed guitarist. I would be paid a few hundred dollars for my time. Oh, and they mentioned Carlos would know nothing about our arrangement. The management trifecta simply wanted songs ready to go in case they were needed. Months later, I did the same for their client Eddie Money with a song I liked quite a bit titled "When the Roses Came Undone." This unique way of managing Carlos seems to be the exact formula Clive Davis used in creating the late-career mega-hit *Supernatural* in 2000, featuring the single "Smooth" with Rob Thomas.

These odd ghost-writing assignments of mine bore no fruit, but I did sign on as a Bill Graham–managed recording artist just in time for them to represent me to A&M Records and my new booking agent, John Huie.

John, true to his word, put me on the road with The Fixx, Let's Active, and two tours with a potent British ska band called General Public, led by Dave Wakeling and the late Ranking Roger, formerly of The English Beat. By mid-May of 1985, touring had ended, and I was back home in Sacramento, writing for my next record, playing club gigs, and filling the occasional support slot on a headliner's concert bill.

I had nineteen songs written, and Philip Bailey of Earth, Wind & Fire was scheduled to produce my second solo album in July. Philip's schedule changed, likely due to the radio success of "Easy Lover," and he was suddenly unavailable. At that point, Bill Graham Management began looking for a new producer, assigning junior manager Marty Diamond the task. By late August, we had interest from UK producer Nigel Gray and the *Saturday Night Live* bandleader, G. E. Smith. My teen-era music hero, Todd Rundgren, passed, and we were still waiting to hear back from a fellow named Dave Evans. Next to his name on the memo was (U2) in parentheses.

I previously mentioned Chris Blackwell, president of Island Records. My compatriots, Brent Bourgeois and Larry Tagg (Bourgeois Tagg), were already signed to Island Records and Bill Graham Management, as well as Island Music Publishing by executive Lionel Conway.

Lionel kindly made me a publishing offer as well.

On the other hand, Doug Minnick, a bit younger than me, was a creative director at CBS Songs, a 1980s iteration of CBS Records' music publishing arm April-Blackwood. He worked out of the Los Angeles headquarters in Century City—high-rise real estate, sleek, well-appointed with a clean, modern 24-track studio. It was everything Lionel Conway's funky, 1970s-style office was not. CBS Songs put an offer on the table too.

Lionel is a consummate music publisher of the highest order. He began with Dick James Music in London, where he helped steward the Beatles and Elton John catalogs. Working for Chris Blackwell and Island, he personally signed Cat Stevens, Tom Waits, Jimmy Cliff, U2, and some of my closest mates, Bourgeois Tagg. Lionel is an industry legend. He was the obvious choice for me, but I leaned toward CBS. I was relieved when the decision was made for me. Lionel's offer was 25 percent lower than CBS's. I was a young man with a family and couldn't afford to leave a little on the bargaining table. It was hand-to-mouth back then.

I became an artist/songwriter with CBS, and like my songwriting inspiration, James Taylor, my songs would be published by April-Blackwood too. I was very close in age to most of the team at CBS and genuinely liked all of them very much. On the West Coast, that meant Doug, Pat Lucas, Dee Thierry, and Teddy Zambetti. And on the East Coast, Deirdre O'Hara and Danny Strick.

I was learning valuable life lessons, on the clock, on my own dime. Mainly this: with great opportunities, the sort that musicians live for, inevitably come difficult decisions.

—

Though my booking agent John Huie had done me an incredible solid, in the end, I wasn't loyal to him. I failed to honor his belief in me. Shortly after signing with his agency and finishing the spring tour of '85, John left FBI. He was starting his own agency, H-1 (no partners this time), and he wanted me to come with him. Ian called me too. He wanted me to stay at FBI, promising he would be my guy.

The band and I were in NYC playing Radio City Music Hall when we visited Ian at the FBI office. He juiced up the energy, showed us a good time, and gave the guys a short tour: "here's where my girlfriend Courteney Cox used to sit and answer the phone—she's the dancer in Springsteen's video. And here's the hot tub Sting once luxuriated in." That sort of thing.

I gave John a no and Ian a yes. The production company I was signed to (Mary Neely and Exit Records) opposed going with John. They said he was starting a Christian music booking agency with Amy Grant, and it didn't fit with their goals for me. This influenced my decision, but only to confirm what I wanted to do anyway.

John went on to reach legendary status in the concert booking business and is the cohead of the prestigious Creative Artists Agency in Nashville. We remain friends, today, though not before I made amends and asked his forgiveness. Even if it had been the right choice to stay with Ian, John deserved better from me. Oh, and staying with Ian wasn't the best career move, after all.

On May 9, 1986, my manager Arnie Pustilnik sent me a letter stating that Bill Graham Management had yet to be paid for expenses and commissions on a tour I'd done almost twelve months prior. Also, they were owed a 15 percent commission on my music publishing deal with CBS Songs.

I took the counsel of an older businessperson I knew. His advice was to pay what I could afford and not worry about the rest. In his view, Bill Graham Management would write the loss off on their tax return. Let them take the hit. They didn't need the money.

There it was, like clockwork. A businessperson, an outside force, changing the course of an already existing, honest relationship, giving me cover to violate the trust of that relationship. He set the plate of self-interest and convenience in front of me, and I sucked it up. No sweet honey from the rock; this was gall, bitter to the taste.

Andi and I were embarrassed. Ashamed, really. We knew better. Our bill should've been paid in full. Bill Graham Management had represented me for more than two years with no payment. All they'd done was serve me and my music faithfully.

Not long after we had moved to Nashville in 1989, I called Arnie and Mick at Bill Graham Management, and just like with John, asked forgiveness and made amends. Their kindness served to remind me that these two men believed in me and had my back. I'd disrespected them and chosen unwisely; a smoother way of saying I was a fool.

Tragically, Bill Graham died in a helicopter crash in 1991. You had to have grown up in, or near, the San Francisco Bay Area to understand the colossal presence and influence this man had on the history of popular music in the twentieth century. He was the architect of concert eclecticism, which influenced so many of us baby-boomer musicians in Northern California. He was the first to put Miles Davis on the same ticket as the Grateful Dead. He mixed blues artists like Albert King with the latest psychedelic pop. All of this sent a signal to musicians of my generation. We were called to learn every kind of American music and play them all well.

I was not close to Bill. His presence was reserved for history-making stars, not the still-yet-unproven or the just well known. Arnie and Mick were the managers. Bill gave me just enough time to feel important and valued, which I imagine was the strategy. Once, Andi and I visited with Bill in his office and received the full legend, story-time hour. A huge photo of me, taken by Michael Jang, hung just outside his door. I also remember Bill coming backstage at the Fillmore West to congratulate me and offer some sage feedback. I'd just finished a set as an opener for Bourgeois Tagg. I have a classic photo from that moment, Bill with his scowling brow (though actually happy), right arm raised with his thumb pointing back to the stage. Me, soaked in sweat, towel around my neck, head down, and drinking in Bill's praise. All with the imprint of my background vocalist Clarice Jones's lipstick kiss stamped on my cheek.

—

I eventually gained some sense and perspective about The Lone Bellow. I could see that my anger was poisoning me from the inside out. In true recovery fashion, I began to let go and let God. Zach and I had gone our separate ways for several years and then, as it so often happens, music put us in the same room again—the Nashville club, Third and Lindsley. It was time to heal from the sucker punch the business hit us with. Once there, surrounded by love, shared meaning, and friends, we put it behind us. Zach was no longer a novice recording artist. Like his former producer, he was now a survivor.

There is a bond that forms between musicians as they spend months together on a project. You're in the studio for long hours every day making music, which also means making hundreds of creative decisions. It's visceral and brainy, fatiguing, and mentally taxing. You're sharing nearly every meal together. The rest of life continues to spin around each of you even when you're trying to give the performance of your life. Or you're five notes away from finishing a bass part but having to answer questions from your tax accountant ("Hey, CP, do you mind if we take a break for a second?").

You're hearing about the spouse at home with the toilet that's broken, or the sick child taken to urgent care in the middle of the night, a tour date that was canceled, a parent coming to visit (the one who has yet to believe you can make a living at music). All of it, the stuff of real life. You tell a lot of stories, and you laugh till you're tearing up, doubled over, and need to take it outside and walk it off as if it were a sprained ankle. It's all of this at once. Music is hard. There's no job like it. No joy like it, either.

When the music is good, it will rise above any difficulties in the making of it. I rise with it, and the levitation becomes medicine through memory. I remember afresh why it is I make music; how it shaped me, took care of me, and gave our family a life we would never have apart from it. No trial or trouble can steal my love of music, my childlike joy in making it, or my gratitude for its extraordinary provision.

For folk/Americana music fans, The Lone Bellow was an unassailable hit. Reporting on the band's 2013 Newport Folk Festival appearance, NPR predicted a bright future for the band, one similar to The Civil Wars, saying, "Don't be surprised if the trio follows in that duo's path to greater success."[1]

No surprise at all.

Debuting on February 2, 2013, the self-titled album was Top 20 in *Billboard*'s Top Alternative, Top Folk, and Top Rock albums, peaking at sixty-four in the *Billboard* 200. *Entertainment Weekly* scored it as No. 4 in their ten best country albums of 2013: "The Brooklyn band's debut album contains traces of gospel-tinged soul and modern folk-pop, but it's a country album through and through."[2]

Veteran critic Holly Gleason, writing for *Paste* magazine, commented, "working with producer Charlie Peacock, The Lone Bellow figured out a way to harness the acoustic-rock template being mined by Mumford & Sons, The Lumineers and The Civil Wars and add a sense of powerful vocal incandescence."[3]

That they did.

—

The year 2013 was exceptional for me as a producer. On that same *Entertainment Weekly* Top 10 list, Holly Williams's *The Highway* ranked No. 6 and *The Civil Wars* was at No. 7—which meant I had produced three out of ten. Also released in 2013 were Ben Rector's *The Walking in Between*, reaching No. 16 on the *Billboard* Top 200, and Brett Dennen's *Smoke and Mirrors* at No. 65.

Though our path to victory was circuitous, Holly Williams and I overcame all obstacles and finished with flair and gratitude. Neither Obama's motorcade nor too little Jackson Browne deterred us in the end. We'd added guests Jakob Dylan and Dierks Bentley, each harmonizing with Holly. After my son Sam recorded Dierks's vocal, the two would go on to have a significant connection. Sam sang all the background vocals on Dierks's breakout hit "Drunk on a Plane," released in 2014.

Holly Williams was both a challenge and a delight. We are two very different kinds of creative, mental processors. She likes to have lots of options set out before her, time to weigh the options, and will even delay choosing one as a caution against choosing wrongly—also known as being thoughtful and full of care.

I'm the opposite, but hopeful that I'm full of care, too. I get a mental picture of the possible choices, and with no delay (à la Malcolm Gladwell's *Blink*), I choose one. I'm not afraid of getting it wrong. I love experimenting, adapting, and editing as much as I do getting it right the first time.

Both of our approaches are equally valid. Except with Holly's, you're not likely to become a record producer.

As a vocation, music production intrinsically requires quick, decisive thinking and action: you're going to make hundreds of decisions in a single day. Athletics is a handy analog here. We have fast-twitch and slow-twitch muscles in the body. Fast-twitch helps with bursts of energy like sprinting short distances. Slow-twitch muscles help with endurance over long distances, like riding a bike for fifty miles. In music production, you need both.

Holly is definitely slow-twitch in the studio. *Rolling Stone* reported that creating the album *The Highway* "wasn't as easy as Williams (daughter of Hank Williams Jr., granddaughter of Hank Williams) thought it would be; what started as a few weeks in the studio with Charlie Peacock of the Civil Wars stretched into nine months." That's not a typo. Nine months for a bouncing baby album.

Yet, when it was finished, Holly told *Rolling Stone* that making the record was "blood, sweat and tears, and the best time of my life, too."[4] I feel the same way. Holly and Chris made me laugh till I choked, especially when Holly told stories on her dad, Hank Jr. She could be funny of the highest order. Table fellowship was just as fun and meaningful. Thanks to Andi, we shared five-star nosh and nourishment with regularity.

Holly was sweet and attentive to Alfie, my ruminant seven-year-old grandson. He called her "H" and made it his business to drop by the studio (thirty steps from Andi, across the garden). Holly would be on the couch, guitar in hand, with her long blond hair falling across the body of her treasured Gibson. Alfie would climb up and quietly sit next to her as we worked. When asked why he liked H so much, Alfie replied, "She's beautiful like a princess."

Sadly, Holly has yet to make another record since *The Highway* (though it remains on the singer-songwriter charts to this day). It's not as if Holly and Chris haven't been busy. Like her friends Reese and Gwyneth, Holly has a lifestyle brand—clothes at H. Audrey—and cool stuff you're enticed to buy at White's Mercantile in the trendy Nashville neighborhood, 12 South. Plus, they've gone and had themselves four children.

Now I understand why *The Highway* took so long.

Growing a baby takes nine months—the ultimate slow-twitch.

Author Gayle Forman has a great line in her book *Where She Went*: "I'll be your mess, you be mine. That was the deal that we had signed."[5] So it is that we are each other's messes. There is no art making, or life making, without a mess. Not only is music hard as a vocation, in that so few artists are able to sustain a lifetime career, but we don't do ourselves any favors by undermining each other and our individual and collective dreams. We do have a unique advantage over most of the population, though. Our ability to organize chaos and restore artistic order and fellowship is unparalleled. No brag, just fact.

eight

A WALKING CONTRADICTION
IN THE LAND OF BELIEF

March 4–17, 1982, I played piano at Lake Tahoe in Harrah's Stateline Cabaret. Some friends and I had taken a one-off gig as a country group fronted by beef jerky mogul Ajay Avery, creator of a chewy product called Montana Bananas. Superstar John Denver was the headliner in the South Shore Room, the big room, with Jay Leno as the opening act.

In 1980, if you'd asked me to take a country gig with a moderately talented jerky mogul, unequivocally, I would've offered you profanity's most succinct reply. I was a star in the making back then, not a jester dancing for dollars.

Circumstances change.

Denver had hired Elvis Presley's legendary Takin' Care of Business band (TCB) with Glen Hardin on piano, James Burton on lead guitar, Jerry Scheff on upright bass, and Ron Tutt on drums. Very briefly, we all shared oxygen with these immortals. Watching James Burton and crew walk through the casino in their TCB leather jackets was transformative. These musicians were storied giants; cool, and worthy of adoration.

Ajay Avery had given our outfit the luminous title of The Montana Banana Bunch. The Bunch received a generally favorable review in *Variety* on March 11, with a positive mention of my piano skills. Steve Voudouris, John Denver's guitar tech, arranged for us to have a few minutes backstage with John. We all chatted, and I left with an autograph for my mom.

On March 18, immediately following the Tahoe gig, drummer Jimmy Caselli and I raced back down the mountain to Sacramento. Jimmy and I were in an actual, serious, and popular band that played its own music, the Charlie Peacock Group. Now that we had a little extra money in our pockets, it was time to get back to headlining Sacramento and San Francisco clubs. We were close to signing a record deal: a symbol of authenticity held by me, if not the whole band.

Hope and optimism were returning to me. I welcomed them. I needed them. Andi and I needed them.

There'd been a particularly dark hour in 1980 when I was separated from Andi and the children. It began with a Greyhound bus ride north to Yuba City and my parents' home. With a substance abuse intervention in mind, my parents hatched an idea for me to check into a hometown mental health facility. I was resistant and left the house for cheap beer at the 7-Eleven and brought the smell of defeat back with me.

I had betrayed my father for the last time. He told me to pack my things and be gone by the morning. After all the misspent words had been spoken, after all the tears and false promises ceased, he came into the guest bedroom where I'd gone to sulk. There was no fight left in him. He laid a Bible on the bed. "Son," he said, "everything that you're looking for is in this book." My only hope. Then he turned and walked out. I left the book where it lay, caught a Greyhound to Sacramento the next morning, and barely spoke to my parents for a year.

It wasn't like I was unfamiliar with the Bible. I'd read it some; mostly a psalm or proverb here and there, usually under duress; or wondering if there might be a song enclosed—a song to be written, that is. Since a child, I'd had a Gideon Bible, like in the Beatles' song "Rocky Raccoon." One of those pocket-sized King James New Testaments with the wisdom literature included.

Inside the cover was a short, printed confession of belief. The Gideons printed a line where you could put your name and date as a concrete affirmative. It said:

"Confessing to God that I am a sinner, and believing that the Lord Jesus Christ died for my sins on the cross and was raised for my justification, I do now receive and confess him as my personal savior."

I signed my name, Chuck 5-30-64, which made me seven years old. I have no memory of this.

This confession was followed by some assurances for the novice, including 1 John 1:7: "But if we walk in the light, as he is in the light, we have fellowship with one another, and the blood of Jesus Christ, his Son, purifies us from all sin."

Years later, inebriated, lost, and sentimental, I wrote these words in the front of that little Bible: "I'm gonna write in here cause many, many years ago this was my papa's bible and I just found out Calvin W. Ashworth first received this bible in the '40s and god bless the souls of the Ashworths and our ancestors, love through Jesus Christ our Saviour."

This time it was signed, Charlie Peacock Ashworth 1979. In the middle of my scrawl, there printed by the Gideons, this unequivocal command: THIS BOOK NOT TO BE SOLD.

Duly warned, I hung on to it. And it may be no coincidence that among my most-traveled, popular songs is "In the Light." That is, "in the light as He is in the light."

By 1982 and the Tahoe gig, my drug and alcohol abuse was in remission. Given an unexpected and undeserved second chance, I'd escaped the grave. Every new day seemed to reveal new grace and previously out-of-reach goodness. The income difference and health of our family in 1981 compared to 1982 was truly remarkable. Sobriety was making a man out of me and giving our young family the first seeds of peace and financial stability. This emerging life made me feel as I did in early childhood, imaginative and free. My inner husband, father, and musical entrepreneur had been set free. Conspicuous failures turned into grateful successes.

Right at the eleventh hour, with no reason to hope, rescue came.

Our marriage had been seven years of youthful fails, uncertainty, chaos, blood-dripping wounds, and deep trauma and pain undealt with. Because of my neglect, Andi had needed help from Aid to Families with Dependent Children (AFDC), a federal assistance program for children of families with low or no income.

Now that my sanity was returning, I wanted us off welfare at the first possible moment. That was my goal. Nineteen eighty-two would prove to be the year that changed everything.

Chapter Eight

One year before, on March 31, 1981, producer (and very briefly my manager) David Rubinson cut me a check for one-half of the two hundred dollars I was paid by Tommy Boyce and Bobby Hart for the music publishing on "So Attractive" (a song cowritten with Steve Holsapple and David Kahne). The other hundred bucks went to my lawyer Lindsey Feldman. David Rubinson, a true mensch, deferred his commission. I was all revved up because the legendary songwriters who wrote The Monkees' songs had bought our little tune.

All the self-generated buzz in the world couldn't change the fact that the Boyce and Hart opportunity had been no real opportunity at all—and that's the way things went for me back then, before I got my head screwed on straight (that elusive outcome my father valued so much). I was perpetually one great opportunity away from making it. Just living only for those vaporous moments.

Even when given a legitimate opportunity, my self-destructive impulses would sabotage it. Like when Juliea Clark and David Kershenbaum of A&M Records signed me to a development deal with David Kahne producing and I was under the influence of everything but imagination and integrity. Or when I was hanging with Tommy Tutone at the legendary attorney Brian Rohan's house in San Francisco and had to be shown the door. Bad form all around.

The dark side of Kerouac's surrogate parenting showed up in spectacularly predictable ways. At twenty-five years old, all my best efforts at life had failed. I was exhausted and in turmoil. I had deconstructed all obligations to friends and family—certainly to institutions. I had used everyone in my life for personal pleasure, ego, and gain. I had declared myself free and found myself in bondage.

A doctor, a Sacramento substance-abuse guru, gave me a prescription. Written on the slip of paper were the initials AA, for Alcoholics Anonymous. Clever. I vacillated, resisted, and after a time, surrendered. It had to be worth a try. Nothing else was working.

I'd left carnage in my wake, including a car accident resulting in a court case and the loss of my driver's license. Unable to drive, I dug out my eighth-grade green Schwinn ten-speed bicycle and pedaled my way to twelve-step meetings, and the 7-Eleven where I bought 3 Musketeers bars to satiate my sugar cravings. Ironically, the bike was stolen outside the front door of a meeting. I like to think some other broken person needed it more than I did. As it's said at twelve-step meetings where they pass the hat for basic expenses: "If you can't put some in, take some out."

Early on, it was impressed upon me by the recovery group that I'd never get, or stay, sober without something called a "higher power." One cranky old man claimed an ashtray as his higher power. He said an ashtray is as good as anything.

When it came time to pick my higher power, it made some amount of sense to circle back around to the God of the Bible. It was obvious that spiritual tourism had borne little fruit. I still had Dad's little Gideon Bible. Hadn't lost it or sold it. As a kind of totem, it still represented something to me. What, exactly, I couldn't discern. Maybe twice I actually tried to read it. No doing. It was word soup. I couldn't see anything. It may as well have been written in Greek or Aramaic.

In the fall of 1980, I admitted I was powerless over drugs and alcohol, especially alcohol. In the light of a little sobriety, it was humiliatingly obvious that my life was unmanageable. Believing I'd be restored to sanity, I turned my will and life over to the care of the God of the Bible.

I prayed to the God of the Bible in the morning and at night. "God of the Bible, please help me stay sober today." Later in bed, "God of the Bible, thank you for helping me stay sober today." That simple. No flourishes. No "thee's," no "thou's." Just "help." And "thanks."

As time went on, I began to elaborate a bit in my prayers, asking the God of the Bible to change my character, my whole way of being. I even began to pray for family provision, for help in my marriage and the whole of life. My prayers were about what was happening under our roof. I figured I'd get to matters of global concern once it was clear I'd live to see the age of twenty-seven.

A twelve-step recovery group is a world unto itself. In a one-hour meeting, you'll hear wet-brain babbling, bitter blame-shifting, and sage advice for the whole of life. For me, the most efficacious of the latter, being: "Get yourself a big notebook and write down everything you ever did or said that was wrong or shameful. It could be breaking a law or a cruel word to an undeserving friend. If you can remember it and it stuck with you, write it down. Anything that hurt someone or something and made you wish you hadn't done it, write it down. Whatever you can recall, from the half-truth to the disgraceful, put it all in there, from childhood till now. Take as long as it takes."

It took a while. I'd said and done plenty I wished I hadn't. These weren't simple regrets. These were choices I knew were wrong. Yet I did them anyway. I wanted to do them. Why? It didn't make any sense.

I had a Kris Kristofferson album as a teenager, *The Silver-Tongued Devil and I*. Kris sang about a man who was a walking contradiction.

> He's a poet, he's a picker, he's a prophet, he's a pusher
> He's a pilgrim and a preacher and a problem when
>   he's stoned
> He's a walking contradiction, partly truth and
>   partly fiction
> Taking every wrong direction on his lonely way
>   back home.[1]

I wrote it all down in a wire-bound notebook, just like they said to. Everything I remembered, I put in the book.

One evening in the parking lot of a restaurant, I read the entire "fearless moral inventory" to my recovery group sponsor. Every word spoke back to me with authority and clarity. I didn't need the caricature of a fire and brimstone preacher to call me a sinner. I chose to cross a line, sear my conscience, and violate laws written on my heart. Repeatedly, I knew the right thing to do and refused to do it. Some part of me was that man. Alcohol and drug abuse didn't help either.

This enlightenment was not the one I had my sights on when I was a full-time spiritual tourist. It wasn't Donovan and The Beatles with the Maharishi in 1967. It wasn't even satori at home sitting cross-legged before a teak table with a little Buddha statuette burning Nag Champa incense. It did have the ring of truth, though, and I'd always said I was after the truth. Reality. I had never encountered anything in my spiritual search that made me feel as if I was known—even if what was known was everything I didn't want anyone to know. This fearless moral inventory stuff, and the upside-down result of it being positive, took me by surprise.

I finally understood why Christians have the sin doctrine. That shit is real. Despite my aversion to the word, sin was simply a descriptor for my condition. Sin and its effects are everything that is anti-God, antipeople, and antiplanet. Sin is the way things shouldn't be. It's the will at work moving in the opposite direction of life and rightness, and all the great human potential of being a lover of good.

—

In between a gig with my own band at the China Wagon in Sacramento on February 17 and the Harrah's Tahoe gig in March, I got a call to sub for a piano player at the top of the Holiday Inn in downtown Sacramento. This was the average high-end cocktail bar gig of the era. I read charts of standards like "It Had to Be You," backed up the singer, and soloed on cue. The leader on the date was a saxophonist named Mike Butera, a monster of a musician.

Mike, a friend of producer David Kahne, had done some recording with Voudouris & Kahne, David's short-lived duo on Capitol Records. Most notably, Mike had been the lead tenor saxophone soloist in a contemporary version of the Harry James Big Band. My dad admired Harry James's trumpet technique and tone. Though arguably famous, to most of our Sacramento community of musicians, Harry James was an anachronism. He did give Sinatra his start, was married to film star Betty Grable, and had Buddy Rich for a drummer. Sixty-plus years ago, this meant something.

The Holiday Inn gig was three hours long, with breaks in between. I knew Mike was a born-again Christian—what the new variety associated with the California Jesus Movement were called back then.

My people, those of the downtown art scene, had little to no admiration or interest in born-again Christians. True, Dylan got a look or two when he professed to be born again, but that's about the scope of it. Generally, Christianity was thought to involve a lot of rule following. That it meant giving up a number of things you enjoyed in order to do a number of things you had no idea whether you'd enjoy or not. There was also a sense that Christians were given to moralizing, an attitude of superiority, hypocritical behavior, and being judgmental. All of that, using the vernacular, was a major *turnoff* for the freedom-loving sort.

My twelve-step confessional inventory had made me soft around the heart though. During a fifteen-minute break, looking for common ground, I let Mike know that I'd been praying for work—appealing to a higher power. I thanked Mike for hiring me, told him I was grateful. He asked which God I prayed to. "The God of the Bible," I replied. I figured he'd be pleased; one point for his home team and all.

Afterward, I left for Lake Tahoe and the adventure with the Banana Bunch crew. When I returned, Mike called to see if we could get together. It was early afternoon. He wanted to know if he could come to my house and pray with me. It did seem a little odd and awkward, but my mind was open. I figured, I pray in the morning; I pray at night; I can pray in the middle of the afternoon, too.

Mike arrived shortly after our phone conversation.

There's a passage in the Bible from Romans 10 that reads: "How, then, can they call on the one they have not believed in? And how can they believe in the one of whom they have not heard? And how can they hear without someone preaching to them? And how can anyone preach unless they are sent? As it is written: 'How beautiful are the feet of those who bring good news!'"

Mike brought me good news that day. I didn't have to work my way to God—a fallacy I'd picked up along the way. In fact, Mike said it was impossible to do so. He said that trying to get to God with good behavior was like trying to swim to Hawaii from California. I knew I couldn't swim to Hawaii, metaphorically or otherwise. Jesus, he said, is the bridge over the ocean of impossibility, doing for people what they can't do for themselves.

According to Mike, the God of the Bible had put a plan in place to deal, once for all, with the exact nature of my wrongs, including the exact nature of any future wrongs, near or distant. I wasn't good Chuck who became bad Chuck who now needed to become good Chuck again. Performance as religion was out, off the table. I could just be me, Chuck. God was coming toward me in and through the person of Jesus. He was bringing me a gift called grace, an antidote to karma.

Mike asked me if I thought I needed a savior. I might have laughed out loud. Yes, I needed a savior, practically, cosmically, and in any other way known or unknown.

Next, he asked, "Do you think Jesus could be that savior?"

Then I knew. I knew more than I could tell. I was experiencing a kind of awareness I had no prior experience with or words to describe.

There was a moment in my imagination when I saw something like a line at my feet. On one side was my life. The one I'd decided I wanted to live, the one I was now finally getting together. On the other, nothing but Jesus and the infinite unknown. I felt a nudge to step over, but couldn't. Somehow, I knew that if I stepped over the line, there'd be no going back, and I wanted to keep my options open. The last thing I needed was to get sucked into some religious craziness.

Then without another thought, there I was, on the other side of the line, standing in the land of effectual belief.

In a fraction of a second I knew love more completely, more extravagantly than I'd ever known it. I felt mercy.

Not everyone does, but I had a very physical reaction. I was overcome with gratitude.

God had heard my cries for help bouncing off his satellites and sent me a saxophonist. Of course he did.

I've heard it said that sin is the only major doctrine of Christianity that can be empirically proven. I agree in part, but disagree with it being the only major doctrine that can be proven. I think human beings are inescapably related to God, and that the doctrine of the image of God in humankind can be proven as well. These two major doctrines, one about the shame and the other about the glory, explain the walking contradiction that is me. I am capable of world-changing good and devastatingly bad behavior; behavior that changes your world and mine down to the most personal of relationships and enterprise. This is what I came to believe when I had no intention of believing it. Christian theologians like it when people say stuff like this. They have names for this kind of sneaky belief: prevenient grace and common grace.

Jesus had been there in my life for decades, as a name, a presence, a story in a book. But the foundation of my childhood Christian belief was cracked and unstable. I questioned everything. I had many roads to walk listening to the blowin' wind, pondering the unsolved questions of my generation. Rilke was right, though. In time, I had lived my way into the answer.

In addition to my Zen hero Gary Snyder, I studied Alan Watts, Thomas Merton, and the greatest interpreter of Zen to the West, D. T. Suzuki. The editor of D. T. Suzuki's *Essays in Zen Buddhism* described Suzuki as "a man who seeks for the intellectual symbols wherewith to describe a state of awareness which lies indeed beyond the intellect."[2] As a young aspiring Zen Buddhist, this concept always hung me up, kept me from fully entering in. I was just acquiring an intellect, let alone one robust enough to know where the intellect ended and the event horizon of new awareness began. Now with the passing of time, I like to think I understand something of Suzuki's bent and desire.

Thanks to friends Steve Garber and Esther Meek, I have a very elementary understanding of epistemology, specifically the pioneering work on this subject from scientist Michael Polanyi. I know the impulse to "seek the intellectual symbols" to describe knowledge that operates at the tacit rather than cognitive level—most artists do. So does Michael Polanyi. Maybe the East and West poles of Suzuki and Polanyi aren't as far apart as some might assume. Both intellectuals were trying to get at something "beyond the intellect"—something more than a little elusive, something that dwells where many words or the scientific process seldom gains traction. Even when wordsmiths and scientists do sneak in and have a look around the Great Beyond, they tend to overcomplicate things. Too much talking, overanalysis, and second-guessing can kill insight and enlightenment on arrival.

Some of us who follow Jesus think this place of knowing (beyond or encircling the intellect) might be what we call faith, even hope and love—all perfectly legitimate ways of knowing. We also think one can hold to this belief without denigrating the intellect.

Unfortunately, there's always some school of thought trying to disengage the intellect from the authentic spiritual life. Even Christians, maybe especially Christians, have an anti-intellectual bias. This is especially ironic coming from a people who profess to know something of the mind of Christ. Where I stand, the best approach to knowing is holistic: use every good and powerful way of knowing, active and tacit, in different measure at different times, all fueled by love.

You can have a real desire to find symbols that describe ways of knowing more than you can tell—at least more than you can tell by using the traditional means of description, argument, or logic. Poetry, art, and music do this symbolic work very well. Especially when they are allowed to speak their own language. It's frustrating when art is not allowed simply to be. People grow dependent on an artist's apologetic or the critic's opinion, and the human ability to know atrophies—description before delight. Instead of knowing more than they can tell, they tell more than they know. Lips are moving, but all we hear is what they've read online or heard on a podcast. Not wholly inadequate sources, but life is more than screen time.

To help people know in fresh ways, Jesus used the spring-loaded power of the parable. Was he trying to communicate with people on a para-cognitive level? Jump-start their hearts? All of this wondering reminds me of how people are always saying something is very Zen or Zen-like. I used to say this all the time. Everyone in our downtown tribe did. "That's so Zen." No one ever asks, "Why is it so Zen?" We're all afraid to reveal our unenlightened state.

Maybe Western Zen-talk is just convenient shorthand for "I know something is real; I'm aware of it, but it's true that either I cannot describe it, or attempting to would be a colossal waste of time and energy. Worse yet, it would take all the fun out of it." To borrow from a common Polanyi illustration, think of trying to explain in exhaustive detail how you know how to ride a bike. I did a little of this one day in the writing of a poem titled "Bicycle Poem No. 1." If you're good at analysis, you might come up with a few fun and clever descriptions of how basic bike-riding gets done. Bottom line though? You probably know more about bike riding than you can tell.

Do you have to know the physics of cycling to ride? No. Yet, your thinking and behavior while riding a bike might give a spectator the impression that you are working out thousands of complicated problems in your head regarding motion, balance, and speed. The truth is, you've gained substantive knowledge of bike riding over time, and this knowledge is more complex and nuanced than you have skill to describe. In short, you just know, right? Or, in Polanyi-ese, you *know more than you can tell.*

I didn't know that coming to belief about the reality of sin would set me on a path of knowing that continues today. Not only was more revealed—my substance-abuse club members said it would be—but more and more is continually revealed. The enlightenment I sought through Zen has come true in the unexpected form of following Jesus in the way of love. Who knew? I didn't.

As much as I liked Zen and Taoism, it wasn't what I needed and it didn't answer the sin problem effectively or provide what I thought was a fully integrated "God, People, and Earth solution." More than anything, I really wanted religious pluralism and syncretism to be my god. It's a fit for my personality and brokenness. I just want everyone to be happy and get along with the least amount of negative drama possible. I understand John Coltrane's search and his struggle. I couldn't stay there, though.

For me, I sorted it out this way. If I could create a god from a mix of gods or religions based on cherry-picking only the aspects I resonated with, then that composite god would never be greater than my own presuppositions, aspirations, prejudices, conscience, and imagination.

As it turned out, transcendence as I understood it was not what I needed anyway. I needed real-time, earthbound rescue. I needed forgiving, reconciling, restorative love.

My life changed forever on the day I was visited by the saxophonist, and I've never turned back from following Jesus in the way of love. For me, love is the most powerful way of knowing and being known. I can say with all confidence that the love of God in Christ Jesus is authentic and trustworthy. I would add that having an interest in what Jesus is interested in is a true and better way to live.

Holding on to this conviction has never been easy, though. At every turn there is someone coming in the name of Jesus misrepresenting his interests, including this writer/musician. Jesus must be the most co-opted character in history. Everyone wants a piece of him. People distort his mission in service of their own. Some are earnest, yet misinformed and misled. Others are downright evil and psychopathic. Some are the snake-oil salesmen of our time. But many, many more who come in his name are good and trustworthy—flawed, broken, and in process like everyone else, but beautiful still, and truly in his company.

I was in the green room, backstage at a U2 concert, several years ago. I stood around a table with friends and listened as journalist David Brooks told a story. The writer had published a very favorable op-ed piece in the *New York Times* about a Christian, a well-known British theologian named John Stott. Not a common occurrence at all. It wasn't long before David heard from a native New Yorker, perhaps one of NYC's and the world's most famous musicians, Paul Simon. The story goes that the musician wanted to know if the writer was for real. Did he really think that any Christian could be taken seriously? Wasn't the very idea of allowing for such a thing antithetical to reason, to pluralism, to the progress of society? And so on.

David set up a meeting between the Englishman and the New Yorker. They met, and the New Yorker was given time to talk about why Christians can't be taken seriously. You can imagine the possible gripes: the unholy alliances, incessant meddling, exclusive truth claims, far-right politics, homophobia, lack of sophistication, warmongering, and just plain ridiculousness. I was told that after a while the Brit acknowledged the occurrence of all of it and said something to the effect of, "What about Jesus? Let's turn our attention to him."

Jesus asked his disciples, "Who do people say I am?" This is the kind of question that reproduces questions. People say many things about who Jesus is. But who do I say he is? What did Jesus say about himself? What can be known about his mission? What are his followers supposed to concern themselves with? Am I living congruent with this mission on earth? And so the questions go.

It is easy to become distracted by all the incongruent and contradictory stories people who claim association with Jesus are telling through their confused and broken lives. Awareness of the wreckage is important. You want to take care in choosing the people you team up with and give your allegiance to. But don't stare too long at the mess. Look to Jesus and carry on. Whenever the wreckage distracts me, I've learned to turn my attention to a sobering question: *What kind of story am I telling through the life I've been given?*

It is also easy to overlook or forget that the life of following Jesus is extended to all people regardless of the quality of their performance as human beings. A merciful, life-changing truth I am so very grateful for. Jesus's gift to the world is rescue, forgiveness, love, and purpose. I've yet to meet anyone that doesn't need a little of these, or in my case, a lot.

> I lived a life of pleasant sorrows, until the real deal came
> Broke me like a twig in a winter gale, called me by my name
> And in that time of prayer and waiting, where doubt and
>   reason dwell
> A jury sat deliberating, all is lost, or all is well
> Home, home, sun on my doorstep, shocks me to find
> I'm a child again entwined in your love, in your light
> In your cool summer shade
> The garden keeps a rose and a thorn, and once the choice
>   is made
> All that's left, is mending what was torn
> Love is like a braid.[3]

I no longer seek only intellectual symbols to describe the sudden state of awareness I experienced the day I started following in the way of Jesus. I'm equally committed to a faithful, sustainable embodiment of that unique awareness in day-to-day life. In all ways, at all times, everywhere and in everything, the love of God, people, and planet (my land of belief) is my work and pleasure. Even if it is now, in the moment, only proximate.

nine

GET READY, 'CAUSE HERE I COME

All musicians are born in a particular place to a particular people surrounded by particular musical influences. There's a reason Jay-Z was so influential in hip-hop and not Texas swing music. He grew up in a housing project in the Bedford-Stuyvesant neighborhood of Brooklyn surrounded by nascent rap and hip-hop music. He could've shown an early interest in Texas swing music, or the five-string electric mandolin innovations of Tiny Moore, but he didn't. Instead, he soaked up the music of his neighborhood and created out of that localized starting place.

I was born to a particular place on earth, Yuba City, California, in 1956 in the United States of America. A significant era in music. A sample of the most popular songs on the radio in 1956 includes such iconic rock 'n' roll classics as "Be-Bop-A-Lula" (Gene Vincent), "Blueberry Hill" (Fats Domino), "Blue Suede Shoes" (Carl Perkins), and "Please, Please, Please" (James Brown). Elvis Presley had no fewer than five major hits that year, including "Don't Be Cruel," "Hound Dog," and "Love Me Tender." Johnny Cash had two that defined his career, "Folsom Prison Blues" and "I Walk the Line." Little Richard rocked the jukebox with "Tutti Fruitti" and "Long Tall Sally."

Though the '50s were clearly the decade that birthed rock 'n' roll, the charts in 1956 included traditional pop vocalists too: Doris Day, Perry Como, Patti Page, Bing Crosby, Grace Kelly, and Pat Boone among them. The Chairman of the Board, Frank Sinatra, was as much a superstar as any human could ever dream of being.

To be born in Yuba City in 1956 was radically different from being born in Tel Aviv, Beijing, or Moscow. American pop culture was not universally ubiquitous then as it is now in the twenty-first century. Today, in the era of global citizenship, a young musician has a whole world of musical influences accessible on his or her phone.

By 1963, at seven years old, I was choosing the music I wanted to listen to—or maybe it was more cooperative; the music was choosing me, too. My first memory of music not directly related to my family story was the classical music played during kindergarten naptime, which I later recognized as Brahms, Mozart, Beethoven, and Tchaikovsky, of *Nutcracker* fame. I also picked up on television show themes from the cartoon/animation composers like Philip A. Scheib, Carl Stalling, Hoyt Curtin, and Raymond Scott, whose music filled our home on Saturday mornings. All of these early, unsolicited, tacit influences revealed themselves again when I took piano improvisation seriously in my late teens. (You can hear them full bloom on the recording Jeff Coffin and I made titled *Arc of the Circle* from 2008.)

My aunt, Karoly Williamson, still a young teenager living at home with her parents (my grandparents), was my music mentor and guide in those early years. Since both of my parents left for work early, I would begin my day with Grandma Lois and Pop. I walked to school in the morning and returned to their house midday. This afforded me ample time to experience a real, live teenager and her music. It was my first exposure to The Beach Boys and The Beatles, as well as all the major singles of the day.

Karoly was always singing the latest hits. She would sing along to Top 40 radio, the *Lloyd Thaxton Show*, and Dick Clark's *American Bandstand*, and she'd let me listen and watch TV with her—that's how I learned to draw Paul Anka's black boots, a style The Beatles wore, too. Like so many baby-boomer musicians, on February 9, 1964, yes, I saw and heard The Beatles on *The Ed Sullivan Show*. Though not entirely accurate, pop mythology lore posits that after The Beatles appeared on *Ed Sullivan*, everything changed. It did, even if there were other significant contributors to change. No doubt, The Beatles were the tip-of-the-spear attack, though. They launched thousands of bands and indirectly sold a whole bunch of guitars and drums.

The Columbia Record Club played a major role in my musical education. It was created in 1955 by Columbia Records as a direct-mail campaign of particular interest to rural music lovers living some distance from big-city record stores. By 1963, it commanded 10 percent of the American record market, and my parents were members (Columbia enticed new members to join by giving them one or more free records). In addition to ordering the records of your choice, the club would often dangle the carrot of free compilations like *The Headliners*, featuring songs by Tony Bennett, The Dave Brubeck Trio, Lionel Hampton, and Johnny Mathis, or *TeenScene* with The Dave Clark Five, Bob Dylan, Chad & Jeremy, The Byrds, and Bobby Vinton. Each compilation had a different catchy title and was filled with a sampling of artists.

The Columbia Record Club compilations provided me with something akin to today's Spotify, Tidal, and Apple Music; my impressionable ears could sample a good bit of music and decide fairly quickly that I liked Thelonious Monk, Johnny Cash, and The Yardbirds, or could pass on Ray Conniff and His Orchestra or The Four Lads. The first record from the club I got to choose for myself was a compilation of Chubby Checker dance hits. I wasn't immune to the Twist, the Pony, and especially the Limbo. What kid doesn't want to bend over backward under a stick while shimmying to a fake island beat?

My hometown caught on, too; little kids started bands. Teens had bands. Live music was everywhere. It was common to hear bands rehearsing in garages and bedrooms. You could buy guitars at the department stores like Sears (Silvertone), Montgomery Ward (Airline), and Woolworths (Teisco). Teddy Karnegas's father used a sabre saw to cut us two fake guitars in the shape of Fender Stratocasters. Ludwig drums were de rigueur. Farfisa and Vox combo organs were available for musicians not ready to take on the behemoth Hammond B3. Occasionally there would be a Wurlitzer or Fender Rhodes electric piano. "Louie Louie" was the first song you learned. Then maybe "She Loves You," "Get Off of My Cloud," or "Little Black Egg."

Not every local band played covers. Some, like Drusalee and the Dead, mixed in originals, too. In 1965, they released a 45-rpm single of Drew's original "Lily" b/w the standard "Exodus," done surf-style (Varden Records). Keeping with the ghoulish theme, posters billed it as "The Morbid Sound of 'Lily.'" Like the other big local names—Freddie and the Statics and Sonny Oliver among them—Drusalee and the Dead gigged often and were openers for all the big acts coming through Northern California.

My dad had written off Drusalee, referring to his band as a bunch of hoods. In the mornings, walking to Bridge Street School, I would pass the band's '47 hearse. Such neato transportation was beyond my ability to comprehend.

By 1965, Dad was employed as the band director at Marysville High School. After the local football games, where his students marched and played, there would be a school dance. One fateful night, with the game over and the band room locked up tight, I accompanied Dad to a dance where Drusalee and the Dead were playing. I saw Drusalee rise up from his coffin, tenor saxophone blazing. The music felt like a huge gust of red-hot wind. Dad collected the cashbox (it was his turn), and we were on our way. I was nine years old and under the spell.

I think this is the way it should be. Every musical child must hear and see it done by others, especially people outside his or her immediate family circle. There has to be some heroic figure (hopefully several) who inspires a youth to imagine himself or herself doing that thing, or something similar—essentially, creating something; saying in the energized imagination, "I want to make that. I *will* make that."

I was fortunate. Before I turned twenty-one, I had already seen Ray Charles, B. B. King, Ike and Tina Turner, Jimmy Smith, Dizzy Gillespie, Thelonious Monk, Art Blakey, Stan Getz, Chick Corea, Al Green, Ella Fitzgerald, Aretha Franklin, and the Staple Singers play live (and that's not all). My imagination and will were energized often.

Today, there are so many sources of inspiration. You can binge-watch the history of music on YouTube, stream the Newport Folk Fest on your mobile device, and make your own playlists on Spotify.

I've always believed artists should keep their eyes and ears open to surprise and inspiration from wherever and whomever. Artists in general ought to be the most curious and alert people in the world.

I began taking trumpet lessons in the fourth grade. Music became mine to succeed or fail at. I was your average absent-minded, sometimes lazy kid. Dad wasn't raising an indolent son, though, especially one that couldn't or wouldn't excel at music. So, I excelled.

By fifth grade I was competing as a young soloist and writing my first melodies. Music had me in its grip—though it didn't stop me from loving baseball and liking girls.

After a decade of renting, my parents paid $19,000 for a brand-new home. This is the time we moved a few miles west from town to the rural community of Tierra Buena, where Mom grew up and my great-grandparents had their small, subsistence farm. We were moving on up.

Our fence backed up to the Shine family (pronounced shin-ee). Bobby Shine was my age and playmate. His older brother, another of my unwitting musical mentors, was named Ralph. Ralph was a musician and played several instruments, including drums, electric guitar, harmonica, and something called an ocarina. I thought Ralph was very cool. He subscribed to *Surfer* magazine, listened to the Wolfman Jack radio show, and had an informative collection of 45s, including "Wild Thing" by English rock band The Troggs. Their name was short for "troglodyte"—cave dweller. Since the band was, in fact, primitive and in the rock business, the name seemed to fit. "Wild Thing" had an ocarina solo. The word "ocarina" can be traced to Italy, where it means "sweet little goose." Bobby and I loved to sit on Ralph's bed and listen to him play the ocarina solo along with the record. It was inspiring. Not to Dad, though. When Ralph would get a little rambunctious, Dad would stand at the fence and yell, "Tune those damn guitars!"

The music Ralph felt most passionately about and excelled at was the blues. He had Little Walter, Paul Butterfield, James Cotton, and early J. Geils records featuring Magic Dick on harmonica. Ralph tried to sing like Freddie King, the bluesman my friend Roger Smith played with early in his career. What Ralph listened to, I listened to. All I had to do was camp out at the fence.

Along with Charlie Musselwhite and Rick Estrin, Ralph went on to be counted among the best West Coast blues harmonica players. Rick Estrin and I have been friends for decades. His band, Little Charlie and the Nightcats, recorded for Alligator Records. We would often run into each other on H Street in Sacramento in the days when people walked around town. The Nightcats were headliners at Maurice's American Bar, where I first began to perform my own songs.

Two of Karoly's favorite songs were the Leiber-Stoller hit "Love Potion No. 9" by The Searchers b/w "High Heel Sneakers," and "Rhythm of the Falling Rain" by The Cascades (and Ricky Nelson). This meant they were my favorites, too. John Gummoe wrote "Rhythm of the Falling Rain."

Decades after the song's breakout success, providentially, John approached me at a BMI Awards show in Los Angeles. "And which marvelous song did you write?" he asked. I think he was only fishing so he could tell me his. I got to meet other writers with marvelous songs that same evening, including Kenny Gamble and Leon Huff ("If You Don't Know Me by Now") and Eugene Record ("Oh Girl")—two songs I had washed many a dish to at the Skillet restaurant inside W. T. Grants department store.

Karoly and I exhausted hours watching *American Bandstand*. I met Dick Clark once when I was hired to play piano for one of his revues featuring Bo Diddley and Peggy Jones, a.k.a. Lady Bo. Dick walked me and bassist Erik Kleven over to the stage. He had that put-together look everyone always talked about. There'd been some sort of miscommunication between him and Diddley. Bo had brought his own band, and we weren't needed. Dick paid us anyway and dismissed us with a smile.

It was exciting to see musicians from our Sacramento tribe in the 1980s play *American Bandstand*. In its thirty-first season in 1988, friends Bourgeois Tagg played their MTV hit "I Don't Mind at All," produced by the wizard himself, Todd Rundgren.

Like *American Bandstand*, the network pop shows *Shindig!* and *Hullabaloo* were fun and life changing to watch. These shows featured artists like The Rolling Stones, Sonny & Cher, the Supremes, The Rascals, and Herman's Hermits. *Hullabaloo* became so popular among teenagers that it caused a commotion at NBC. They had to move the show out of the Wednesday-night time slot. It was competing too much with *The Beverly Hillbillies*, starring Buddy Ebsen. *The Beverly Hillbillies* had a theme song entitled "The Ballad of Jed Clampett": a song most '60s kids could sing in its entirety even today. It was composed by Paul Henning and performed by bluegrass stars Lester Flatt and Earl Scruggs.

Aunt Karoly went to local dances, too, for which I was too young. One such dance featured The Beach Boys at the Marysville Auditorium, with Freddie and the Statics opening, just across the river from Yuba City. The band had five major hits by then: "Surfin' USA," "Surfer Girl," "Little Deuce Coupe," "Be True to Your School," and "In My Room," all songs I first heard in Karoly's bedroom. I loved to study the album covers. As a tradition, the week before every new school year, my mother would take me to Sears. I would beg her to outfit me in striped shirts like The Beach Boys wore.

The date of The Beach Boys dance in Marysville was November 22, 1963: the infamous day when President John F. Kennedy was shot and killed. Nineteen-year-old Fred Vail was the promoter. Somehow, Fred found his way to Nashville, where he created Treasure Isle Recorders, a much-admired studio.

Freddie Singh of the Statics recorded for the Vardan label along with Drusalee and saxophonist Sonny Oliver (related to my brother-in-law, Boomer Williams). Years later I would play in Freddie's band on the way to making my own music. He played in the house band at the infamous Gazzarri's on Sunset Strip in the '60s. Freddie was shot at close range in San Francisco and lived. He was a survivor. He had something of a residency at a bar in Marysville called Eddie's Lounge, owned by Ahmad. That's where I joined Freddie's band. As usual, I was pretty good at improvising, but stubbornly refused to learn any actual parts, a temperament that made playing a highly arranged song like Stevie Wonder's "Sir Duke" impossible.

Being underage and playing the bar circuit was always something of an abbreviated experience. California had a bandstand law that allowed underage musicians to work in a nightclub, as long as they were on the bandstand performing. I was subject to this decree for a few years. As the rule dictated, at break time, a bouncer would escort me out to the sidewalk. After fifteen or twenty long minutes elapsed, I'd be ushered back in. Playing my Fender Rhodes electric piano in a cover band was not the destiny I envisioned. I wanted to write songs, record and perform them. Eddie's Lounge was nothing more than a quick stop on a longer journey.

In high school, three primary songwriters stirred my imagination: James Taylor, Jackson Browne, and Paul Simon. These were buttressed with the British influence of The Beatles and Donovan, and the Motown influence of Smokey Robinson, Supremes, The Temptations, and Marvin Gaye. Top 40 radio from 1965 to 1973 lives in me. I had an AM radio glued to my head during this period. I was listening to two very young DJs on KOBO in Yuba City: Dave Camper (Tony Cox now) and Rick Gibson.

I had just turned fifteen when Rick took me for a drive in his El Camino and played the 8-track tape of Todd Rundgren's *Something/ Anything*. The Chevrolet was fitted with JBL speakers in custom cabinets behind the bench seat (a big deal at the time). It turned our little spin around town into a full-frequency rock concert. I had to have my own vinyl copy of this record, immediately (and, eventually my own JBL speakers too). Once in hand, I loved the music, but couldn't get enough of the photograph of Todd at work in his makeshift apartment studio. I wanted what he had.

Rick, an amateur recording engineer, offered to help me realize the dream. A few weeks later I was recording with him in an unkempt ranch-style home hidden within a peach orchard. It was the "band house" of a local rock group named Whitefire. Rick was already set to track the band and kindly squeezed me in for a late-night recording session. I only had a couple of songs—"Hey Lady Love" and "Needless to Say," ones I'd written for my new girlfriend, Andi Berrier.

Hey lady love don't shine your light upon this poor boy's head.

I have no idea what that meant, but my unconscious and naïve James Taylor imitation was spot-on.

This was my first "studio" experience. I remember my gut, clenched, queasy, and full of butterflies; an unfamiliar mix of fright and euphoria that I would come to know very well. It didn't take long for Andi and music to become my reasons for being, my purpose, my oxygen. Music became the means by which I could express myself in ways that felt perfect and transcendent. Inside music, I could just be. Andi was my home base of heart and mind. We shared everything, and still do.

The songs Rick recorded for me in the makeshift, orchard studio in the spring of 1971 were the first tangible evidence that I might actually follow in the path of Todd, or other songwriting heroes James Taylor and Jackson Browne.

Cassette tapes in hand, I was left with the only logical next step—to take them to music impresario David Geffen. I'd read an article about Asylum Records in Los Angeles. A label founded by David Geffen and Eliot Roberts, two former agents at William Morris, a talent and booking agency. They were releasing records by Joni Mitchell, Linda Ronstadt, John David Souther, and my favorite, Jackson Browne. His debut album for Asylum came out just after the first of the year in 1972. I was spellbound. The article said that Jackson had been at it since he was a teenager. I was a fifteen-year-old teenager. Maybe David Geffen would want to sign me, too.

While vacationing in Morro Bay in late June of '72, Dad agreed to drive me to Los Angeles so I could give my tapes to David Geffen and Asylum Records. (And I mean, literally my tapes, as in the same exact cassette tapes Rick had given me at the end of our recording session.)

We drove four hours to 9130 Sunset Boulevard. I informed the receptionist why I was there. Then I handed her a brown lunch bag with my name and address on it and the two cassettes inside. Dad and I went for a hamburger and drove four hours back to Morro Bay. Several weeks later, I received a package in the mail. My cassette tapes and a kind rejection letter were enclosed.

Eighteen years after the fateful drive in Rick's El Camino, I met Todd Rundgren backstage at the War Memorial Auditorium in Nashville. My friend Larry Tagg introduced me as the cowriter of "Stress," a song Todd had produced for Larry's band, Bourgeois Tagg. "Oh, yeah, a big hit," said Todd, raising his eyebrows to emphasize the sarcasm. Coming from a onetime musical hero, this hurt a little. Not

much, though, considering Todd had just come off stage after tossing
confetti, condoms, and inflatable toys to the audience.

This is the way it goes when you trace the trajectory of an artist's
life: you look at the stories. In the stories you find the glory and the
shame—and the absolute absence of neutrality in human choices.
The old saying "one thing leads to another" holds true. In the early
1980s, a rock group from England called The Fixx had a *big hit* with
this idea. "One Thing Leads to Another" went to No. 4 on the US pop
charts. (Somehow, in the grand scheme of things, I ended up their
opening act in 1984.)

—

My discovery of the blues on the sanctuary piano at my grandparents'
church was no mere accident. Most of my generation could play some
form of the blues before just about anything else. The blues were the
foundation for whatever future house you'd build in your musical
life. Ironically, coming from America, where blues is an indigenous
music, I devoured British blues, especially John Mayall and the many
groundbreaking players that came through his band (e.g., Mick Taylor, Eric Clapton, Marc Almond, and Jack Bruce). Paul Butterfield,
Gregg Allman, Phineas Newborn Jr., B. B. King, and Ray Charles
were my earliest American blues influences.

My musical menu had expanded since Saturday morning cartoons.
Every horn band from Tower of Power to Ten Wheel Drive, includ-
ing the more popular Chicago and Blood, Sweat & Tears, formed
me. Al Green, Sly and the Family Stone, Gladys Knight, Parliament-
Funkadelic, Curtis Mayfield, Joni Mitchell, and Stevie Wonder were
my mothership connection. For country music and southern rock,
I listened to Kris Kristofferson, Johnny Cash, Merle Haggard, Willie
Nelson, and the Allman Brothers.

All of these many influences, whether Todd Rundgren or the blues,
came under the headship of Miles Davis and the unprecedented stream
of pioneering musicians he recruited for his landmark recordings: Wyn-
ton Kelly, John Coltrane, Bill Evans, Tony Williams, Herbie Hancock,
Wayne Shorter, John McLaughlin, Chick Corea, Ron Carter, Keith Jar-

rett, and so many more. Miles was the ultimate magnet for talent, a wonder at turning the screws of intensity while opening the gate to unexpected creativity. He was peerless and innovative, and his preference for risk and his confidence that it would produce previously unheard results were absolute magic to me. He became my organizing principle, the blueprint for casting musicians and keeping my productions unique.

Every song I've written (and will ever write) has some blend of all these diverse influences. They are seminal. By absorbing their history, songs, styles, and nuances, I have irrevocably influenced all that I've become as a musician, songwriter, and producer.

If the music of the family story and place I was born into is my bedrock, the whole of influences is the framing and walls of my musical house. This is why when people ask me, "How do you write a song?" I can answer, "How can I not?"

As an artist, songwriter, and producer, I've had the opportunity to meet, and on occasion work with, a number of people I've mentioned. Almost all of these artists, musicians, and songwriters are seven or more years older than me. Jackson Browne being a good example, born October 9, 1948 (eight years older). Or Herbie Hancock on the far end, born April 12, 1940 (sixteen years older). When you're inspired by someone's music, the age of the one making it is meaningless. Every successful, sustainable career is built on the maxim "you're only as young as you feel." You're ageless if what you create, decade after decade, is meaningful, inspired, and able to keep your very first audience while drawing new listeners to the particularity of your evolving musical vision.

Not everything you learn along the way is artistic philosophy, either. Sometimes you get the most practical advice from musicians a little older than you. At sixteen, I was playing my Wurlitzer electric piano in local saxophonist Rod Battaglia's band at a restaurant bar, Pasquini's. I believe it was a private party. Pasquini's is at the bend on Highway 99 just short of Live Oak, California. There used to be a cling peach grading station there when Dad and I graded peaches for the State of California. This general area is where mass murderer Juan Corona buried his dead. My family still eats at Pasquini's.

Before we'd played a note, Rod gave us younger men some important instruction: "When the fight breaks out," he warned, "keep on playing and don't leave the bandstand."

Not if. When.

It was during our version of Rare Earth's "Get Ready."

We were.

—

Dad played a post-swing-era style of trumpet, a cross between Harry James and Chet Baker, with a little Roy Eldridge in the mix. He was a West Coast improviser more in the style of an eight- or twelve-bar solo, or two-bar trumpet break. Not the longer impassioned solos of Clifford Brown, Lee Morgan, or Miles Davis (though he was a fan of Miles).

One of Dad's jobs in the Air Force was to play in a dance band—a racially integrated one, at that. This meant playing the hits of the time: some rock 'n' roll, swing, and ballads. He preferred his music cool, swingin' and a tad bit more orderly. Our home hi-fi played the AM radio and the records of Sinatra, Tony Bennett, Doris Day, Perry Como, Ella Fitzgerald, Miles Davis, and Dave Brubeck. Rock snuck into our home via the radio (especially KOBO broadcast from Yuba City) and those wonderful Columbia Record Club compilation albums. As much as he disliked rock music, Dad reserved his worst snobbery for country music, then called country and western.

Along with rock 'n' roll's national emergence, country music was very popular in California in the 1950s. There was even a successful country music television show, *California Hayride*. Cottonseed Clark hosted it, and Sacramento's KOVR broadcasted it to the valley and to anyone with that sort of predilection. KOVR was one of the stations I would eventually appear on when my career first got going.

I produced a short film tribute for the performing rights society BMI and music publisher SonyATV featuring the legendary songwriter Hank Cochran. Many of Hank's admirers assembled to pay tribute: Elvis Costello, Cowboy Jack Clement, Merle Haggard, and more. Hank got his start on the *California Hayride*. When Hank passed, he left behind some memorable, evergreen songs such as

"I Fall to Pieces" and "Make the World Go Away." He's also credited with giving Willie Nelson his first big break. Hank was the quintessential, Dust Bowl hillbilly done good.

At the film shoot, Willie Nelson was enlisted to call Hank on the telephone. Clay Bradley stood by to put it on speaker so everyone could hear (and my engineer Richie Biggs could record it). Willie told the story of how Hank had been offered a raise by his publisher, Pamper music. Instead of taking it, Hank got Pamper to sign Willie and give him the money that would have gone to Hank.

As the conversation came to a close, Hank said to Willie, "I hope to run up on you again someday."

The Okie migration had no small effect on California.

A respectable number of the migrant populace had come to Northern California and the Central Valley from states like Texas, Arkansas, Kansas, Louisiana, and especially Oklahoma. Though history credits the Great Depression and the Dust Bowl for this historical diaspora, some folks just wanted to see what all the California fuss was about.

My mother's family, the Williamsons and Millers, left Durant, Oklahoma, in 1939 to pick fruit in the orchards around Yuba City. Though Grandpa Ashworth arrived in California in the early 1920s, by the time of the 1930 census he was working a sawmill in Merced Falls for the Yosemite and Sugar Pine Lumber Companies. Merced Falls is approximately forty-five miles from Modesto. Three years later, the Ashworth family was back living in the Oroville–Feather Falls area, sixty-five miles north of Yuba City—now with a new son, my dad, Lil' Willie.

Dad never met his fiddle-playing maternal grandfather, though he had one photo of him with fiddle in hand. I framed it and still keep it close. Dad knew his uncles George and Tommy, both Louisiana transplants to the Golden State. Tommy, like my great-grandfather George Reilly Baggett, played with the fiddle held to his chest. Since most folk and fiddle tunes can all be played in the first position, holding the fiddle to your chest and not your neck works just fine.

I have several childhood memories of driving up to Oroville to visit Uncle George (referred to as Bo) and Uncle Tommy. Every visit ended with fiddle tunes and Chiclet gum. Once and only once did my sister and I bring home two live chickens. Each grew up to be ornery as hell. I believe we took them back to Uncle Bo, where I assume they became dinner.

Though my maternal grandfather, Marvin Williamson, didn't play an instrument, he loved to lean into you and sing a bit. Mostly "Froggy Went a-Courtin'" and various songs he made up. He sang the old Irish-Scottish, American hillbilly melodic shapes along with the three chords so common to Okie folksongs. This classic Okie lyric from "Why We Came to Californy" exemplifies the style well. I can hear grandpa's voice now:

> Here comes the dust storm, watch the sky turn blue.
> You better git out quick, or it will smother you.
> Here comes the grasshopper, he comes a-jumpin' high.
> He jumps across the state, an' never bats an eye.

California continued to make important contributions to country music throughout my childhood and the second half of the twentieth century. The Bakersfield sound, developed in the late 1950s, was popularized by Buck Owens and Jean Shepherd. A few years later, after serving his time at San Quentin prison, Merle Haggard added his own unique flavor to the sound, and the rest is country music history.

I was backstage with Merle for a brief minute at the Hank Cochran filming. Takamine had provided acoustic guitars for all the performers to use. I watched Merle walk up to each guitar, upright on a stand, and strum an open chord with his index fingernail. He did this four times to four different guitars and walked away. I took it as mild disinterest, so I asked him, "You wanna' play a Gibson?" No verbal response. He looked at me with a cobalt-eyed stare and lowered his head about three-fourths of an inch. I handed him my son Sam's Gibson J-30. He strummed a chord, kept the guitar, and walked out of the room. (That guitar has a way about it. Bono played it when he came to our house several years ago.) Artists tend to know when an instrument holds music and invites you to discover it. Sam's J-30 does both well.

Merle closed that day by singing a Willie Nelson song, "Back to Earth." A moving and compact, genius of a song, if I've ever heard one.

It's difficult for a record producer to capture anything of lasting value if an artist doesn't have a unique essence. The Hag had essence in spades. Engineer Richie Biggs and I put a mic in front of him and got out of the way. You listen to a voice like Merle's, and for a moment you can hear the history of America. Not all of it, but some of it, and that's no small grace.

None of us choose the musical story we are born into. Yet, as we grow and mature, we do begin to choose new stories and storytellers. These new personal musical choices are never neutral. They're just as formative, if not more so, than the influences children are born into. In every way we receive and create a musical story we'll inhabit and work from our whole lives.

I believe a portion of the world's population is born magnetized to music. It sticks to them and them to it. Generation after generation, these called and fortunate ones do their work. They create from communally constructed musical stories and live openhanded and openhearted, ready to be influenced by new ones. Once discovered, the influences animate them like wind in the trees, ripple on rock. New music is born.

ten

IN THE LIGHT

In 1997, at the Ryman Auditorium in Nashville, I brought my teenage son Sam backstage to meet pianist Herbie Hancock and saxophonist Wayne Shorter. The two legends had just performed a sublime set of duets. This was Sam's homeschool. Nothing turns the light on, creates the aha moment like being in the presence of greatness. Béla Fleck and Jeff Coffin, two of Nashville's remarkable improvisers, were backstage, too. I introduced myself to Herbie. We had history, which I wasn't foolish enough to think he'd remember.

Decades earlier (1978) I'd spent a day with Herbie at a preproduction rehearsal for trumpeter Eddie Henderson's album *Mahal*. I'd been at Eddie's home in the Berkeley Hills the week before. He had graciously invited me to audition for the piano spot in his band.

I sat down at the piano and played the Steve Swallow tune "Hullo Bolinas," borrowed from the Bill Evans album *The Tokyo Concert*. (Steve, a remarkable bassist, recorded the duet "After All These Years" with me in 2020.) I also played one of my own instrumentals for Eddie. He responded to my hesitant performance by dropping the needle on some rare Miles Davis vinyl. Which was cool, but confusing. Several years later the lights came on and I understood the subtle hint. He was gently showing me I wasn't ready.

He wasn't done with me yet, though. Eddie graciously guided me and Andi to an upstairs bedroom. He sat us down in front of the very first video player we had ever seen. It would be a decade before VCR models worked their way into consumer consciousness. Eddie pushed play on this massive machine from the future (or at least Japan), and the image and sound of the famous John Coltrane Quartet came to life. I had grieved that Coltrane had passed and that I'd never see him perform. There he was. Serious, luminescent. Playing the most unique version of "My Favorite Things" the world has ever heard. As Coltrane mused in words, "I've found you've got to look back at the old things and see them in a new light."

Eddie left us in the room alone for at least an hour. I could not believe the unmerited favor I was experiencing. I became John the Revelator caught up in a bright vision of jazz paradise.

I drove away from Eddie's home with the address for Studio Instrument Rentals (SIR) in San Francisco. He had invited me to join him the following week. I was twenty years old and already hanging with my musical heroes. Surely this was the beginning of great things.

This opportunity gave me no choice but to quit my job at Bremer's Hardware. How could I turn down a day spent soaking up the funk with Herbie, Eddie, Paul Jackson, Julian Priester, Bennie Maupin, Howard King, and M'Tume? No gig ever came of it, but the experience was seminal.

Forty-four years later, on October 19, 2022, in NYC, Eddie and I would finally work together. We recorded an EP of songs as an homage to '90s acid-jazz and hip-hop (think US3's big hit "Cantaloop [Flip Fantasia]"). Our recording featured LA rapper Dangerboy. At eighty-one, Eddie was still bringing his A game. And those records he made in the '70s? Sampled by Jay-Z, Pete Rock, and more.

As for skipping out on my hardware store gig, I was a disinterested employee anyway. Instead of resigning in person, I sent Bremer's a postcard of a fisherman in a little boat. The sportsman was reeling in a gigantic catch bigger than the boat. It said: "I got the big one." Either Andi or mother picked up my check for me. That was that.

Only a few years later I would record at the Automatt studio across the street from where Eddie's rehearsal had been. I didn't know it at the time, but my future mid-'80s managers, the legendary Bill Graham and associates Mick Brigden and Arnie Pustilnik, had offices just around the corner. Fast-forward decades, in Brooklyn, I recorded a song titled "Automatt" with musicians Jeff Coffin, Ben Perowsky, Hilmar Jensson, Tony Miracle, and Jaco Pastorius's gifted son, Felix. It was released on the album *When Light Flashes Help Is on the Way* in 2018.

—

Backstage at the Ryman, Herbie Hancock saw that my young son Sam was carrying a drumhead.

"Whatcha got there, man?"

Sam showed him the Remo drumhead the late drummer Tony Williams had signed for him ten years earlier in Sacramento at the Crest Theatre. Drummer Aaron Smith and I had taken Sam to hear Tony's band. Sam must've been seven years old.

"Would you sign this for me?" Sam asked Herbie.

"No, man, you don't want me to put my name on there. That's Tony Williams."

"I know," Sam argued. "It'll be even better if you and Wayne sign it, too."

Herbie smiled wide and nonchalantly passed the drumhead over to Wayne.

"Check it out, man."

"Anthony Williams," said Wayne, nodding his head slowly. "Anthony Williams. Anthony Williams." And he kept on. He must have said Anthony Williams ten or twelve times in every possible inflection and pitch. It was like he was composing a follow-up to "Nefertiti."

"Anthony Williams. Anthony Williams. Anthony Williams."

Eventually both men signed it, but not before Wayne told some Anthony Williams stories. He especially delighted in recalling how, at just seventeen, Tony was playing with Miles Davis. According to Wayne, people just didn't understand what Tony was doing on the drum kit.

"Couldn't get no respect. Just like Coltrane in Philly. Coltrane was like Jesus—couldn't get NO respect in his hometown!"

No respect in the City of Brotherly Love? That's not right. In the Bible, Philadelphia is the sixth of the seven churches God speaks to in John the Revelator's vision. They have been a faithful gathering of Jesus followers. Jesus said, "You have kept my word and have not denied my name."

Keeping of the word is multifaceted, but in Jesus's summary, clear as pure light: love God and neighbor. Denying God's name? Also clear: there is no other name but Jesus given to humankind through which salvation is made real. Salvation? That's a bit more complicated and mysterious. Thankfully there are openhearted and openhanded people humbly working to get at living definitions.

Let me introduce you to two of them, Ned and Leslie Bustard. I met them on June 25, 1988, at a music festival in Gardner, Massachusetts. I was opening for Amy Grant and Take 6. Ned and Leslie were college students and unmarried. Somehow, as both love and lark, I agreed to sing at their wedding. It was, I believe, a decision made for me before the beginning of time—such is our connection.

In the next century, on April Fool's Day, 2005, our plane landed in the great city of Philadelphia, not in ancient Turkey but in the USA. Andi and I had been invited by the small but tenacious imprint Square Halo (founded by Ned, Leslie, and friends) to speak at their conference in Lancaster themed "The New Humanity: Christian Mysteries for Everyday Saints." We have published several essays with the imprint, including Andi's contribution to *A Book for Hearts and Minds: What You Should Read and Why*. Stitching the tapestry of interconnectedness even tighter, the "Everyday Saints" conference in 2005 was just down the road from Lititz, where John Sutter had retreated after fame and gold derailed his profitable, name-making train. In our musical worship that day we sang "I Thirst, Thou Wounded Lamb of God," written by Nicolaus Ludwig Zinzendorf, the Moravian patron of Lititz.

> I thirst, Thou wounded Lamb of God,
> To wash me in Thy cleansing blood,
> To dwell within Thy wounds; then pain
> Is sweet, and life or death is gain.
> Take this poor heart, and let it be
> For ever closed to all but Thee!
> Seal Thou my breast, and let me wear
> That pledge of love for ever there.

It had been my plan to visit John Sutter's grave in Lititz while at the Square Halo conference in Lancaster. As it happened, we ran out of time. We had a plane in Philadelphia to miss. The drive from Lancaster to Philly International is an hour and forty-five, and car trouble shattered that window.

I must have said, "Unbelievable!" fifty times. The repetition of a merely adequate word is sometimes all you have left. A cab had dropped us off at the airport Hilton just before dark. We reluctantly checked in. It was April 2, 2005, and the evening news reported the passing of Pope John Paul II. Revealing my Protestant-centric vision at that time, he was the first and only pope of whom I ever took serious notice. We watched the news late into the evening. Had we made the plane, we'd have lost the moment.

Pope John Paul II, born Karol Józef Wojtyla, was the 264th pontiff of the Roman Catholic Church and the only Polish pope. He first caught my interest in 1990 when I was asked to join a group of artists heading over to Poland for a series of concerts. Pope John Paul II said of Jesus, "We live in the light of his Paschal Mystery—the mystery of his Death and Resurrection. We are an Easter People and Alleluia is our song!"[1]

On November 9, 1989, East Germany said enough already. They began letting people cross into West Berlin. This world-changing decision started a party, and the Berlin Wall began to fall. Nashville music executive Jozef Nuyens, a Belgian native, showed producer Brown Bannister and me a little piece of the concrete history he'd brought back to the States. Nine months later, on my way to Poland from Amsterdam, I saw the wall for myself. Not a lot left by that time, but enough to feel the heat of history. By October of 1990, Germany would be reunified.

Our tour bus of mismatched musicians on the way to Poland included Jesus music pioneers Rez Band, Darryl Mansfield, The 77s, and fresh-faced upstarts dc Talk. After driving all day and night, we arrived in Katowice on August 19, 1990, just in time for dinner. The meal was mysterious and stretched us beyond our imaginations. It left us hungry for something predictable, like bed.

In the morning, we woke to noses full of black soot and knew for sure, as if there was any doubt, we had just bumped into another world. It was August 20, my father's birthday. We arrived on the scene of a country in the starting gate of reinvention and renewal. In another three months, the former car mechanic and Nobel Prize winner Lech Walesa would ace the presidency. His victory would signal the end of communism's grip on Eastern Europe.

Infrastructure was the first order of business: telecommunications, to be exact. In the morning, you would sign up at the hotel desk to make a phone call. Nine hours later, they would let you know your line was ready. Everything was upside-down from our privileged lives. We hit the streets to learn more. I had six musicians traveling with me, my trio members Vince Ebo and Jimmy Abegg, along with bassist Tommy Sims, keyboardists Roger Smith and Blair Masters, and drummer Aaron Smith. Four out of the six band members were Black. A parade of Polish people followed them through the streets. All of us were asked to leave several businesses.

This was a great band of characters and talent. I'd known a few of them since I was twenty years old and living in Northern California. Roger Smith, a giant on the Hammond organ, was born to become a member of the band Tower of Power. He's been with them since 1998. As a young musician, Roger was fortunate to have Philadelphia's Jimmy McGriff, the Hammond B3 legend, show him some signature blues songs, "Down the Road a Piece" and "Little Red Rooster." That was all it took. He was hooked.

While living in Austin, Roger formed a band with guitarist Eric Johnson. From there he moved on to Freddie King's band and others of that era, including Gladys Knight and Jeff Beck. He also played in the house band on the legendary *Soul Train* television show.

At twenty years old, Aaron Smith was drumming for producer Norman Whitfield at Motown in Detroit. Aaron played drums on The Temptations' psychedelic soul song "Papa Was a Rollin' Stone." The track, produced by Whitfield, was recorded in Studio A of the Motown studio, Hitsville USA. After a long tenure with The Temptations in the studio and on the road, Aaron left to study with Alan Dawson at the Berklee School of Music. That's where I first connected with him—at least I tried to by telephone. Alphonza Kee, bassist and older brother to gospel legend John P. Kee, had given me Aaron's number. Al and I had a steady jazz gig at the Bull Market in Sacramento and later played in The Runners together. After washing out at Cal State Sacramento, I was thinking about moving to Boston to attend Berklee. I was also interested in attending the Creative Music Studio in Woodstock, New York, for the fall session of '77 to study with Anthony Braxton, Lee Konitz, and Carla Bley. The administrator discouraged me, saying, "It would be very difficult and expensive for you with a spouse and baby to board here."

I wanted Aaron to give me the same straight talk about Berklee. Al Kee was living just outside Marysville, California, and studying music theory with my father at Yuba College (as did John P. Kee). Al had played with Aaron in bassist Miroslav Vitous's band after Miroslav left Weather Report. Al played the low notes on bass while Miroslav played the higher-pitched melodies on bass. Two basses. Unusual, unless you're Phil Spector. He had two of everything.

At the time of our trip to Poland, bassist Tommy Sims had no idea what good fortune awaited him. We would do a record together in 1991 titled *Love Life*. While I made the album for Sparrow Records (known as a gospel label), I wanted to see if we could find a distribution partner in the pop world. My friend and future *American Idol* judge Randy Jackson was working as A&R for Columbia Records at the time, as was David Kahne. I sent *Love Life* to Randy for consideration. He called me. But it was a case of "not interested in you, but who is that incredible bassist?"

Randy had played on the Bruce Springsteen session for the song "Human Touch." Bruce wanted Randy to tour with him. The timing was off. But maybe this amazing bass player on Charlie's record might be interested. He was.

Tommy played with Bruce in 1992–1993 and coproduced with Bruce and Chuck Plotkin the song "Streets of Philadelphia" from the Tom Hanks film *Philadelphia*. The song went on to win the Oscar and Golden Globe for Best Original Song as well as four Grammy awards. The closest I got to this red-hot project was renting my Sony digital multitrack machine to Columbia Records and engineer Tom Laune for some of Tommy's overdubs. There you go. Our tight circle of session musicians were very happy for Tommy (if not a little jealous).

For years I'd been collecting ideas about art, creativity, imagination, and such. I always had something quick to say about the subject, asked or not. But Poland at that time was a better teacher than a thousand books. Katowice was proof that the value of art wasn't merely didactic. Art could just be. It could take its place in the community; add to the beauty without making a fuss. In 1990, Katowice needed color, light, and shadow. Everything was soot-stained gray. Even the limited art and colors looked like they'd ceased caring. This was a time of radical change and renewal. I was confident that a brightness would return. Free people have a way of lighting up the darkest places.

Our trip also included a visit to Birkenau and Auschwitz, two of three major death camps in a larger Auschwitz complex. Standing in an observation tower at Birkenau, I noticed a black, brooding spider the size of a fifty-cent piece. It gripped its web stretched tight across the window. A big droning fly, magnetized to light, foolishly landed in its grid. The fly was venom-pumped and wrapped, dead and dangling on arrival. Such was my view as I looked out across the grounds of one of history's cruelest chapters. All of us stood quietly—my band, Polish Jews, Japanese tourists.

I wondered what Roger, Vince, Aaron, and Tommy were thinking. Their generational heritage was nothing if not suffering at the hands of others—likely white people. This was years before I learned about my own African ancestry and our family story from enslavement to freedom. Then I turned to the Japanese folks. A nuclear weapon, "Little Boy," was dropped on Hiroshima on August 6, 1945, followed by "Fat Man" on Nagasaki on August 9, 1945. Frederick L. Ashworth (no relation) was the weaponeer for "Fat Man." Nine and half months earlier, Ashworth had reported to Los Alamos. Right off the plane, Thanksgiving Day of 1944, he went to a cocktail party/square dance at Oppenheimer's pad.

My eyes focused on the spider web again. How long would the strong be allowed to prey on the weak? The prophet Habakkuk (1:13) asked God,

Why then do you tolerate the treacherous?
Why are you silent while the wicked swallow up those
more righteous than themselves?

A few days later, back in England at the Greenbelt Festival, I mentioned this to vocalist BeBe Winans. "Thankfully there are rays of hope," he said. He believed one was Nelson Mandela. That man turned South Africa on its head.

At Birkenau, a guide pointed out the high-voltage electric fence surrounding the camp. It was constructed, he explained, to prevent the escape of prisoners, yet prisoners routinely used it as a means of final escape. When a prisoner reached the breaking point of despair and hopelessness, he'd run to the perimeter and throw himself upon the wires. People thought of the method as "escape" and never used the word suicide. They just called it "running into the wires."

My friend and longtime vocalist Vince Ebo, present on this particular trip, ran into the wires in 1993. I still don't know for sure what it was that made him despair unto death. I don't know about final escape with respect to a Jewish man or woman imprisoned at Birkenau. That's a reaction to a category of evil that is impossible to imagine. That is also true of suicidal motivation as a whole: it's hard to inhabit the space of that heavy a despair. It's a horrifying mystery for both the people who suffered atrocities at Birkenau and for Vince. From my experience with Vince, a close friend and collaborator, I know that suicide is the rocket that launches a stream of unending question marks out into the universe and beyond. It mucks up the peace and makes you stare without seeing.

It was no different when Chris Cornell took his life on the day of our wedding anniversary, May 18, 2017. A true artist, and certainly in the top five best vocalists I've ever recorded. In "Black Hole Sun" he sang of a heaven that could send hell away. And no one sings like you, Chris, anymore.

After Birkenau, we went to Auschwitz proper, where we made ourselves sick with seeing and imagining. Strangely, we found some upside-down brightness in the dank, closed basement of Block 11, a compound prisoners spoke of as "the Block of Death." Carved into the wall of a tiny prison cell was an icon of the crucified Jesus on the cross. Made me think of the fellowship of suffering; the senseless murder of the innocent. Then on to Romans 8: "Who shall separate us from the love of Christ? Shall trouble or hardship or persecution or famine or nakedness or danger or sword?"

Being the curious man I am, I've read a few of the voguish atheists, including Christopher Hitchens, Richard Dawkins, and Sam Harris, who once said, and I'm paraphrasing from a journal entry: "Forty years from now, we'll realize that taking religion seriously was like taking astrology seriously."

David Dark, in his book *Life's Too Short to Pretend You're Not Religious*, offers an opposite view: "All religion, all the time." To this, he explains, "I call myself religious in an effort to be more exactingly honest with myself concerning what I'm up to. I'm never not worshipping. I'm never not confessing my faith."[2]

David's bottom line? Every human has one or more objects of worship. Every person, a faith. We are all religious. In David's definition of religion, even Sam Harris. When we really value the fellowship of humanity and its trajectory, we must, I think, be as David suggests: *exactingly honest concerning what we are up to.*

After touring Auschwitz, I was one of the first people back at the bus. I was shut up and blank-eyed trying not to dwell on what I'd seen, but feeling I should. Selfishly, I was glad to head back to the city and to music—the original reason we came to Poland. Although, perhaps the tour of the death camps had a deeper purpose. As Denver Moore, the subject of the film *Same Kind of Different as Me*, once told me after recording some of his songs: "Maybe you didn't get what you wanted. But I hope you got what you needed."

On August 21, we played Spodek, which means "saucer" in Polish, and the arena does in fact look just like a flying saucer taking off. I used to keep a picture of it hanging in the hallway of my Art House studio. Spodek is a big, multipurpose arena and the largest indoor venue of its kind in Poland. Having hosted many Western musicians including Elton John, Green Day, Pearl Jam, Sting, and U2, Spodek is the place to play. Story goes that the saucer was constructed on a coal-mining waste dump. Possible cave-ins under the foundation were a real concern. To relieve any safety fears the public might have had, endurance tests were conducted. This included marching 3,500 soldiers into the hall, where their good vibrations were measured and approved.

All was well the night we played. Our concert was one of the most unusual I've ever been part of. I didn't have much confidence at the start. My voice was weak and scratchy from the nasty coal soot and rising early to tour the prison camps. But there was a defining moment in the concert. We collectively stopped trying to make it happen, stopped trying to overcome weakness and just let go. The band began to improvise new sections, explore fresh territory in the music we hadn't discovered before. Even our Polish interpreter, on stage with us, had good rhythm and style. It was something transcendent happening through the music. Only God knows for sure.

A little less than a year later, we were back in Poland playing an outdoor stadium in Krakow. BeBe & CeCe Winans were on that trip; also, the stunning vocal group Take 6 and the Nicaraguan American guitarist Tony Melendez. This was to honor the pope's first trip to the homeland since the collapse of communism. Like the pope, composer Frederic Chopin had made a similar pilgrimage in 1849, though he toured in a jar filled with cognac. On his deathbed, Chopin requested that his heart be sent to his homeland of Poland. And that's where you'll find it, sealed inside a pillar at Warsaw's Holy Cross Church.

Born without arms, Tony, a thalidomide baby, had learned to play guitar with his feet— he did a whole lot with his feet. Tony came to Poland with some papal notoriety, having played for the pope in 1987. But he was just a regular musician. I'll forever have this image of all of us in the basement of a Polish resort, late at night, stories flying, guitarist/artist Jimmy Abegg sitting with Tony at the bar, Tony drinking a pint with his feet while Jimmy argued loudly with an even louder young Russian woman (one of our handlers, I think).

Jimmy: "This country is a pit."

Russian woman: "You weak, worthless Americans. You think Poland is bad? You wouldn't last a second in Russia."

In 1999, US president Bill Clinton and First Lady Hillary welcomed Pope John Paul II to America at Lambert International Airport in St. Louis, Missouri. A papal youth rally was held, and twenty-two thousand kids got in on a mile-long "Walk in the Light" march from the Arch to the Kiel Center.

The group dc Talk performed my song "In the Light," which I heard on CNN later that evening. I was humbled to have my song find its way into the festivities—to hear thousands of kids singing it. Seven months later, Andi and I would be living in St. Louis, studying at Covenant Seminary. It wasn't but a few years earlier that my sister Terri had called me from Arco Arena in Sacramento: Billy Graham was reading the lyrics to "In the Light" from the podium.

The pope's youth rally was a bookend to that honor. George Costanza's line from *Seinfeld* would have worked nicely right then: "That's it. I'm outta here!"

I'll always appreciate how dc Talk gave my song a second chance at life. The first time I recorded it on *Love Life*, sales peaked at an underachieving, by industry standards, forty thousand. Still, I was grateful for the forty thousand listeners. The dc Talk version sold somewhere north of 3.5 million copies, all-in. Sales are always welcome, but not the greatest reward. For most songwriters, including myself, the honor is in having a song, any song, well received and multiplied into the world.

Ironically, the album *Love Life*, which included "In the Light," was rejected by a significant number of Christian music gatekeepers. One distribution company sent their order back to President Bill Hearn at Sparrow Records with a note: "When Charlie Peacock starts making Christian music again, we'll start selling it." It was Christian enough for the pope and Billy Graham.

eleven

THE PATH OF THE PRODUCER POLYMATH

The first record producer I ever laid eyes on was Skip Drinkwater in 1977. He had a minor hit with an artist named Norman Connors on Buddha Records—a song called "You Are My Starship." My brother-in-law Boomer Williams hipped me to it. Drinkwater was also trumpeter Eddie Henderson's producer. I never met Skip, just watched him work that metamorphic day in San Francisco. More accurately, I watched Skip Drinkwater watch Herbie Hancock lead Eddie's band through the new material.

I talked to Herbie backstage at the Rose Bowl for U2 on the 360° Claw tour. He seemed slight in height. Smaller than I remember from the last time I visited with him at the Ryman with my son. Maybe that's how it goes. When I was coming up, everyone I admired was a giant. As I found my own way, told my own story, my heroes grew smaller.

The next record producer I fell in with was David Houston, someone I'm still friends with today. David founded a studio in south Sacramento called Moon Studio. It was his parents' garage outfitted with foam, egg crates, an ARP 2600, ARP Omni, Mini-Moog, Mu-Tron Bi-Phase, Baldwin electric harpsichord, 1/2" Tascam/TEAC 8 Track, and a whole load of Sacramento street cred.

In late 1968, David's band Public Nuisance signed a deal with record producer Terry Melcher, movie star Doris Day's son. Then it all fell apart. Terry had been living with actress Candice Bergen at 10050 Cielo Drive in Benedict Canyon, Los Angeles. They moved out and director Roman Polanski and actress Sharon Tate moved in. Then, in August of 1969, 10050 Cielo Drive became a tragically infamous address.

That whole slice of history is carved into my hippocampus.

I was baptized with my mom at First Christian Church in Marysville, California, April 6, 1969. By July 20, Neil Armstrong was walking on the moon. That same day on earth, the San Francisco Giants played the visiting LA Dodgers at Candlestick Park. I was there in the stands. Giants Bobby Bonds, Willie Mays, Willie McCovey, and Gaylord Perry all played that day. Gaylord, the pitcher, with a batting average of .109, hit a home run. Giants manager Alvin Dark had previously declared, "They'll put a man on the moon before Gaylord ever hits a home run." True story. We arrived back in Yuba City in time to watch Walter Cronkite's very fuzzy broadcast of Neil Armstrong take his first steps and speak these words: "This is one small step for [a] man, one giant leap for mankind." The same day I was backstage at the Rose Bowl with Herbie Hancock, who should be there too? Buzz Aldrin, Neil Armstrong's traveling companion on that historic trip to the moon.

After the Manson murders, Terry quit all his music endeavors, including Public Nuisance and another Sacramento band called Redwing founded by my friend Tom Phillips. Some think Manson ordered his followers to Terry's former address in order to murder him; Manson was angry at Terry for refusing him a record deal. David Houston remembers, "I don't know how true it is, but the story is that the people who went there were after Terry Melcher, not the people who were there."

David finally got a more life-giving brush with fame when The White Stripes covered one of his songs from that era. There's more, too. The album Public Nuisance recorded for Melcher, *Gotta Survive*, was released in 2012 by Jack White's label, Third Man Records. The label's marketing called it "A masterpiece of American, late-Sixties garage rock," adding, "Sacramento-based Public Nuisance laid down gritty, baroque psychedelia that was too hard for the hippies and too poppy for the punks. The end result is the perfect amalgam of all that was great about the era."

Ruby Amanfu, who married Sam in 2017, was a member of Jack's all-female band, The Peacocks, in 2012. Ruby sang "Love Interruption" with Jack on the 2013 Grammy telecast. Beyoncé came calling, and Jack produced a song on *Lemonade* with Ruby singing background to Beyoncé. I agree with NPR pop critic Ann Powers, who once said she's "all about the chills when Ruby Amanfu sings." Me, too.

David Houston's still at it today, producing mostly indie artists, those left of center enough to understand his ethos and quirkiness. From 1978 through 1982, I played piano on many recording sessions where David engineered or produced. I couldn't even name them now. They've all blended together into a stew of singer-songwriter demos, aspiring pop artists, TV themes, industrial films, commercials, and public service announcements. Drummer Jim Caselli and bassist Erik Kleven were often on these sessions. More experienced than me, they taught me what the session musician's role was.

First, you're on the clock, on someone else's dime. Respect this. Get to a workable part quickly. If you don't like the music, this changes nothing. Find a way to contribute one or two fresh ideas without dismantling and reinventing the client's project (though I did do this a few times). You're on the gig because you play with a unique combination of imagination and music history, accuracy and feel. So lock in with your session mates rhythmically, but make it feel good. Getting the style vibe on target trumps precision. And be a good hang. Laughter, being a uniter not a divider, and sharing a story or encouraging word can turn an average session into a better one. It's about the music and your growth as people while you're making it.

I had a lot of growing to do. In the beginning I played a piano part and kept quiet. As confidence bloomed, I tried to shoehorn my musical mind brimming with ideas into everyone's music or project. It was too much. I learned that hoary cliché, *less is more*. A strong foundational part with a little special sauce mixed in was plenty. Few car commercials needed my jazz odyssey meets new wave at full force.

What I remember most about David Houston is his tempo. Not his music tempo, but the pace at which he carried himself. A producer is in charge of the tempo: tempo of the track, tempo of the heart, tempo of the discussion, tempo of the lunch and dinner. It's all the intentional measure of time and pace, and the producer is the conductor. A good producer knows how to bring the peace and stir the chaos.

I went to visit producer David Kahne at his SeeSquared studio within Avatar on West Fifty-Third Street in NYC—this was late 2012. Avatar is the magical studio where I recorded my *Love Press Ex-Curio* record with Ravi Coltrane, James Genus, Joey Baron, Ralph Alessi, and Kurt Rosenwinkel, as well as a Ladysmith Black Mambazo track with James and the percussionist Don Alias. The Avatar location started out as a power substation, then a soundstage for the TV game show *Let's Make a Deal*. In 1977, it became the Power Station and the studio home of hit after hit.

Before taking the elevator up, I popped my head into Studio A where the brothers Carney were working. I had a thin connection to them; just enough to say hello. Reeve Carney was starring in Bono and Edge's Broadway production *Spider-Man: Turn Off the Dark*.

Reeve and Zane had performed during an emerging music night I sponsored at Molly Malone's, a club in Hollywood. Little sister Paris Carney was part of an artist's retreat we held at our home and studio in Nashville. All very talented and approachable artists.

David Kahne was the third record producer I watched work. It was 1980. This time, I was the artist, recording my first songs for a major label, A&M Records. Over time my relationship with David developed to where he enlisted me to write with him for Hiroshima, a band he was producing. I don't remember much other than David's frustration with me and the one important thing I learned that day.

David kept saying, "We just need one idea." I thought songs were made of many ideas. Which they are. That's not what David was talking about.

He was talking about something like dirt. Dirt is a big idea. If you start with it, all sorts of things can happen. Things that previously did not exist will appear as touchable, edible matter on the planet. All any artist ought to need is one idea. It's a guarantee and an earnest deposit. From one effectual idea all others will pour forth, like dirt, water, and seed becoming rice, becoming meaningful labor, becoming food, becoming income, becoming assets to support more dirt, seed, and water.

David Kahne was way out in front with his understanding of cosmic symmetry and the soil of creation.

The one big idea is elemental. So is problem solving, and there's always an element of puzzling out solutions with songwriting and music production. My friend Reed Arvin is bold enough to say there's no creativity without a problem to solve.

And even though we all love a firestarter, an aha moment, causing creativity to fly at the speed of light, it doesn't always go that way. Like farming, music production is often about delaying gratification. Dirt, seed, water. Basic stuff. You have to sow before you reap. Wait for it. There it is.

Yes, songwriting and production include the one magnetic idea that draws all goodness toward it. And problem solving with multiple solutions at your fingertips. Plus, delaying gratification with a smile on your face, knowing that various species of creativity have different gestation times. It's all this and much more.

—

Work in the peaches is what kept food on the table of my great-grandparents Robert and Maggie Miller. They first came to Yuba City in Sutter County from Durant, Oklahoma, in the 1930s. Peach juice is in my blood. Hands down, the peach is the most significant fruit I've encountered in this life. Next to the skin of my mother, the fragrance of a ripe peach is the oldest scent I know. Sutter County once proudly declared itself the Peach Bowl of the World (still would if it weren't for urbanization). Sometime in the 1880s, two agribusiness types, Abbott and Phillips, developed the Phillips Canning Cling Peach.

When my mother and her folks first migrated to California in 1939, they lived off Harter Road, in houses provided by Harter cannery. Twenty-five years later, I would attend school with a Harter descendant named Matt Piner, architect and inventor of the GoBagger, a sandbagging tool.

Matt's mother, Loadel, was a Harter and a Mills College graduate (class of '50). She's got a famous cling peach eponymously named after her. This peach is an extra-early variety that ripens by mid-July. Still a winner today. Loved for its stems, leaves, and fruit, the Loadel is grafted by pomologists into a dwarfing rootstock like Controller 5. This creates smaller trees with a more than decent yield of peaches and cuts down on labor costs for pruning, thinning, and harvesting. Like football, peach farming is a game of inches.

So is songwriting and music production. A single imaginative word in a song or the perfect drum hit is the lyrical or musical inch. Songs and productions are filled with these small but essential advancements in the direction of goodness and finishing well—getting the ball over the goal line, becoming the fruitful tree that holds the weight of its own creation.

We come from a rural farm community, so "cultivate" is a word I'm very familiar with. In the farm setting, it means plowing or tilling the ground, that is, breaking up the surface of the land so that natural (and applied) nutrients, such as fertilizer, can more easily do their work. And of course, water is hugely important. In the case of farmers who work outside organic guidelines, pesticides are used to discourage and kill pests that might otherwise damage the crop.

With respect to trees, pruning plays a big role (my great-grandfather's gig). An unpruned tree will develop slow-growing and nonfruitful shoots. You want the tree to be filled with shorter, fruit-bearing shoots. You don't want the tree to grow so high you can't easily reach the fruit. And you want to create space within the tree for sunlight and air. A tree that grows too much fruit is a problem. The branches and shoots cannot support the weight. Branches will snap and the fruit will fall to the ground and ruin.

Cultivation is the rhythm of observation, improvisation, action, and patience. It's an extremely engaged, present way of being. You can't half-ass it. It is intentional, time-consuming, labor-intensive work. It is embracing what you make, what you steward, and caring for it as described above.

Farming is also risky business, all the more reason to be prepared. Wear the crown, be the king of contingency. Never have just one answer to a problem.

It may be Kerouac's inspiration that allows me to risk and fail so easily. I'm still searching for something new. I'm willing to make mistakes. I feel no compulsion to land on the best choice the first time.

I can always correct. I'm happy to tweak my choices a thousand times until I can say, I love that. I didn't have this freedom as a session musician. And I suppose the hunger for it is the reason I became an artist and producer.

Along with the pleasure of unfettered imagination and creativity, I've also learned to create music that's closer to craft than invention. I've lived long enough to identify the DNA of most any music and break it down to the molecular level. Once I learned to do that, it was no big chore to put it back together again and nuance the result as desired.

In my lifetime there's been two basic kinds of record producers: the one I've just described—the musical molecular scientist. And then there's what I'd call the talent scout, fan, and encourager.

The first ought to have some of the second. The second can succeed without the first. If you're the second, though, you must hire inspired, expert musicians and engineers, ones that will fill the holes in your imagination, skill, and ability. You are absolutely dependent on them for your success. Historically, this sort of producer is both uncommonly lucky and committed to a simple recipe for success: only work with artists that make you look good, which are almost always artists who need very little help in the *very special and one of a kind department*: Billie Holiday, Miles Davis, The Beatles, Joni Mitchell, Paul Simon, Nina Simone, James Taylor, Aretha Franklin, Bruce Springsteen, Sting, Nirvana, John Mayer, Beyoncé, Adele, and Ed Sheeran. Artists of that ilk. Put a mic in front of Al Green. You know what you get? Al Green.

To produce talented yet mere mortals, producers need to be skilled in the art of cultivation and pruning. When problems arise and the artist doesn't have a solution, a producer should already have multiple options ready to offer. Fail at this, and you fail at producing. Someone has to have the one idea or the fifteen fixes. Imaginative, creative solutions to musical and artistic problems must be within reach within seconds. The producer is hoping the artist will provide the mind-opening one idea, but it doesn't always work that way.

I always set out to help the artist create a record that will get released, find an audience, or add fans to an existing one. The amount of shelved, unreleased records by big-name producers is bewildering. Some unreleased records are the fault of the artist—they simply fail to deliver the songs or the performances. Sometimes it's the joint failure of artist, producer, and marketing.

Confession: I should have walked from a few projects, and maybe that's what some of these other producers know. I confess it felt like failure to me to even think it. I felt that it was on me to pull the rabbit from the hat—I know better about myself now. I'm not the musical superfixer I perceived myself to be. My need to prove my skill and worth, never conceding defeat for artists and projects not fully my responsibility, was my undoing. I laid my body down, made myself sick with overwork, to prove a point no one had pressed.

Yes, I was driven and very skilled at finishing records on time, on budget, with the requisite quality for mass-market release. Which has nothing to do with art, community, and well-being. All things I value more. I learned that my need to prove my value—even that I deserved to be alive—too often overrode what I truly value. Improved mental health has made this clear and put me on a path toward wholeness far less dependent on performance. Especially finding my worth in solving seemingly insurmountable problems and organizing chaos.

This said, there's still a time to put the blame for musical failure where it belongs—with the producer (myself included). Unwillingness to fully invest in the project, lack of skill and ability, or crazy unforeseen circumstances might be the cause of producer failure. Whichever reasons, it's failure to deliver what the artist, management, and record company have asked for: help us make a better record than we could possibly make on our own.

For the majority of projects, I believe I've fulfilled this requirement, even if I'm not always satisfied with the results. If I produce an artist and the music is unconvincing (to me or others), it's because inherent artistic problems have gone unsolved. Sometimes they can't be resolved. The artist has reached the ceiling of his or her skill, or the money and the clock have run out. No one gets it right 100 percent of the time. Still, a reasonably high percentage is expected and essential.

In 2003, I produced half of a record entitled *Worldwide* for the rock band Audio Adrenaline. Along with my son-in-law Mark Nicholas, I was A&R for the project. I'd worked with the band in 1999 on *Underdog*, where I also cowrote one of their popular songs, "Hands and Feet." During *Underdog*, lead singer Mark Stuart was experiencing voice problems. Engineer Shane Wilson and I were accessing all known digital triage. I'd always known Mark to have a scratchy speaking voice. Now his formidable, cut-through-the-guitars singing voice was in trouble. I had the band's very young and talented guitarist, Tyler Burkum, give Mark a little help. Tyler sang unison lines with Mark and added vocal harmony parts behind him—that sort of thing. Problem solving.

By the time we started *Worldwide*, Mark was in serious voice meltdown. I kept telling label head Greg Ham, "I don't see how Mark can possibly sing. He's in bad shape. We have to get him over to the Vanderbilt Voice Clinic right now. A steroid shot is not going to fix this." My son-in-law Mark was equally concerned for his friend and artist.

Greg loved Audio Adrenaline and was worried for Mark, too. Even so, Greg had a company to run. Audio Adrenaline was a best seller. *Worldwide*, in effect, already existed. It was locked in and already on the Forefront and EMI Distribution release grid. Sales projections had been made. Marketing and promotion teams were already at work, busy setting up this hit record we'd yet to write or record. Mark, fully aware of the seriousness of his vocal condition, remained the positive and big-hearted person he is. Somehow, the work would get done.

I could not believe we were actually going forward with the record. The situation was that dire. It felt like I was handed an unsolvable problem.

Worldwide won the Grammy for Best Rock Gospel in 2004.

—

When you start out as a musician, you're in love with every note of music you hear. You're incapable of understanding all the glory and shame, problems and solutions, fails and fist bumps a project goes through from inception to earbuds.

When I was fourteen, I read the credits of *Donovan's Greatest Hits*, saw producer Mickey Most's name, and wondered what does a producer do? I liked all the twists and turns of instrumentation on the Donovan songs, "First There Is a Mountain," "Wear Your Love like Heaven," and "Hurdy Gurdy Man." Did Mickey Most have something to do with all these otherworldly sounds?

More was written about producer George Martin than most other producers. I soaked it up. Listening to George and The Beatles turn the recording studio into an imaginarium was cathartic. I wouldn't know to what degree until I began my own career.

It was watching producer David Kahne at work, up close and epiphanic, that sealed the deal for me. His skills and methods became the gold standard for what I thought a music producer should be. An engineer, cowriter, confidant, song doctor, multiinstrumentalist, mixer, background vocalist, string and horn arranger, conductor, programmer, A&R person, accountant, and part-time acupuncturist. Though overwhelming in scope, I understood this to be the minimum requirement—minus the acupuncture.

In 1979, one year before meeting David, I produced my first commercial record, "Chumps" b/w "Auto-erotica"; a 7-inch, 45-rpm single for the Sacramento art-punk band Labial Fricative. (More accurately, coproduced with my *mad for life* friend, Steve Holsapple.) Though I did in fact wear a fur-lined motorcycle jacket then, I was hardly a bona fide punk. I'm not sure Labial Fricative was either, with the possible exception of the lead singer, Marya Curry, a six-foot-tall bodybuilder and girlfriend to Mike Curtis, the bass player.

Andi and I did attend a Dead Kennedys show once, and we'd been to San Francisco's ground-zero punk/new wave club the Mabuhay Gardens. In 1979, the Mabuhay was punk bona fide. Hardly enough to tip my cred scale, though. At the time, Andi was pregnant with our son Sam. I don't recall much about the Dead Kennedys except for lead singer Jello Biafra's intensity and East Bay Ray's disarticulated, if not earnest, guitar playing. Strangely, I once had an orchestration lesson from Jello's father-in-law, a classical composer at UC Davis.

One of my greatest coproductions, daughter Molly, born in 1977, gestated to funk and jazz along with the punky new wave that followed in the wake of The Sex Pistols. At three years of age, Molly wore a button that read "Shut Up and Dance," the title of a song by our favorite San Francisco punk/new wave band, Pearl Harbor and the Explosions, featuring our friends Peter Bilt (Dunne) and John Stench (Hanes), who daughter Molly affectionately called Goofy. David Kahne produced their full-length for Warner Brothers in 1980.

Jimmy Griego, Rick Daprato, and David Lynch rounded out the members of Labial Fricative, my maiden voyage production on 45-rpm vinyl. Rick played drums and owned Esoteric Records, trading in mostly used vinyl. Jimmy (drums too) had played with the Sacramento art-crowd favorite, The Runners. For a short time, I'd played my Fender Rhodes in the band. The Runners were decidedly not punk, rather funk.

Labial Fricative was my first production gig, and of course, there had to be two drummers. In this world or any world to come, that's at least one drummer too many. I had a jazz-fusion musician on guitar. Shouting for singing. I can see myself sitting at the console, disturbed by what I was hearing, and having no clue how to make right what sounded wrong. I'm sure coproducer Steve was saving my arse right and left.

Thirty-five years later, drummer Rick Daprato sent me a message, saying, "Time has apparently rendered it worthwhile, since copies of the 45 are selling for $30 and a record label wants to reissue it." Fast-forward a few more years, and the very rare single is now selling for $200. One blogger allowed that the band and its recording might qualify for a short list of Sacramento's "fathers of the punk scene." Along with Ozzie, The Twinkeyz, The Mumbles, and Permanent Wave.

David Houston produced The Twinkeyz. I used to run into The Mumbles at Maurice's American Bar quite often—Frank French (the friendliest), Richard McGrath (a true punk), and Mike Palmer (still playing bass today in the NorCal band Mumbo Gumbo). I took over Ozzie's rehearsal space when they moved to LA. The band left behind a cheese jacket made entirely of single-wrapped American cheese squares sewn together.

There's no good reason that Labial Fricative should have asked me to produce their single. Maybe because I hung out at Rick's record shop and talked music with him. Maybe because I knew Jimmy and played with him in different ad hoc groups. Likely, it was Steve that got us the gig. I'd done recording sessions as a musician. But I knew nothing about producing records, yet.

Occasionally someone will ask how I became a record producer. Generally speaking, a whole range of influence and circumstance caused it. At the tacit level it was the land where I grew up that prepared me to become a producer. This is usually not the answer people are looking for. They'd rather know about my first big break and all that sort of thing. I remember what it feels like to be young with the whole world in front of you looking for a map to take that first step. So, I bend toward their wants. Then I address the true need: a clear vision of how people and place shape you and how the grace of God sustains you. I was twenty-five years into a career before I truly understood and accepted that God's love and proximity to a particular people and place are the unequivocal answer to why I became a musician, a songwriter, and a producer.

twelve

SOMETIMES IT'S THE WINNING

Incense cedar trees dot the landscape of the coast and interior of California and Oregon. The tree is aptly named for its pleasing fragrance, which has medicinal properties. I've known these trees my whole life. There's a stretch of Highway 20 outside of Nevada City where you really begin to gain altitude and the smell of this unique cedar teases your nose. I always make a point to lower the car window and take it in. It sings to me, and I breathe its song.

These trees aren't bothered by pests. The aroma fends them off. An Incense cedar boasts a remarkably impenetrable bark too—but only when it's mature. Its biggest source of danger is dry-rot fungus making a meal of its heartwood. When this happens, the durable wood that refuses to decay becomes a crumbling mess. The trees die long before you see them fallen.

One of the most intriguing things about this particular species of tree is that it doesn't easily splinter. Its wood is great for pencils because, unlike other types, it can be sharpened in any direction. Incense cedars also make excellent windbreaks. Plant them in a line outside your home, and they make cold winters more bearable.

Some moments are like Incense cedars. The wisdom of longevity and uniqueness of experience protect and deflect potential disaster. Or a bright future is consumed in what seems like an instant. The thing is, these moments begin like any other—you don't know when the atmosphere will shift—you just have to turn into each moment as it comes. Stay sharp.

I had just enjoyed a remarkable year with The Civil Wars. The debut album, *Barton Hollow*, was a critical favorite and a No. 1 best seller on *Billboard*'s Digital Chart. We had two Grammy nominations, Best Folk Album and Best Country Duo/Group Performance.

All good, but I feel most alive, most grounded, when I am in the process of creating, reimagining, and refining sound. Awards play their role in moving a career along in a positive direction, but the studio and the process of imagination and creation are what ground me. I was ready for more work with new people in new places.

Andi and I flew from Nashville to Los Angeles on Wednesday, February 8, 2012, and checked into Mosaic, a boutique hotel in Beverly Hills. A convenient location from which to branch out for meetings during Grammy week.

The next day started at breakfast with producer Mike Elizondo, also A&R at Warner Brothers. Mike and I admired each other's work. We had Switchfoot in common. I discovered the band, signed them to my re:think label, and developed them through their first three albums (with the deft marketing direction of Nick Barré). On the fourth album, this time for Columbia Records, I received a coproduction credit with John Fields on the smash single "Dare You to Move." A song featured on both *Learning to Breathe* and *The Beautiful Letdown* (where producer John Fields hit a home run with his reinvention of the song). Mike came onboard for the band's seventh and eighth albums: the Grammy-winning *Hello Hurricane* and the follow-up *Vice Verses*.

I started the *Hello Hurricane* project with the band in August of 2007. We recorded thirteen songs at Big Fish, a studio in the coastal hills above Rancho Santa Fe, California. It was an experiment that failed. The band was simply not ready to make a record. Certainly not the one I hoped for. The band agreed. Manager Bruce Flohr from Redlight Management agreed. History proved the diagnosis true.

Mike jumped in after a few more false starts and changes, including the band's exit from Columbia Records. Eventually the band self-produced another version of the album at their newly constructed studio. It was Mike that brought the indefatigable project to completion. Rob Cavallo signed the band to a new contract, tweaked a few songs, and released *Hello Hurricane* on Atlantic Records. One of the songs I produced at Big Fish, "Mess of Me," eventually emerged on the album *Building a Hurricane*.

After our breakfast meeting, Mike and I headed over to Warner Brothers Records to visit with Lenny Waronker. After a long absence, Lenny was back at Warner's in something of an emeritus A&R position. He'd been an essential player among Warner's history-making collection of executives, A&R people, and producers going back to the late 1960s. Names like Mo Ostin, David Geffen, Joe Smith, Ted Templeman, and Russ Titelman. They were disruptive change agents. Some of my favorite records were created under their tenure, and especially the production collaboration of Lenny and Russ on *Gorilla* by James Taylor and Rickie Lee Jones's eponymous debut.

What Lenny and I had in common was the artist Sal Valentino and a love for The Civil Wars. Sal Valentino was a founding member of two bands signed by Warner Brothers Records—The Beau Brummels and Stoneground. Lenny had produced *Triangle* and *Bradley's Barn* for The Beau Brummels. When I stepped into his office that day, the first thing I noticed was a painting by his daughter of the album cover for *Bradley's Barn*, forty-four years after the album's inception. I was just a little kid when I saw an animated cartoon version of The Beau Brummels. They were featured on *The Flintstones* television show in 1965. Renamed The Beau Brummelstones, they sang their national hit "Laugh Laugh." How could my nine-year-old self possibly conceive that fifteen years later I'd be performing the oldie-but-goodie with Sal?

I played piano in one of Sal's post-Stoneground bands in 1979. This included some recordings where Sal covered one of my songs, "Not Tonight." Our crowning achievement was opening for Bob Marley & the Wailers at Freeborn Hall, University of California at Davis. Sal would let me sing a couple of songs in the set. I still remember the newspaper review: "The keyboardist sang a few selections to a smattering of boos." *A Smattering of Boos* sounds like the title of a Richard Brautigan novel.

Lenny's got some stories. Without a wisp of guile, he'll describe critical moments in pop music history. All of which he took part in.

I'm especially fond of one:

Warner Brothers signs an African American teenager named Prince. The eighteen-year-old wants to produce himself. The record label has never allowed artists to self-produce.

Lenny wants a handful of Warner's folk, including Russ Titelman, to watch Prince at work in the studio. This, Lenny thinks, will erase any lingering doubts. It's not an audition, more of a musical hang. The team already knows they're getting in the Prince business. Not backing out, just want a look-see.

Lenny books a studio and Prince flies out. Immediately it's obvious that Prince has serious production skills, knows his way around the studio, and plays every instrument well. At some point Prince is sitting on the floor against the wall with his legs stretched out. It's very crowded in the studio. To move around, Lenny has to step over him. As he does, Prince stops him and says, "Don't make me Black." It's not that Prince sought to obscure his Blackness; he simply refused to be creatively pigeonholed by the limited imaginations of music execs solely because his skin was brown. A box too small was his bridge too far.

Lenny's production partner, Russ Titelman, had become friendly with the pop band Sixpence None the Richer. They had a breakout hit, "Kiss Me," produced by my good friend Steve Taylor for his Squint label. The band covered "I Won't Stay Long," a song written by my son Sam when he was a teenager. For his homeschool senior project, Sam recorded a full-length album titled *Sauté*. Russ liked it and flew out to Nashville to stay with us and hear Sam play at J.J.'s, a corner grocery store with a stage.

Russ was easygoing. He didn't balk at sleeping on the twin bed in our odd little bedroom/bathroom affectionately called the Hobbit Room. Though his visit was about Sam, I enjoyed visiting with Russ. Hearing him lift the veil on music that defined my teenage years was pure pleasure.

I wrapped up my visit with Lenny and Mike. Lenny was hardly stuck in the past. He was overseeing Kimbra and Gary Clark Jr., among others. Mike was at the top of his game, a bona fide hit-maker. Now all we needed was a project to work on together.

The next day, I was back on the meeting track. This meant driving all over town. Every mile and wasted hour was a reminder of why I don't like Los Angeles. I took a meeting with Jay Landers at Universal. Producer David Foster had just taken over the subsidiary, Verve Records. In its golden years, the label was a jazz institution. Founded by Norman Granz in the year of my birth, it was home to Ella Fitzgerald, Billie Holiday, Stan Getz, Nina Simone, Charlie Parker, and my favorite, Bill Evans.

Like many historic imprints, it'd been bought and sold and repackaged infinitum. Now at Universal, Verve was all about deep jazz catalog, classical and adult pop, including the kind of music David Foster does so well, like Josh Groban and Michael Bublé.

Jay Landers worked under David as his principal A&R. Both of them liked The Civil Wars, or at least liked the success story. As the *Los Angeles Times* ardently put it, "Through bands such as The Civil Wars, a new music industry is born."[1] Jay encouraged me to bring something similar to Verve. I had no interest, but didn't tell him that.

"Think about it this way," Jay advised. "If T Bone Burnett would sign it, we want a look at it."

While hurriedly leaving Jay's office, David turned and pointed in my direction. "Are you as good as me?" he asked.

This gave me considerable pause. "I would put myself in the same category as you in terms of skill and ability."

I think that was about fifteen words more than he was looking for.

"Come work with us," he said. "Don't work for anyone else."

I've never heard another word from David Foster.

Not every creative opportunity is mine to have. Equally important, not every gig is right for me. I've learned which situations are a fit and which aren't. More than that, I have learned to protect my ego from disingenuous flattery. It saves me from a ton of drama.

Parsing the disingenuous is a learned skill. You begin with naïveté, then experience hurt and confusion by people who praise you and forget you in the same breath. Now you're suspicious, cynical. Next up, you have to live a little, meet enough people in order to learn the characteristics of genuine interest and respect, over against blather and selling. You find your people. You have a baseline. Now you don't have to be cynical. When the disingenuous flattery appears, your brain and ego process it accordingly—as my dad often said, "In one ear and out the other."

I don't know how to do consequential artistic work around men that are too aggressive, a little too light on humility and too beguiled by power and money. They shut me down and leave me uninspired.

I've got my own share of issues: ways I speak and act that shut others down. I can find my alpha male. I think most of my honest friends would agree.

There are some things I'm just not good at, though, like hanging with artists for fringe benefits or just to close a deal. I've got no hype or inauthentic enthusiasm to give. As an artist, I've been up close and privy to disingenuous excitement. I've sat with executives, artists, and producers who can blow hot air interminably. Most of them live in Los Angeles. Their game is at a fiendishly genius level. I swore I'd never be that guy.

If I need to meet up with an artist again and again for drinks and conversation, then I'm out of the running. I can't compete with a label or person who's willing to sell when an artist's ego needs selling to.

I wanted to sign country star Jake Owen to a production and publishing deal. This was when Jake was a part-time golf caddy. Hadn't made his first record. I recorded some song demos on him and enlisted producer Jimmie Lee Sloas to work with Jake. Mine wasn't the only company interested in the would-be singer. The competition excelled at the man-hang. Consequently, I lost Jake. And he wasn't my first miss. Ironically, fifteen-plus years later, Jake signed a trio that I'd discovered and developed, Daves Highway.

Artistically, there's no meaningful work for me in an environment defined by gamesmanship. Making the effort to fit in would be a wasted effort. I don't like myself when I tiptoe into the murky pond of unrestrained ambition and flattery. I actually think there are things in the world worth failing at. Sometimes it's the winning that dry-rots your soul.

From the top story of the Mosaic Hotel, you can see the Beverly Hilton at the intersection of Wilshire and Santa Monica Boulevards. It's the fancy hotel I stayed in when I came to LA in 1984 to mix my first solo album, *Lie Down in the Grass*, with engineer Larry Hirsch. I've stayed there and attended several industry events over the years. All I remember from that first stay in '84 is the $4.00 fresh-squeezed orange juice. Back then you could buy a family-sized meal at Taco Bell for that amount.

Late in the afternoon, Friday, February 11, 2012, there was an emergency going on down at the Hilton. Less an emergency than a dreadful discovery: Whitney Houston had been found dead in room 434. By all accounts, she was planning on attending the annual Grammy party held downstairs and hosted by her mentor, Clive Davis.

Her death was truly heartbreaking news. Everyone in the business had unrelenting hope that Whitney would find her way to sobriety and the music again. Once upon a time she'd been a megastar with peerless talent deserving of every accolade.

Within minutes the story seemed to be everywhere. A sadness spread out from the Hilton and draped the city. I couldn't help but think of David Foster, the music man I didn't click with. Now he was a man who was likely pretty stunned. I prayed comfort for Whitney's family and for people like David, with whole chapters of their lives shaped by Whitney. Especially so when she was in her prime and emotionally spot-on. Her voice could make your eyes leak and your whole being say thank you. Whitney's unprecedented performance of "The Star-Spangled Banner" at the 1991 Super Bowl was one of those times. A clinic on how to put chill bumps on a nation.

Randy Jackson and Bongo Bob Smith were two friends who'd worked with Narada Michael Walden on Whitney Houston's first hit records. Bob had played on the No. 1 smash "So Emotional." All of us longtime Sacramento friends were happy for him. Now I was thinking what a jolt this news must be.

The annual Clive Davis soiree at the Beverly Hilton went on as planned. Stars gathered downstairs while Whitney's body remained upstairs with the coroner.

—

All over town, people continued to get ready for music's big night. We relocated to the Ritz-Carlton to be next to L.A. Live, site of the Grammys. Once settled, we connected with our party and headed out to the Twenty Ten Music dinner at A.O.C., a restaurant and wine bar.

In 2010, I formed a music production and publishing company with my friend David Kiersznowski, a Kansas City businessman and philanthropist. I gave it the obvious name of Twenty Ten Music. Inaugural and simple. My love of naming usually took me in a more imaginative direction. Apparently, I'd learned something from a young band I'd signed.

When I discovered a trio of surfer/musicians from San Diego, they were known as Chin Up. A name that had to be changed. I asked, what about some surf terminology? When they landed at Goofy Foot, I asked for clarification.

"It's when you switch your feet."

"Surfers are simple," they added.

Switchfoot it was.

Twenty Ten Music had provided some funding in the early days of The Civil Wars. This allowed me to work on spec and provide studio time for the project.

Dave and Demi Kiersznowski (cofounders of their company DEMDACO) had flown in for the Grammy party and Sunday ceremony. My aunt Karoly, uncle Clark, and Andi were there too.

Screenwriter and producer Allan Heinberg came with our mutual friend, artist Butterfly Boucher. Her 2009 release *Scary Fragile* was produced by David Kahne. I had worked with Butterfly on *Any Day Now*, a tour documentary of the Nashville artist collective Ten out of Tenn, founded by Kristen and Trent Dabbs. Along with Butterfly, some of Nashville's most influential indie and major label artists have run through this celebrated group. Mikky Ekko, Erin McCarley, Joy Williams, Matthew Perryman Jones, Katie Herzig, Andy Davis, and Mat Kearney, among them. This was Nashville's answer to Hotel Café, the Los Angeles ground zero for songwriters early in the twenty-first century.

Another guest at the table that night, Cary Brothers, was a front-runner among the Hotel Café crowd. Cary is known for the song "Blue Eyes" from the Grammy Award–winning, platinum-selling *Garden State* soundtrack, a film and record that brought exposure to indie-rock artists like The Shins. My son Sam and I admired The Shins' cover art for *Chutes Too Narrow*. We hired the same artist, Jesse LeDoux, to create Sam's cover for *Gonna Get It Wrong before I Get It Right*.

What all these Ten out of Tenn and Hotel Café singer-songwriters had in common was a mountain of TV/film sync placements—the use of your music in film, television, trailers, and every sort of digital media application.

One afternoon I was visiting with Allan Heinberg at the ABC Television lot on Prospect Avenue in the Los Feliz neighborhood of LA. Allan said, "I've got something I want to show you." We passed some editing suites and stepped through one of the doors. The editor pressed play, and a scene from *Grey's Anatomy* came on. For three and a half minutes, an emotional montage unfolded, all supported by my production of the unreleased Civil Wars' song "Poison & Wine." I was ecstatic. No studio versions of the song were available. Allan, a trusted friend, had been given our unreleased master.

Joy and John Paul found out about the placement four days before the episode aired. The management team quickly uploaded our studio version to iTunes. My son fast-tracked a suitable music video. We were watching the *Grey's Anatomy* episode while the video uploaded to YouTube. Our small but meaningful project had just been exposed to a national audience on the No. 1 television show in America.

Thank you, Allan.

One new fan in particular got very excited about "Poison & Wine."

Taylor Swift put it on her official iTunes playlist and sent a Twitter post heard 'round the world. "I think this is my favorite duet. It's exquisite."

We were happy that Eric Volz was able to join us at the restaurant. He was living in Venice Beach and traveling around the world as a crisis manager and advocate against wrongful imprisonment. A subject Eric knew all too personally. He'd been arrested in Nicaragua for murder and sentenced to thirty years in prison. Eric spent fourteen grueling months in confinement. Our best friend, and Eric's mother, Maggie Anthony, was relentless in her pursuit to see Eric freed. Finally, she received game-changing support from the White House. During a speech, US Secretary of State Condoleezza Rice mentioned Eric's false imprisonment. The secretary's word had immediate effect. The Nicaraguan appeals court signed release papers for Eric that very day. He was on his way home.

Along with producer/engineer Eric Robinson and photographer Allister Ann, we had three actors at the table. Molly Quinn from *Castle*; Charity Wakefield, an English TV and film actress (*Wolf Hall*); and Gethin Anthony from an HBO show that was just taking off, *Game of Thrones*. He played a character named Renly Baratheon.

Rounding out the guest list was the band The Daylights and their girlfriends. Drummer Svend Lerche brought his fiancée, Angela Hudson, sister of pop star Katy Perry. When Katy was still Katy Hudson, she had come to visit me at the Art House in Nashville for career advice. I have no memory of what I told her. If it was move to LA and become a megastar, then my advice might actually be worth something.

The Daylights were fronted by the enormously talented twin brothers, Ricky and Randy Jackson. Twenty Ten had funded four songs for them. Each song had earned multiple TV and film sync licenses, including *Rabbit Hole* with Nicole Kidman.

Sunday, February 13, I had coffee with dobro legend Jerry Douglas and a few of the Mumfords. Then went back up to my room and got into my Billy Reid suit, tie, and shoes. Artist rep Shelly Colvin had hooked me up.

Andi and I met Dave, Demi, Aunt Karoly, and Uncle Clark over at the Staples Center for the *54th Annual Grammy Pre-Telecast*. Like pretelecasts so often are, it was a no-nonsense machine doling out seventy awards as quickly as possible. When it came time for The Civil Wars, we were all surprised to win Best Country/Duo Group Performance for "Barton Hollow."

Were we making country records?

Then just like that, we had a second one for Folk Album of the Year. Two for two. Now we could breathe.

It was a good year to be in the audience for the main telecast. A Whitney Houston tribute, Bruno Mars on stun, Taylor Swift doing her anti–Bob Lefsetz song "Mean" from *Speak Now*, and the forever young Paul McCartney singing a silly love song to his new wife.

In 2013, we were surprised and happy to see an official tweet from Paul: "The last albums I bought were Kanye West, The National, The Civil Wars and Jay-Z." Rewarding, but my favorite McCartney story is about my friend Jude Adam. When she was at the BBC, Paul had come in for an interview. Her job was to greet the Beatle and make him comfortable.

"Welcome. My name is Jude."

"Jude, as in, 'Hey Jude'?" Paul asked.

I had no real choice but to snag Paul's response and use it as a song title on my jazz album, *Lemonade: Collected Solo Piano Improvisations*. If you were to step into my piano room, you'd see a framed letter in a young girl's handwriting. "To Paul McCartney only" it says. Andi had written to Paul on August 4, 1964. Her mother never mailed it.

The Civil Wars were allotted sixty seconds on the televised broadcast to sing "Barton Hollow." That's it. Yet, from that one tiny performance the duo received a huge Grammy bump in sales the following week. Selling 35,663 copies, up 178 percent and second only to Adele's *21* sales—which no one could touch. She and producer Paul Epworth won so many Grammys that night I lost count. We were just happy to have The Civil Wars on the cover of *Billboard* and be well on our way to a gold record.

There's one more meeting from that whirlwind Grammy week.

In 2012, I loved the minimalist production mode I was in, capturing live performances and keeping the production from getting too heavy-handed or tricky. I was having success with this approach. I still wanted to produce pop music, though, like Mike was doing with Kimbra.

I already had a young artist in mind.

After the morning at Warner Brothers, I met Christina Grimmie and her manager Mandy Teefey (Selena Gomez's mother) at Sushi Dan in Studio City. I'd been talking with Christina via email and phone about her music and where she wanted to go with it. I told her that if she was game, I'd love to work with her.

Young singers were uploading versions of Civil Wars' songs "Safe and Sound," "Barton Hollow," and "Poison & Wine" daily to You-Tube. Christina was among them. Because of her famous daughter, Christina's manager, Mandy, had seen everything the world could throw at a young artist. I'd have to go through Mandy's firewall before any music would get made. She needed convincing that I was one of the good guys, and not a letch or a leech on her client's talent.

I passed the audition. Christina was lovely. Humble. Eager for life. Christina would come to Nashville for several days of writing. I shared my confidence in Christina with Jeff Sosnow at Warner Brothers, and of course Mike, showing them performances of Christina on her You-Tube channel. I was certain that she would grow beyond her status as a YouTube star or Disney artist. After all, one of the biggest stars in pop music, Justin Timberlake, had transcended his Mouseketeer beginnings. I believed in Christina as a person. I saw no reason why we couldn't make a great, legit pop record together.

I went home to Nashville and created five song-starts for the upcoming writing sessions. These went into a folder on my computer titled "Christina Grimmie Songs." We were ready to begin. All that was left was to iron out some logistics.

Mandy co-managed Christina with her then-husband Brian. He took over when it was time to discuss terms. I explained that there would be some basic recording costs surrounding Christina's visit. Nothing extravagant. A studio engineer and a few musicians. I wanted her to finish the week with songs that were fully realized and mixed. I'd learned not to trust the imagination of music businesspeople or most artists. There was a time when a songwriter or a producer could make a simple demo. With a little skill and imagination, people could extrapolate from the demo what a master would sound like.

That time had passed.

I knew if I was going to get this gig, I couldn't hand in anything but tracks that sounded finished (even if I knew there was still more work to do).

I agreed to pay half the costs for the week, with the idea that either Christina or her management would pick up the balance. In my experience, and by Nashville standards, this was fair, even generous.

Brian wanted me to pay for everything. That didn't make any sense to me.

The standard I was taught and followed was one of equal risk and reward. Developing recording/touring artists is a speculative business. There are some hard costs involved, but many people in the creative loop at the beginning of an artist's career work on spec—they don't get paid until the artist begins to make money. Following this pattern, I wasn't requesting to be paid anything. I was requesting that Brian or Christina join me in paying half of any hard costs involved in sending her home with finished recordings. If the music found a home, then maybe someday, we'd all be rewarded.

Brian had his version of reality. I had mine. We couldn't find any common ground, and the writing session had to be canceled. I felt very bad for Christina. I wished this sort of tangle wasn't so commonplace, but I couldn't find a path forward.

The next time I saw Christina was at the Village Chapel, a Christian church in Nashville. I turned around and there she was, sitting with her mother. They were visiting the city. Sunday came around, and somehow, they'd ended up at our fellowship.

Christina went on to make more commercial recordings. She toured with Selena, increased her YouTube fan base, and even acted in a film. She came in third in season six of NBC's *The Voice*. All the coaches immediately turned their chairs for Christina—as they should have. Adam Levine promised to sign her regardless of whether she won.

On June 10, 2016, Christina was murdered by an obsessed fan following a concert in Orlando, Florida. Cut down. So young.

Sometimes, you'll see Internet or newspaper copy with the words "senseless killing" or "senseless murder." It's a redundant descriptor. Murder by its very nature is senseless. It shouldn't make sense. It's nonsense. Those who loved Christina will never get over this. It was not God's will that she be murdered. God did not take her because of a pressing need for a soprano in the heavenly choir. A sick man took her breath from her.

It's true, a grieving person can be comforted by the belief that human destiny is more than just this life. As far as I know, this is a cornerstone of Christian doctrine. Even with great faith, it's perfectly sensible to weep and to ask why—even wrestle with God. And it's inevitable that no earthly answer will be entirely sufficient.

Every once in a while, I'll be searching for some music on a hard disk or server, and there'll be that folder: "Christina Grimmie Songs." Though her death is inexplicable, I like to remember how much sense her young life made.

Our friend and neighbor, Irishman Keith Getty, wrote a modern hymn with Stuart Townend titled "In Christ Alone." All over the world, this hymn is as ubiquitous as a hymn can be. I had the honor of recording a version with Kristyn Getty and the peerless Alison Krauss (a remixed version nominated for a Grammy in 2023). "In Christ Alone" touched Christina in a profound way. In April 2012, she uploaded her own simple, live version to YouTube, a video with millions of views.

> No guilt in life, no fear in death—
> This is the pow'r of Christ in me;
> From life's first cry to final breath,
> Jesus commands my destiny.
> No pow'r of hell, no scheme of man,
> Can ever pluck me from His hand;
> Till He returns or calls me home—
> Here in the pow'r of Christ I'll stand.[2]

thirteen

MAD TO LIVE

In the Sacramento Valley, dirt is everywhere. Remember, the community I grew up in is Tierra Buena—good earth. When I look at the fields, I see clods. A clod is just a lump or chunk of dirt. There are tractors and plows working the fields leaving clods and Pigpen-trails of dust in their wake. If you want a clod, you've got to plow. A disc plow slices up the earth, turns the slice upside down and then crumbles it. Those crumbles might be anything from rich, loamy soil to claylike clods.

Preparing the soil is the first step to growing anything. This is what living in this place taught me. Preparation. Planting. Patience. Then more patience and lots of care and nurture. Harvest, then more care. Like pruning and plowing, even burning off the chaff. Then doing it all over again, year after year. A life of repetition, yet not without surprise. There's always something remarkable to give thanks for, and drought, fire, and plain bad luck to ponder and move on from.

If I had my way, I'd send students to four years on a farm instead of university (and I'm someone who created an entire curriculum for a university music program). Though a hard sell to the parents, students would likely learn as much teasing music from the dirt as just about anything else. Interdependence of all you see, touch, and feel would be the underlying pedagogy. Students would practice extrapolating outward from the dirt to other subjects. Finance, nursing, poetry, law, music, and a thousand other things. The dirt's a good teacher. Hands down, better than Kerouac. That's unfair. It was Kerouac that taught me that the best teacher is experience. This influence must've made it into a lyric: "You can only possess what you experience." A phrase that has a little of the theologian A. W. Tozer on it too.

The experience of farming is at the heart of our family's life and story in California. I came up knowing what it was like to grow your own food in a garden, raise chickens, and work in the orchards and fields. Everyone learned to succeed at growing something from the earth. This makes you one kind of citizen of the world and not another. It can even make you an artist, a jazz piano player, a record producer.

All that work of calling forth green from the earth takes water. Water quenches thirst, makes stuff grow, and puts me at peace. Rivers, lakes, streams, canals, and ditches—water for life, water for play—fishing, boating, waterskiing, duck hunting, swimming. Like rich soil, water is everywhere to be seen, enjoyed, and remembered.

Soil and water get at something very human and ancient. We go from dust to dust with time in between living in a body made of at least 70 percent water. That's no crazy coincidence. I think of the water surrounding my hometown, and every name becomes a memory: Jack Slough (fell in when I was a little kid, big channel cats and landlocked salmon), Ellis Lake (fishing and catching fifty bluegill the size of a credit card and the drag boat races), Boyd's Pump (boat launch on the Feather), and Hank & Mickey's (boat launch on the Sacramento River—big striped bass).

Outside Marysville, on the right side of the levee is a dump—that smelly designation where trash goes to die. Going to the dump was a rite of passage. It stirred my imagination. The smell is forever mine to bring to mind. On every trip to the dump, I'd imagine finding an abandoned go-kart. I'd rescue it and bring it back to life. I never did find one. What I did learn was to never let failure or unbelief have the final word.

There is a deep weave of land, place, and people, and how I know what I know. The knowing is in the light sweetness of the air around the Sutter Buttes near harvest time; the scaled slotted bark of live oak scraping my palm; the gurgle of the Feather River, then the Yuba. It's more than I can say, so close and yet beyond my grip, this knowing. Atoms of veracity, unseen and undeniable. It is, if you let it be, in the prose of Jean-Louis Lebris de Kérouac, simply *mad*.

Kerouac yearned to be in the company of "the mad ones, the ones who are mad to live, mad to talk, mad to be saved, desirous of everything at the same time, the ones who never yawn or say a commonplace thing, but burn, burn, burn like fabulous yellow roman candles exploding like spiders across the stars."[1]

To be *mad to live and desirous of everything* is a way of seeing. It is life on the road, swivel-headed, never missing the ecstasy camouflaged as mundane. It is seeing it, delighting in it without preconceptions, and moving on to the next micro-enlightenment. Even the act of seeing something/anything with *shoshin*, or beginner's mind, doesn't quite do the "burn, burn, burn" justice, though. To be *mad to live* is to actively see the relationship between God, people, places and things, and ourselves, our stories. It is being present in the world as one who aspires to be seamlessly integrated with God, people, places, and things without ever being less or more than human.

Kerouac, in *On The Road*, wrote: "I saw God in the sky in the form of huge gold sunburning clouds above the desert that seemed to point a finger at me and say, 'Pass here and go on, you're on the road to heaven.'"[2]

There's a road trip I've taken more than all others. On it, I pass from here and there, mad to live, with the interconnectedness of all things ablaze. It begins by heading west to east from Sutter County in the middle of the state, just above Sacramento, and zigzagging my way uphill into the grand Sierra Nevada range.

—

If you cross the Feather River from my hometown of Yuba City to Marysville, you can connect with Highway 20 and drive northeast for several miles along a great expanse of flat farmland; fields of rice, prunes, and cattle. I know this gateway out of the valley into the eastern foothills well. The land holds memory all the way to Truckee, Tahoe, and a dot on the map called Chilcoot. One nexus after another of history and music. Spiritual pursuit and the heart of darkness.

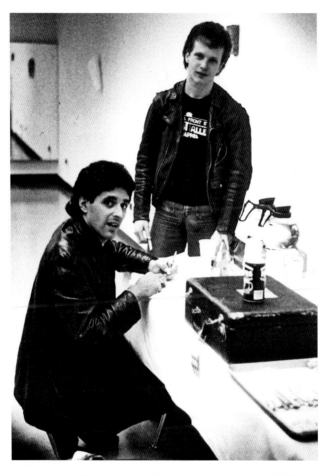

Sal Valentino (Beau Brummels) and me backstage at UC Davis, California, before opening for Bob Marley, December 1, 1979

Mentor Steve Holsapple and me at Moon Studios, Sacramento, California, circa 1979

Always a gig, always a photo needed—Erik Kleven (bass), John Hanes (drums), the fearless leader, and Pat Minor (guitar)

I opened for British Ska band General Public on two USA-Canadian tours (1984–1985), including this stop at Radio City Music Hall, New York City

1981, The Charlie Peacock Group with Jim Caselli (drums), Mark Herzig (guitar), Erik Kleven (bass), and Darius Babazadeh (saxophone)

Press photo on signing with Island Records, 1986. Left to right: Mary Neely, President of Exit Records, Joel Webber, Island VP of A&R, me, Jim Swindell, Island VP Sales & Marketing, and Lou Maglia, President of Island Records. Island founder Chris Blackwell skipped out early for the airport.

1987, backstage at The Fillmore in San Francisco with the legend, manager Bill Graham

Island Records recording artist Brent Bourgeois, best friend and collaborator, sharing a treat in the Exit studio

In the studio with bassist and future television star, Randy Jackson

Great band of brothers and sisters, opening up for Bourgeois Tagg at The Fillmore. Left to right, starting with the back row: Bongo Bob Smith (percussion), Michael Roe (guitar), Aaron Smith (drums), John Weber (keyboards), Eric Heilman (bass), Shelley Burns (background vocals), me, and Clarice Jones (background vocals)

A 1987 short-term Sacramento supergroup called Emperor Norton featuring old friends. Left to right: Henry Robinett (guitar), Larry Tagg (vocals, bass), me, Brent Bourgeois (vocals, keyboards). Not pictured: Aaron Smith (drums) and Bongo Bob Smith (percussion).

The coveted Tower Records end-cap—what marketing called "price and positioning"

Much of the 1980s was spent hitting it in the clubs, back when people danced to bands. Next to me, Clarice Jones and the great Vince Ebo. To quote Vinnie, "We tore it up." John Weber was poking out in the back.

Somebody found a stylist! A great version of my 1980s era band featuring Darryl C. Anders (bass), Bruce Spencer (drums), John Weber playing all the keyboard parts I didn't want to, and dear friend and collaborator Jimmy Abegg (guitar)

Jimmy Abegg and me during the late 1980s acoustic trio era—our third man, vocalist Vince Ebo, is out of the frame

NorCal musicians at Studio D in Sausalito, 1988. Margaret Becker, my first production for Sparrow Records. Jimmy Abegg (guitar), Margaret and me up top—bottom, left to right, Mike Urbano (drums), Larry Tagg (bass), and Roger Smith (keyboards).

Musican meets mentor. Producer Brown Bannister and me at our stations, working on multiple records at Castle Recording Studios, Nashville, 1989.

Producing Scott and Christine Denté of Out of the Grey at my Kaleidoscope Sound Studio in Bellevue, Tennessee, 1991

My first platinum record—one million of five million total on Amy Grant's *Heart In Motion*. Left to right: Bill Hearn (President, Sparrow Records), Mark Williams (VP Publishing), the songwriter, and Peter York (VP of A&R).

Art House and re:think staff and spouses party, 1996—David Dark, Jay Swartzendruber, Sarah Masen, the boss, Shane and Stacye Wilson, Katy and Scott Krippaehne, Molly Ashworth (Nicholas)

Revealing the secrets of the universe to Switchfoot—Tim Foreman, Jon Foreman, and Chad Butler

Art House and re:think staff and spouses party, 1997—Nick Barré at bottom; left to right in the middle row are Molly Ashworth, Katy Krippaehne, Andi Ashworth, Shane Wilson, Jay Swartzendruber, Russ Ramsey; left to right in the top row are Brent Milligan and Douglas Kaine McKelvey

Wrongly bearded record producer with the great Joseph Shaba-lala, leader/founder of Ladysmith Black Mambazo, 2000, Louisville, Kentucky

Amy Grant and Bono in conversation at our home, The Art House, Nashville, Tennessee, December 9, 2002

Bono, playing son Sam's J-30 Gibson, and leading us in "They'll Know We Are Christians"

The most significant landmark in Marysville is actually a water-mark, Ellis Lake. Named after W. T. Ellis, the architect of the Marys-ville levee system, Ellis Lake is a memory-drenched place for me. I remember the time a tow truck driver called our house to say he had our 1963 Ford Falcon. He'd just pulled it out of Ellis Lake, he said. If we wanted it back, we'd have to pay the tow charge. Strange call since we'd sold the car years before. The new owner had never changed the registration. There's a W. T. Ellis monument engraved with his words "Always Watch the Tricky Yuba." It's impossible not to. The Yuba River will be on the right the whole way.

Just out of District 10, headed due east, there's the house where Bob Lebhart, my dad's piano player, once lived—they were in the Air Force band together. This stretch is the doorstep to Loma Rica and the foothills. *Loma* is a Spanish geographical term meaning something like "low, small hill." Right before my early exit from high school as a junior, I worked in Loma Rica for Mr. Arronson, a genius engineer and bleeder. I helped him clear a home lot by hauling small boulders on the chrome rack of my Honda Trail 90—they were sup-posedly Oligocene, Miocene, and Pliocene volcanic rocks. I recall that Mr. Arronson had trouble clotting after being cut, and he was cut often. Everything he touched had a little of his blood on it.

Where the hills start to roll is Spring Valley Road, on the left, once the home of the Japanese American Picnic. Japanese Americans are a tough, resilient people. God knows they've got a right to be indig-nantly bent out of shape. But mostly they're not.

Roosevelt's March 30, 1942, executive order called for all legal Cal-ifornia residents of Japanese ancestry, including the native-born, to surrender themselves for detention. Many of the parents and grand-parents of kids I grew up with obeyed the order. Family names like Tokunaga, Hasegawa, Nakamura, Nakagawa, Kinoshita, and Tahara. The Marysville Assembly Center, a temporary detention camp, held 2,451 of the eventual 97,785 Japanese Californians imprisoned during World War II. All of this just a few miles from Yuba City.

My songwriting guru, Steve Holsapple, graduated from Sacra-mento State University. He codirected and edited two award-winning films aimed at telling the Japanese American story, *Children of the Camps* and *From a Silk Cocoon*. Steve was part of an influential generation of Northern California multimedia artists who came out of Sacramento State University and UC Davis between the late '60s and early '70s, inspired and often taught by José Montoya, Ruth Rippon, William T. Wiley, Wayne Thiebaud, Robert Arneson, and Roy De Forest. I met Steve when he was writing songs for Bonnie Raitt, Dave Mason, and a Sacramento band called Barrelhouse. In addition to his mixed-media artwork, he was also a part-time recording engineer at Moon Studio in Sacramento.

Barrelhouse was a local Sacramento band that had moved to LA to seek their fortune, and Steve followed them. Singer Fred Marrone and Steve cowrote "Keep This Heart in Mind," the lead cut on Bonnie Raitt's *Green Light*. The song, recorded at Shangri-La in Malibu, peaked at No. 39 on the charts. Shangri-La would one day become Rick Rubin's studio, where The Civil Wars took a brief run at working with the famed producer.

Barrelhouse had signed to Family Productions and Homegrown Music in Los Angeles, companies owned by Artie Ripp, notorious for signing Billy Joel to a one-sided publishing and record deal. Musically, Ripp's most egregious act was mastering Joel's debut, *Cold Spring Harbor*, at a pitch higher than it was recorded. Barrelhouse's most memorable night at Ripp's Fidelity Sound Studio in LA would have to be when Phil Spector barged in, pistol in hand, and accused the band of stealing his pizza. They say alcohol and guns don't mix. You can add pizza to that.

Steve wisely returned to Sacramento. He had a destiny to fulfill. It was time for us to meet.

I was gifted a couple hundred dollars to record some songs at David Houston's Moon Studio, my first time in a studio since my two-song fail with Asylum Records as a young teenager.

Steve engineered. I paid for two sessions. After that, he told me there'd be no charge in the future. He'd record me for free. Mutual risk and reward. We started writing songs together. Steve taught me about crafting a lyric and the timing of melodies, especially anticipating or pausing for effect. He's a true brother in imagination and creativity. And, he's one of "the mad ones, the ones who are mad to live." For many years, Steve's painting *Rehearsal* graced the entryway to my Art House recording studio in Nashville. In Steve's unique style, the collage has two major subjects, trumpets and trout. Both dominant themes in my life, thanks to my father and the Yuba River.

I take the Spring Valley Road exit and park at the memory of the Japanese American Picnic.

How fun it was to be invited to the picnic, to play games and hang with our friends and, most deliciously, eat sweet rice balls called onigiri. To this day, fifty-five-plus years later, Andi talks with one of her best friends, Joanne Tokunaga, for a couple of hours on Zoom every four to six weeks (along with two other besties, Jenae and Lynne). My sister, Terri, and I still stay in touch with the Hasegawa family. We were back-fence neighbors in our school days and shared life together.

Another friend I still correspond with is Joanne's cousin, and a former student of my dad's, Phil Nakamura. Phil played several songs at our wedding in 1975, including "Something" by James Taylor and guitarist John McLaughlin, from *One Man Dog*. Phil and his cousin Brian Nakagawa were genius with James Taylor impressions. Brimming with satisfaction, I played trumpet at their Acoustic Electric Concert in 1973. The horn parts on Chicago's "Saturday in the Park" never sounded so enigmatic.

When Andi and I met James Taylor decades later, I believe I may have mentioned his song "Something" and our wedding. (I was babbling and he was kind—that much I do remember.) JT's cowriter, John McLaughlin, had a spiritual guru, Sri Chinmoy, who renamed him Mahavishnu. This led to McLaughlin's band name, Mahavishnu Orchestra. (I was in a band that competed in a 1973 high school battle of the bands with songs from Mahavishnu's *Birds of Fire* and Miles Davis's *Jack Johnson*. Records like these set the standard for musicianship. We offered a teenage approximation.) Chinmoy also gave spiritual names to Carlos Santana (Devadip) and Michael Walden (Narada). Waxing on Sri Chinmoy, Santana told *Rolling Stone*, "I am the strings, but he is the musician. Guru has graduated from the Harvards of consciousness and sits at the feet of God."[3]

Farther up Highway 20, there's the Browns Valley exit and a very faint reminder of the Barbaccia boys' racetrack. I played in a band with Phil Barbaccia, saxophonist and son of a prune farmer—and another student of my dad's. Mr. Barbaccia built his boys an asphalt track for their small-scale race cars. Over the years the elements swallowed it whole. The last time I looked for it, all I could make out was an impression, and not the thing itself.

I performed at a party in the same area for Shakey Johnson, the West Coast pizza pioneer. Other area mavericks I've played for are the late Tower Records founder Russ Solomon and eccentric litigator Melvin Belli (played on his yacht as it sat docked on the Sacramento River). Men like these kept the Old West bravado alive in the late twentieth century.

In 1968, when I was twelve, the last dredge on the Yuba River at the Hammonton gold field was shut down. Phil Barbaccia, David Parker, Craig Kearney, and I played a gig in a field off Plantz Road in the Hammonton area maybe four years later. Probably made twenty bucks each making nice at a high school student's senior party.

Gold fields run all along the Yuba River, pocking a patchwork landscape of westerly flowing water. There are hundreds of dredger ponds, and an incalculable amount of gravel and rock, dredge, and hydraulic mine debris. The Yuba was the most heavily mined of any watershed in the Sierra Nevada. More gold has been taken out of the Yuba River than any other river in the Lower 48. Mining camps lined the Yuba from Marysville up to the towns of Grass Valley, Nevada City, and beyond.

Hydraulic mining is what really changed the shape of the watershed, though. Gold panning was always the most primitive means of getting at the shiny stuff, and factually, panning is really prospecting, not mining. By the 1870s, miners used water cannons to break up the canyon walls. With plenty of water, they could blast the hell out of the countryside, and they did, catching the gold in sluice boxes while the rest of the sediment washed into the Yuba. It's said that three times as much earth washed down the Yuba River than was excavated during the construction of the Panama Canal. In some places the mining waste caused the riverbed to rise as much as eighty feet.

Unfortunately, it took a decade or more for people to realize hydraulic mining was not a sustainable activity unless, of course, your goal was total destruction of the earth. In 1884, Judge Lorenzo Sawyer put an end to hydraulic mining for good. All that's left now are the many scars of a radically bad choice. Thankfully, in the ensuing years, Gary Snyder and his like have given the land needed TLC via the Yuba Watershed Institute.

At seven hundred feet above sea level, the road is increasingly steeper.

Just down from the Parks Bar Bridge I drive through a wisp of a Gold Rush–era town named Smartsville. There's a calm stretch of the Yuba where Andi and I once skinny-dipped. I remember fearing that my neighbors, pilots Capt. Don Stanley and Major Bowles, might be flying overhead in their SR-71 spy plane. With superior magnification, or infrared, they might detect us unclothed. I needed to stay on Captain Stanley's good side: he loaned me his Teac 4-Track reel-to-reel tape recorder—a marked improvement over my pawnshop recorders and sound-on-sound setup.

Detection from the sky is not as far-fetched as it might seem. I was raised with the SR-71 spy plane looming as a ubiquitous icon in the clouds. With Beale Air Force Base nearby, the sound of a sonic boom was commonplace. It's one of the most significant sounds of my childhood, next to the trumpet and my grandma Williamson calling my name like you'd call a cat at dinner time.

Proximity to an air base can be dangerous.

In 1961, when I was five years old, the crew of a B-52 bailed out at 10,000 feet over our Yuba City. Crash imminent, the commander stayed with the aircraft, steering it away from us. The two nuclear weapons on board were torn from the aircraft on impact. Safety devices worked. No nuclear contamination.

I included a song I wrote, titled "Climb a Tree," on my *Everything That's on My Mind* album in 1995.

> So I went back to my little town, climbed a tree and had
>   a look
> There goes ol' singing John without his helmet on and the
>   rice fields are burning
> The Feather, she's a-churning under the 10th street bridge
> And there's an SR-71's vapor trail, and you come to
>   my mind.[4]

Risking hubris, I'm pretty confident no other song in the known world name-checks this particular spy plane.

Next up along Highway 20 is the mining camp, Timbuctoo, then Hammonton-Smartville Road. The road is the back entrance to Beale Air Force Base. As newlyweds, our second house was on Hammonton Road near Yuba College. Wasn't really a house. It was a Quonset hut, likely one sold as surplus from Beale. Andi's mother cried when she saw where we were living—prescient tears. The hut was rodent-infested. We used the oven exactly once. The smell of toasted mouse was one strong culinary buzzkill. My favorite memory of the hut was drummer Craig Kearney in our "living room" reading aloud from Richard Brautigan's *Trout Fishing in America*, amplified by our band's PA system. We eventually would move on to Sacramento and our destiny after a few months in the mousy, musty hut.

Further up the foothills, University of California Sierra Field Station is just off Scott Forbes Road. This is the general area where bassist Dan Barth lived for a short time. I don't mean in a house. This was the 1970s. This land once belonged to Hill Nisenan, a tribe of Southern Maidu. When I heard Dan was camped out up there, I imagined him in the shade of an old oak tree, creekside, grinding acorns into meal.

With a fire and an old-school coffee can, you can heat water to pour over the conical acorns and draw out their natural bitterness. Dan might have had a little wheat flour or germ for baking a primitive bread of sorts. If you know what you're doing, you don't need anything but what the foothills provide. Every plant has meaning, every meaning a shade of color, and every color a contribution to the uniqueness of place. Just find yourself some acorns, berries, willows, deergrass, and wild onions. There are some broadleaf maples, and some foothill pines like the gray, but most trees are blue oaks or live oaks—the source of the acorns. Interior live oaks are evergreen while blue oaks are bare come winter. The hills are marked with chaparral species like manzanita, and madrone. Dan knew all this sort of information and still does, I imagine. He's all about conservation. For years he fought to keep the Sutter Buttes free of commercialism and development.

Dan was the first bass player in the first real band I ever played in, Blind Horse. Dan was a few years older than me, had a car, a Fender bass, and, like my Kerouac guide David Parker, knew secrets.

Dan was the one who taught me about KPFA in Berkeley and KSAN in San Francisco and how to put up an antenna in my bedroom window to draw in their signals. Once dialed in, I had access to the world I wanted to inhabit. I wasn't landlocked in my little farm town anymore. Rock and Roll Hall of Famer "Big Daddy" Tom Donahue worked at KSAN back then. He'd been responsible for signing The Beau Brummels to his Autumn Records. Staff producer Sylvester Stewart produced their hit "Laugh Laugh." Later, he did all right: changed his name to Sly Stone. As a DJ, Donahue was the original architect of underground radio. Sacramento's KZAP modeled themselves after KSAN. Years later, Tom's widow, Rachel, allowed me to write at the house she shared in Los Angeles with keyboardist Murphy Dunne of Blues Brothers fame. He had a Wurlitzer electric piano in the house. A 200-A, like my first electric piano.

Dan Barth introduced me to possibilities far beyond my zip code, yet taught me to appreciate the beauty under my feet. Dan taught me how to tie-dye and how to make bread in a coffee can. He was the first to play me Coltrane's *A Love Supreme*. He took me to Oakland to hear Ray Charles and Ike and Tina Turner. His tutelage was righteous and life changing. I owe him a debt of thanks—he gave me a bigger world than I was born with.

Pleasant Valley Road is the exit for the Bridgeport Covered Bridge spanning the South Fork of the Yuba River. Go that direction and you're driving on what used to be the Virginia Turnpike Company toll road. It ran between the Nevada County mines and the Comstock Mines in Virginia City, Nevada (which was still Utah Territory when silver was discovered in 1858). I once saw a photo of Comstock miners with the caption, "To Labor Is to Pray."

Indeed. Like a lot of created things during that time, the covered bridge (and toll road) came into being because a whole lot of gold and silver came into view. It's been called the longest single-span covered bridge in the US, but apparently that claim stands or falls on how you measure it. Measure wrong, and there's one in New York State that'll beat it, and another one in Stanislaus County, California. There are many human supremacy claims of a tenuous nature. The longer you live, the more apparent this becomes.

When I think of Bridgeport, and that's what we called it, I think of only one thing: skinny-dipping. We used to park at the bridge and walk upstream a bit to what amounted to a beach and an ad hoc gathering of uninhibited folks. That place erased any remaining mysteries surrounding the human form. (In retrospect, it would have been better to let mystery prevail.) Bridgeport is still going on today, though, and on occasion people get their panties in a wad about it. At least they're wearing panties. As I recall, one disgruntled director of a local pro-family-values group asserted, "If you believe in God and family, you're not going to go along with people running around naked." Fair enough, but one person's "God and family" is, well, not quite another person's God and family.

With this sort of debate on his mind, a traveler can be assured that Nevada City is near.

In Nevada City, at 2,500 feet, they've been tinkering with God and family since the electric kool-aid acid test began its decline. Hippies and back-to-the-land types saw Nevada City as the antidote to the unlovely love-in that San Francisco had become. The counterculture and communes took to the hills. Even the preeminent Dharma Bum himself, Gary Snyder, set up camp on the ridge in North San Juan (outside Nevada City) practicing the Zen life and deep ecology at a place he named Kitkitdizze. During the Gold Rush, the ridge played a dominant role in hydraulic gold mining. It was a nexus for water sent by flume out of lakes up around Bowman and then distributed to various mines downhill.

In my day it was the closest counterculture nexus; a place to get gigs playing original music; and the home of KMVR, a free-form public radio station (the first to interview me and Steve Holsapple and play our single "No Magazines"). Friends I played in bands with nearly fifty years ago, Scott Usedom, Lorraine Gervais, and Larry Casserly, still live there making music—and Larry, a DJ at KMVR.

I bought Snyder's Pulitzer-winning *Turtle Island* at Lawrence Ferlinghetti's City Lights Bookstore in San Francisco in 1975. It remains a tacit requirement that every disciple of the Beats make the pilgrimage to City Lights, and preferably purchase a book or a Kerouac book bag. Andi and I have never had any trouble buying books, even as paupers. My son-in-law has suggested that we do a deep purge before shedding our mortal bodies. We'll take it under consideration, later. (As providence would have it, we are blessed to have author Ann Patchett's Parnassus Books just around the corner from our Nashville home. She makes off with our money, often.)

We were introduced to the multihyphenate agrarian writer Wendell Berry after our eventual move to Nashville in 1989. I took notice that our alternative newsweekly, the *Nashville Scene*, liked to quote and name-check Mr. Berry and a fellow named Will Campbell. With that, our bookshelves expanded to fit their works, and in particular, the Wendell Berry canon. Wendell reminded me of what I admired about Gary Snyder with his adoration of the confluence of land and art. (Of course, there would be a direct link between where I'd been and where I was going.) Just for pure fun, I name-checked Mr. Berry in the song "Wendell Berry in the Fields at Night" on my 2018 jazz release, *When Light Flashes*.

I'm never surprised anymore who reads and respects Mr. Berry. I observed songwriting legend J. D. Souther perusing our bookshelves one afternoon, "Ah, Wendell Berry," he said. I didn't name-check J. D. Souther explicitly in a song, but I did reflect on the writer of such American classics as "Heartache Tonight," "Best of My Love," and "New Kid in Town," in my song "Deep Inside a Word":

> Tall and thin, he bends with the wind
> At every place a body breaks he bends
> And the stories, such stories he tells
> From a view very few know well
> Oh the humor, the insight, and the will to never age
> He's a Texas troubadour, a California sage.[5]

And then the universe gets set right in some significant way with this factoid: Gary Snyder exchanged over 240 letters between 1973 and 2013 with Wendell Berry. They are bound together in *Distant Neighbors: The Selected Letters of Wendell Berry & Gary Snyder*.

Two men, distant neighbors, in the great Membership of the Neighborhood. Both integrated with the land—wise, artistic, and word stewards of the highest rank. Both making evident a new mindset of openness and generosity to people and place. One, a Christian in Henry County, Kentucky, the other a Zen Buddhist up on San Juan Ridge in the Northern California of my birth.

> I come into the peace of wild things
> who do not tax their lives with forethought
> of grief. I come into the presence of still water.
> And I feel above me the day-blind stars
> waiting with their light. For a time
> I rest in the grace of the world, and am free.[6]

Also on the San Juan Ridge is Ananda Village, a commune based on the teachings of Paramhansa Yogananda, author of *Autobiography of a Yogi*. In my generation, it was de rigueur for musicians on a spiritual search to read at least a few chapters of this book. Swami Kriyananda (J. Donald Walters), self-proclaimed "direct disciple" of Yogananda, founded Ananda Village in 1968 with the dream of a cooperative spiritual community shaped by "plain living and high thinking."

Gary Snyder, Swami Kriyananda, and poet Allen Ginsberg purchased 160 acres of land on the ridge in the late 1960s. The plan was for each one to build a simple home. Snyder didn't anticipate that Kriyananda had in mind a three-hundred-person spiritual community. It had been his understanding that all Kriyananda wanted was a personal cabin. Not quite. Ananda is now 900 acres and hundreds of residents, complete with complex living problems, like cult-busting lawyers and nosy sociologists.

In 1975, Andi and I toured Ananda Village up on the ridge. We were on a field trip with a group of sociology students. While only mildly interested in the swami's teachings, the yurts, geodesic domes, and other alternative housing options captured us.

Suburbia would not do for Andi and me. We held the economically untested belief that one's dwelling should, as much as possible, represent the way one views the world. In our case, that meant almost anything other than the status quo. That day at Ananda, *Whole Earth*

Catalog, Foxfire, and a book titled *Woodstock Handmade Houses* had no small effect on us.

In 1992 we created a hybrid home/studio out of a country church—the place where we lived and moved and had our being for twenty-five years. Long before our residency, the old Methodist church in Bellevue, Tennessee, housed a small commune of families. According to longtime residents of Bellevue, the commune folks were often seen "runnin' around naked." Though we had some experience in such things during our Bridgeport days, I must say it never caught on under our watch.

Nevada City is the end of the road but not the story. Paraphrasing Kerouac, *what's to come is too fantastic not to tell.*

Like the interconnectedness of Snyder and Berry, there's a through-line from Ananda and Paramhansa Yogananda on San Juan Ridge and the rock band Switchfoot and their hometown of Encinitas.

When working or vacationing in the San Diego area, I love to eat breakfast at Swami's Café on the Pacific Coast Highway (PCH) in Encinitas (the word "swami" means teacher or guide). It was Switchfoot singer-songwriter Jon Foreman that first took me there for the best açaí bowl around. I signed Jon, brother Tim, and Chad Butler to my record label re:think in late 1996, and Switchfoot was born with their first release in 1997, *The Legend of Chin*. The love I have for these three men is infinite. We changed each other's lives for the better and, by common report, added more to the beauty than detracted from it.

If to be *mad to live and desirous of everything* is a way of seeing, what you see across the street from Swami's is the Self-Realization Fellowship, the site of Paramhansa Yogananda's Hermitage, where he lived for many years and wrote his famous *Autobiography of a Yogi*. According to biographer Walter Isaacson, Steve Jobs read the book as a teenager. Then reread it on a trip to India, and up until his death, had read it every year since. Attendees at Jobs's memorial service were each given a small brown box. Inside, a copy of the book. I wonder if Jobs ever visited Ananda Village on the ridge or the Hermitage in Encinitas?

I took a class at Covenant Theological Seminary with a student born in Sri Lanka named Ananda (meaning "extreme joy and happiness"). He told me his favorite song of mine was "In the Light"—a song about the duplicity of trying to find a life on your own apart from God, yet desiring to be in the light as God is in the light. According to my classmate Ananda, "In the subcontinent, the name (Ananda) is as common as John." You may recall that former Motown drummer Aaron Smith had once been a Yogananda disciple. Aaron plays drums on both mine and dc Talk's version of "In the Light"—a fact that gives me *extreme joy and happiness.*

Just across the Pacific Coast Highway, next to the Hermitage, is Seacliff Roadside Park. Here you can climb down the steep stairs to the beach known as Swami's—something I did once with Ruby before either of us could have imagined that one day she'd be my daughter-in-law.

This stretch of the PCH—Cardiff, Encinitas, and Carlsbad—is Switchfoot ground zero. We've made some lifetime memories in this place, so different from any locale in my ancestry, except for Sangano Beach outside Luanda, Angola, which uncannily resembles Swami's Beach. Not only has our life been deeply enriched by our connection to Switchfoot, but we count Jon and Tim Foreman's parents, Jan and Mark, as some of our favorite people. We are student-followers of the same teacher, Jesus. In the Jesus way or tradition, the honorific in English is Teacher or, in the Aramaic language of Jesus, Rabboni. Very similar to the Hebrew Rabbi.

This deep history is why it made perfect sense to invite Mark to attend the ASCAP (American Society of Composers, Authors and Publishers) Pop Awards in Los Angeles, May 16, 2005. Switchfoot and our publishing company received an airplay award for the hit song "Meant to Live" (reaching No. 6 on *Billboard*'s Mainstream Top 40 Chart). Because the band was on tour, Mark received his son's medals of honor for the achievement. We sat with Eddie DeGarmo from EMI and in general had a good time, with one exception.

Neil Young received a lifetime achievement award, and the Indigo Girls sang one of his songs in the tribute. But the talented duo's performance was uncharacteristically dismal. Overwhelmed by empathy, I thought I might go into cardiac arrest—no exaggeration, my chest was tightening. Which reminded me of attending a 1981 William Burroughs and John Giorno reading at Keystone Korner in San Francisco, where Old Bull Lee (Burroughs) read from "Twilight's Last Gleaming" and used the phrase "cardiac arrest" with unrestrained liberality.

Every performing artist knows the embarrassment of a dramatic failure or two. The Indigo Girls' lasting career has more than redeemed this skip in the time/space continuum. I claim the same for my own all-too-human embarrassments. Including the time I sang a duet with Ashley Cleveland at an EMI sales conference, disassociated, and warbled absolute nonsense lyrics to "Slippery Pearls," a song I cowrote with Douglas McKelvey.

As for the rest of the awardees, Mariah Carey was a star, Jermaine Dupri was elfish and seemingly vainglorious, and Mo Ostin, former president of Warner Brothers Records, with wisdom and eloquence in a speech honoring Neil, proved they don't make them like Mo Ostin anymore. I told producer Narada Michael Walden (a Mahavishnu Orchestra alumni), sporting his Hammer-time '80s getup, that he should start playing jazz again. I think he agreed, and in fact has (though I suspect not due to my encouragement). Then Mark and I left the building. Mark to the south, me to the south, but different definitions of the south.

If you're ever at Swami's Beach in Encinitas, look out to the horizon and you might see Mark Foreman, in the surf on his longboard, waiting in the lineup for the next epic wave.

Aren't we all.

I began this road trip of interdependence and nonneutrality with dirt and water, then traveled alongside a riverbed of rock and water, and ended with sand and water, the great Pacific Ocean. Each combination of nature having a glory and a woundedness. Each one, home—a locale for learning and memory making. They are, *people and place*, so entwined in ever-evolving community and story as to never be ripped from the grip of history—certainly not my memory.

The interdependence of all I see, touch, and feel—all I encounter with every stitch of my person—makes me *mad for life and desirous of everything*. This curiosity and passion "on the road to heaven" set the stage for good—bearing fruit in music, art, and the Membership of the Neighborhood, here on *tierra buena*.

fourteen

EVERYONE AND EVERYTHING, A ROLE TO PLAY

If you follow the Sacramento River from Shasta to the San Francisco Bay, you will see the river make a little jog west around the Sutter Buttes. It's that stretch of river, out past the town of Meridian, that I know best. Farther downstream, on the west bank of the river about forty-five minutes south of Sacramento, is Rio Vista. In 1985, a forty-foot, eighty-thousand-pound whale named Humphrey swam under the Golden Gate Bridge into the bay, up the Sacramento River past the Rio Vista Bridge, to Shag Slough, west of Sutter Island. Nearly beached in the shallow slough, sixty-nine miles from the Pacific Ocean, Humphrey the Whale became the most famous humpback in the history of the species. "It's a federal whale," said a government official overseeing the historic rescue.

The Feds spent some money and hired a musician as part of their rescue plan. In order to entice him back to open waters, Bernie Krause, a bio-acoustician, played recordings of the feeding sounds of Humphrey's kin. Krause, former member of the folk group The Weavers, got Humphrey turned around. Prior to working with the whale, Krause's credits included Country Joe and the Fish, George Harrison of The Beatles, The Monkees, and Jane Goodall, naturally. I once consulted Bernie for a gig I was doing with Paul Blaise and the Art Directors and Artists Club (ADAC) in Sacramento. Before I was a legit record producer, I won a dozen or more ADAC Awards for such enigmatic musical compositions as Crystal Dairy Sour Cream and Caltrans's "Small Orange Cone."

People lined the banks of the Sacramento River for miles to cheer on the homeward-bound Humphrey. Inspired by the familiar sounds of family and the prospect of dinner, he had turned around and was returning to open water. We followed the action on TV from the comfort of our living room. At Nantucket Fish Co., a restaurant in Crockett near the Benicia Bridge, whale watchers waited patiently for Humphrey's appearance. When the wayward whale came into view, restaurant help and customers gathered on the pier outside. They cheered and partied and felt lighter in the world for having paused to care for and delight in something other than themselves.

How do you explain such a skip in the universal flow of things? Whale-ologists suggested a sickness, perhaps parasites on the brain, or an inner ear infection. The fact is, whale or man can find themselves on the wrong side of the river, stuck in the shallows. Yet somehow, lost mammals large and small are shown cosmic favor to turn and return. As the eminent theologian J. I. Packer once explained rhetorically to Andi and me, "It's all of Grace then, isn't it?" Grace is a river, too.

The Sacramento River in Northern California is a long 447 miles, flowing south from upstate near Mount Shasta in the Cascades. The river acts like a person who has lived long enough to know when to reserve speech. No great, world-changing utterances, just a steady flow of who and what she is. The Sacramento can be brooding but never menacing. That is, unless you dive to the bottom and sup with the giants: white sturgeon capable of living well over a hundred years, growing to eight to twelve feet and a thousand pounds or more.

I've spent many a fishing hour out on the Sacramento with my dad and one of two uncles—either Uncle Ron the Barber or Uncle Walt the Engineer. We were normally on the hunt for stripers or salmon. If you're using sardines for bait, you can hook a sturgeon now and again. Uncle Ron the Barber had a clever trick. He doused his hands with Vitalis before tying the sardine on the hook. He said it kept suspicious fish from detecting human scent. A man ahead of his time. Vitalis, normally used for healthy, handsome hair, repurposed for grander achievements. Genius.

If you really want a sturgeon, though, you should go sturgeon fishing, which means you should be prepared to actually catch one. Most fishermen are not. We certainly never were. You know you've hooked a big sturgeon when it peels the line off your reel. If your line doesn't break (it usually does), then you let the prehistoric monster pull you up and down the river for about an hour. I say an hour because most people can hold a dream in their hearts for at least an hour. Usually, after an hour, with no sign of the fish ever rising from the bottom, you lose your dream to a consigned realism. The hopeful thought of landing the largest freshwater fish in North America degenerates into "I don't know, man, why don't we just cut the line?" Every bone and muscle aches and you're sweating like a stuck pig, but it's not all loss. You've got yourself a good story, and stories are good medicine.

One day, my dad, Uncle Walt the Engineer, and I were fishing for stripers out on the Sacramento when we heard an awful wailing. At a distance, echoing down the river, it sounded like a woman or child in horrible pain. We pulled up anchor and headed toward the sound. Soon we could see the cry for help wasn't human at all. In a flash, I understood the colloquialism "sweatin' like a stuck pig." Hopelessly tangled in the Himalayan blackberry vines covering the riverbank was, in fact, a stuck pig and, given the ninety-degree heat, likely one sweating. The bank was so steep and the vines so thick there was no way of rescuing the poor creature.

With the full faculties of my twelve-year-old mind, I pondered that pig a while. My grandparents or great-grandparents never bothered with pigs that I knew of. There were chickens, turkeys, and goats for me to know and to develop opinions and reflections on, but no pigs. Still, you pick up things along the way, bumping into pig knowledge, especially pig physiology. For example, a pig's penis is shaped like a corkscrew, the spiral taking the form of a left-hand thread. Also, you will never meet a star-gazing pig. While standing, it's physically impossible for a pig to look up into the sky.

My wife and I had a beloved history professor at Covenant Seminary in St. Louis who collected pig likenesses to aid in remembering the church's most egregious heresies. Dr. Calhoun used drawings of a Gnostic pig and a Donatist pig—that sort of thing—the latter pig guilty of requiring that only the purest of priests administer the sacraments. If you know anything about Christianity, you know that pure moral character, as in completely undiluted, is a fantasy.

—

The first possible impression any person might have going north on Highway 99 from Sacramento is that they're right in the center of a very flat valley, filled with farms stretched thin east and west all the way to the foothills. Two-story stucco houses and condominiums with a yardstick of space between them encroach on the rice fields from the south. With the coast range to your left, the Sierras to your right, and the Sutter Buttes at about ten o'clock, it's all farmland from Sacramento to our hometown of Yuba City. Yuba City and its little sister, Marysville, are threaded by Highway 20, the gateway out of the valley into the foothills and on to the Sierras, where granite and pine build a nest for the snow.

Listed in federal records as the World's Smallest Mountain Range, the Sutter Buttes silhouetted against the horizon are as familiar to me as anything from my childhood. Los Tres Picos, South, North, and West, a geological trinity keeping watch over all of life. It's said that a Spaniard named Gabriel Moraga was the first European to see the Buttes in 1806. Each time I steer the rental car onto 99 north, I'm watching for the Buttes to appear on the horizon. Sometimes, if the rice fields are burning, it takes a while to see the Buttes' glory. Eventually they emerge, and what I've always counted on in an uncertain world is known again.

The Maidu people called the ranges Histum Yani. Translated, it means "Middle Mountains of the Valley." For some it meant "Spirit Mountain," giving weight to the story that after death, the spirits of the Maidu would rest in the Buttes. In the stories my people hold close, our spirits go to be with Yeshua the Christ, Emmanuel or God with Us, and our bodies rest at the foot of the Buttes in the Sutter Cemetery.

Swiss-German immigrant John Sutter is credited with setting something in motion that my family participated in—the making of Sutter County agriculture. This is especially true of my mother's family and the first four generations who worked the orchards and canneries (which includes me). It was Sutter's wealth that created the footprint for fruit and nut trees in Sutter County. Even today, on the exact site of Sutter's farm is Sierra Gold Nurseries and miles of young trees supplying orchards in and around the state. All the old names, like Sutter and Fremont, so ubiquitous to home and place, drip with meaning (not always the good kind).

Because the Sutter Buttes are mostly private property, they're not a place you visit easily, except to circumnavigate, which I've done in memorable fashion: one dark night, driving to the Gridley Fair, a chunk of meteorite crashed to earth in front of our car. Scared the hell out of all of us—me, my aunt Karoly, and Uncle Jim Durbin. We looked around for UFOs—but none in sight. This encounter with matter from beyond is as visceral today as it was then.

We'd gone over to Gridley to see Kenny Rogers sing "Ruby, Don't Take Your Love to Town." Pat Buttram (Mr. Haney on *Green Acres*) opened up for Kenny. Mr. Buttram, from rural Alabama, the son of a circuit-riding Methodist preacher, wasn't as far from home as he might have thought. The only difference then between rural Alabama and rural Gridley, California, was about two thousand miles. I'm sure it suited Mr. Buttram fine. He'd worked with Gene Autry, the singing cowboy, and understood firsthand the humor of the rural (and even cowboy) life. My uncle Jim was a cowboy then—still is. Back then, in the late sixties, Jim worked for a San Francisco doctor who owned a ranch in the Buttes and a small herd of cattle. Most of the ranch was planted in alfalfa or grain hay (oat or wheat). You plant in the fall and reap in May. It's good habitat for pheasants, the ringneck variety, first introduced from China to the Willamette Valley in Oregon in the year 1881. I've fished the Willamette River for trout and steelhead, and it's beautiful country. South Dakota named the ringneck its state bird. In Sutter County every good bird has its season. September is dove, October is duck and geese, and November is pheasant.

Several ranches that spill out from the Buttes double as hunting clubs of some variety of bird during late summer and fall. I recall that iconic crooner Bing Crosby, once a frequent hunting visitor to the Sutter Basin, called the season "The time for the ducks and the quail and the pheasants, and for getting reacquainted with your dog."

Uncle Jim's vocation as caretaker and cowboy was my good fortune. It allowed me access to the Buttes, and over time, took a little of the fright and mystery out of them for me. I'd always been scared of the rock fences said to be built by Native Americans and Chinese. Those fences chilled my insides. Did they whisper a tale of subjugation that my "sensitive kid" radar picked up on? It didn't help that hunters tied the skins of dead coyotes to the barbed wire that ran for miles as a nasty helpmate to the stacked volcanic stone. Ranchers paid hunters a fair price to keep the Buttes clear of varmints. If it weren't for Uncle Jim, those dead skins would've kept me clear.

Dry and rocky, the Buttes always appeared old and from another time. They were like a scar on your skin that holds some long, complex story you don't bring up unless someone asks you about it. Some of us knew the history of the Buttes and the Maidu stories. Some of us knew the Buttes were west of town, and that's about all. That's the way it is with most kids, though: you don't care much about history until you get some of your own.

—

There's a landscape painting, *Hock Farm* by William Smith Jewett (1812–1873), depicting a view of the Butte Mountains from the Feather River looking west. Jewett's painting illustrates something of the grandness of the legendary farm of John Sutter, with the outline of the Buttes in the background (which didn't officially become the "Sutter" Buttes until 1949). Art is good at making monuments and markers. It's good at truth telling and good at stretching the truth. Sometimes art adds more glory to a place, person, or thing than it deserves; sometimes it mutes it or hides it altogether. Artists by their nature tinker with reality. They expand and contract what is. In this case, the painting mutes the early Spanish and Mexican colonization of the land taken from the indigenous people and the foreboding future of Hock Farm. John Sutter, like Humphrey the federal whale, would be caught in the shallows and far from home soon enough.

Mexican California was ripe for a man with big ideas. Like entrepreneurial immigrants before him, Johann August Suter changed his name and planned for empire building. "Suter" became "Sutter," and the land of peaceful Maidu was quickly taken over by agriculture, industry, and the darker ambitions of the human heart. Sutter learned everything he needed to know about the stuff of a self-interest economy: cheap labor, cheap materials, and influential friends. This is something every person in the business of making a name for himself or herself knows. Despite Babel's warning, history is a parade of humanity desperate to make a name for itself. Sutter's imaginative and creative choices, as self-serving as they were, set in motion the mass population of the West, shaping the territory into a jewel in the crown of the United States of America. Sutter made a name for himself, all right. One that people today, especially in California, are happy to co-opt for their own name-making purposes, from the promotion of wine to health care. Between Yuba City and Sacramento alone, the number of times Sutter's name is appropriated for monetization and branding would astound the first-time visitor.

When someone's name is that pervasive, you've got to ask why. What makes some personal fame timeless? What kind of spirit embeds itself in words and names to give them oomph? Mother Teresa and the Kardashians are all famous, but for wildly different reasons.

The story goes that one year after arriving in California, John Sutter became a naturalized Mexican citizen. This qualified him for a land grant, which he obtained the following year. The governor granted Sutter forty-eight thousand acres of land to the north and east of Yerba Buena (later to be named San Francisco). Sutter got more than land; he received power, too. The governor authorized Sutter to function as judge and jury, and by all means "to prevent the robberies committed by adventurers from the United States, to stop the invasion of savage Indians and the hunting and trapping by companies from the Columbia."

How Sutter came about such authority so quickly can only be explained by a very old method of making life work: pure deceit. At one time or another, most of us feel compelled to be someone or something other than who or what we are. Perhaps, especially so, those in the entertainment business. I know this temptation well. It's easy to think that being me is not good enough. I have to be me plus something. Sutter was no exception.

It is a strange by-product of life that a lie often feels safer, more reliable than the truth. I've known many people who would rather believe the lie they know than the truth they've just met (not excluding myself). Somewhere along the way Sutter, the bankrupt adventurer, imagined for himself a military career, that of a captain of the Swiss Guards of Charles X of France. He parlayed this self-appointed, imaginary military title into several impressive letters of recommendation that he used to establish credit and enlist support. He was nothing if not industrious. Then, as today, name-making achieved through lying is acceptable for the attainment of power. Even more acceptable, thinks the liar, when the power one seeks is believed to be righteously motivated.

In order to truly change the world, though, history shows you've got to have a fort. My childhood in Sutter County was filled with the construction of all manner of forts. It seemed as if we built forts in order to learn to build a life. Sutter built a thick-walled adobe fort with the sweat of Hawaiian, Kanakas, and indigenous American enslaved and indentured labor. Sutter named his settlement New Helvetia (New Switzerland), but it didn't stick. As with the river, the emerging city was eventually named Sacramento after the most holy sacrament, the Eucharist (or "thank you meal"). It's an irrevocable irony that a city named after the Christ-memory and the promise of freedom and forgiveness for all is in fact built on the backs of the enslaved and underpaid. I think this is why the theologian Cornelius Plantinga Jr. described sin as something/anything "not the way it's supposed to be."

John Sutter ruled over the intersection of immigrants coming west from the Great Salt Lake and south from Oregon. As faulty as his motivations were, the broad scope of Sutter's authority and infrastructure laid the groundwork for millions to venture west, including my family eighty years later. His empire included thirteen thousand head of cattle, a tannery, acres of Castile roses, a distillery, and the aforementioned agricultural utopia known as Hock Farm on the west bank of the Feather River (just south of what is now Yuba City).

Like Yuba City, Hock Farm was built on the site of a Nisenan (Maidu) village. Subjugation of the indigenous people and anyone else with brown skin was the business plan. With his achievements and new wealth, John Sutter's initial misfortunes had been more than reversed. Life was working again. Then came the pivotal, cosmic moment. The shout heard round the world.

On January 24, 1848, a millwright named James Marshall discovered gold at the Coloma sawmill Sutter had partnered with him to build. Marshall rushed down the hill to give Sutter the news—and the shape of California and the West changed forever.

The Gold Rush ruined Sutter. His workers left him for the gold fields; squatters took over his land, destroyed crops, and helped themselves to his prodigious herds. By 1852, Sutter was in no better shape than when he left Germany. He wrote in his diary: "By this sudden discovery of the gold, all my great plans were destroyed. Had I succeeded for a few years before the gold was discovered, I would have been the richest citizen on the Pacific shore; but it had to be different. Instead of being rich, I am ruined, and the cause of it is the long delay of the United States Land Commission of the United States Courts . . . but I hope that justice will be done me by the last tribunal—the Supreme Court of the United States."[1]

There is perhaps no human temptation so great as the temptation to put your hope in wealth. Sutter proved to the watching world just how human he was.

Sutter's optimistic naming of the territory New Helvetia brought him no lasting good fortune, strength, or power. Fable speaks of the ancient Helvetii (Sutter's ancestors) as a strong and powerful people. I can't confirm that, but their modern descendants, the Swiss, do keep a fastidiously clean country. Old names and tools weren't enough to overcome justice or gold fever: the reckless and blind ambition that glittering yellow flakes stirred up within dreamers and desperate men. The luckless New Helvetia was dismantled and Sutter bankrupted, proving once again that when humans are tested, it's best to plea for mercy, not justice. Blessed is the person that deserves the latter and receives the former.

Following a devastating fire at Hock Farm, the imaginary captain (and by now calling himself major general) moved his whole lot to the Moravian Christian community at Lititz, Pennsylvania. Moravian theology predisposed the sect to offer hope to fools and losers, those who didn't just sin but were in fact sinners. Their hero, at least the one they owe their very beginnings to, was a preacher and scholar named John Hus. Hus was a Bohemian. Not the bongo-playing variety, but a resident of Bohemia, what would become Czechoslovakia. Hus was an important Christian reformer who predated and forecasted the Protestant Reformation. This knowledge I owe to the uniquely satisfying, pig-analogy-employing professor, Dr. Calhoun. Every field of endeavor has its own humor, though I suspect church historian humor is among the most dry and arcane. Musician humor tends toward the less subtle: "You know how you get a musician off your porch, don't you? Just pay him for the pizza, he'll leave."

There's nothing funny about John Hus, though. Hus was rector of the University of Prague and preached from the pulpit of the chapel of Bethlehem. The archbishop of Prague, a critic of Hus's, convinced the pope to silence Hus's preaching. But Hus disobeyed and continued to preach. Within a year he was excommunicated. Though John Hus respected the papal office, he sharply disagreed with Pisan antipope John XXIII's selling of indulgences. According to John Hus, the Bible left no wiggle room for such things. Hus wondered how one could sell what only God could freely grant.

And so it went for Hus; calling for reform and receiving rebuke. Eventually, papal authorities dressed him in the garb of a priest, shaved his head, and donned it with a demon-decorated paper crown. Then they tied him to a stake and burnt him alive. In the tradition of Saint Stephen, it is recorded that he prayed, "Lord Jesus, it is for thee that I patiently endure this cruel death. I pray thee to have mercy on my enemies."

Over time, the Hussites, a powerful group of Bohemian reformers influenced by the martyr, gave birth to a splinter cell, the Unity of Brethren, later called Moravians. It was this group, now in America, that Sutter found refuge with. The Moravians in Lititz, Pennsylvania, had received generous help from Count Nikolaus Ludwig von Zinzendorf, the godson of Philipp Jakob Spener, the father of pietism. Through the patronage of Zinzendorf, and a generous gift of property from George Kline, the community of Lititz was founded, taking its name from the Bohemian castle that provided refuge to Moravians in the time of Hus. Once again, the old world had come to the new.

All ideas and actions have consequences. Every life is a history-changing life. Here I am, a musician in the twenty-first century writing about the interconnectedness of John Hus, the Moravians, John Sutter, Lititz, Yuba City, and me. The ability to ferret out the interconnectedness of people, place, thing, and idea, and see their present and future connectedness is not only the purview of a writer, but one of the most important tools in my musical and artistic toolbox.

Every musical creation I participate in is the imagination intersecting with history. They are all a paradox, simultaneously original and derivative. Observant artists cultivate a curiosity to discover, know, and use the interconnectedness, the interdependence. The ability to combine global, pan-generational musical and lyrical ideas is often the very thing that inspires curious musical artists to create work that is fresh and unique.

I remain very curious as to how Sutter received an invitation to join this community of Moravian Christians. It is lost to history (for now), though I'll never stop looking (I recently purchased a dozen more books looking for the answer). Whatever the story, there's no record of Sutter ever trading the dream of a New Helvetia for the hope of New Jerusalem, the city of the great King. From his refuge in Lititz, Sutter mostly schemed ways to reverse his gold rush misfortune. He was still trying to recover the wealth. Please do not read judgment into that last sentence. Recovery of wealth is the lasting temptation of any musician who was ever extravagantly paid and now isn't. Who wouldn't want, one more time, to write a song and earn $1.5 million for it in a single year? Who wouldn't want, one more time, to play one gig and earn $1 million for a fifty-minute set? Yes, this really happens.

Though the new state of California granted him a pension of $250 a month, Sutter ultimately failed to convince the US government to honor his Mexican land claims. He died from general disappointment in a Washington, DC, hotel in 1880. His body was laid to rest in Lititz, and for the next 150 years the township appropriated his name for tourist trade—there was even a wooden statue of his body that stood at rest in front of the General Sutter Inn. Then George Floyd and the summer of 2020 happened. Celebrating and monetizing oppressors had, for at least half the nation, become shameful and untenable.

On June 18, 2020, the 140th anniversary of Sutter's death, a crew removed the statue. "Just let him drop," one of workers said. News outlet *LancasterOnline* reported: "There was a quiet cheer as the statue fell face-first onto the ground."[2]

As California grammar school students, what we learned about John Sutter was selective, superficial, and void of any ache—Sutter's or anyone else's. I can't speak for today, but in 1967 elementary school, American history wasn't shaped to reveal anything diverse, comprehensive, or transparent. The same oft-noted Euro-American immigrant pioneers got all the ink. I was taught history as information, facts without a context, and far too often, communal lies agreed to and perpetrated by those in power. The bulk of what we studied charted our American progress this way: we discovered a rough-and-tumble land inhabited by uneducated, often violent savages and shaped it into a paradise with our goodness, intellect, imagination, determination, weaponry, know-how, and our assumed affiliation with the one true God. Sadly, a curious child was hard-pressed to learn anything of the incivility and absence of neighbor love that built much of America.

Age-appropriate truth telling is better than lies. Decades later, when the well-researched facts of John Sutter's story were revealed, it angered and sickened me. Jack Forbes, UC Davis American Indian studies professor emeritus, has unreservedly called Sutter "a rapist and enslaver," joining his voice with other academics and researchers in response to all the Sutter branding and memorializing that's gone on for 170-plus years.

In *Slavery and Freedom in Texas: Stories from the Courtroom, 1821– 1871*, Gonzaga University law professor Jason Gillmer has written the most carefully researched narrative on my third great-grandfather, Tapley Abner Ashworth, and the Ashworth family in Texas in the 1800s. His next research project? Race, rights, and the law during the California Gold Rush. With the Sutterness-of-all-things so attached to my personal story, I look forward to Professor Gillmer's take on this decisive era of Northern California history.

Does a careful look at the name making of John Sutter really matter? If I point the spotlight on my own name making, does it matter?

It all matters—every dream, molecule, action, and inaction. Whether you're creating a song or a country, there are no neutral creative choices. Ideas and decisions intersect and affect the whole. Artists tend to come by this way of knowing more naturally since they are always making something that is present, right in front of them. Their work bears witness to the idea that every action and inaction matters. It preaches to them (if I might use the vernacular).

There is a gravity to our personal decisions, to the fruit of our imagination and creativity. Choice by choice, implicit and explicit, in what we commit and omit, we are history makers. Not one person, place, or thing is excluded from making history, from telling a story of presence. Whales and pigs, mountains and rivers, bio-acousticians, and Moravian immigrants all have a role to play.

Sutter County, with its agri-centric culture, shaped a story within me that includes the influence of its namesake, John Sutter. Close proximity to Sutter history had both informed and skewed my perception of him. As a student it was simple to understand him on the whole as a pioneer, fort-builder, founder, and major player in the Gold Rush. It's all right there in the textbook and on the road sign. This is a mental shortcut, a way of quickly organizing what is known into a one-and-done assessment. To understand him in the fullness of his broken humanity is to allow for the kind of cognitive overload that comes with taking in a complex amount of data and trying to make sense of it in a fixed amount of time. Adding frustration to it is the admission that my best efforts at truly knowing Sutter are like the mayfly landing on the eddy of a stream—I have only broken the surface.

I hope I haven't put you off your Friday evening bubble bath, good book, and glass of Sutter Home Chardonnay. Please, carry on.

In America, I sense that concern over the accuracy of the stories we tell one another about our past and present is amplified (maybe even a new season when facts triumph over fiction). Marginalized and once-ignored voices are helping give a fuller, more diverse, and factual account of American history. I welcome this, even when it's shameful, personally. As it is in my own family where great-grandparents came to English America enslaved, then enslaved others generations later in antebellum Texas.

Everyone and Everything, a Role to Play

I want the world to know that my third great-grandfather, Tapley Abner Ashworth, a "free negro ... of African descent" from "the largest free black family in Texas," pioneered the republic and the state, and cattle ranching in particular. He also enslaved at least four other human beings of African descent. Black scholar Carter G. Woodson, who documented my extended Ashworth family, has made the case that arrangements of mutual benefit were made between free Blacks and enslaved Blacks (a means of protecting the enslaved from white ownership). I'd like to think this was the case with my own great-grandfather, but I have no way of knowing or proving it. It is just as likely, reports Woodson, that the existence of a free Black enslaver was fruit of the caste system that existed among Blacks and a form of assimilation to white cultural norms.

Maybe it's the proximity effect again, just my brain tossing out the distractions and getting right to the sum of family = forgiveness. I do find in myself the ability to analyze Great-Grandpa Tap, speak truthfully, and hold out the open hands of forgiveness, of grace. I can imagine a time-traveling episode of sitting with him at supper, hearing his story (perhaps his confession), marveling at how there's a little bit of his voice in my voice. Maybe I'm so bold as to tell him he's wrong about slavery and offer a just and generative way forward.

Will my imagination do the same for Johann August Suter?

It must be obvious by now that I believe in a challenging and often befuddling interconnectedness of ideas. Human failure, call it sin, is a certainty. Perfection, impossible. People (and whales) lose their way. They get lost in the shallows. The friction of skin on circumstance makes the simple twist of turning and heading back to deeper, safer waters seemingly impossible.

Yet, there is a beauty and goodness to humanity (and whales), and the irrepressible will to adapt and live. The imagination and its fruit, creativity, when fueled by love, are immutable, world-changing forces. I've seen a simple cry for help become the first notes of a concerto of courage and change.

I believe in grace, not karma. I can hold to this and still believe we are responsible actors in an earthly drama where ideas and actions have serious consequences. Even when consequences are punitive,

207

grace is on alert, eager to initiate redemption—to bring forth "beauty from ashes." Forgiveness is not forgetting. Grace is not giving up on change. The two in tandem prepare my heart to be the person I want others to be for me.

None of this diminishes or excuses the monumental crimes of commission and omission we have inflicted on one another across time. Ferreting out and telling a deeper, truer, and diverse story of America are the work of the patriot who knows that the American ideal of freedom for all is not achieved through ubiquity and power, or opportunity and wealth for only a few. Only *We the People* will do.

My confession holds out the hope that any one of us, at any time, may have ears to hear. Recognizing the familiar music of our kinfolk, we can turn and return home to be known and nurtured. Even in the first ratcheting clicks of the 180, the communal choir of grace begins to sing a song of promise and invitation. Take my hand, follow my voice. We will turn and return together.

This world and its people are a collaboration, both improvisation and orchestration. Sometimes it sounds like noise and the end of the world as we know it. Count the din of danger as real, but don't be fooled into thinking the music has ended or the voices of good-willed people have been silenced. Sit up straight and focus your hearing. A flute-like sine wave will emerge from the white noise and bloom into new, full frequency, curiously captivating and inspiring music. You won't be the only one hearing it. Or the only one acting on it, making your presence known in a dizzying number of ways.

The best future of art or nation will be created by people who are neither bully entrepreneurs nor pacifists, but activists. Folks who are actively engaged with people and planet, listening and learning, seeking to know and nurture, to imagine and create for the cosmic betterment of everyone and everything.

I tell myself, forget making a name for yourself. That's so 1849. Make a name for others. Make history. Make it good.

fifteen

THE ACADEMY OF THE OBSERVANT LIFE

Ambrose was the bishop of Milan in the fourth century. Among his many achievements, Ambrose championed the antiphonal chant, a European music device not unlike African call and response. His most famous student was Augustine, the world-weary saint with a mind that refused rest. Augustine wrote: "In order to discover the character of people we have only to observe what they love."[1]

I met a contemporary Ambrose once during a trip to New Orleans, just a year before the tragedy of Hurricane Katrina—I call him the Bishop of Transportation. I was on the move visiting musician/actor brothers Jonathan and Richard Jackson on the set of Miramax's teen-horror film *Venom*, a straight-to-DVD/streaming and don't-pass-go release. (If you watched the television show *Nashville*, then you know Jonathan. He played "dead sexy East Nashville hipster" Avery Barkley.)

In 2012, I was contacted by Russell Ziecker at Lionsgate Television to coach Australian actress and singer Clare Bowen, for *Nashville*. Clare's character, Scarlett O'Connor, was scripted to partner in a successful but contentious singing duo with Gunnar Scott, played by British actor Sam Palladio—an obvious nod to The Civil Wars ("obvious" mostly because they said that's exactly what it was). A week passed, and either T Bone Burnett or Buddy Miller (the show's music overseers) decided Clare would be fine without me. Still, Clare and Sam became friends of the family, and I went on to write music for the show, as did Sam and Ruby, who also acted in the final season.

After our rainy visit, Ambrose, a cabbie, ferried me from the French Quarter to the airport. He talked. I listened. He was a street philosopher, a PhD with tenure in the academy of the observant life. Ambrose explained that Al Capone's second in command once managed Louis Armstrong. News to me, but it made a certain kind of jazz sense. He also knew a lot about Dr. John, Pinetop Smith, and Professor Longhair. He told me Fats Domino (born Antoine Dominique) was still living in his original neighborhood, the Lower Ninth Ward: "built that big house, you know."

Three days after Hurricane Katrina, the whereabouts and fate of Fats Domino were still unknown. Yet, because of meeting Ambrose, I understood the Lower Ninth Ward and the context for the unfolding story. Finally, Fats and other family members were rescued by boat, leaving his mansion of pink, yellow, and lavender to the dark fate of mud, mold, and ruin.

Eighty-one-year-old blues icon Clarence "Gatemouth" Brown wasn't as fortunate. He lost his home in Slidell, Louisiana, and then his life in Orange, Texas. Though Brown was already seriously ill with lung cancer when he evacuated Slidell ahead of Hurricane Katrina, it's believed that stress hastened his death. The singer's agent Lance Cowen told the newspapers: "He lost everything except his Firebird guitar and a fiddle."

My music collaborator and Art House North cofounder Sara Groves took her tour bus to Slidell filled with diapers and formula. A young mother herself at the time, it was her way of making neighbor love real. Sara described the area along the east shore of Lake Ponchartrain: "[It was] unbelievable. The houses on the right side of the road were on top of the houses on the left side of the road. A mile inland there was a houseboat in the median of the highway."

That Blues Hall-of-Famer Clarence "Gatemouth" Brown would have to cross the Sabine River from southwest Louisiana only to die in the East Texas town of Orange could not escape my mind. This short trip across the river of cypress has been common for people of color for centuries, going back to before the Louisiana Purchase, and soon after it with the establishment of the Neutral Ground (1806–1821), a.k.a. No Man's Land. My own family, the "fabulous Ashworth clan," zigzagged between No Man's Land on the Louisiana side and the various iterations of Texas, often, to save their very lives.

Tapley Abner Ashworth, my third great-grandfather, is buried in Harris Cemetery in Orange, only four miles southwest of Gatemouth in the Hollywood Cemetery—a Black burial ground closer to the Sabine River. Adding insult to injury, when Hurricane Ike flooded the region three years after Katrina, Mr. Brown burst forth from the grave, though not like Lazarus. According to an Associated Press article, "The top of Brown's vault had popped off, and his bronze casket had floated away. But three jars of Bama grape jelly remained by his aluminum marker."[2] Why jelly? One of the Grammy Award–winner's best-known songs is "Grape Jelly." It was his favorite condiment; he even added it to spaghetti.

One hundred fifty years earlier, my Grandpa Tap Ashworth experienced his own unique insults and injuries. In February 1840, Texas Congress set forth the Ashworth Act, "An Act concerning Free Persons of Color,"[3] which ordered all free Blacks to leave the republic within two years, unless granted an exemption by Congress. No exemption? Refusal to leave? Free persons would be sold into slavery. Legislators buttressed this bit of lawmaking with the argument that the mere presence of free Black people living as responsible, contributing citizens to the Republic of Texas undermined the contention that Blacks were inferior. White settlers, seeing Blacks as fully human, might begin to question the legitimacy of slavery. Which many citizens did, especially as it applied to our family. For several decades in the early history of Texas, the Ashworths and other free persons of color catalyzed both lawmaking and lawbreaking.

The Board of Land Commissioners and various citizens of Jefferson County petitioned the Senate and House of Representatives of the Republic of Texas to exempt Grandpa Tap and his brothers because they were "industrious and orderly"—men who would never have been forced to leave "had there been no taint of blood in their veins." Most notably, the petition informed the Senate and House that the Ashworths came by their Blackness through "great and embarrassing circumstances."

While this language should've been embarrassing and shameful for its racism, it is an artifact of free Black history in the Republic of Texas. These free Black families had little to no agency over their own narrative. Their supportive yet racist white neighbors were their public voice.

In 2005, in the aftermath of Katrina, the great and embarrassing circumstances truly belonged to the US government. Once again, politics and law, race, color, status, and land dictated matters of compassion and compensation. And just as the governing powers chose not to deal with such things back in the days following the Louisiana Purchase, they chose not to deal with such things in our day. The mass displacement, languishing unresolved property damage, and slow movement toward repair in Louisiana post-Katrina went from bad to worse, and quick. As the oft-repeated aphorism goes, *If you want to respect law or sausage, don't watch either one being made.* The laws and policies of governments, both federal and local, failed so miserably it was impossible not to observe that they did not love the safety and wholeness of Black people any more than in Texas in the 1840s.

Like Sara Groves responding to the aftermath of Katrina, love implicates me in every story I have eyes to see. Whether the story is 1840 or 2025. The observant life gives birth to the active life. "Keep your eyes peeled," my father used to tell me. And so I have. Like seeing, listening has never been more important.

Ambrose the writer, the art curator, the street hustler, and the war hero all have something to say. Listen.

At the time of our conversation, Ambrose the cabbie had no idea of the fate that awaited him with Katrina. I hope he lived to tell.

I remember him telling me that "music's good for the soul." I agreed, thinking he had the elder Ambrose, and surely Fats Domino, on his side with words like that. Along with our love of music, the cabbie Ambrose and I had in common that we were both grandfathers, too. We chatted the little ones up with excitement and broad, toothy smiles. The irony of conversing with a stranger is that your individual lives always look very different and personal, but then you strip away the nuance to find a common likeness buried inside a diversity of experiences. Take away money and geography, and we're all just flesh and blood and soul. We're all dealing with sin and forgiveness, love and hate, glory and shame. The big ideas and the challenges they represent remain. Life creates another day of history, and the babies keep on coming. People dream their dreams. The young grasp at reinventing the wheel, and the maturing masses learn to let go of such reinventions one breath at a time.

In the poem "211th Chorus" from *Mexico City Blues*, Kerouac wrote: "I wish I were off this slaving meat wheel and home in heaven, dead."[4] Sacramento guitarist and friend Pat Minor used to quote Jack's verse often. Pat smoked unfiltered cigarettes like he was playing the blues with Gatemouth and could go jaw to jaw with Jay Leno should the need arise. Pat had a special way about him when he encountered absurdities or extraordinary foolishness. Unique to him, Pat's 6 foot 3 inch frame would take on the shape of a question mark. One eyebrow would rise to an Olympic height, and his smile would sparkle outward into the world, his head bobbing as on a spring. Then, with a slow, exaggerated tone, he'd ask anyone who might be listening: "What were they thinking?"

His was the art of being human, of being Pat. For twenty-seven years, Pat worked at the Crocker Art Museum in Sacramento. He hung the shows, painted the walls, and finessed the lighting so that art might have its day. Pat once described a Persian antiquity as "So light, it felt like a thought."

With wisdom he added: "You always have to have reverence in your hands for everything."

A quiet peace filled Ambrose's cab, and I remembered something beatific from the day before. I was shuffling down Canal Street when I heard some mad character ask: "Anybody know where I can get my watch repaired? I'm a hustler and I gots to have my watch." So much of the art of being human is knowing how to tell the time.

On my flight home to Nashville, I was seated across the aisle from a fellow working his own hustle.

He was an American soldier, a heroic traveler of the war in Iraq. Injured in combat, both legs were replaced by prosthetic devices so high-tech you'd think NASA or SpaceX had designed them (maybe they did). He was an airplane-loud-talker, preaching about his two recent appearances on Fox News and dragging director Michael Moore and his film *Fahrenheit 9/11* through the mire. Though amped, positive, and on-mission, the soldier had his bad days too. That's what he told a seatmate (and everyone within earshot).

He exclaimed that Sharon and Ozzy Osbourne had visited him in the hospital—gave him some T-shirts and CDs. "They were cool," he bellowed. "But I don't need Sharon Osbourne to teach me about foreign policy."

Regardless of their political parties or positions, musicians and entertainers can remain cool in the mind of the public as long as they don't engage the world as citizens, or speak the totality of what they believe. Not all artists, but many, are embedding belief in their art all the time, though. The art is always speaking life, telling some story. In short, to know their art is to know them, at least in part. Some of the public get this. They have the reverence. They know what time it is. Others are incapable of picking up the signals—it is not how they perceive art or music, not how their radar works.

Text-friendly social media platforms have changed the game somewhat. Fans follow their favorites online only to discover the songwriter-sherpa who took them to the top of Rock 'n' Roll Mountain has been deceived by dark powers. "Did you read that stupid tweet?" they moan. The wayward sherpa is about to get corrected and put in his or her place. Cue cliché: "Hey, artiste, stay in your lane." Then there's the racist version of stay in your lane, like telling LeBron, "Shut up and dribble."

It might just be me, but I don't think artists are generally known for staying in prescribed lanes. Certainly, LeBron isn't. And, as it relates here, no human needs such admonishment.

The summary of human vocation in the Old Testament's Micah 6:8 has fresh meaning and application:

> And what does the LORD require of you?
> To act justly and to love mercy
> and to walk humbly with your God.

Learning to see justly often precedes acting justly. Which requires reverence for everything, merciful love and humility. And everything ain't no lane.

On October 13, 2022, tragedy hit our Nashville community and beyond. One of our own, writer/editor/publicist Jay Swartzendruber, died suddenly of a heart attack in Charlotte, North Carolina, where he was employed by Billy Graham Evangelistic Association (BGEA). He was only fifty-two. This was unthinkable. I had known Jay as a college student in California in the 1980s. After transferring to Wheaton College in Illinois, he'd become our summer Art House and recording studio intern in Nashville. Then, over time, a coworker, best friend, and family.

Jay was a glorious mess of passion and idealism; a true superfan of me, Steve Taylor, Bono and U2, the Tennessee Titans, the Atlanta Braves, and more. He was genius at over-the-top physical responses to average occurrences—clear some space, he's about to get excited!— and we all loved him for it. All-in, a unique and beautiful human.

At Jay's memorial service, respected artist and Jay's former boss, Steve Taylor, asked all the right questions: "Can you think of anyone who brought more enthusiasm to his passions than Jay? Can you think of anyone who was a better listener than Jay? Can you think of anyone who cared more about the meaning and precision of the words he spoke than Jay?"

I cannot. Every inquiry, Steve reminded us, always ended with, "Does this make sense?" Translated through Pat Minor's earlier question, it might read: "What do you think about what I'm thinking?" Communal pondering for cosmic betterment.

As much as Jay loved Jesus, music, and sports, he wanted to love one woman, too. The most transparent person one could ever meet, Jay told his close male friends everything about the women on his mind. Which was good. Some of Jay's operating assumptions about love and dating were just skewed enough to partially deter his chances. When Jamie came along, Jay's advisors (particularly Nick Barré, Doug McKelvey, and me) affirmed her greatness, lovingly warned Jay "don't blow it," and set this once-in-a-lifetime couple up to win. We fell in love with Jamie as much as we had Jay, and marriage, like the rising of the sun, was inevitable and right. They were as good a team as I've ever witnessed.

Author David Dark had known and worked with Jay since the inception of the Art House in 1991. I cannot improve on David's remarks in memoriam: "He was a publicist of every form of goodness he discerned. In this, he was determined to BE the publicity he wanted to see in the world, a relentless agent for and of Beloved Community."

Create the contrast. Always have reverence in your hands for everything. An A student in the Academy of the Observant Life. That was Jay. And because that was Jay, in 2002, he was right up in the center of a world-changing story, and he took us all with him.

The story began with a letter written to Bono in the fall of 2002; you can read about it in Irishman Steve Stockman's *Walk On: The Spiritual Journey of U2.* I'd rather tell you the deeper, longer tale—the one with unexpected twists and turns. The one that begins and ends with a letter.

Bono, a big-idea person if there ever was one, had several in a row. First, in the spring of 1999, Bono pitched President Clinton on America joining the worldwide Jubilee 2000 celebration, inspired by ancient Jewish culture (see Leviticus 25:8–24). In the year of Jubilee, Hebrew prisoners and the enslaved are freed, debts forgiven, and the mercies of God are embodied for all to see. For America, Bono was suggesting unrestrained generosity, relieving the debt of countries suffering emergency level poverty, famine, and widespread illness. Through the support of a range of unlikely collaborators, America's contribution to Jubilee 2000 got done. Next up was a big idea called DATA, or Debt, AIDS, Trade, Africa. This is where Jay and I got involved.

We had heard through the media and our mutual friend, Mark Rodgers, that Bono was planning a whirlwind seven-day (mostly speaking) tour billed as the Heartland of America Tour for early December 2002. The whole purpose was to take this new idea (DATA) on the road and tell the story of sub-Saharan Africa's debt, AIDS, and trade emergency. And, most critically, to find and inspire American activists in every corner of life, including politics and the Christian church.

Our circle of like-minded friends loved the Heartland idea and wanted in. Surely, Music City, the oft-noted buckle of the Bible Belt, filled with every manner of musician and home to Senate Majority

Leader William Frist, would need to be a key stop on the tour. Jay, being the writer/publicist and student of Bono, drafted a letter requesting that our home and studio, the Art House, be a stop on the tour. I helped Jay edit the letter to essentials only and assured Bono and management we would fill the room with an influential mix of artists and others involved in the Nashville scene, including well-known recording artists with the ear of the American Christian church. With the letter polished, Jay and I signed it, and Mark Rodgers put it in Bono's hands.

The gathering had the potential to generate great good for years to come and equally great disappointment should something change in the U2 command center, and the date suddenly be canceled. Good reason for concern. It was on and off again a few times, then suddenly full speed ahead. "Bono will be here December 9 (2002)."

So, what happened?

First and most importantly, the Spirit of Justice blew through Music City, and people felt the wind blow. Then came a messenger dressed up as a rock star, riffing on two-thousand-year-old words like "Do to others as you would have them do to you" (Luke 6:31).

The messenger gathered together a room full of artists in the business of making a name for themselves. He told them, and I paraphrase: "History is watching. It's taking notes. When the story of these times is written, we want it to say that we did all we could."

It was a long and fruitful talk that day at our house, one filled with laughter, collective moral seriousness, and a few rounds of "What were they thinking?" Band management insisted it not be recorded. Often noncompliant, why I adhered to this order is a mystery.

Then Bono prayed, because prayer is a way of breathing when the worst of disease, hunger, and poverty has sucked the oxygen out of people and planet. You talk to God about matters of mutual concern— it's a conversation about goodness and health becoming present in the world. Prayer is showing up for the life you've been given; a way of saying to God, Thank you. I'm here, I'm listening, and I'm ready to move. Tell me a story. Point me in a good, life-giving direction.

In closing, Bono picked up my son's Gibson J-30 acoustic and led us in singing:

We are one in the Spirit, we are one in the Lord
We are one in the Spirit, we are one in the Lord
And we pray that our unity will one day be restored
And they'll know we are Christians by our love, by our love
Yeah they'll know we are Christians by our love

We will work with each other, we will work side by side
We will work with each other, we will work side by side
And we'll guard each man's dignity and save each man's pride
And they'll know we are Christians by our love, by our love
Yeah, they'll know we are Christians by our love.[5]

Because the Spirit of Justice is never just blowing through one person or one town, all sorts of people simultaneously met and heard similar messages bouncing off God's satellites. Grass roots and grass tops both were inspired. It was a strange assortment of people mobilizing across America and the planet to fight the worst of disease, hunger, and extreme poverty. Political enemies put down their blue/red, left/right banners and rhetoric. Christians who previously groaned that AIDS was nothing but a sex problem became infected with the love that Christ has for the poor and afflicted. They turned and returned to a better way of being human—one that cares for all that God loves. Countries, institutions, and corporations released some of the brain trust and wealth they had stored up for themselves. They offered it for the good of people and planet.

By November of 2003, the Global Fund to Fight AIDS, Tuberculosis and Malaria welcomed the support from British prime minister Tony Blair and US president George W. Bush to increase their cooperative efforts in the fight against HIV/AIDS. The US alone committed to $15 billion over five years in the fight against AIDS. Here on the ground in Nashville, I can attest that the generosity of time, talent, and funding was present and effective. The fruit of the awakening continued for years with local projects like singer-songwriter Dave Barnes's Mocha Club, an online community of people pledging the cost of two mochas a month ($7 in 2009) to fund relief and development projects in African nations. Bill Hearn, the president and CEO of EMI Christian Music Group, was involved with Healing Waters International, an NGO working to reduce water-related illness and death.

In short, for a moment in time, an ad hoc gathering of people sought justice and loved mercy, and those who named it as such woke each day to walk humbly with God and pray, saying: "You're doing this. Thanks for letting us get in on it."

Then real change happened on the ground in the worst-hit areas of sub-Saharan Africa (e.g., Botswana, Kenya, Mozambique, South Africa, Uganda, and Zambia) and in the hearts of the American church and American politicians. For a time, people who could never agree on anything locked arms to work for the restoration of rightness and the reconciliation of people and planet. But it wasn't about charity. It was about justice. It's worth repeating Bono's words from the Fifty-Fourth National Prayer Breakfast, February 2, 2006:

> Six thousand five hundred Africans are still dying every day of a preventable, treatable disease, for lack of drugs we can buy at any drugstore. This is not about charity, this is about justice and equality.
>
> Because there's no way we can look at what's happening in Africa and, if we're honest, conclude that deep down, we really accept that Africans are equal to us. Anywhere else in the world, we wouldn't accept it.[6]

Bono said this about the African health emergency, but it's prescient and applicable to Black/white polarity of America in general, the history of my own family in the making of America, and the racial justice awakening in the summer of 2020.

So much good and life-giving change can be traced back to the December 9 gathering. The diversity of it is well documented and goes far beyond my intimate knowledge and pay grade. (For example, in his 2003 State of the Union address, President George W. Bush asked Congress to commit the $15 billion referenced above over the next five years to combating HIV and AIDS in Africa. The President's Emergency Plan for AIDS Relief [PEPFAR] was born.)

Keeping it personal will keep it simpler in the telling. Along with many other Nashville activists, artists, and executives, including Steve Taylor, Margaret Becker, Michael W. Smith, and Jars of Clay, Andi and I helped DATA and the next iteration, the ONE Campaign, in several ways: hosting Jamie Drummond and President Tom Lane for follow-up meetings and filling the room with activists ready to work; helping Steve Taylor produce video and audio materials to broadcast Bono's appeal on the big screen at music festivals; contributing a chapter ("Taking It Personally") for *Mission Africa: A Field Guide*, and another to *The Awake Project: Uniting against the African AIDS Crisis* (under the guidance of editors Kate Etue and Jenny Eaton-Dyer); and joining Republican senator Bill Frist, then the Senate majority leader, in vocal support, photo ops, and television coverage of the bipartisan efforts to awaken Americans to the African health emergency.

This was our music community's first lesson in sausage making (I mean activism), and how to effect change within the American political system. It took an Irishman to stir our hearts, but we got there. Most importantly, hurting and dying global neighbors got desperately needed, tangible help from America.

—

There you have it. Seeing justly led to acting justly. Well done, everyone. Can someone get me a red bow to put on this thing? One more round of *they will know we are Christians by our love!* Uh . . . no. Let's go back to Washington, DC, January 20, 2005.

I felt out of place and a bit disingenuous at having accepted Mark Rodgers's invitation to attend President George W. Bush's second inaugural ceremony. I was moving from cautious ambivalence regarding the war in Iraq to genuine concern for its justness, not just its efficacy. In short, American foreign policy, what it means and where it comes from, held my thoughts. Seeing justly, leading to acting justly, and all that.

But, admittedly, like a lot of Americans after 9/11, I wanted revenge, an eye for an eye. Unless, of course, I'm the perpetrator; then I want everyone to leave my eyes alone.

The week before the inaugural, I experienced a hellish five days, attempting yet failing to close a music business deal. Weary and wandering, I thought, *Why not?* Let's go to Washington and take in a little of what Shakespeare called the "Pride, pomp, and circumstance of glorious war." Boy, was I not thinking straight.

Despite my reservations about President Bush and the war, I thought I'd be moved by the history and ritual of the inaugural event. Nothing. I had no impulse to shout "hurrah!" or grumble "har-rumph!" I did have a kind of tight-eyed wonderment as to whether the president was actually saying what I thought he was saying: *A declaration to end tyranny around the world?*

This sentence, and what seemed like very explicit religious references to Christianity, Islam, and Judaism, raised my brow and wrinkled my forehead. It sounded like a call to war without end, in the name of God. Even Peggy Noonan, speechwriter for George H. W. Bush, called it "dreamy and disturbing." But Noonan also called the speech "God-drenched," which, by historical standards, I don't think it was. (See the speeches of Lincoln, Wilson, Kennedy, or Reagan.)

In 1961, John F. Kennedy swore his oath before "Almighty God," telling his country that "the rights of man come not from the generosity of the state but from the hand of God." He closed by asking for "His blessing and His help, but knowing that here on earth God's work must truly be our own."[7]

Sociologist Robert Bellah observed this about Kennedy's speech: "The whole address can be understood as only the most recent statement of a theme that lies very deep in the American tradition, namely the obligation, both collective and individual, to carry out God's will on earth."[8]

God's will. I think that's why President Bush chose to recognize the three major world religions that live and die to see the will of God on earth as it is in heaven. The very word "Islam" means submission to the will of God. President Bush affirmed "the truths of Sinai, the Sermon on the Mount, the words of the Koran" as "ideals of justice and conduct that are the same yesterday, today, and forever."[9] A nod to the Koran in an American presidential inaugural speech? First time I'd heard that.

After the inauguration, we ate tapas with Steve and Meg Garber, then attended the Pennsylvania Ball and caught a cab back to the Holiday Inn. "O Lord, in thee have I trusted: let me never be confounded" go the words of Ambrose's famous *Te Deum*. Yes, I was trusting. But not confounded? Hardly. I was looking for Buechner's rock again.

Five months later, on May 14, 2005, Andi and I flew back to Philadelphia to hear Bono and U2 prove again that they were the world's biggest rock 'n' roll band. Our friends at DATA and the ONE Campaign provided us with tickets and green-room passes. The industrious Mark Rodgers had arranged for a group of us to meet up before the concert at Popi's Italian Restaurant on South Twentieth near the arena. Tom Hart (then president of ONE Campaign) and author and *New York Times* columnist David Brooks were in attendance. As were Steve and Meg Garber, Mark and Leanne Rodgers, and Michael and Dawn Gerson. Mark and Steve hosted, steering the conversation toward Bono's lyrics and trying to answer the question: Is U2 a prophetic voice for our time? (Steve had contributed a fine chapter to *Get Up Off Your Knees: Preaching the U2 Catalog*.)

I was seated next to Michael Gerson, speechwriter for President Bush and author of a significant portion of the president's second inaugural speech Andi and I had heard in person. Shortly after the inaugural, Michael was named by *Time* magazine as one of "the 25 most influential evangelicals" in America. This was before all residual significance had been squeezed from the word "evangelical." In its purest noun form, "evangelical" simply means a messenger of good news. Now, "evangelical" is just as apt to be used for racial and political distinctions as theological. When millions of people are doing the former, it is not good news.

By 2007, Michael Gerson had retired from the Bush camp. He warned his political party to take seriously the obligation to "order society in a way that protects and benefits the powerless and suffering." Taking a prescient tone, he wrote: "A Republican Party that does not offer a robust agenda on health care, education reform, climate change and economic empowerment will fade into irrelevance." As history would make clear, Gerson could see something of the future, though not the complete dismantling and reimagining of his party yet to come. By 2022, he would have this and much more to say:

Leaders in the Republican Party have fed, justified and exploited conservative Christians' defensiveness in service to an aggressive, reactionary politics. This has included deadly mask and vaccine resistance, the discrediting of fair elections, baseless accusations of gay "grooming" in schools, the silencing of teaching about the United States' history of racism, and (for some) a patently false belief that Godless conspiracies have taken hold of political institutions.[10]

Back at the Italian restaurant in 2005, I had to smile when Michael shared that the last big pop concert he'd been to was Amy Grant's in 1986 or '87, the era when Amy was wearing the leopard-print jacket and on pop radio with Peter Cetera of Chicago fame. They had a No. 1 *Billboard* smash with "The Next Time I Fall" produced by Michael Omartian.

Still, sitting next to the president's speechwriter was no small thing.

A U2 appreciation dinner was not the time or place to discuss my confounding during the inaugural, or the speech Michael had helped write. We had an Irish rock band's body of work to appreciate and dissect. The lively conversation around the table anchored me in the present for a time. Dinner concluded, and U2 and the green room were next. It was good to say hello to Jamie Drummond and Lucy Matthew again, pioneers with Bono in Jubilee 2000, DATA, and the ONE Campaign. U2's chaplain, Jack Heaslip, gave us a warm greeting. Jack was also kind to visit with a roomful of folks in Nashville at a Wedgwood event a few years later, sharing something of his unusual relationship with the once-scruffy band from Dublin. After Jack's death in 2015, Steve Taylor's good friend Martin Wroe, a British poet and theologian, filled the band's chaplain role.

The Philadelphia U2 concert was everything I'd come to expect from the band: a commitment to artistry and global change for good. We followed our handler and her flashlight out to the VIP platform in front of the mix console. Questlove was already inside the roped area making it a true Philly experience. Then U2 did what only they could do on this earth of ours—at least back then.

Was it just a coincidence or did something in the atmosphere cause a Bono stage prop to line up so neatly with part of Gerson's Bush speech from earlier in the year? Bono put on his "CoeXisT" headband: the *C* bent into the shape of the crescent of Islam, the *X* the Star of David, and the *T* the shape of the cross of Christ. Bono's message: these three world religions all believe in the God of Abraham—and we are all sons and daughters of Abraham, hence we ought to find a way to CoeXisT.

Remember, in Bush doctrine 2005, the very ideal of freedom is "sustained in our national life by the truths of Sinai, the Sermon on the Mount, the words of the Koran, and the varied faiths of our people." Foreign and domestic policies, right? As if possible, right at that moment I could feel a tangible uneasiness creep across the American evangelical church. I could see the I-dotters and T-crossers demanding clarification that the Bible teaches that no person comes to the Father of Abraham except by grace through faith in Messiah Jesus. Imagine being Abraham, able to watch this long "six degrees of Abraham" drama revolving around your slice of history, your home of Iraq, and your genealogy. The Genesis 12 promise of "all the peoples of earth will be blessed through you" hung—hangs, really—by a ragged thread.

The Gersons kindly gave us a ride to the hotel. I wasted my opportunity to ask Michael's thoughts on the similar Abrahamic emphasis between the speech and Bono's headband. Mark Rodgers had asked me a question in the car. I lost myself in the answer, rambling on about the role of imagination and creativity in cultural and political renewal. I should have played my introverted musician card, shut up, and listened.

—

On July 2, 2011, for a few minutes on a steamy, southern, "cat on a hot tin roof" evening, Andi and I reconnected with Bono. U2 was in Nashville on their 360° Tour. We had the privilege of introducing him to Joy Williams from The Civil Wars. Hugs, kisses, and photos for all. A quick chat with Rick Hall of FAME Studios fame ("the father of Muscle Shoals") and more photos. But most importantly, Bono and

I connected on what drew us together in the first place—justice for all. "That really changed things, that was a pivotal moment," he said, referring to the gathering at our home, the Art House, in December of 2002.

Later onstage, recalling the event, Bono was kind enough to give me a shout-out from the Claw. Ancillary, but no less important to the tale of interdependence, I (with Lucy Matthew and Mark Rodgers) was able to play a small role in helping scholar David Taylor put our friends Eugene Peterson and Bono in the same room for the film *Be Brutally Honest: The Psalms.* Eugene called Bono "a companion in the faith." Bono called Eugene a poet and scholar. Indeed.

Shortly after his death, Jay Swartzendruber received a letter from Bono. Full circle. Steve Taylor read it to the mourners gathered at Jay's funeral and those streaming from home.[11]

Funny how something as simple as writing a letter can change history. Like if you write a letter to Amnesty International and someone in some prison cell in some country you're not that familiar with, gets to know you've remembered them. And someone who has locked them away, becomes just a little uneasy about who knows what. And maybe eventually, the letter is the key that unlocks the door of their cell.

I'm always writing letters to people, wondering if I can persuade them to join me in unpicking another locked door in history.

A letter holds power, like the letter Jay and Charlie wrote to me nearly twenty years ago.

I got to hang out with Jay and so many passionate believers involved in the arts in Nashville, but more important than that I got to meet some co-conspirators.

People who wanted to move the political dial in the US, people who knew we could make a difference in the fight against a pandemic—a pandemic not like the current one, a pandemic that the rich world was not taking seriously.

You receive a letter and you never know what impact it may eventually have. This one helped fire up a movement in the battle against HIV/AIDS. It unlocked another door in history.

I love the way that Jay called the action of faith groups in supporting PEPFAR a "shining moment."

Thanks for writing to me Jay. May we all have such shining moments in our life.

Bono

The day after Jay's passing, Chris Blumenfeld, a colleague at BGEA, was sitting at Jay's desk trying to figure out what he needed to give to Jay's wife, Jamie. When Chris opened an office cabinet, he saw a printout of an email taped to the inside door—one I'd sent Jay two years earlier. We had shared a remarkable evening of reminiscence and laughter with Jay and Jamie and three other couples, including our hospitable hosts, our daughter Molly and son-in-law, Mark. Along with Jay, guests Nick and Krista Barré and Doug and Lise McKelvey had all been essential players in the creation of the Art House work and story.

I had written to Jay to clarify something. Once home, standing in my closet, fumbling to put on pajama bottoms, I realized I had missed an opportunity to let Jay know that I considered him "peerless in sincerity, humility, curiosity and graceful open-heartedness." My life, I wrote him, is "infinitely richer for knowing you."

I closed by saying, "If I could give you a note to keep in your pocket till Jesus calls you home it would say: Jay, rest in the knowledge that you are loved beyond measure by the friends who gathered around you and Jamie tonight."

Once Jamie and Chris reminded me of this email, I went searching my laptop to see if the conversation had continued. I found Jay's response.

"Thank you for putting this down in writing. I'll probably have to read it multiple times for it to sink in. Friday night was truly epic. So much love, so many laughs. That combination remains unrivaled in my life when it comes to those of you gathered around that table."

By posting my note on his cabinet door, he had committed to letting it sink in, one glance at a time, one day at a time.

We are strange creatures, hungry for love and to be known. Yet, even in our deepest longings for time and attention, we can avert our eyes from love, somehow feeling unworthy to look its unconditional version in the eye; to let it fully sink in. Even more strange and unreconcilable is our capacity to avert our eyes from love's pursuit while directing loving eyes toward our neighbors in need, even our neighbors across the ocean. What's the quote again? *To discover the character of people we have only to observe what they love.*

For me, there is no faithful human or artistic life that isn't full enrollment in the academy of the observant life. Seeing and acting in love for cosmic betterment. The vocation of history making.

The best version of unlocking the doors of history is never a power move, a grift, or an exercise in name- and myth-making, though. Or sausage making, for that matter. It's a movement of love, formed and actualized by weak and broken people intent on good despite their imperfections. It's taking all of life personally. It's implicating yourself in the creation of the world. *Be the publicity you want to see in the world.* Thank you, David Dark, for this good witness. In honor of everyone with eyes to see, from Ambrose to Jay and the Irish rock star, this is my new motto.

sixteen

IMAGINATION, INTERDEPENDENCE, AND THE BONDS OF AFFECTION

Andi and I were married in our hometown in an outdoor ceremony at the fairgrounds on May 18, 1975. I was eighteen; Andi, nineteen. We rented a one-bedroom house just over the Feather River on Rubel Street in Marysville, across from Eastpark Lake and the railroad tracks, near the grocer, where in 1964 they sold copies of *Meet the Beatles*, and around the corner from Marysville High School, where my father was band director.

Living near the Feather, Yuba, and Sacramento Rivers taught me lessons about the interdependence of things; how we come to be a confluence of who we meet and what we learn, the choices we make in concert with place and people. The river's abrasion, hydraulic action, solution, and attrition are ongoing; she keeps moving in order to live, and as she moves, she shapes the land she cuts through and is shaped by it.

We are what we take with us, and what we leave behind.

That summer I worked as a peach grader for the Department of Agriculture, tended a large vegetable garden, meditated, read Alan Watts, listened to pianist Keith Jarrett's *Facing You*, and wrote poetry. I bound the poems together in a chapbook clothed in soft leather with wooden beads I'd crafted.

I was of a mind that my hometown was the kind of place you left. The capital city of Sacramento was calling to us.

My artist radar picked up any signal remotely related to jazz, or the Beat writers and poets such as Michael McClure, Anne Waldman, Lew Welch, Gary Snyder, Richard Brautigan, and of course, the reluctant and haunted progenitor, Jack Kerouac. Eventually, inevitably, these magnetic waves escorted us to a café in downtown Sacramento called Monica's. It had nearly everything of importance to our imaginations. Clean food and ground coffee, feminism, jazz, art, and poetry. On our second visit, I brought my poetry chapbook for the open-mic and read "Old Hunker's Blues" with derivative tone and staccato cadence, channeling Allen Ginsberg and a ride cymbal.

We had found our people. Or, at least knew with some certainty, that people who valued what we valued could be found in Sacramento. In less than a year, we joined them.

I had some inkling of this possibility for us, when at age seventeen I met Charlie Weiss, a Sacramento musician and disc jockey. We were students together in an electronic music class at Yuba College, out near the Air Force base, a forty-minute drive from Sacramento. I didn't know it at the time, but many of Charlie's friends and coworkers at the alternative radio station KZAP would eventually become my friends and coworkers as well: Dennis Newhall, Jeff Hughson, Mick Martin, Helen Meline, Captain Carrot (Cary Nosler), Viola Weinberg, and Lindy Haber (who managed my band for a time). Another handful of new friends were in a band—maybe more a collective—with Charlie Weiss, called Orphans of Love: Les Haber, Pat and Kathleen Minor, D. R. Wagner, and the aforementioned Lindy.

The piano player in the jazz trio at Monica's was Kent Lacin, a gifted photographer and musician. A few years later, I would meet Kent properly and visit his studio with our mutual friend Steve Holsapple. Kent took the photos for my first album, *Lie Down in the Grass*. More famously, Kent took a photo of himself, Steve, and another artist, Chuck DeLost, sitting on a sofa, each reading a newspaper on fire, leaping flames and all. Who needs Photoshop?

One of the young chefs that passed through Monica's was a talented woman from the East Coast named Kathi Riley, a best friend of the disc jockey Meg Griffin, a radio legend celebrated in the Rock and Roll Hall of Fame. Kathi, herself no underachiever, was on track to follow the path of many great chefs who apprenticed under Alice Waters, Berkeley's farm-to-fork pioneer. I met Kathi after our inevitable move to Sacramento. First, through Steve Holsapple, and later through her boyfriend, Bongo Bob Smith, percussionist with the funk/world music band The Runners (featuring Skip Moriarty, Henry Robinett, Keith Jefferson, Jimmy Griego, Alphonza Kee, and more). This anthroposophy-meets-Parliament unit provided the soundtrack to Sacramento's downtown art crowd and the small cadre of steadfast hippies lingering about, refusing to concede.

Fast-forwarding decades from those halcyon days, Kathi, Bob, and their daughter Natalé remain some of our family's oldest and most treasured friends. Kathi and Andi have been cooking together since the early 1980s. Kathi's presence and influence are tightly woven into several events we've hosted at our home in Nashville. She's been part of retreats in Vermont (OQ Farm) and Texas (Laity Lodge) and holds two important distinctions: (1) joining Andi and other dear friends in cooking meals in our home for eighty or more people! and (2) gently mentoring our granddaughter Bridget in all things sous chef at the Vermont songwriter's festival we hosted.

I picked up a phrase from reading Zen scholar D. T. Suzuki: *"ji-ji-mu-ge,"* which means something like "the interdependence of all things." I remain friends with everyone I've mentioned, even if only through Facebook and the occasional face-to-face. Engaging in this sort of Kevin-Bacon-game storytelling reminds me there is no neutrality on earth. Every choice matters. Every person you meet becomes some part of your story, and you, theirs.

—

Early in the twenty-first century, a policy research group in Washington, DC, brought me in for a panel on film and music. During downtime, Andi and I were free to explore the National Museum of American History, the Vietnam Veterans Memorial, and the Lincoln Memorial.

Andi was delighted to have unlimited time at Julia Child's kitchen, re-created so wonderfully at the museum. I watched videos of the chef while Andi took in every detail of Julia's famed workspace. I was reminded of Julia Child's great gifts, strong opinions, flexibility, and good humor—all of it making for an iconic creator and person of influence in the culinary arts. Moving through the food exhibit, we were proud to see a poster for Pallido olive oil, bottled exclusively for Corti Brothers grocers in Sacramento, and another for the Acme Bread from Berkeley. Signs, symbols, and touchstones, firing off like fireworks. We had once lived around the corner from Corti Brothers, shopped there often, and chef Kathi had recently brought Acme bread to Andi for a food retreat in Texas. There was the book *Diet for a Small Planet* that had influenced our thinking so much in the 1970s. And of course, there was a tribute to Alice Waters too, being the farm-to-table pioneer that she is. Alice went from good to good, founding the world-renowned Chez Panisse, then becoming a national public policy advocate for school lunch reform.

In the 2010s, a delegation of Sacramentans and their mayor, Kevin Johnson, visited our city of Nashville to study the sights, sounds, and imaginative ethos of Music City. Their hope was to take back to Sacramento good and useful ways of being and doing; ones they could apply to Sacramento as a farm-to-table capital. Nashville was honored to host them, and I was enlisted to create an *Only in Nashville* music experience for them at the top of the AT&T building (we call it the Batman Building).

The National Museum's Edison exhibit was equally fascinating. Imagine creating such mind- and life-altering inventions. There's no neutrality in a lightbulb. It came with the power to change everything, and it did.

As did a certain Greensboro, North Carolina, lunch counter (on display at the museum). In 1960, racial segregation was still legal in the United States. On February 1 of that year, four African American college students sat down at Woolworth's "whites only" counter and asked to be served. They were refused and told to leave. They didn't, and their sit-in became national news. It cast a bright light on inequality and played a significant role in moving the nation toward the Civil Rights Act of 1964. One lunch counter, four seats of imagination and courage. There's even a Nashville connection: the young men had been in communication with Nashville's civil rights leaders who'd been training for sit-ins. This is, in part, what prompted them.[1]

Of course, for me as a musician, I was also inspired to see the great John Coltrane's tenor saxophone and score for *Love Supreme*.

These are a few of many good American stories represented in the museum. All, in different ways, testifying to the glory and the shame of America and our remarkable ability to change course, problem-solve, empathize, invent, and persistently and imaginatively overcome our greatest follies, adversities, and differences. It brought to mind Bono calling America *one of the greatest ideas in human history*.

Before leaving the museum, we listened to a short concert by the Air Force Strings. Given my dad's history with the Air Force dance band in the 1950s, I felt duty-bound to give the musicians a listen. It was a gift I didn't know I needed. The band was tastefully musical and technically flawless. From memory, they played sturdy yet elegant arrangements of American composers Brubeck and Strayhorn, and patriotic repertoire like "America the Beautiful" and a medley of armed forces theme songs. We cried. I saw afresh the simple unifying power of music to entertain, to stir righteous emotion, and to cause human flourishing. All achieved without an ounce of marketing or monetization—music for a better economy (hat tip to Wendell Berry's wisdom). I was humbled. I kept saying to myself, "People are great."

We ended our day at the Lincoln Memorial. In the closing to his first inaugural address, Abraham Lincoln reminded the nation: "We are not enemies, but friends. We must not be enemies. Though passion may have strained, it must not break our bonds of affection." As Wendell Berry so powerfully said in his 2012 Jefferson Lecture of the same name: *It all turns on affection*. And so it does. With that, I'll let Mr. Berry bear witness further: "As imagination enables sympathy, sympathy enables affection. And it is in affection that we find the possibility of a neighborly, kind, and conserving economy."[2]

—

Soon after moving to Nashville in 1989, Andi and I founded a nonprofit called the Art House, later, Art House America. Our mission was and is simple: champion imagination and creativity for the good of all, and nurture anyone looking to explore an artful, faithful life. At Art House America, we trust that the person and story of Jesus represent a new way to be human, and so affirm his ways.[3]

All this background information is a setup for what follows next—a Texas-sized aligning of people and history.

It begins with a celebration: the fourth anniversary of Art House Dallas. Brad and Holly Reeves, along with Jenny White-Green, founded the Dallas group. Andi and I are so grateful for the imaginative and faithful ways they've served their community. We eagerly joined in to provide words of confirmation and encouragement. It was a short, twenty-four-hour stay, though. Next up, Laity Lodge in the hill country of Texas near Leakey. Laity is a magical, oasis-like locale in a canyon on the Frio River in central Texas (overseen by our friend Steven Purcell). The family behind H-E-B Grocery and Central Market set the whole thing in motion years ago. We have visited there often and count the people and place essential to life. Laity is known for many good things, not the least being you get to the lodge by driving down a shallow stretch of the Frio and its bed of solid rock. A highway of H_2O.

I was the guest musician. Our son Sam and banjo virtuoso Matt Menefee (of Mumford & Sons) joined me. The retreat featured the poet Christian Wiman (*My Bright Abyss*) and the late pastor/author Eugene Peterson (*The Message, Eat This Book*). And so it was, that the Art House Dallas event inaugurated four days of the most remarkable interconnectedness of people, place, and story I've ever experienced.

Consider all this: The late author and sports management icon Bob Briner introduced me to Laity Lodge in the late 1990s. Andi and I quickly became regulars at the lodge and introduced the leadership to a wealth of gifted friends—musicians, artists, writers, speakers, and more.

I met Texan Jenny White-Green through her work in Washington, DC, with my friend Mark Rodgers. It was Mark who first introduced me to Bono and writer/commentator David Brooks, and invited me and others, including Steven Garber and David Kierznowski, to help create a cultural investment group called Wedgwood Circle (named after Josiah Wedgwood). David Brooks joined us for the retreat.

Also in attendance was Nathan Tasker, an Australian musician. Years before, Nate had come to live in Nashville part time and attended our Art House events. Nate and Cassie Tasker eventually took over leadership of the on-site Art House Nashville work. It was Nate who introduced me to Brad Reeves, and from there, Brad took an interest in all things Art House. I, in turn, introduced Brad to Wedgwood Circle. Then, when our good friend Mark Rodgers wasn't looking, Brad and I enticed Jenny back to Texas to launch Art House Dallas, which she did, with great hospitality and imagination.

Steven Purcell grew up listening to my music (think *Lie Down in the Grass*). Later I knew him as the director of an annual arts retreat at Schloss Mittersill in Austria. In 2006, I was delighted to be one of many who recommended him for the executive director position at Laity Lodge, where he leads to this day. Steven introduced Andi and me to Eugene and Jan Peterson via the Chrysostom Society. And, as you might imagine, I love the humble connection between Bono and Eugene. Along with Eugene and Jan, Steven and Amy Purcell were with us for the retreat.

The author and educator David Dark was also present. He is a founding participant of Art House in Nashville. David, like Jon Foreman of Switchfoot, married a Masen sister from Michigan (Sarah Dark and Emily Foreman). I've had the honor of producing two records for Sarah and a few singles much later in life. They all met at the Art House, swirling around friendship with our daughter Molly Nicholas during the early days of Switchfoot. The band connected with the filmmaker Brandon Dickerson to direct their first videos. Brandon and his wife, Kirsten, had moved to Austin to do artful work there and around the world. And so it was that they were in attendance, too.

Author Andy Crouch introduced me to filmmaker Nate Clarke (present at the retreat). Jerry McPherson, Sam Ashworth, and I orchestrated a film for Nate titled *Wrestling for Jesus*. From London, author/poet Steve Turner introduced me via email to singer-songwriter Kelley McRae (also with us).

I first met the extraordinary NYC-based children's book writer Sally Lloyd-Jones at Hutchmoot in Nashville. She is a friend of many, but very close to our Australian friends Nate and Cassie Tasker. We love her so because she's unique, but also because she has written the absolute best children's Bible, one our grandchildren loved to read. Scholar and arts pastor David Taylor sought me out years ago, and we've been friends ever since. We were delighted when he found his match in the artist Phaedra Taylor. Sally and the Taylors joined in, with David coleading the retreat with Steven Purcell.

So, is it too much to claim that I was with many of these people (and more, like Andrew Ripp, Arthur Boers, Malcolm Guite, Paul Soupiset, Robert Feuge, and Chris Domig) in the great state of Texas over a four-day period? I was indeed. How in the world did this happen?

There's that compact Zen phrase again, *ji-ji-mu-ge*, interdependence and harmony within diversity. Then there's serendipity—chance or the happy accident affecting people and events for good. In Christianity, a complementary thought is that of Jesus being the agency of creativity and holding all things together. Christianity also has providence, a similar phrase to *ji-ji-mu-ge*, though much more personal and particular in definition: providence is God going ahead of a person or persons, preparing the way for future eventualities and interdependent connection of people and place.

I believe this is precisely why and how these four days in Texas came to be. As fun as it is to chart the interconnectedness, there's more going on here than name-dropping or list making. Remembering and writing it down is a kind of prayer—one means among many of saying to the Creator of interdependence and harmony, "I see what you did there! Thank you."

There is no neutrality to people or place. Antebellum Texas and white supremacists had a violent and disastrous effect on my family in Texas in the 1800s—one I'm still dealing with in the present. Four days in Texas with people who change your life for the better is re-demption—a gift from Christ the Redeemer.

I named the late Bob Briner as starting it all for me with Laity. True, but our friendship began with a fax from the sports legend. "How can I serve you?" Bob asked. This one question changed my life. Bob, then a stranger, was selflessly saying, whatever gift I've been given, whatever resource I steward, is yours. Bob became a lifelong friend and champion. In the past, God sent me a saxophonist with life-altering good news. With Bob, he sent a "tubby Texan" (Bob's own words) to make me a better man—to model magnetic humility, generosity, kindness, and the art of graciously investing in people and place.

All the people named here have had similar effect. Their art, words, friendship, and life in general have shaped me as a human and an artist. Whether through conversation or music, it's always about learning to listen, to hear a voice, a sound, a silence, that doesn't emanate from you. Every opportunity to practice this is a grace, and in my mind, essential to becoming a fully human person. After all, we are, essentially, inspired dirt, animated through our connection to God, creation, and one another.

—

One summer, Andi and aforementioned best friend Kathi Riley Smith attended Laity's Food Retreat. Along with Laity staff, they cooked the late Judy Rodgers's famous recipe for roast chicken. Judy and Kathi came up in the nascent farm-to-table movement with Alice Waters, and both cooked for Alice at Chez Panisse in Berkeley—later working together at Zuni Café in San Francisco, where Judy's chicken came to fame—and where Kathi returned briefly as guest chef early in the decade 2000–2009.

One of the guest speakers at the Food Retreat was Ellen Davis, a biblical scholar from Duke Divinity School. Ellen's most beloved riff is encouraging an agrarian reading of the Bible, specifically that part of the sixty-six books of the Bible that Christians share with the Jewish people, the Torah. I heard a podcast where Ellen talked about being a teenager living in Israel. She said the land became so familiar to her that even today she cannot read the Bible or exegete a text without seeing the land in which the story took place. Ellen Davis reminds me of Wendell Berry in her examination and honor of place. In America at least, Wendell is a clear, sane, agrarian voice weaving together God, people, and place in a farmer/artist way. Quoting Wendell, Ellen believes the Bible is *the story of a gift*. What Ellen Davis, Wendell Berry, and others like Wes Jackson and Norman Wirzba have in common is a deep respect for the land and the Giver of it. To hear from any of these people is to hear clues to a faithful way forward stewarding all that God has entrusted to the human family, including dirt, land, and place.

Some years back I opened my email to see a *NoiseTrade* advertisement for My Brightest Diamond, the recording moniker of artist Shara Worden. I've watched Shara from a distance for several years. She is one among a few recording artists of her generation that are truly unique in thought and execution (she's also been Sufjan Stevens's collaborator). According to a *Huffington Post* interview, Shara moved to Detroit so she "could be a part of the urban gardening movement that is happening in the city."[4]

I heard a story that Shara's friend, artist Erin Martinez, dug up roses from empty lots where houses were torn down in Detroit and replanted the roses in a garden. That way, all was not lost, and what someone once loved and cared for was loved and cared for again— and the dirt held it all together.

Jesus spoke of a way of rightful being and living with God, people, and place. He gave it a name that the people of the time would understand—the kingdom of God, and then he turned their notions of kings and kingdoms upside down and inside out. His talk of the kingdom was not a once-for-all, clear-as-a-bell theological declaration. It is, however, a creative means to reorient, even reestablish, what it means to be God's kind of fully human person; that is, a person alive to a healthy relationship with God, his people, the land and all that is in it.

I see in the land of my youth the Greensboro Four, the farm-to-table movement, Laity Lodge, Coltrane's lifelong influence, Judy Rodgers's roasted chicken, Alice Waters's Edible Schoolyard Project, the Air Force Band playing Billy Strayhorn, Ellen Davis, Wendell Berry, Wes Jackson, Norman Wirzba, the greening of Detroit, Shara Worden and her friend's reimagined roses—the story of a gift, for our time. And for this man, all good reasons to say thank you to God through Christ Jesus.

Chapter Sixteen

Sometimes the reasons for gratitude are so uniquely strange I couldn't possibly anticipate them. I bear witness in some vignettes: the story of 1½ pianos, an art-centric watering hole, a relative and a new friend, and two million vinyl records.

In April 2010 I was in Los Angeles having dinner with Svend Lerche, and Randy and Ricky Jackson of The Daylights. I was working with the band on film/TV placements and had recently placed the song "Oh, Oh" in *Rabbit Hole*, starring Nicole Kidman. After dinner we headed to the band's house in Studio City to listen to new songs. Like every band house I've ever visited, this one was stuffed with gear, including three upright pianos. They gave me the Craigslist story on the instruments and pointed to a little dining alcove, saying, "We've got an old electric piano over there."

Vintage electric pianos always get my attention. I turned and moved toward it. Not ten feet from the piano, I spoke clearly and without hesitation: "That's my piano." And it was. I knew it was. At the speed of Malcolm Gladwell's *Blink* thesis, I knew.

Of course, I had to prove it to the guys, which was not that difficult. It was the right era, a Fender Rhodes Mark I Stage (1969–1975), specifically 1972 vintage—manufactured by CBS (who purchased Fender). I bought it used in 1976 and customized it by installing a MXR Phase 90 into the metal front panel between the volume and bass EQ knobs and the center logo.

I sold the piano in 1978 while living in Northern California, probably to make rent. I couldn't believe I was seeing it again after thirty-two years. We celebrated, high-fived, and exclaimed, "No way, dude!"

The band offered me the piano. Maybe someday, I said. Right then, I was content with the unexpected reunion.

Stunning. Later that night, driving to LAX airport, I wiped tears from my eyes, reflecting on the odds of my working with a band in Los Angeles that would somehow be in possession of my first Fender Rhodes electric piano from thirty-two years earlier. I could feel the love of God, as if no detail in the universe was overlooked. No stray molecule, no Fender Rhodes piano unaccounted for.

The electric piano I rediscovered at The Daylights' house had been quite the tourist. Ace keyboardist Korel Tunador (Goo Goo Dolls and Katy Perry) was given the piano in Pittsburgh by his uncle Barry Gilmartin, who purchased it up in Eugene, Oregon, in 1979. Korel took the piano to Boston and the Berklee College of Music. Eventually he brought it out to Los Angeles, where he asked The Daylights to keep it for him. He didn't fancy carrying it up and down his stairs anymore. A thankless task if there ever was one.

In 1978, I bought a new Rhodes Mark I Suitcase (1975–1979 era). This is the piano I owned in 1979 when I first started playing my own music at Maurice's American Bar. I'd sing a few songs like "Springtime in Israel" and "So Sentimental." Mostly the band and I devised sons-of-Miles *Bitches Brew* improvisations. Guitarist Robert Kuhlmann and bassist Erik Kleven were in that band. Blues harp legend Rick Estrin and jazz pianist Jessica Williams were in the audience back then. Tower Records founder Russ Solomon would stop by, as would the Zen governor of California, Jerry Brown. My close friends Pat Minor, Steve Holsapple, and singer-songwriter Bob Cheevers were always in the house, as was Joan Didion's niece, Julie Didion. I could count on them to champion whatever naïve experimentation of mine was making the needle bounce.

Maurice's was the perfect creative environment to develop as a young artist. Art was front and center, and it was there that I took my first baby steps as a solo performing artist. I had found my people.

One evening at Maurice's I was verbally sparring with pop star Roger Voudouris ("Get Used to It"). Out in the parking lot, closing time, we kept it up. All good-natured with just a little sting. We had history.

Roger signed to Warner Brothers Records in 1978. I auditioned for his touring band. He told me I got the gig because my fingernails were clean. As quick as I got it, I lost it. Despite my tidy manicure, Roger didn't like what he was hearing. I wasn't copying the record. I'm positive that was true. Roger Smith, a fantastic keyboardist and friend, took my place.

The keyboard player I was supposed to be copying was producer and session ace Michael Omartian. He'd filled the record with major eleventh chords and substitute bass changes and had provided charts for the touring musicians. It really deserved to be played as written. I was doing my own thing.

Chapter Sixteen

A few years later I was auditioning guitarists for a tour opening for The Fixx. Joe Satriani had made this ingenious record where he played guitar, drums, and bass—yet all created from the sounds of his electric guitar. Bongo Bob Smith and I immediately thought of Joe and called him to audition. Disappointment. We sent him back to Berkeley with a no. I asked Bob, is it my imagination or was Joe playing chords a flatted fifth away from everything we were doing?

Very gifted musician but wrong for the job. Just like I was wrong for Roger's gig.

After we moved to Nashville, I met Michael Omartian. Nicest man. Hugely humble. Like Brown and Keith Thomas, Michael also produced tracks on the Amy Grant best seller *Heart in Motion*. Given my noncompliant piano playing with Roger Voudouris, failing to imitate Michael, this was a full-circle moment. Complete with *ji-ji-mu-ge* and surprise.

We were having dinner at Michael and Stormie's home, along with the Bannisters. I remarked on Michael's grand piano. He responded, "Yeah, man, I got another one just like it down in the basement studio. Yamaha gave 'em to me."

I was thinking, I'm no Michael Omartian, but if Yamaha would give him two pianos for free, they might give me one-half of one. And they did. With Michael's recommendation to Yamaha, they gave me a 50 percent discount on a new Yamaha C7 grand piano. I still have that piano. It represents redemption. And like my dad's tiny Gideon Bible, it is "not to be sold." Once again, the love of God in unique form. No detail overlooked.

I once read a book, *The Fabric of Faithfulness*. I was so impressed with it that I sent a note of respect and appreciation to the author, Steven Garber. He kindly wrote back saying he'd be in Memphis soon. Perhaps he could stop in Nashville for a quick visit? We were delighted to host him. We ate a lunch of BLTs and talked as if we'd known each other our whole lives.

Steve's father was a scientist for the University of California at Davis (UCD). My dad's older brother Lee Jackson Jr. ("Jack") was a scientist at UCD too. His focus had something to do with soil and helping to cultivate healthier cotton. Steve and his family had lived in Shafter, just around the corner from Bakersfield—the epicenter of cotton farming in California. My Ashworth cousins had lived in Shafter, too. We visited them on a trip to Los Angeles in the 1960s. Quickly, the co-incidences became too much. Once Steve learned I was an Ashworth and not just a Peacock, the random pieces took order and quickly presented themselves as an uncovered and integrated story.

Steve's father was my uncle's lab partner. Whenever we heard of Uncle Jack's achievements in academia and agriculture, we were hearing of Steve's father's work too. When we had played with our cousin's best friends in Shafter fifty years ago, we were likely playing with neighbor Steve. Wildly unexpected threads were cinched tighter that day, and all in Buck Owens's backyard. To this day, Steve and I remain best of friends and work alongside each other as often as able.

Lastly, the blue-ribbon winner for providence—a story I never tire of repeating.

My high school classmate Sharon Minchuk is in Istanbul, Turkey, on vacation. Imagine Sharon sitting in her hotel room watching the news on Al Jazeera International. A segment on the Brazilian collector of vinyl records, Zero Freitas from São Paulo, comes on. He's the biggest collector in the world—has over two million albums in his collection, fully cataloged in a massive São Paulo warehouse. The reporter pulls out one cataloged album as part of his close. And as Sharon shared the story in her post on Facebook: "The album is none other than Charlie Peacock, our own Chuck Ashworth!"

I love this trajectory: Yuba City High School classmate—Istanbul, Turkey—Al Jazeera—São Paulo, Brazil—two million vinyl albums. And the one album the reporter pulls from the rack? My second solo album on Island Records from 1986. Never sold more than twenty thousand copies. Bam!

I shared the story with Alfie, my then nine-year-old grandson. He picked up on the word "Brazil," saying: "I want to go to Brazil."

Why? I asked.

"That's where the statue is," said Alfie.

Of course. Christ the Redeemer.

I hold to a story that brings order and meaning and redemption to the serendipity and interdependence—like the analogy of an or-

Chapter Sixteen

chestra conductor artfully cueing musicians and musical events—and of course, the musicians must play their part with skill, interpret, and build upon their experience. I don't think any of this tapestry of providence and collaboration is an accident—more like an invitation. Neither do I think the interconnectedness will prosper and profit unless people show up with intention and imagination for the life that is unfolding before them. My fate is determined by my neighbors, and theirs by mine. Everything, everyone, everywhere turns on affection. It is our bond.

seventeen

ARC OF THE CIRCLE

Unlike the one-and-done legendary blues artist Robert Johnson, I used to think that I'd experienced four major musical crossroads. The first, around age twenty. Would I perform and compose jazz exclusively or become a pop star? I chose the latter.

The second was the *Sacramento or Music City conundrum*: Should I leave behind the pop music mission of the Warehouse and Exit Records in Sacramento for new and potentially meaningful opportunities in Nashville? A choice that meant associating with the phenomenon then known as contemporary Christian music (CCM). At the time, I needed to regain control over my vocational choices, wrong or right. *Music City, here I come.*

The third evolved in and around my tenth year in Nashville. It was less a crossroads than a complicated cloverleaf freeway interchange navigated over a few years.

The fourth, I'll save till later.

As for the third, I was burnt out from CCM. What I now know as fatigue, anger, and resentment. After many fun, meaningful, and productive years, the bloom was off the daisy—genrefication and arbitrary corporate policies had become my nemeses. Regarding the music, I primarily worked with two excellent, imaginative artists: Margaret Becker and the duo Out of the Grey (Scott and Chris Denté), producing four albums for each artist. Though the list is long,

I want to highlight a few more artists I've yet to mention: Avalon, Warren Barfield, Lisa Bevill, Bob Carlisle, Eric Champion, Cheri Keaggy, Scott Krippayne, Rich Mullins, NewSong, Nichole Nordeman, Aaron Spiro, Michelle Tumes, and Tony Vincent. Also, there were many multiartist projects, including the two *Coram Deo* projects filled with talented artists, for example, CeCe Winans, Michael Card, and Steven Curtis Chapman, and Christmas projects with Amy Grant, Michael W. Smith, and Cindy Morgan (see the "Selected Discography" for a deep dive).

—

Finally, there was the era of re:think Records—the Sarah Masen and Switchfoot years (1996–1999). With distribution to both mainstream pop and CCM, the stakes were higher, with more staff on the property and more responsibilities than ever. The re:think crew included engineer Shane D. Wilson; executive assistant Katy Krippaehne, who introduced my daughter Molly (Sarah's roommate and touring companion) to her husband, Mark Nicholas; publicist Jay Swartzendruber; and head of marketing and promotion, Nick Barré. As the nonprofit Art House correspondent, soon-to-be-author David Dark occupied an office corner answering cosmic questions from the curious around the world. David and Sarah would go on to marry. We also signed three songwriters who've made a significant mark on music and literature, Tony Miracle (Venus Hum, Blue Man Group), Brent Milligan (producer, educator, and longtime collaborator of Steven Curtis Chapman), and Douglas Kaine McKelvey (award-winning songwriter and author of the *Every Moment Holy* series). All-in, a stellar team.

EMI (the British music giant, home of The Beatles) had purchased the Sparrow Records label, retained the leadership, and reinvented it as EMI Christian Music Group (EMI CMG). Sparrow, founded by Billy Ray Hearn in 1976, had a storied past—one I'd joined up for beginning in 1989, when I signed on as an artist, songwriter, and producer. By 1996, I was ready to *sign* my own artists.

Having been part of the pioneer (post–Jesus Movement) wave of mainstream pop artists that were Christians, I was ready to take the next generation into the street, not just the sanctuary. I'd developed a very strong opinion about something called "crossover." I needed to see if my instincts were right or not.

What I observed was that recording artists signed to explicit Christian labels had no opportunity for their music to be heard by everyone, everywhere, until they'd sold a significant amount to Christians only (in the 250K to 500K albums range). If they could get to those elevated sales numbers, their record company might opt to increase their cultural reach by making a deal with one of the mainstream labels—hence, crossover from one genre or distribution system to another. There had been successful partnerships like this in the past—Denice Williams, BeBe & CeCe. But once Amy Grant's *Heart in Motion* exceeded all expectations with A&M Records' enthusiastic promotion (5 million sold), crossover was a business plan for those that qualified, like dc Talk with Virgin Records.

I understood this business-wise but disliked it theologically. I definitely didn't think artists who were followers of Jesus needed anyone's permission to do their jobs, for everyone, everywhere. The label re:think would represent this conviction—from thesis to praxis.

Bill Hearn, my boss and record company president of EMI CMG, agreed. He graciously funded my re:think label experiment. Instead of crossover, I'd sign new, unproven artists that were *simultaneously* promoted to Christian audiences and mainstream pop audiences.

Instead of crossover, I was doing old-school A&R and talent discovery: "I got a feeling about this artist. They're the real deal." There was no scouting of influencers and indie artists with millions of streams on Spotify then. It was all Gladwell's *Blink* and a gut feeling. Risk and reward or risk and ruin.

My first signing was Sarah. A remarkable singer-songwriter from Michigan in her late teens, she was the most fully evolved artist for her age I'd ever met. Sarah checked every box: curious, iconoclastic, a lover of language, void of cliché, inventive, pop market ready, likable, and people wanted her to win. And she did. Out of the box we had significant radio-play at the adult album alternative format and at Christian pop radio with a song titled "All Fall Down."

But it was the 1990s, and I needed a band.

In 1996 I was running on the treadmill at a gym trying my best to lose twenty pounds. The overhead speakers were blasting modern/ alternative rock radio at ear-bleed levels: Spacehog, Soundgarden, Oasis, Dishwalla, Pearl Jam, and Foo Fighters. Guitars had made another rock 'n' roll comeback. In a fraction of a second, I knew. I'm going to sign a band like this to re:think.

Unbeknownst to me, a few months earlier, a regional sales rep for EMI named Buz Buzbee had dropped off a cassette at my office. I was sitting alone in the front office one late afternoon and happened to look over at the window sill. It was filled with the cassettes of aspiring artists. Most of them, I'd yet to listen to. The spine of one cassette jumped out at me. It said Chin Up. I reached for it and placed it in the cassette player. There it was. Just like with Sarah. *Blink* and gut. All boxes checked. This was the band I was looking for.

I'm not sure I even finished the first song, "Chem 6A," before calling the number. I talked to parents and finally the band, Chad Butler and Tim and Jon Foreman.

I took a scouting trip to San Diego, where the band was from. They were young, fun, artistic, and very much the real deal. We recorded some songs direct to a 2-track tape machine. Demos for archive purposes and listening once back home in Nashville. The tapes never made it there. The one time in my life I put recording tape in a suitcase, American Airlines lost it.

To this day, Jon will tell you, had the tapes made it back to Nashville with a chance to be reviewed, I would've passed on signing the band. Not true. Our friendship and musical destiny were written into history before any of us were born. I'm convinced of that.

Twenty-five years later Switchfoot (not Chin Up) is still going strong. And the tapestry it began? Beautiful.

As for all my rethinking and desire to innovate? Sure, some of that clearly happened. Historian Leah Payne, PhD, described my experiment with re:think and Steve Taylor's with Squint Records this way: "Taylor and Peacock won praise for creating art that aimed to be divinely good rather than supremely useful."[1] That we did. This is the positive side of her appraisal. The negative being, many consumers of Christian music wanted to know what was Christian about it. Unable to clearly discern this goal, it failed the usefulness test.

As it turns out, the name *re:think* does appear to have been endowed with enough goodness to be useful— almost thirty years later. EMI was absorbed by Universal Music in 2012. Always a top property, EMI's Hollywood-based Capitol Records remains a potent brand label today (though under the umbrella of Universal's Capitol Music Group [CMG]). This group contains legendary, history-making record labels, such as Blue Note, Astralwerks, Priority, Motown, and Capitol Christian. The latter has its own music group: Motown Gospel, Capitol CMG Label Group, and Re:Think, the distribution and label services arm of Capitol CMG.

I recognize only 5 percent of the artist names linked to Re:Think on the Capitol CMG website. With a few clicks, it's obvious they are predominantly worship leaders or worship artists, many with church fellowship affiliations. Two from churches with pastors and agendas I would never endorse. Capitol found a new use for one of its legacy assets and repurposed the name.

The re:think concept and dream? Obviously, that's been co-opted, institutionalized, and, in reality, vaporized. They have every right to do with re:think anything they desire, though. They own it. I sold it to them. They can even change the capitalization of the name.

Music *is* hard. Reversals of fortune aren't always about money and fame. Sometimes, they're about meaning—the loss or the replacement of it with another mission.

When I first saw the Motown, Capitol, and Re:Think logos strung together on the website, I was stunned by the irony of it. Motown artists, such as Smokey Robinson and The Temptations, and The Beatles and The Beach Boys on Capitol were my classroom for how to write a pop song—with Aunt Karoly spinning the vinyl. Each one of these labels was started by a songwriter. Motown: Berry Gordy; Capitol: Johnny Mercer; and me with Re:Think. Not bad company. I'll rest in this realization and be grateful I survived.

—

With re:think, hypervigilant stress was the norm. I had dramatically overworked, overthunk, and spent my resilience reserves. For therapy, I returned to practicing the piano with some consistency. *Shedding*, as it is called by jazzers, referring to much-needed alone time practicing in the woodshed. Though a self-taught pianist, as a teenager I'd used the method books of the era to learn chord voicings and practice modes, patterns, and scales (thank you, John Mehegan, Jerry Coker, and Dan Haerle). This was de rigueur for any serious student of jazz. Like training to play in the NFL or becoming a heart surgeon, playing jazz at an authentic level requires serious commitment. You have to put the time in. There are no shortcuts.

My dad, the music educator, had used the Jamey Abersold method of play-along recordings, memorizing the solos of the greats and the practice of scales, modes, and patterns in all keys for his jazz pedagogy. And, of course, immersion: playing in small and large ensembles and gigging. No substitute for that—which in my era meant playing from something called the *Real Book*, a kind of jazz canon of tunes to perform and base your improvisations on. A little of this rubbed off on me. But what I quickly realized about myself is that I loved the outsider artists and the inventors/innovators most—musicians that I imagined wouldn't get near an Abersold method book (though I've since learned this isn't entirely true). What I felt most intuitively about jazz was the freedom of composition and improvisation. I had moments where I pretended to sound like pianists Bill Evans, Keith Jarrett, or Andrew Hill. And to this day, I can do a tiny imitation of each. But I quickly moved off the idea that I had to momentarily become someone else to become myself. Instead, I wanted to see what sort of individual sound would emerge over time without copying, without memorizing solos. A goal that has taken a lifetime and is best represented on the EP *Blue for You* (2022).

When I began shedding again in the late 1990s, I just played, inventing challenges to overcome problems and increase technique—putting in the work to help my hands articulate the music I was hearing. That's how I practiced. A time arrived when I returned to my youthful skill and ability and then surpassed it. Engineer Richie Biggs set me up to record myself on the 7 foot 6 inch Yamaha C7 piano in the big room of the Art House. I improvised for hours and edited the best of my performances into a dozen songs or so. Fifteen years later, in 2014, they were released as *Lemonade* and debuted on *Billboard's* Traditional Jazz Chart at No. 4.

In 1999 and early 2000, I finished the last of my production work before taking a break. This included a new vocal solo album of my own and producing Audio Adrenaline, Switchfoot, Darwin Hobbs, Twila Paris, and Ladysmith Black Mambazo. The third crossroads was afoot, though. Two old narratives had returned, the jazz and the pastor story lines. Prayers were spoken. Choices were pondered and made.

When I returned to jazz and the improvisational music story line, saxophonist Jeff Coffin, then of Béla Fleck and the Flecktones, and bassist James Genus (The Brecker Brothers, Herbie Hancock) were my guides.

I met Jeff at the famed Nashville club the Exit/In. Roger Smith was in town playing Hammond B3 with the legendary East Bay horn band Tower of Power—he still does. The band has been a part of my musical vocabulary since early high school. I was hooked when I heard Andi's sister Paula playing the debut record the summer between freshman and sophomore year. The first full-length was recorded for San Francisco Records, a label founded by producer David Rubinson and promoter Bill Graham, two men who figured into my life a decade later—each would manage me for a time.

I recognized saxophonist Jeff Coffin from a Flecktones promo photo and approached him after the concert. He was interested in doing some playing, perhaps recording. I knew I couldn't play at Jeff's level, let alone record with him. His prowess was frightening.

I doubled down and practiced for months. Once confident, I called Jeff and set up a recording session. Having never played a note together, we recorded for two hours. Then ate lunch and recorded a bit longer. The second session didn't touch the first in spontaneity. I used very little of it. The result is *Arc of the Circle*—a recording of our improvisational duets with special guests added later, including guitarist Marc Ribot and drummer Derrek Phillips. It was not released until 2008.

I met James Genus on a New York City homeschool outing in the late 1990s with my son Sam. One of our stops was to hear guitarist John Scofield at Iridium. James was playing bass. A solid gentleman and masterful musician, James visited with us, and we traded information. You can watch him on *Saturday Night Live*. He's the always-visible musician to the left of the guest host during the monologue. I hired him to play on the Ladysmith Black Mambazo record (with the late great Don Alias on percussion), Twila Paris, and my own *Kingdom Come* recording.

As for the pastor narrative, there was the year we kept an apartment in St. Louis to attend seminary. My plan was to earn an MDiv and keep practicing the piano. Once again, I needed to move. This time backward. Choosing to dive back into jazz was fun and no harm. Revisiting seminary and possibly becoming a pastor at forty-five years old was the definition of nonneutrality. It turned out different than planned, but the difference was fruitful. I went home with a fresh perspective, new friendships, a disturbing goatee, an adventure with Andi, and some education (she went on to complete an MA in theological studies). The bottom line verdict for me from all the theologians and profs was, "Stay if you like, but honestly, you're already doing what we hope to train people to do. The autodidact life is working for you. Carry on."

By 2001 we were back in Nashville. I returned to what I knew: creativity, movement, dissatisfaction, and cyclical illness. The stress continued to build. Gone for nearly a year, I needed well-paying work, and soon. I worried that I'd squandered my music career looping on the pastor fantasy, ignoring the obvious and being obviously off-course to some degree. I married off a son, lost an appendix, and raised my blood pressure. Had frequent anxiety attacks. I worked as a VP for EMI for a year, wrote another book, passed a kidney stone, and kept practicing the piano.

It was time for a trip to the beach.

On the beach in Seaside, Florida, small planes fly along the ocean's rim with banners in tow. They're meant to draw the attention of beachgoers to restaurants with enticingly cheap deals on shrimp and steak or shops shilling boogie boards and flip-flops. You can't help but notice the banners trailing from the Piper Cub. You're sitting under your umbrella reading the latest Jack Reacher tale and hearing the little putt-putt aircraft motor before you see anything. When the plane appears, you look up and give the advertisement two seconds of your life. Then you go back to reading or tanning or both.

My plane, the banner I paid for, read, "Come home, music. My soul is lonesome. I'm so sorry I took you for granted."

Before the seminary trip, I'd been producing too many pop/gospel records and writing too many three-minute songs with the same form, function, and predictability. What I needed was to step back to move forward. My intuition to return to improvisation-based music was spot-on. It freed me from my music business resentment and, most importantly, musical stagnation.

Thankfully the music was willing to come back. The adage is true. *Take care of the music, and it will take care of you.*

My new music, filtered through the grid of hard-won experience, had healing in every note. Just the imaginative task of naming my new jazz/improvisational compositions was so freeing it almost felt noble: "Be Well Johnny Cash," "Downstairs Room of You," "Dodo's Whim," "The Brightness of Peter Berger," and "Frank the Marxist Memorial Gong Blues." The latter was named for a mentor, Frank Kofsky, an American Marxist historian and jazz critic who played drums in a raggedy outsider-artist version of Elvin Jones.

When it was time to make my recording of *Love Press Ex-Curio* (released in 2005), James Genus made it happen. With his imprimatur paving the way, Ravi Coltrane, Kurt Rosenwinkel, Joey Baron, and Ralph Alessi came on board for a session in NYC. Jeff Coffin, Tony Miracle, Victor Wooten, Jerry McPherson, and other friends joined in Nashville. My old-school Sacramento collaborators Henry Robinett and Roger Smith got in on it too.

I felt like an artist again. I'd recaptured that youthful singular feeling of creating music without thought to use or success. The fortune was in the forgoing of all that music-business thinking.

The NYC sessions were incredibly intimidating, though. I had spent two decades out of the loop, singing for my supper or producing artists. I was not, by any industry definition, a jazz musician. I didn't hang in jazz spaces with jazz cats. I wasn't immersed in the scene. I was in my teens and early twenties, but after that, no. These guys were the real deal. One with a Coltrane surname—geez. I was nervous, sweating, and exuding imposter syndrome. They were kind and professional, and we made it through five songs in six hours.

I had not realized that several compositions were challenging, even for this crew. The producer in me quickly assessed there'd be editing to do. Trumpeter, Ralph Alessi? "That cat," as my dad used to say, "could read fly shit." Without Ralph's stellar sight-reading ability, we would not have accomplished what we did. On the subject of dung, one of my favorite moments of the session was during the fade of a song when drummer Joey Baron yells out, "Holy shit, man, you think any of that is usable?" *Of course, Joey. This is what I do. I move the ones and zeros around till every musical choice plays nice with the other. Leave it to me. I'm licensed. Seriously, I do this for a living.*

Jazz critic Mark F. Turner wrote on the fruit of our labor: "Like a sound chemist, Charlie Peacock mixes acoustic jazz with electronica to create some interesting music on *Love Press Ex-Curio* (Loves Pressure Exhibits Curiosity). The pop and gospel Grammy-winning producer/artist now proves his passion for jazz, and the results are impressive."[2]

With my passion proven and no jazz police at the door, I felt like the first musical crossroads had finally been merged, redeemed (or deemed unnecessary). I composed and played jazz, wrote and sang songs, and the bonus: I became a record producer, a label owner, and a music publisher too. The whole pop star thing was never my path. Artist, yes.

As for a summary of the second crossroads: I did leave Sacramento, and Exit Records' pop ambitions, for Music City. I exited to work with Christians on what I knew was music almost exclusively named gospel or Christian. What was the first thing I did on arrival, though? Write a hit pop song for Amy Grant. My dream of writing songs the whole world sings and creating music for the Christian church had also come true.

Still, I wasn't comfortable being fenced within any genre's playground. Ten years working within Nashville's Christian music community confirmed this. My trip to seminary and return to improvisational music inspired broader personal and musical changes. Admittedly, this third crossroads required a lot of circuitous hiking and wandering. I eventually found the path and a handle on my identity.

I was an autodidact, polymath, musician. An artist. A follower of
Jesus, open to creating everywhere, in everything, for everyone, and
helping others to do the same. My motto? No worthwhile music and
art making, no good dreams, were off-limits. Bring it on.

This meant I could still work with my much-admired artist friend
Sara Groves on her projects, gig with Jeff Coffin opening up for the
Sun Ra Arkestra, continue developing recording artists, take another
seminary class or two if I wanted, write a book, cofound a collective
of patrons and artists, champion the ONE Campaign, do speaking
gigs, and produce films on legendary songwriter Hank Cochran and
Nashville's indie music community, including the winsome, inventive
artist Brooke Waggoner.

Longtime collaborator and friend Scott Denté joined me in the
creation of a production/publishing company and sometime label, Runway Network, from 2005 to 2008. We did admirable work developing
artists and stewarding songs, including artist Andy Davis and the Sixpence None the Richer catalog. But being in control of my music business destiny held no sway over the control my insides had on me.

We spent a small fortune with little to show for it by music industry standards. Runway Network was indie to a fault. I wanted major
label results—a big story, like I'd had with re:think and Switchfoot.
The thrill of going from a bunk-bed band to international hit-makers
was intoxicating. Disappointed with Runway's results, I wore a mask
of cranky, judgmental dissatisfaction on my face. I was making those
I loved, like Scott and Andi, miserable.

Scheduled to travel to China with Dave Kiersznowski, I canceled
at the last minute. I was too sick to move, let alone get on a plane.
I got in bed and slept for a week. Then I came to. Awake. I'd had a bad
case of amnesia and *the body keeping the score*. Some people can get
their mogul and their music on simultaneously. I would eventually
learn I'm not one of them. We closed up shop.[3]

Then 2009 happened. The era of The Civil Wars duo had begun.
And with it, a new season of *Producer for Hire*. The big story I craved
had come around again.

Though the music business is historically unpredictable, there's
one aspect you can always count on. It lives for the sound of applause

and the ring of the cash register (or the ping of a cash app). Make your own record apart from a big-time record label and sell a half-million as The Civil Wars did, and the business comes calling. They're thinking, *Hmmm, maybe you know something we don't and we should purchase or license it.*

This time I was going to be a bit wiser. Dave Kiersznowski and I set up Twenty Ten Music (TTM) as a publishing and production company, mixing patronage and profit. I'd look for ways to develop artists while producing friends I loved or major label projects that intrigued me. Dave and I invested in the family—my son Sam and future daughter-in-law Ruby. Along with The Civil Wars, we worked with The Lone Bellow, k.s. Rhoads, Zeke Duhon, Brooke Waggoner, Anna Gilbert, Daves Highway, Nathan Tasker, The Daylights, Joseph LeMay, actress/vocalist McKenzie Mauzy, and many more. I took meetings with everyone and fielded all calls, including Christina Perri, Kristian Bush of Sugarland, Mary Chapin Carpenter, A. J. Croce, Rickie Lee Jones, Regina Spektor, Buffy Sainte-Marie, and Colbie Caillat.

Ultimately, for production work, I ended up investing my time in The Civil Wars (2009–2013), Keith & Krystin Getty (featuring Alison Krauss), Chris Cornell, my own *No Man's Land* vocal record, Holly Williams, The Lone Bellow, Brett Dennen, Kris Allen, *TURN: Washington's Spies* (theme for a TV show on AMC featuring vocalists Joy Williams and The National's Matt Berninger), Jon Foreman, Joy Williams's *Venus* solo album, Selah, Scott Mulvahill, and Angelica Garcia (an artist that Warner Brothers' A&R executives Lenny Waronker and Michael Howe brought me).

By fall of 2014, I was toasted to a crisp (again) and back in therapy. *Producer for Hire*, that old song and dance, was still more problem than peace. I offered the same diagnosis of the music business from fifteen years earlier: *There's too little reciprocal respect anymore. And with their dramatically one-sided policies, these entertainment corporations' business affairs (legal) departments have taken all the fun out of it. And the nature of artistry has changed in ways I no longer connect with.*

My therapist offered his own diagnosis: *You're very angry and lonely.*

True enough. I was angry about the state of the music business and lonely in my marriage, as was Andi. It was a season of taking one another for granted. Of finding more wrong than right. A story we documented in our cowritten book published in 2024—gratefully, a tale that ended in an enriched marriage and friendship.[4]

Before redemption arrived, while angry and lonely, I did what any reasonable person would do. I took a job creating a commercial music program at one of the most inflexible, befuddling, insular institutions known to humanity—the American university. That's how clever I am. Apparently, it had been a bit since I'd read my creative writing journal from my sophomore year of high school: "I tend to shy away from the institutional schooling system."

I kid, of course. I jest. But, no. Not really. I was proud of the music program we built. I made lifetime friends with colleagues. Hired many talented people still there and thriving. Absolutely loved my students. Then there was the other 95 percent. Good thing I'm a fire-startin', short-distance runnin', quick-twitch kind of guy. A twitch is about how long my body lasted.

My tenure included consultant/artist in residence from fall 2014 to summer 2015 while I created the program, built a studio and classrooms, and recruited faculty and students. During the 2015–2016 academic year, I was director of the Commercial Music Program. From 2016 to 2017, I was that, plus the director of the entire School of Music *and* overseer of the newly acquired Sound Emporium Studios (think, *O Brother, Where Art Thou?* soundtrack).

I was homebound on sick leave for nearly all of my fourth semester of employment. By the summer, it was apparent I would not be coming back. The Mayo Clinic diagnosis: *central sensitization*. A name for my cyclical illness, now a constant. Escaping institutional life was a relief. Disappointing the students and letting down colleagues and families I'd made commitments to—heartbreak. Now, I'm just a memory, a fancy man: *Founder and Director Emeritus of the Commercial Music Program, Lipscomb University, Nashville, Tennessee.*

Ironically, with every imagined treatment modality for my disorder, music became my core therapy. Somehow, the way the brain works, I was less obsessed with the 24/7 disabling, migraine-level headache if I was working on music. *Take care of the music, and it will take care of you.*

At the end of the 2016 fall semester, my music publishing agreement with Steve Markland and Downtown Music was wrapping up. I'd already determined not to renew even if asked. Apart from cowriting an Elle King song for a Reese Witherspoon film (*Hot Pursuit*) and working on the *Nashville* TV show, it had been an overall fail. Most importantly, nothing about the relationship played to my strengths, and sadly, I had no more patience for being a sixty-year-old man sitting in writing rooms with twenty-something songwriters.

The younger songwriters have an edge in that they naturally hear the language, melodies, chords, and rhythms of their time. This is why the bulk of popular music is created by younger people. The sixty-year-old's advantage is being possibly skilled enough to hear the song elements of their time *and* all the subsequent generations (though almost always with an incrementally diminished ability with each passing year, for example, having the ability to access the uniqueness of Seattle-esque grunge more than Drake-era trap). Pragmatically, the more experienced songwriter imagines and hears the options for all the directional elements of a song quicker than a younger counterpart. It's this latter bit that caused my patience to stretch thin. Turning the writers' room into a songwriting lecture, exhibiting impatience, not allowing your fellow songwriters to evolve at their pace, and taking over the song to get it done, is a bad look. One I increasingly made visible and was shamed by.

I turned in the last of my required songs and pronounced it the end of my thirty-five-year corporate music publishing career. I'd been with CBS Songs (April/Blackwood), SBK, SparrowSong, EMI, SonyATV, and Downtown Music Publishing.

The very next day I received a call from Brent Bourgeois. Ours is a long-running friendship, personal and musical, going back to our nightclub roots in the late 1970s and nascent recording careers. We've seen it all. Been competitors, collaborators, and each other's champions and producers. One of my favorite embarrassing memories with Brent is November 27, 1985. We were sitting on the steps of the Fillmore Auditorium in San Francisco, talking about ourselves after exiting the building. Inside, promoter/legend Bill Graham's Fillmore 20th Anniversary Concert (1965–1985) was under way. We were two of his young artist management clients, and Brent was cofounder of the band Bourgeois Tagg ("I Don't Mind at All"). Our sizable egos needed a little "me time" break from the hippie lovefest going down inside the auditorium.

Interestingly, the Bill Graham invite we received had a born-again theme, though not of the Jesus-type: "Obviously, this is a reunion for many of us who've been fortunate enough through these years to have been a part of very special time in space. For whatever the reason, the soil of the Bay Area seemed to be chosen; and, out of a seed that was planted here, all of us seem to have been reborn."

Inside the Fillmore, Country Joe McDonald was singing "Feel Like I'm Fixin' to Die Rag" from Woodstock fame. The Sons of Champlin, Jefferson Airplane alumni (Kantner, Balin & Casady), John Lee Hooker, Bob Weir from the Dead, It's a Beautiful Day, and Buddy Miles were all there, jammin', bringing back the '60s, complete with the original acid light-show pioneers. Legendary rock 'n' roll history. What a drag it was for us, forced to hang out with all these old people and their irrelevant music.

We've matured a bit since then. We're the older people and finally understand the privileged context we'd been invited into.

Brent was calling to tell me about his new gig with Facebook as a writer/producer/A&R person, and ultimately wonder aloud, *Would I be interested in writing and producing for Facebook?* What? Facebook and music? That sounded like the ultimate corporate mess.

Back in our nightclub performer days in Northern California, there was a musician named Will Littlejohn from the band Leo Swift, and Leslie Barton, a savvy music-lover and fan of ours. Will went on to cofound WaveGroup Sound, producing such ubiquitously popular video games as *Rock Band* and *Guitar Hero*. Leslie Barton? VP of sales and marketing. Our mutual friends, guitarists Lance Taber and Lyle Workman, were involved, too, executing those noodly licks and chunky power chords.

In 2014, WaveGroup became Facebook's official in-house sound and music design team, and the Facebook Music Initiative (FMI) was born. Enter Leslie Barton, Pamela Roberts, and Brent as A&R handling the talent. They began inviting their friends and music producer/artist favorites to contribute.

This brings me to the fourth musical crossroads. When Brent asked me if I'd like to be part of FMI, I had a choice to make. Was I ready to completely disconnect from the music business that I'd given my entire life to? Could I live in a musical world devoid of ego strokes, scorekeeping, and gold records? This gig was about creating music for the world's largest social media platform (2 billion plus), essentially a music library for users to include with video and animation posts. You know, dancing cats, birthday notices, and those weird ads that appear when the ghost in the machine knows you've been shopping for a pair of blue Nike trainers with custom gold lettering?

Actually, the invitation was the one I'd waited my whole life for. It just came from a source I could've never predicted, but guided by friends I trusted. I was asked to reveal the full width and depth of my musical interests, meaning, and skill. To make what I love. To play as a child with the experience of a music biz survivor.

I accepted and headed down the road. There were some minor creative bumps, entirely of my doing. A few times, I leaned too hard into an old-school music library trope, not trusting that I was being asked, without qualification, to simply "do my thing." Once I accepted reality, freedom came. It was a remarkable multi-year experience that involved creating all the jazz I dreamed of and much more (orchestral pieces, pop songs, and film soundtracks). And all without even a moment of corporate disrespect, distrust, or self-serving financial or legal shenanigans on Facebook's part. Indeed, a dream come true. Brent and Leslie, my main reports, were encouraging and always professional. For me, it was a drama-free zone.

In 2019, I was asked to be the pilot artist for an FMI streaming program. Instagram had jumped in and begun incorporating the music on their own Meta-owned platform. This is where FMI really took off—especially with Reels. Since millions were enjoying our music and using it off-platform, FMI decided, *If you can't beat 'em, join 'em.* Why not let all these new Facebook- and Instagram-generated fans listen on Spotify, iTunes, Tidal, Pandora, and all the rest? Goodwill, right?

The first release was *Jazz Composer, Vol. One*, featuring my compositions performed by Nashville's finest jazz musicians, including long-time collaborator Jeff Coffin; trumpeter Matthew White, who played on my 2018 jazz release, *When Light Flashes*; drummer Jim White; bassist Matt Wigton; and pianists Chris Walters and Matt Endahl. This allowed me to compose bebop and Miles Davis, *Kind of Blue*–era styles—something I'd missed out on back when I was younger. To hear them played authentically was, in bebop vernacular, "a gas." I grew up on this music, but apart from my dad's record collection of Miles, Monk, and Brubeck, the style I was into as a teenager was funkier and more experimental: Miles's *In a Silent Way* and *Bitches Brew*, along with Herbie Hancock's *Headhunters* and Chick Corea's *Light as a Feather*.

I loved Bill Evans and the mind-expanding improvisations of Keith Jarrett, but it would be a long time before I had my own concert grand piano. I did have a Fender Rhodes electric piano, just like Herbie and Chick, complete with wah-wah, phase shifter, and delay pedals. The FMI opportunity allowed me to dust off the past and regain my inner-1970s, funky Rhodes chops. I brought them into the future as often as possible, especially with the album *Paisley Crusader*, on the title cut, "Try to Stop Us," and "Le Grande" from the EP *Eye on the Spy*. No contemporary recording features my electric piano offerings more than *Keep Movin'*, the collaboration with trumpeter Eddie Henderson, a veteran of Herbie's band and a significant jazz solo artist in his own right.

I was able to release a solo piano follow-up to *Lemonade* titled *Trout Creek Ranch* and my most adventuresome jazz/improvisational music recording yet, a true acoustic quintet titled *Blue for You*, featuring John Patitucci, Eric Harland, Chris Potter, and Marcus Printup. Writing this paragraph makes me smile. I'm forever grateful. Because of FMI (now called MMI, incorporating the Meta title), I have a larger, more active audience for my music than ever.

This riff on the FMI experience, my music, and those I made it with could fill pages. From this point on, I defer to the discography. I have other, more cosmically consequential things to write than lists and mic drops.

Though I've used the *crossroads* as a metaphorical device from music history, to be accurate, there never was one, let alone four. The crossroads concept is conjured from the stuff of blues legend. When applied to me, it reveals stops along the road of immaturity, insecurity, and for decades, yielding to misdirection and not accepting the obvious. A sort of panic and confusion: *Something is happening. Better give it a name and make a big deal out of it.*

Away with the crossroads metaphor. Here's another travel option that feels more applicable to the long and winding road.

Look at any map. Even the longest stretch of interstate highway isn't straight or flat, is it? It will still get you from here to there, though. Or drop pins on any two points of a circle, and you have an arc, correct? Ironically, it's all arc of the circle, though, isn't it? Circumnavigate the circle once or a thousand times. It's the same track, but maybe you see things differently and experience the repetitive trip differently.

For years I let myself be tortured by well-meaning voices hoping to temper my artistic eclecticism and curious interest in *too many things*. Not suitable for building a brand, they said. Focus. *You're at a crossroads, choose well or fail at something/anything.* Just being my myself wasn't enough. Yet it is. Entirely enough.

Narrowcast brand-building is just name making in a new suit. And name making, as I've stated elsewhere, is in the top five of the world's most exhausting and inhuman undertakings. Storytelling, fine. But telling stories in the form of relentless PR to "build a base" toward the goal of name/brand "ubiquity" for profit? Or dialing in your artistic focus tight enough to fit into a marketable genre or niche? Count me out. I'm just a simple farm kid. I focus on fruit bearing and offering the firstfruits of the harvest from several crops. I really am the great-grandson of Bob and Maggie Miller. Got my own subsistence art farm.

Returning to the directional road metaphor—I'm focused on finishing the race. Completing the long-lived task that my teacher, Jesus, has given to me. The work of witness through my imagination and creativity to the astonishing, life-altering story of the grace of God for humanity and the entirety of creativity, known and still yet to be discovered. This is my gig. This is who I am.

Andi with Switchfoot members Chad Butler and Jon Foreman

Musicans from the Love Press Ex-Curio sessions at Avatar Studios, New York City, 2004—Joey Baron (drums), James Genus (bass), Ravi Coltrane (tenor saxophone), Ralph Alessi, seated (trumpet)

Multi-day artist retreat at our home, The Art House, September 10, 2008

Reunited with my Fender Rhodes electric piano

The Art House, Bellevue, Tennessee

Joy Williams and John Paul White of The Civil Wars recording the *Poison & Wine* EP, The Art House, 2009

Andi with songwriting legend JD Souther and dear friend, longtime recording engineer Richie Biggs—Art House 20th Anniversary, 2011

My longest, most prolific session musician relationship is with this talented character, guitarist Jerry McPherson

Producing The Lone Bellow debut, live at Rockwood Music Hall, New York City, 2011

Producing Jackson Browne for Holly Williams's 2013 recording, *The Highway*

Jeff Coffin, rock legend Al Kooper, and the artist at The Red Room, Berklee College of Music, Boston, 2012

Producing Chris Cornell and Joy Williams, The Art House, Nashville, Tennessee, 2013

Performing on the *Late Show with David Letterman*, December 16, 2013. Chris Cornell and Joy Williams sang "Misery Chain"—Elf showed up backstage

Two trusted friends and confidants—Steve Taylor and Allan Heinberg

Andi and me with the source, my teenage songwriting hero, James Taylor

It's your birthday, Allan Heinberg—cake wranglers, left to right, Butterfly Boucher, Katie Herzig, Andi Ashworth

Music legacy, father and son, the Oscar- and Grammy-nominated song-writer, Sam Ashworth

The adult children, a formidable four at the Grammy Awards 2021 —Sam
Ashworth, Ruby Amanfu (Ashworth), Molly and Mark Nicholas

Friends for life—Dave Kiersznowski and Steven Garber

Autodidact producing the master, trumpeter Eddie Henderson at Orchard Studios, New York City, October 19, 2022

Peer pressure—fellow producers and friends, Mike Elizondo and Tommy Sims

With John Huie, co-founder of CAA Nashville at the iconic Exit/In night-club, October 24, 2023, almost forty years after he first booked me on tour with The Fixx and General Public

Interviewing legendary guitarist Peter Frampton for documentary, 2023

Vince Gill, filming documentary—two survivor/thrivers, one famous, the other just well-known, both chronically music-centric

It began and ends with live music. Rudy's Jazz Room, Nashville, Tennessee, 2023—The Charlie Peacock Quintet featuring Brian Blade (drums), the artist (Fender Rhodes electric piano), Scott Mulvahill (upright bass), Roger Smith (Hammond B3 organ) and Jeff Coffin (soprano saxophone).

eighteen

THE SECRET OF TIME

Our move to Nashville in 1989 was the right place, right time, with the right people and the right tools. Providence; a seamless interdependence of people and place, musicians and music, imagination, and creativity with few limitations. And then, the wholly undeserved gift of succeeding at it and providing for my family and studio teams.

"You will never stop working." Sparrow Records executives Peter York and Bill Hearn were doing their part to make good on their earlier promise. In between gigs with Brown, they contracted me to produce Margaret Becker's *Simple House*, the follow-up to our first successful collaboration, *Immigrant's Daughter*. The first three albums I made for Sparrow—these two, and *The Secret of Time*—were nominated for Grammy Awards. I remember asking Peter, "Hey, man, should I be going to the awards ceremony?" He replied with a "No, babe," and "not much chance of winning." I wasn't offended. I didn't have time to attend, nor could I afford the expense. I put my head down and got back to work. Not only was I writing for *Love Life*, the follow-up to *The Secret of Time*, and touring, I was back with the Brown crew working on Amy's *Heart in Motion*.

In Sacramento, we had lived busy, productive lives. I was always in the studio, performing Northern California clubs in the evening, and on occasion in the UK or Europe touring or recording. In one season, I toured the US and Canada with The Fixx and General Public, among others. It was difficult for our young family. Andi heroically took on nearly all the work of family and home, and I created the music. I was a loving father and husband, but too often absent. Even when present, my mind was occupied creating the next thing or puzzling out a labyrinth of problems.

Even dreams come with tension and trial. We were naïve to the challenges that would present themselves in Music City. The complexity of family and nonstop production, tempo of busyness, necessity of travel and expensive studio gear—every rhythm doubled and tripled. A little over a year had passed since moving, and I'd already worked on six albums (and toured Europe, the UK, and the USA, and built a home in a subdivision in Bellevue). I was on fire and loving every minute of it—except the stress and loneliness it produced in Andi.

I needed a studio of my own, something minutes from the house so I could be close to the family, eat dinner together, tuck the kids in with Andi—practice presence more faithfully. Bill Hearn's father (Sparrow Records founder), Billy Ray Hearn, provided rescue. He called the label's Nashville banker. "Charlie Peacock," he told the eager-to-please banker, "is going to be hugely successful and make a lot of money for us. Give him whatever he needs." This directive was less a mafia don affectation than using language his banker understood; a case of lending his own successful, respected imprimatur, saying *you have my guarantee*. I learned from this and would (in later years) lend my imprimatur to the musically gifted in need of help and encouragement.

By that afternoon I had a check in hand for $100,000 (a five-year loan). Back to work at Omnisound Studios, I began querying Brown and every other engineer in the studio as to what gear I should buy. I needed a building in Bellevue near our home. More work on top of already too much work. Still positive, I was temporarily taking on the extra, hoping a more human, life-giving work/family balance would emerge.

On Amy's *Heart in Motion* album Brown had assigned me various arranging and track-building responsibilities, and I got to it, concentrating on "Every Heartbeat," including the song's horn arrangement and another for "Hats" (adding his own special sauce, trombonist Chris McDonald took my rough ideas and turned them into a readable, playable arrangement).

Along with Amy the star, and Brown at the helm, the musicians on "Every Heartbeat" were Chris McHugh (drums), Tommy Sims (bass), and Jerry McPherson (guitars). I handled keyboards, drum programming, and horn arrangements, with additional keys from Blair Masters and Robbie Buchanan. The horn section consisted of Mark Douthit (sax), Barry Green and Chris McDonald (trombone), and Mike Haynes (trumpet). Backing vocalists were Chris Eaton, Kim Fleming, and Vicki Hampton. Jeff Balding recorded and mixed. Daniel Abraham added additional production to the radio and remix singles.

This circle of excellence and creativity grew me, attuning my ear and my resolve to finer points of musical—and managerial—creativity. I had for so long hoped for a mentor who embodied the obsession and skill that could transform an abstract, chaotic idea into a layered, distinct, and infectious piece of music—a mentor willing to teach. And now here I was, surrounded, learning, and working on more projects than my Dodge and Bellevue bungalow could handle. Provision arrived in the form of a very practical new minivan and new home.

Sadly, though, the Brown Bannister production apprentice chapter was coming to a natural end. I learned so much from this talented and loving man. I wasn't on the runway anymore, though. I was flying at thirty-five thousand feet with my Nashville artist, production, and soon to be record label/publisher career—soaring to more opportunities than I could possibly fulfill.

I had finished Margaret Becker's *Simple House* during my time with Brown and crew, but I count another musical act as my Nashville solo-producer beginning. Scott and Christine Denté met at Berklee College of Music in 1985 and were married in October 1987. Soon after, the couple moved south to Nashville to pursue a music career, and like thousands before them, waited tables. Peter York from Sparrow heard a demo and scouted them. He wondered, would I be interested in producing the duo, soon to be named Out of the Grey? We all met at the Californian-friendly restaurant Slice of Life, across the street from Omnisound at 1806 Division Street to discuss.

Providentially, Fleming McWilliams, a vocal performance student at Belmont College, waited on us and introduced herself. She recognized me. Over the next thirty-three years, she would join her husband to be, John Painter, in the duo Fleming and John, make records and tour, create the wildly successful music camp Voice Up Loud (which my two granddaughter vocalists have attended), and become mother to Roxy (my grandson Alfie's best friend). Only in Nashville.

I connected with Scott and Chris Denté from the jump; they proved to be highly skilled soulful musicians with big, open hearts, eager for life. I told Peter, "I'm in." I had to complete my new studio in Bellevue so we could get to work.

And so it all began in earnest; because of the opportunities Brown and Mike Blanton created for me, and Peter York and Bill Hearn living up to their promises, I did not stop working for ten years. None of the Brown crew did, nor my own crew of first-call musicians and engineers. According to *AllMusic* (industry standard for album credits), I produced well over seventy records between 1989 and 1999. All-in, I have over one thousand credits on albums and singles. Not numbers as much as history, and *whoa, that was a lot of work.*

For so many of us musicians and would-be producers, during that short period of time, Brown was our Miles Davis. He spotted our talent, cultivated the best in us, and teed us up to have our own remarkable careers. Brown opened up a world to me filled with a unique cast of characters that changed the course of my life for the better—and the lives of many more in the process. Though his deep connection to the success of Amy Grant's early career puts him at the center of contemporary Christian music's mainstreaming, a just and wise world recognizes him as a producer's producer, capable of any style or genre of music, who represents in word and deed what an actual Christian is. But a "Christian producer"? No. For me, as a genre tag, it is far too limiting and inaccurate. Brown's crew, his acolytes, would have nothing of it, and their careers prove it.

Genre typecasting is the curse of every musician, composer, and producer eager to faithfully create music that the whole world sings.

Instead, we aspire to be (as I believe for myself) God's musical person, everywhere and in everything. This doesn't exclude making music specifically for the Christian church—it naturally includes it as an expression of musical faithfulness among thousands of options.

Consider a few of the Nashville songwriters, musicians, and producers in the original Brown studio crew from 1989.

Wayne Kirkpatrick is a singer-songwriter and producer often linked to Michael W. Smith and Amy Grant, and rightly so. He co-wrote many of the songs Christian people associate with these artists. The whole story? Wayne has written songs for Faith Hill, Garth Brooks, Babyface, Joe Cocker, Martina McBride, Wynonna Judd, Trisha Yearwood, Bonnie Raitt, Peter Frampton, and Eric Clapton, whose version of the Wayne Kirkpatrick/Tommy Sims/Gordon Kennedy song "Change the World" won the Grammy Award for Song of the Year and was a Top 40 hit in over twenty countries. Wayne developed the country band Little Big Town, producing and cowriting, including their signature hit, "Boondocks." With his brother Karey, Wayne cowrote the lyrics and music for the hit Broadway musical *Something Rotten!*, nominated for ten Tony Awards. The Kirkpatricks went on to do the same for *Mrs. Doubtfire*. Bet against Wayne in music and art, and you're going to lose.

Tommy Sims, Gordon Kennedy, and Chris McHugh have a similar story. Once members of the "Christian rock band" Whiteheart, each musician exited to live a much larger, musical narrative. Tommy, bassist/songwriter/producer, became bass player to the stars, including Sheryl Crow and Bruce Springsteen. Chris is a first-call session player with a deep list of rock, pop, and country credits and a long tenure as drummer/music director with superstar Keith Urban. Gordon, the son of the legendary session musician and producer Jerry Kennedy, has kept the legacy alive as a multidecade musical partner to Garth Brooks and Peter Frampton.

As far as ubiquity goes, one musician from the Brown camp may have achieved more influence than all others: guitarist Jerry McPherson. *AllMusic* tallies Jerry playing on over 1,300 albums and singles, including those by Faith Hill, Don Henley, and The Civil Wars. (And we know this tally is incomplete. Despite the advent of competitive independent music from 2000 to 2009, *AllMusic* has yet to find a way to keep up with the millions of digital releases not affiliated with major labels.)

This sort of musical evolution and diverse influence is the norm, not the exception. Turn the page on all these musicians connected to Brown Bannister and Nashville in the late 1980s, and you'll see a similar story arc: Dann Huff, Jimmie Lee Sloas, Blair Masters, Eric Darken, Chris Eaton, Kim Fleming, and Vicki Hampton are only a few.

The same evolving narrative, from Christian music beginnings to well beyond, applies to the many remarkable people that have been my first-call crew over the years, including engineers Tom Laune, Rick Will, F. Reid Shippen, Shane Wilson, and Richie Biggs; and musicians Steve Brewster, Tony Miracle, Brent Milligan, Scott Denté, Tim Lauer, Andy Leftwich, Ken Lewis, and Mark Hill. How Mark and I met is a story.

The first time I worked with Mark, I asked him to basically be someone else. Tommy Sims was my guy on bass, absolutely brilliant. One of Tommy's parts on the Out of the Grey record had been accidentally erased. It was time to mix. He was on tour and unavailable. I'd heard great things about Mark, a skilled touring musician with few recording credits, so I took a chance and called him: "Mark, I've got good news and bad news. I'd love to hire you to play bass on a record, one song. The bad news is I need you to copy Tommy Sims's bass part verbatim." Thankfully, we had a work tape to pass on to Mark. He memorized it and nailed it note for note, feel for feel. I wish I remembered which song it was. What's the old adage? "Luck is when preparation meets opportunity." Check *AllMusic* for credits—Mark has over eight hundred, including Kelly Clarkson, The Lone Bellow, and Dierks Bentley.

I could take days to mention the hundreds of Music City contributors to the tunes the world knows and enjoys. It would be an honor and guaranteed to fill several books. No argument, just fact. The foundation of a significant portion of contemporary Nashville music finds its genesis in Brown Bannister and the Christian music era of the 1980s and early '90s. That's what you find if you peel the onion on Garth Brooks, Taylor Swift, producers Keith Thomas and

Dann Huff, the pop hits of Sixpence None the Richer, Jars of Clay, Switchfoot, BeBe & CeCe Winans, and so many more. Research the bands Paramore or Chagall Guevera, or Emmylou Harris's longtime collaborator Phil Madeira. It's undeniable and the list is long.

As for Amy Grant and the music Brown produced on her, simply peruse the media reports surrounding the 2022 Kennedy Center Honors for evidence of influence. Amy was an honoree. Sheryl Crow and Brandi Carlile both spoke of the seminal power of Amy's music and her character. I was honored to watch the broadcast from home, holding hands with Andi, listening to "Every Heartbeat" in the tribute film segment.

—

On June 26, 2022, Andi and I gathered at Møxe studio outside Nashville with a small group of friends to celebrate our mutual bestie Allan Heinberg's birthday. We seized the opportunity to recognize his latest contribution to filmmaking, *The Sandman*. Allan, a screenwriter and showrunner, had been working overtime with author Neil Gaiman to bring the sprawling, much-beloved story to Netflix. It was finally airing, and Allan had in hand the latest trailer for us to watch. Producer and studio owner Jordan Brooke Hamlin hosted. Singer-songwriters Katie Herzig and Butterfly Boucher were with us, along with Ruby, and Wayne and Fran Kirkpatrick. It had been thirty-three years since Wayne sang background vocals on *The Secret of Time* and we cowrote "Every Heartbeat."

Allan graduated from Yale in 1989, moved to NYC, and first pursued acting before a stage play titled *The Amazon's Voice* helped launch his writing career. While we were beginning our new adventure in Music City, Allan was beginning his in the Big Apple. Unbeknownst to me, Allan, or Wayne, the interconnectedness of our lives had already begun through Amy Grant's music. Allan was a fan, and in 1991, there was no more galvanizing, fan-supported Amy Grant record than *Heart in Motion*, featuring five hit singles, none more ubiquitous than "Baby Baby" and "Every Heartbeat," which Allan fondly remembers as "a gloriously produced three minute and thirty-five second blast of pure pop joy."

For over three decades now we've been playing a long game of reciprocal admiration, delighting in and celebrating each other's hits, and even our misses. It's fun—and good for business—to have audiences applaud your work, offering their approval via cash, subscriptions, and views, but the soul of affirmation is found in friendship, where every good dream is championed, regardless of its reception in the marketplace. To know and be known is a good economy unto itself.

There are moments we experience with a dual consciousness; part of us participating in the present, while another part of us plays historian, absorbing the sensory and sentimental memories. Those moments are sacred. This celebration of Allan represented so much to me: the circles of affirmation and affection cultivated through a passion for the arts, the culmination of years of friendship, and the choice to love the music and to love my family, and let that love keep me curious and, hopefully, humble. Anger has always been in my blood, but also, fierce loyalty. And always, music. Divine providence used what I had to save me.

Eager to catch up, Wayne and I shared a long, meaningful conversation about why we continue to dream and create and believe our best work is still ahead of us. Both of us expressed gratitude for the tapestry of people that make up an artful life, including Amy and Brown. We also agreed that the opportunity to pivot away from the traditional music business has been good for our mental health, having grown weary of business practices sapping the fun from the artmaking, replacing it with irrational attorney-speak and anything but fair play.

Wayne shifted to Broadway musicals, a novel, making clocks, and a film on the history of board games. I helped to create Meta's 13,000-plus song library for its Facebook and Instagram platforms; amped up my jazz discography; created mixed-media art; wrote a book with Andi, a novel; and began developing *REDBONE*, a streaming series based on our family in antebellum Texas, 1856 (which Allan advised me on and kindly pointed me to the story-coach team of Rebecca Bloom and Pamela Weiss).

Wayne and I talked about our mutual Louisiana roots—his in Baton Rouge, mine in Singer, near Lake Charles—and how disturbed it makes us to see so much of the South go backward, including Tennessee where we live. The country progresses, and regresses, in cycles. For far too many generations, it's taken resistance, stubborn imagination, and bloodshed to propel us toward a more perfect union, to thwart the inertia of greed and prejudice. Ideally, the art we make points toward a better world, calls out hypocrisy, and tells the truth. So many times, art is prophecy. And it costs.

After dinner, we gathered in the media room to watch *The Sandman* trailer. Before beginning, we asked Allan to set up the story for the epic comic series novices in the room (which were most of us): Dream (the Sandman) is one of the magical siblings known as the Endless. Dream rules over the realm of sleep and his kingdom, the Dreaming. However, the series kicks off with Dream spending a century in captivity (away from the Dreaming), and so begins an odyssey of self-reflection and change, where Dream questions his past choices regarding love, family, and relationship with humanity. And he's beaten down. Once free, Dream returns to the Dreaming but is too weak and powerless to restore his kingdom. He's never been so vulnerable and humiliated. Dream comes to realize who he is without his power. No spoilers, but in his new reality, Dream contends with the best and worst of humanity, his relationship to Death, his ability to serve as he reigns, and the supremacy of change.

Okay. I was engaged.

I'd spent the last seven years weak and beaten down from a neurological disorder called central sensitization, manifesting in an intractable headache. Yes, one headache 24/7, for years. I no longer possessed the powers of endurance, resilience, pluck, and daring that I based much of my identity on. My empire-building and -maintaining days were behind me (thankfully). I'd been in the mode of evaluating my life choices in light of my weaknesses—I was coming to terms with who I was without these powers. Strangely, I liked my life and myself much better, even with the headache. I felt at peace.

Years ago, on the album *The Secret of Time*, I wrote "Experience," a song I previously mentioned: "You can only possess what you experience / truth to be understood must be lived."[1] This was a classic case of me (the artist) speaking through my art something I understood in part but had yet to live in full. I'd been living with a form of disintegration. Intellectually and spiritually, I knew I wasn't a boat left adrift at sea; that I was loved, safe, and had people to rely on in my weakness. My body, having kept the score though, didn't receive the message, or couldn't process it.

In my body, the fight-or-flight reaction of that sixteen-year-old trying to leave home, trying to survive, kept panicking, kept striving. He still lives in me, and I bear his scars, but I am changing. I am making a home for that sixteen-year-old where he can practice rest. I am learning how to say no to so many things in order to say yes to a few essential things, like Andi, family, friends, naps, vocational pursuits that are meaningful and pleasurable and stoke the fires of joy and peace. Even with the headache, I've made more of my own music in my sixties than any previous decade. It is a gift. The best and worst lives in my DNA. Fight and survival, too. I am my family tree, and the boy from Yuba City. Epigenetic codes can change us, though. So can brain plasticity and providence. I believe we can unlearn our pain and know joy.

> Deliver me from strategy, from endless clever thinking,
> Set my sights upon the shore, keep this boat from
> sinking down,
> Let me taste of a fresh wind of reason and stir the
> gift within,
> For I am not a boat left to drift at sea,
> I remain in you and you remain in me.[2]

Jordan pushed play, and we were immediately wooed into the imaginary world Neil Gaiman first envisioned and Allan helped bring to the screen through his deep writing gift and affinity for Neil's story. The post-trailer comments and analysis picked up steam with every friend contributing a sublime combination of smiles, laughter, and seriousness. After all, knowing Allan as well as we do, it was clear he had located the beating heart of Neil's masterpiece. In Allan's words, "*The Sandman* is an exploration of what it means to be human. To be mortal and therefore vulnerable. Capable of being hurt, but also capable of loving and being loved."

Maybe because the small party was composed of people who've been God-haunted, curious about Jesus, or confident in his person and story, a question was floated and somehow landed in this partially-seminary-trained person's lap. I felt safe answering, knowing most if not all of us were actively working at how to stay close to Jesus and as far away from the hate and bigotry of many national movements appropriating the name Christian.

In light of Dream's story of human failure, and our vulnerability in general, how would you define sin?

I answered:

Sin is everything that is contrary to love and a truly, good human identity. It is anti-human, anti-God; the way things are not supposed to be in a "love of neighbor-centric" world. Sin is certainly choices we make, but it is also something like a cancerous ethos in the wind, dividing us from God and each other, breeding hate, greed, racism, exploitation, and bigotry. Sin is incapable of empathy, hope, mercy, forgiveness, and unconditional love. Most baffling of all, is how sin works in us against the good we not only know to do, but genuinely, passionately want to, and yet don't.

As I've said before about the Beloved Community, it all turns on affection. In my path of following Jesus and his love-of-neighbor mission, affection is everything. To whom and what have I given or loaned out my affection? That night at Allan's party, I hope it was given to Allan, my friends, my community of dreamers trying to leave the world a better place than when they first arrived.

Decades ago I sang a declarative prayer to Jesus in the benediction of "The Secret of Time" lyric. It is as authentic now as it was then, but more meaningful and tested over the wealth of time since. I have lived it before Andi, my children, and my community of peers—proximate, never perfect. I am not a younger man auditioning new theologies. I'm living the eternal now transformed by inexhaustible love.

Chapter Eighteen

The moment I found out who you were, I found out who I was,
The silence covered me and the tears began to fall,
I could see what a great and grand act of affection it's all been,
(Time that is, time that is, talk about time that is, time that is)
My history is written through the choices I make,
Let me sing just ten true words, I'd rather sing just ten true words
Than a hundred words that in the end amount to nothing,
absolutely nothing.[3]

POSTLUDE

It's the Grammy Awards 2020; our stretch limo eases into space on the street just outside the red carpet. We exit one by one—son Sam and daughter-in-law Ruby; three of our grandchildren, Bridget, Alfie, and Brinsley; and us, Honey and Papa, as we've been dubbed (our official grandparent names). The kids and Andi are so striking and fab. Every detail of their look is a diamond unto itself. I'm a little like a bulging sausage—too much meat, not enough skin. This is the last time I'll ever dress like this—tricked out in the garb musicians wear on stage and at awards shows. I do like my shoes, though. I painted them with acrylics. Formerly ankle-high green leather chukka boots, I turned them black. Then went all Jackson Pollock on the toes and back quarters.

We are the proud parents. Sam and Ruby are the stars. Both are up for Song of the Year, with Sam nominated for Album of the Year, too. They've cowritten the hit song "Hard Place" with the breakout artist H.E.R., personally known as Gabi Wilson.

Gabi and her producer, Swagg R'Celious, attended a songwriter's camp and festival I curated at OQ Farm in Vermont in the summer of 2016. The three-day gathering was funded by the music-loving philanthropists John and Jean Kingston. There's a righteous song on the H.E.R. album *I Used to Know Her* titled "The Lord Is Coming" that Gabi, bass phenom Scott Mulvahill, and Alanna Boudreau wrote at the festival.

Once we are out of the car, the swarm of photographers/videographers makes their mental calculations: *Who are you? Are you somebody? Should we care? Do you belong in our publication or on our broadcast?* Sam and Ruby are saved by someone with a clipboard and cell phone. They begin the red carpet stroll. The rest of us are escorted around the tent in an outside parallel lane. We plan to wait at the end of the red carpet and rejoin Sam and Ruby as they come out of the tent. Reunited, we'll enter the Staples Center for the evening awards ceremony and broadcast.

The only problem is that security repeatedly motions us to keep moving and enter the building. I explain that our adult kids are nominees on the red carpet, that we're watching their minor children, and that we need to wait for the parents to join them. Some people are very gracious and understanding. One even shows us the least obtrusive place to stand. We watch Sharon and Ozzy Osbourne shuffle back and forth, seemingly lost. No one motions for them to move along. They are recognizably famous and have a handler.

There are only two seats for our grandchildren on the event center floor with Sam and Ruby. Alfie will be with us in the balcony. The plan was to have one grandchild on the floor change out with Alfie halfway through the broadcast. We don't know exactly how this will be executed; we just know our party needs to stay together. I'm devoted to seeing that each grandchild has quality time sitting among the Jonas Brothers, H.E.R., and BTS. Nothing matters to me more than making this happen for my grandchildren. They are each dressed for prime time, adorable, and polite to a fault.

Then, as happens in all dramas, the antagonist enters stage left. He's a big man. Maybe 6 feet 3 inches and at least 250 pounds—classic club bouncer type. I've seen this shape of man since I began playing music professionally in my early teens. They are multifunctional and can be allies or nemeses. Usually not strong conversationalists. Girth and height, a second language.

It begins with "Keep moving."

As I've already done five times with other security, I tell Keep Moving my story. I'm cheerful, polite, and concise. I expect nothing more than comprehension and respect. What I get is, "Keep Moving." We couldn't have been more far apart in our understanding of the moment.

This is why artists only go to these events with a handler, a manager, or a publicist going ahead of them, a person to interact with the immovable forces uninterested in their story, telling them to keep moving.

The irony of the bouncer's command is that I've been moving nonstop since I was a teenager, trying to find where I belong, where I would be understood and respected, a place to stand unharried. Being told *You don't belong here and keep moving* at such a late date in my artistic journey triggered all feelings. Anger, heartbreak, insecurity, anxiety, shame, hurt, and fear—all six decibels too loud in the mix.

I kept moving.

—

In the fall of 2023, film producer Zach Hunter called with a passion project. I joined up, signing on as an executive producer for a television streaming series titled *Stage Left*—a wide-angle look at the essential nature of small musical stages (clubs, theaters, etc.) to culture—specifically, to the creation of world-changing styles of music, such as folk, jazz, country, rock, R&B, hip-hop/rap, and pop.[1] Many cities, stages, and artists contributed. My job was to deliver the *only-in-Nashville* experience. I called in family, friends, and favors for eight days of filming interviews and performances. Every bit of it is good and meaningful.

Some of it went deep inside me and rooted around the library of my decades on earth. *What was the experience looking for in my experience?* I remember waking up too early on most of those eight days of filming. Eyes still closed, covers tugged tight, swimming in a mental sea of wonderment and prayer.

The first day of filming began on a Saturday at Vince Gill's house and studio—a peer, same age, Oklahoma background, exceptionally affirmed. With twenty-two statuettes, Vince has earned more Grammys than any male country artist in history. The music keeps coming. While in the middle of a tour as a member of The Eagles, he was tracking new songs during his off week. Vince graciously sat for an interview and played a new classic, "The Whole World."

It feels like the whole world has got a broken heart
We sure could use a brand-new start
How the hell did we wind up so far apart?

Monday morning, I interviewed recording artist Peter Framp-ton. I couldn't help but think of the day I spent with one of his best friends, artist Gary Wright, so long ago. Or Peter's close association with guitarist Gordon Kennedy. Or of my family's next-door teenager neighbor in Tierra Buena, California, 1975, blasting Peter's "Show Me the Way" out his bedroom window. This was one year before Peter's Billboard No. 1 breakout album, Frampton Comes Alive! When the ubiquity/fame formula took hold, the British guitar standout became an international superstar, breaking all sales records for a live rock album—8 million in the US alone.

Monday evening, I was down on Lower Broadway in Nashville with country legend, eighty-five-year-old Whisperin' Bill Ander-son. Bill is the longest-serving member of the Grand Ole Opry show (sixty-two years as of July 22, 2023). We were doing a walk and talk to rival any scene on Aaron Sorkin's West Wing. The setting was the inexplicable commercial madness that three city blocks of Nash-ville's history have become. Thousands of people walk the street to nowhere, somewhere. Present, if only to say they'd been there, done that. Some folks are genuinely moved emotionally, happy to take it all in. Others are making a wobbly beeline to the next bar named after a country music celebrity.

With two to three bands playing in each building, from street level to the rooftop, the ambient volume is that of an NFL game or jet runway. I could tell Bill was trying to put a sharp point on his voice to cut through. No time for whispering.

Both of us wearing lavalier mics on our shirt collars, we braved the sidewalks of this cacophonous national attraction so Bill could narrate a firsthand account of honky-tonk history on Lower Broad-way—legacy joints like Tootsie's Orchid Lounge and the Ernest Tubb Record Shop where after-hours jam sessions occurred. A songwriter and performer with hits in seven decades, Bill was quickly recog-nized, and tourists lined up for photos. He treated every request like it was the first time he'd been asked. Everyone got a smile for the ages. Eventually, his manager called a halt to it, and we escorted Bill back to the parking garage. Once inside the safety of my car, Bill finally whispered, "That's the last time I come down here."

Being with these three men for a few hours each, hearing and processing their stories, had a lasting, revelatory effect on me.

Peter is six years older than me. I was just beginning my artistic journey at the height of his fame. Though Peter has a long and varied career, he can't shake that window of time when he rattled and rocked the world. Everything vectors to that tipping point in the 1970s when Peter was in his midtwenties (though in the UK, he'd been a pop star since his teens). He can't do an interview (even mine) without necessarily mentioning the breakout smash and his revered 1954 Les Paul Custom guitar (nicknamed Phenix) used on the historic record. Or the origin and use of the Heil Talk Box first introduced to him by Nashville pedal steel player Pete Drake (while the two were recording *All Things Must Pass* with George Harrison at Abbey Road Studios in 1970). The Talk Box sound defined the Frampton hit "Show Me the Way."

That same year, Jerry Kennedy played with Pete Drake on Ringo Starr's second solo album, *Beaucoups of Blues*, recorded in Nashville at Music City Recorders on Music Row (Elvis Presley's famed guitarist, Scotty Moore, engineered).

Peter has been a Nashville resident for many years now. He is an immigrant who went as far as he needed for meaningful work, to be understood and respected. Peter could live anywhere. But Nashville music and history is in him, and he's in it. (Peter and pal Gary Wright played the Tennessee State Fairgrounds in Nashville on July 4, 1976.) Nashville is where Peter can be the talented boy who grew up in a musical home to become a world-class guitar player and musician's musician. He wasn't raised to be a one-and-done superstar. He likes playing the guitar. There's no place on this *tierra buena* that gives space to the guitar like Nashville.

As I reflected on Peter's oversized, shiny moment in music history, I was grateful that the few moments I can count (albeit not so lustrous) are spread out among the decades—not anchored in one.

While I cannot match Bill Anderson's hits in seven decades as a songwriter (who can?), having *Billboard* hits in various roles across three decades from 1991 to 2013 is more than sufficient.

This includes the Nashville Christian music decade (1989–1999) with many radio hits and awards as an artist, songwriter, producer, publisher, and record company president. At the beginning and middle of this decade were Amy Grant's pop hit "Every Heartbeat" (1991) and "In the Light," a hit for dc Talk (1995)—both the fruit of my first love, songwriting.

The Switchfoot discovery and development came to commercial fruition beginning with the gold-certified soundtrack of *A Walk to Remember*, starring Mandy Moore (with Mandy singing one of Switchfoot's songs, "Only Hope"). Next up, Switchfoot's Top 20 pop hits, "Meant to Live" (2003) and "Dare You to Move" (2004), with "This Is Your Life" hitting Top 30, all from *The Beautiful Letdown* (3x platinum). Rock and pop radio wasn't done with the band yet. The next album, *Nothing Is Sound*, included the hits "Stars" (2005) and "We Are One Tonight" (2006).

The satisfaction of having heard the seed of goodness in a youthful San Diego bunk-bed band and watching them bear fruit in the world is indescribable. Then something similar happened again. Only this time, it would be a rocket, up and down. Not the long haul of multi-decades of touring and recording Switchfoot is now known for.

On April 7, 2009, I went to the French Quarter Cafe in East Nashville to hear my friend Joy Williams's new duo, The Civil Wars. And so began our role in the indie Americana music boom and the next shiny season of *Billboard* hits, gold records, and Grammy Awards.

We, Peter, Vince, Bill, and I, have backstories that don't make it into the bios and blurbs. You never hear or read headline descriptions like "Fired Piano-Player Charlie Peacock," "Broke with a New Baby Vince Gill," or "Difficulty Matching Prior Success Peter Frampton." If you did, a publicity firm would likely be fired. No, we're all "Grammy Award–Winning Charlie, Vince, and Peter," with "Grammy Award–Nominated Bill." That's the way we choose to roll and rock. There's a practical reason for this.

There are significant life stories written long before the shiny objects appear. Objects that are effectively yearly awards from a trade association (could just as easily be a Century Breeder Award from the American Hereford Cattle Association). Type any award name and capitalize each word. It's just name-making with fonts masquerading as gravitas. But it still matters for personal reasons mostly associated with untold, prior stories.

When Soundgarden vocalist Chris Cornell came to record with me and Joy Williams in 2013, he made a frank but surprising comment: "Hey, you have all your awards up."

Wondering what was implied but not said, I stumbled into a reply. "Yeah, I didn't used to, but years ago, my good friend Maggie chastised me, saying, 'Put 'em up, enjoy the fruit of your labor—you're not taking them with you.'"

Chris told us, "I keep mine out of sight."

I can't speak for Bill, but having been to Peter and Vince's studios, I can tell you they don't. And I consider them fully affirmed, self-aware, humble people.

I learned to read music and play the trumpet in fourth grade. Treble clef lines on the staff: *every good boy does fine.* Spaces: *face—F A C E.* I did fine, but not without tears running down my cheeks. Scales and rhythms, working through Robinson's *Rubank Elementary Method* book, all to get to a decent "Mary Had a Little Lamb."

Not that I would've even thought of the question then, but as I've alluded to several times: Was I learning music or learning how difficult it was to reach the bar my trumpet-playing father had set for me, for himself?

I was nine years old.

Then, a lifetime of family and music progressed, and I passed through one circle of affirmation after another—from one place of belonging to the next. Constantly moving, ever aware that the people who held the keys to my future (my family's future) almost always saw me only in terms of my last best story, the most recognizable, recent achievement. The shiny moment.

Dad's version of *nothing ever good enough* was slow-pitch softball to the 90 miles per hour fastball that the actual music business was. They weren't playing tough love. Mostly just tough. A few kind-hearted people put some love in the mix. But once "real money" was spent, the scrutiny level tripled. It wasn't just about competing for a spot on a roster with your music and performance. It was also about how you presented—attitude, clothing, hair, fitness—whether the sales and marketing people liked you and wanted you to win. And don't dare think of turning down an opportunity. This is how we lost our first set of wedding rings. I pawned them for music business trips to Los Angeles and couldn't afford to buy them back.

In the fall of 1991, I was at Merchant's in Nashville, a swanky restaurant on Lower Broadway, long before tourism dramatically altered downtown. It was a regal table of Sparrow A&R and music publishing folks, including Bill Hearn, Peter York, Brown and Debbie Bannister, and Andi. I was presented with my first platinum album plaque for Amy's *Heart in Motion* and celebrated my first top-of-the-pops, bona fide *Billboard* hit song.

I was thirty-five years old. I'd been married for seventeen years with a thirteen-year-old daughter and a ten-year-old son. I'd logged thousands of hours in the studio, produced many records, been on major record labels as an artist, and was nominated for a Grammy Award. I'd performed in every rock club and theater in America, from the Roxy in LA to Radio City in NYC. I'd toured in the UK and Europe. All of this was the preamble.

By music industry standards, where the bar was set back then, with one singular platinum achievement, I'd finally delivered on the promise of my talent.

From trumpet novice to hit-maker, it only took twenty-six years. It was a long, exhausting road. Not just for me but for Andi, too. We were finally at the beginning. Not by our standards but by the standards of those who controlled (in part) the standard of living for a family whose vocation was popular music. I inhaled, exhaled, and got to the business of repeating it. Who wouldn't want to? The financial benefit is evident to everyone. The most essential benefits and their nuances might not be as clear.

Straight up, it's about freedom. The freedom to choose what you want to work on and with whom. The freedom to turn down projects. The freedom that comes with having your own capital so you aren't always explaining to a nonmusician why your musical dreams are worthy of funding.

That same year (1991), Vince Gill was awarded his first platinum album for *When I Call Your Name*, which was released in November 1989. It took a year and some change, but Vince got there. With the help of producer Tony Brown, Vince Gill dialed in the iconic, high-lonesome sound that eventually ushered him into the Country Music Hall of Fame. And that undeniable sound, plus the commercial success, was what the fans and gatekeepers noticed. Vince, too, was finally at the beginning. Like me, Peter, and Bill, this celebrated arrival occurred after decades of Vince faithfully doing the work, honing the craft, and making enough to live on till the next big opportunity or cash advance. For Vince, this meant singing Pure Prairie League's Top 10 *Billboard* hit, "Let Me Love You Tonight"; joining Rodney Crowell's band, The Cherry Bombs; writing songs for others; and playing recording sessions.

It's called paying your dues. With dues paid and shiny objects obtained, here's an inside look at the mind of the musical artiste: "Now, if you would, music business, with my debt settled, kindly get out of my way and let me carry on with faithfulness to the art and heart of music. Fair enough?" There it is again: looking for a place to stand, respected and unharried.

This is what it's all for. Freedom, sustainability, and the unfettered ability to imagine and create at the level we envision without corporate permission or their money. In the artist's mind, we have more than satisfied the corporate criteria. Does this mean that entertainment corporations cease their performative orientation and benchmarks? Uh, no. But we can. We have earned the right to rewrite the script and reimagine why we do what we do, how we do it, and most essential, how we measure success in the whole of life.

Because technology has democratized music making and business so radically, a young musical artist creates music, artwork, and videos on a laptop then uploads to streaming services and social media platforms. If they go viral, an entertainment company will likely come knocking. The new breed of musical artist is more likely to be independent of the entertainment corporations. Many are happy to remain independent and often do very well on their own or with their own handpicked team. (Apart from productions, this has been my approach for twenty years.)

I came up in an entirely different world, though. One where you fought for and had to earn every bit of artistic and financial freedom. A plaque on the wall can be a reminder to breathe, to rest, and to wisely and imaginatively enjoy the freedom you've both earned and been gifted with.

What my three artist subjects (Vince, Peter, and Bill) have in common is they've all survived the razor edge of fame. Just as I've survived being well-known—a slightly less dangerous enterprise, but not by much. While it's difficult to moderate the survivor instinct, if the thriver in the survivor will eventually take the lead, goodness and wisdom become welcome companions and priorities. What Bill said about walking through the cacophony of Lower Broadway can be said of many things that hurt more than help: *That's the last time I come down here.* And mean it.

I've collected a broken heart full of incidents and accidents I refuse to repeat. This commitment has created space to allow for all that I wish to repeat—for everything I will take with me when my days on earth are done. Specifically, family, friends, and all that I made that was truly good and useful to people and planet, that which honored my teacher Jesus and communicated (somehow, some way), "Charlie Peacock? That husband, father, grandfather, friend, and artist? Yes, he's with Jesus."

I love every new day with Andi at home in Nashville, rising each morning to read and pray through the Book of Common Prayer and then busy ourselves making food, music, books, hospitality, blog posts, friendships, art, films, and all the goodness of life. I also really love talking with my children and grandchildren. Their thoughts and stories are oxygen, and I delight in their ordinary and extraordinary daily work and play.

Whether that be Molly and her long, faithful tenure with Nashville Public Radio, her unimpeachable reputation, or her care for our grandson Robert; Sam's overflowing musical talent with Oscar, Grammy, and Golden Globe nominations; son-in-law Mark, wisely stewarding the songs the worldwide membership of Jesus sings; or daughter-in-law Ruby, lending a helping hand to generative societal care and snapping up two Grammy nominations for Song of the Year.

Proud, yes, but there's no performative agenda at play. They can bring home shiny or dull objects. It doesn't matter. There's nothing they can do to make me love them more, or love them less.

Andi, these grown children, my grandchildren, my sister Terri and her family, all the artistic collaborators, loving relatives, and dear friends—including everyone who has ever dared to give *the boy making his tapes* a kind listen—these are the people and memories that last longest and matter most. When I take my last breath on God's *tierra buena*, I will take this trustworthy truth with me. It is a reasonable exchange. Trading the perishable, shiny object for imperishable, graceful goodness.

It all comes down to love, to knowing and being known. To have gained the world and not have loved or been loved is meaningless. There's an ocean of space between what people consider your artistic, cultural moment and your actual cultural contribution. Which is your interdependent, nonneutral, whole life of loving, as proximate as it may be—including loving music. This is what you want to be famous for.

—

For the docuseries *Stage Left*, I gathered with my people at Rudy's Jazz Room in Nashville on that week of filming to record and perform a new composition for the cameras. When I say *my people*, I mean those who speak the language of improvisational music with deep imagination and ability. It is music rooted in West Africa strained through the grid of history to become American blues and jazz— and then through the power of imagination and every shifting generational skill, to become something altogether different, yet never growing too far from the mother tree.

Along with me on Fender Rhodes electric piano, the musicians included: *Jeff Coffin* on soprano saxophone, my longtime collaborator, beautiful solo artist, and a member of Dave Matthews Band; *Brian Blade*, drummer extraordinaire with a wide range of artists, including Joni Mitchell, Bob Dylan, Wayne Shorter, and Norah Jones; *Roger Smith* on the Hammond B3 organ, a veteran member of Tower of Power; and upright bass phenom *Scott Mulvahill*. I was privileged to coproduce his debut album, *Himalayas*, in 2018.

Postlude

The five of us had never played together before. We opened up the windows, and the Spirit blew through. Listen to our performance from that day. Lean in; turn up the volume.

Ding, ping, swoosh and swell,
O rhythm of the line, the long line
of snares and cymbals and snares.
The sound of cargo. The sound of fieldwork.
The sound of war. The sound of freedom.
A sliver of land, the river, the gathering of the unwelcome
people.
Huddle 'round the fire. We are ablaze, Woman says.
Get warm, get ready.
I'm ready said the saxophone. I am fire. The fire of Coltrane.
The fire of me.
Am I welcome?
You are welcome said the drum.
I will touch this and that with whimsy and no other purpose
than to surprise and delight you.
I do not know a rigid rhythm. Such things are, how do I say,
anathema.
I agree said the organ.
There's a box named Leslie behind me roaring with flame and
flexibility.
Clear a space and let me sing and dance—bear witness.
I learned this move from such and such, how to prance,
how to tease the flame
from my hands to the box to the ear, to the body
through and through.
Don't skip the heart nor the booty, Woman says.
Good trick, huh—I see you!
Nothing like a history lesson.
Let me express my gratitude, said the upright bass.
I am fire and fireproof, 'bout to get my best on.
I lay down my own surprise, low with a sparkle.
Look at the faces. Everyone tickled.
No sadness. No gut-twisting cares.

Postlude

"Nothing but blue skies."
The promise of fellowship kept.
This is exactly how I knew it would be, said the electric piano.
Not a note out of place. Trustworthy.
No stray molecules, fools or rules. Only grace.
Which is why I, the piano player, will try to play
something I hear
that has never passed through my hands
to the keys and tines before. Not once.
Here it comes. There it is. There it goes.
It found the soprano saxophone. It found the rooted ones.
It found the Woman of history. It found the land, the trees,
and the river.
It found the beating drum.
It found the upright bass and organ, saying, How do you do?
Each in unity spoke back a blessing.
Just fine, brother.
Pleased to welcome you.[2]

Is there any feeling better than welcome? Of belonging? Of mutual respect and love? Or of creating something musical, extraordinary, and spiritual that did not exist before and will never live again in that particular molecular shape? The latter is nothing less than cosmic, mystic magic. That I, the great-grandson of a grandfather born in Mystic, Louisiana, have been able to be smack-dab in the middle of the mystical and mysterious so often is more than I can process. The poem will have to be my sufficient witness.

There is so much goodness in music. Goodness from the Creator, who has brought it into being, goodness from the blessed ones who make it, and goodness from those who receive it and pass on the story of the music, neighbor to neighbor.

This is why I made the music. And why I will always make it.

RECOGNITION AND GRATITUDE

I begin with the one I have loved for fifty-plus years. Eternal gratitude to you, Andi Berrier, who conceded to take on the surname of Ashworth just as your husband and his Peacock name game took flight. We are skin and heart entwined, yet two individuals with unique views and approaches to life. Thank you for showing me how differentiated unity is the better, more respectful way. I am wildly grateful for your kiss, companionship, resilience, and inexhaustible patience. We did it, and we know where all credit belongs. This unity of gratitude is strong. Even so, our story's unbreakable thread is who you are, what you truly value, and how you care for those you love. Thank you for lavishing me with your love, collaboration, care, and respect.

To my beloved children and their spouses, Molly and Mark Nicholas, Sam and Ruby Ashworth, and the grandchildren, Robert, Bridget, Alfie, and Brinsley, in one thousand ways, this book is for you. Of all the stories in the world, yours are the ones I value most. But they are yours to share. I have left you some of mine, hoping they will be helpful and enjoyable to you or those who come next. Be at peace. Create the contrast. I love you, always.

In the category of *the author wishes to thank*, there would be no book without longtime editor/author friend Elisa Stanford and her introduction to the energetic and ever-truthful Sharifa Stevens. Sharifa, as an editor and sounding board, your big heart and precise expertise have demonstrably influenced and improved this manuscript. Big ups! Any remaining misses before the last edit are all mine to claim. Elisa, thank you for your insights and polish. To my indefatigable agent, Don Pape, thank you for being a true believer—honest but always hopeful. I also want to thank Allan Heinberg, Rebecca Bloom, and Pamela Weiss. Your help on the REDBONE series pitch deck contributed insights I incorporated herein. Lisa Ann Cockrel (Eerdmans Publishing), you were the acquisitions editor that truly understood this book and the perfect eyes and intellect to offer last tweaks. Lisa, you made it a better book (no small thing), and for that I will always be grateful. A sincere *well done* to everyone at Eerdmans who worked to make this book a reality. Thank you, Mike Gowen, Jessica Bonner and the team at Milestone Publicity. Jordan Wetherbee you nailed the cover art first time!

Since roots are at the heart of this work, I give respect and honor to the memory of my parents, Bill and Alice Ashworth; my in-laws, Marilyn and Arnold Ickes and George and Barbara Berrier; and to my grandparents, Lee and Ella Ashworth and Marvin and Lois Williamson. In like manner, respect and gratitude to my great-grandparents and their following surnames. Paternal: Ashworth, Baggett, Clark, Burgess, Dial (Doyle, Doll), Evans, Hodges, Insall, Goins (Goings, Gowen), Perkins, Drake, and Buxton. Maternal: Williamson, Miller, Bryan, Finley, Bond, Pruitt, and Phillips. A recognition of grief for the West African names that are lost to time and circumstance.

A special thanks to my aunt Connie Wise (Dad's sister) for uncovering the Ashworth story. Verna Thompson, I'll always be grateful for your research, especially for identifying our correct great-grandfather, Tapley Abner (not Moses). The following researchers and authors, though not always in agreement, are short-listed as indispensable in any research of our family: Ric Murphy and everyone involved with the Society of the First African Families of English America, the Redbone Heritage Foundation, Allwyn Barr, W. T. Block, Laurie Constantino, McDonald Furman, Henry Goins, Tim Hashaw, Paul Heinegg, Milton S. Jordan, Terry Jordan, William Loren Katz, K. I. Knight, Marilyn Baggett Kobliaka, Henry Louis Gates Jr., Jason A. Gillmer, Bruce A. Glasrud, Don C. Marler, Shelley Murphy, Frederick Law Olmstead, Harold Schoen, Quintard Taylor, Patricia Waak, Stacy R. Webb, David A. Williams, Carter C. Woodson, and Ramona Young. *Note: This is a brief list of contemporary and past researchers. Nevertheless, a good start.*

As for the rhythm recognition, I must begin with my great-grandfather George Reilly Baggett, the Louisiana fiddler, and my father, teacher of teachers, Bill Ashworth (trumpeter, composer/arranger, and educator). Thank you, men, and Grandma Ella for the genetics and the high bar of excellence. Mother, Alice, your skill at rhyming rubbed off. Bless you. Dean Estabrook, thank you for the cornet lessons in grammar school and music theory classes in high school. It's unlikely that many high schools teach Schoenberg anymore.

I have tried to build moments of specific recognition into the book, and where I've failed, or brevity and editing won out, I offer the following general, but no less enthusiastic, thanks:

Gratitude and recognition to the Yuba City and Marysville musicians I grew up with, playing everything from backyard parties to the bar on the corner. This includes Tierra Buena Elementary, Yuba City High School, and Yuba College performance groups. A special shout-out to the inspiration of Drusalee and the Dead, The Owens Brothers (The Jades)—and to Freddie Singh, and Rod Battaglia for employing me—as well as KOBO DJs Dave Camper (Tony Cox) and Rick Gibson.

To my Sacramento community of musicians, record labels, music stores, production companies, nightclubs, ad agencies, bookers, managers, recording studios, artists, and Tower Records—I offer a huge but still insufficient thank you. It would be a cosmic crime not to call out some of you personally. Stephen Holsapple, you understood me first and opened your artistic world to me, including friendships with a mad cast of characters, such as Bob Cheevers, Les Haber, Lindy Haber, David Houston, and Pat Minor. Steve, we are brothers for life!

Tom Boucree, Rodney Byrd, Larry Casserly, Lorraine Gervais, Craig Kearney, Gerry Pineda, Brad Smith, Scott Usedom, Tim Volpicella, and David Zook, you were my first serious jazz/improv and Top 40 (money, money, money) bandmates. Then the Kee brothers, led by Alphonza, and on into The Runners. Darius Babazadeh, David Watts Barton, Jimi Beeler, Shelley Burns, Mike Butera, Jim Caselli, Bob Cheevers, Steve Dallas, Eric Heilman, Mark Herzig, Steve Homan, Pat Minor, Skip Moriarty, Doug Pauly, Henry Robinett, Michael Urbano, Robert Kuhlmann, Aaron Smith, Bongo Bob Smith, Roger Smith, Lyle Workman, and more, we are still friends today! That's no small thing. May our brothers and sisters rest in peace: Richard Oates, Jimmy Griego, Vince Ebo, Joyce Diamond, Skip Maggiora, Roger Voudouris, D. R. Wagner, Jessica Williams, Clarice Jones, and Keith Jefferson—to name a few. I would call out Erik Kleven among the departed as one who tolerated much from me and never wavered as a friend, bandmate, or my champion. Brent Bourgeois and Larry Tagg, I considered you my only real competition (wink). You set a very high bar. Love and respect. Regarding the Exit Records era, a few names must be mentioned and thanked: Jimmy Abegg, Daryl C. Anders, John Golden, Steve Griffith, Colin Hart, Moss Hudson, Joan Kudin, Don McKenney, Michael Miller, Julissa Neely, Mary and Louis Neely, Keith Rintala, Michael Roe, Steve Scott, Joe Sogge, Bruce Spencer, Duane and Jil Temme, Jan Eric Volz, Ruth Walden, John Weber, and Daryl Zachman. Larry Lunetta, thank you for the trumpet solo. I would also like to thank Paul Blaise of Blaise Media, Carol Gale, Russ Martinez, Pat Melarkey, Dave Mering, Randy Paragary, Maurice Read, Bo Richards, and Peter Torza, for helping with instrument purchases, booking, and employing me. John and Laura Cowan, I still remember.

Then there's San Francisco, Los Angeles, New York, and London in the 1980s. Where would the music business and my career be without them? Sincere gratitude for your help and encouragement, small and large: Herb Alpert, Arma Andon, Seline Armbeck, Martin Bandier, Chris Blackwell, Benjamin Bossi, Mick Brigden, Kim Buie, Kevin Burns, Juliea Clark, Lionel Conway, Ian Copeland, Marty Diamond, Maureen Droney, Peter Dunne, Lindsey Feldman, Ken Friedman, Gil Friesen, Bill Graham, Nigel Gray, Richard Green, John Hanes, Eddie Henderson, John Huie, Randy Jackson, Michael Jang, Leslie Ann Jones, Tonio K, David Kahne, David Kastens, David Kershenbaum, Ken Kessie, Frank Kofsky, Charles Koppelman, Pat

Lucas, Lou Maglia, Marc Maron, Doug Minnick, Jerry Moss, Lynn Arthur Nichols, Deirdre O'Hara, Arnie Pustilnik, David Rubinson, Elliot Scheiner, Al Scheslinger, Bud Scoppa, Joel Selvin, Bonnie Simmons, Annie Stocking, Michael Stone, Dee Thierry, Sal Valentino, Tom Willett, Kurt Wortman, Donna Young, Teddy Zambetti, Michele Zarin, and Michelle Zieminski.

Lastly, Nashville and beyond, beginning with recognition of those who got us there, in a home, and helped us build a future: Brown and Debbie Bannister, Michael Blanton, CBS Songs, Gary Chapman, Melissa Clough, Amy Grant, Barbara Haynes, Bill Hearn, Billy Ray Hearn, and Peter and Michelle York. Special thanks to Jim and Michelle Abegg for joining us on the journey. The Hearn family, Sparrow Records, and Amy Grant put wind in my sails I still feel today. I am eternally grateful to you all. Thank you to the entire staff of Sparrow, EMI Christian Music Group, CCMG/Universal, and any iteration to come. Respect to Bill Hearn for these words regarding my signing of the band Switchfoot: "I don't hear it. But I trust you, and if you hear it, then I'm behind it." That's what used to be called *a real record man*. I also want to single out Peter York for his belief in me and for gently coaching me through the first Margaret Becker record. Thank you, Peter, for everything. Scotty Smith, with your partnership in the Art House beginnings and grace emphasis, our Nashville life was more inspiring and free. Thank you.

Record producers are only as good as their talented recording engineers and various assistants. I've been privileged to work with the very best. First, specific thanks to a few Nashville engineers I've collaborated with over consecutive years: Jeff Balding, Richie Biggs, Steve Bishir, Bill Deaton, Ciel Eckard-Lee, Russ Long, Craig Hansen, Kevin Hipp, Tom Laune, Bryan Lenox, David Leonard, Graham Lewis, Garrett Rockey, F. Reid Shippen, Glenn Spinner, James Sweeting, Kevin Twit, Terry Watson, Rick Will, and Shane D. Wilson—as well as these additional mix engineers—Chuck Ainlay, Craig Alvin, Brandon Bell, Michael Brauer, Tom Elmhirst, Jacquire King, Chris Lord-Alge, Manny Marroquin, Elliot Scheiner, and Spike Stent—and mastering engineers Eric Conn, Richard Dodd, Bernie Grundman, Ken Love, Bob Ludwig, Steve Marcussen, and Michael Romanowski.

A nod and thanks to Richie Biggs for achieving the longest-running engineering and mixing relationship with me. Much respect. Golf claps and smiles for these world-class assistants (studio, Art House, and admin), in order of appearance: Lee Brewster, Jonathan Beach, Jay Swartzendruber, Nick Barré, Katy Krippaehne, David Dark, Russ Ramsey, Jessica Graeve, Amanda Shoffner, Jamie Swartzendruber, Edie Spain, Janice Soled, Leah Payne, Mark DiCicco, Andrea Howat, James Sweeting, Carly Ripp, Cassie Tasker, Ciel Eckard-Lee, Jac Thompson, and Bridget Ashworth. If it had to be constructed or fixed, Richard Kapuga nailed it, literally.

Whether growing the flowers to grace a table, creating a life-altering meal, giving an artist a listening ear, writing our story, or paying the bills, Andi was on it. Everyone knows her as the glue and the grace. I'd also be remiss to not mention the assistant roles my daughter Molly and son Sam played over the years, whether in the studio or on the road. Thank you, kids.

During the short re:think Records era, our staff interacted with EMI distribution, marketing, and promotion. Thank you to Rich Peluso, Hugh Robertson, Troy Vest, and everyone who made it happen. I'd also like to thank my record business colleagues (often the competition) who were breakfast and lunch buddies or a phone call away: Blanton & Harrell, Don Donahue, Darrell Harris, Terry Hemmings, Jeff Moseley, and Steve Taylor. And to anyone who ever tried to manage me—thank you for trying! This includes you, Dan Raines and Creative Trust. And thanks to Jeff Roberts and crew for fly dates and tours. You too, Wes Yoder. The following festivals alone put me on the performance map. Many thanks to JPUSA and Cornerstone, Creation, FlevoFest, Greenbelt, and NewSound. (Dan Russell, you were in from the beginning, remember Let's Active at the Paradise in Boston?) A loving and grateful shout-out to all the Sparrow employees from the early days that gave 110 percent on my music and my productions for the label and what became EMI Christian—a few I'm remembering are: Barbara, Jenny, Lucy, Kyle, Marlei, Cora, Richard, Christiev, Steve F., Marie, Casey, Danny, Greg, Steve R., Rod, and Matthew—so many more though.

Before I wrap up all this reckoning and thanks, I'm going to allow myself a *Potluck for 50*, the random selection of folks whom I wish to thank for very diverse reasons: Meg Anderson, Al Andrews, Dane and Maggie Anthony, Martin Ashley, Loren Balman, Jerram Barrs, Leslie Barton, Kenny and Laura Benge, Wendell Berry, Traci Sterling-Bishir, Bono, Doug and Terri Bornick, Brent and Mary Ann Bourgeois, Andy Boyer, Clay Bradley, Wayne Brezinka, Bob Briner, J. Mark Brinkmoeller, Anastasia Brown, Bruce Brown, Dave Bunker, T Bone Burnett, Ned and Leslie Bustard, Michael and Julie Butera, Buz Buzbee, David Caldwell, Beth Nielsen Chapman, Jeff Coffin, Jennifer Cooke, Mike Cosper, Jeremy Cowart, Kristen Dabbs, Tim Dalrymple, Craig and Judi Daniels, Bill Decker, Andrew DeFusco, Guy and Marissa Delcambre, Joanne Devine, Mike Elizondo, Mike Fernandez, John Fields, Leslie Fram, Mako Fujimura, Steven Garber, Holly Gleason, Troy and Sara Groves, Os Guinness, Tom Gulotta, Denis and Margie Haack, Greg Ham, Richard Headen, Allan Heinberg, Lisa Jenkins, JPUSA, Regina Joskow, Tim Keller, Dick Keyes, David Kiersznowski, John and Jean Kingston, L'Abri, John La Grou, Larry Lauzon, Ken Levitan, Keith Lindner, Will Littlejohn, Roland Lundy, Lynne Lyle, Steve Markland, Bruce McCurdy, Charles McGowan, Jenae Medford, Bill Milkowski, Russell Moore, Lynn Morrow, Stan Moser, Brian Quincy Newcomb, Mark Nicholas, Brad O'Donnell, Bridgett O'Lannerghty, Mary Oliver, Andy Olyphant, Scott Parker, PASTE (Joe Kirk, Josh Jackson, Nick Purdy, Tim Regan-Porter), John Patitucci, Erik Petrik, Jon Phelps, Steven and Amy Purcell, Brad Reeves, Malaika Rhea, Mark Rodgers, Scott Roley, Edith Schaeffer and Francis Schaeffer, Phil Sillas, J. D. Souther, R. C. Sproul, Matt Stevens, Susan Stewart, John Stott, John Styll, Nate Tasker, David Taylor, Rod Taylor, Steve and Deb Taylor, Jim and Kim Thomas, John J. Thompson, Jemar Tisby, Troy Tomlinson, Dave Trout, Steve Turner, Lenny Waronker, Alicia Warwick, Jody Williams, Joy Williams, Paula and Boomer Williams, Isabel Wilkerson, Dallas Willard, N. T. Wright, Nate Yetton, Clark and Karoly Zaft, and Jim Zumwalt.

If an artist, producer, cowriter, or musician's name appears in the "Selected Discography," I offer recognition of and gratitude for that person's contribution to my musical life. To all the songwriters and artists that our various companies funded and developed, I hope you were cared for well and progressed in your art making in meaningful ways. I'm grateful for the privilege of knowing and serving you. I trust you're all still creating the songs the whole world sings.

I'll close by highlighting a few of the extraordinary studio musicians and vocalists I've worked with since leaving California in 1989. It will not be exhaustive, but complete enough to recognize and celebrate those gifted ones who substantively contributed to my career. A full-frequency round of applause for: Sam Ashworth, Mark Baldwin, Bruce Bouton, Tom Bukovac, Gary Burnette, George Cocchini, JT Corenflos, Scott Denté, Kenny Greenberg, Jeff King, Jerry McPherson, Paul Moak, Bryan Sutton, Guthrie Trapp, and Derek Wells (guitars); Brian Blade, Steve Brewster, Chris Brown, Fred Eltringham, Shannon Forrest, Mark Hammond, John Hammond, Eric Harland, Evan Hutchings, Chris McHugh, Miles McPherson, Greg Morrow, Dan Needham, Aaron Smith, Aaron Sterling, and Nir Z (drums); Barry Bales, James Genus, Mark Hill, Brent Milligan, Scott Mulvahill, Craig Nelson, Danny O'Lannerghty, Felix Pastorius, John Patitucci, Matt Pierson, Tommy Sims, Jimmie Lee Sloas, and Victor Wooten (bass); Tim Akers, Pat Coil, Tim Lauer, Phil Maderia, Carl Marsh, Blair Masters, Tony Miracle, Roger Smith, and Reese Wynans (keyboards, synths); Eric Darken and Ken Lewis (percussion); Roy Agee, Tom Ashworth, Jeff Coffin, Mark Douthit, Barry Green, Mike Haynes, Philip Lassiter, Sam Levine, Chris McDonald, and Matthew White (horns); Ruby Amanfu, Sam Ashworth, Bob Bailey, Brent Bourgeois, Ashley Cleveland, Christine Denté, Nirva Dorsaint, Chris Eaton, Vince Ebo, Tabitha Fair, Kim Fleming, Vicki Hampton, Nikki Hassman-Anders, Darwin Hobbs, Tiffany Palmer, Janna Potter, Joey Richie, Chris Rodriguez, and Nicol Smith (background and guest vocals); Béla Fleck, Matt Menefee, and Ilya Toshinskiy (banjo); Jeff Taylor (accordion); Andy Leftwich and Jonathan Rudkin (fiddle, mandolin); Buddy Greene, Charlie McCoy, and Terry McMillan (harmonica); Bruce Bouton, Dan Dugmore, and Russ Pahl (pedal and lap steel); David Davidson, Tom Howard, Ron Huff, and Kristin Wilkinson (string arrangers); Nashville Recording Orchestra and Nashville String Machine (orchestras).

SELECTED DISCOGRAPHY

This is a selected discography, approved by me (accurate from 1979 to 2024). The idea was to compile a robust discography composed of the "first use" recordings and some esoterica for fun. Many recordings are missing that can be found on AllMusic.com and Discogs.com. This discography spares you from trudging through the mistakes, the NOW, WOW, "Best Of" records, and the endless compilations such as '90s Party Hits!, Hipster Hymns, and Chartbuster Karaoke. Also, most of the independent recordings I produced from 1979 to 1983 are now lost to time and memory. Additionally, while a few films and soundtracks are mentioned, TV/film/ad productions are not included (Tunefind.com is a good source for the latter). Also noteworthy: in 2017, with Meta Inc., I began creating unique projects and casting guest artists (three-hundred-plus songs). Consequently, many of these "productions" appear in the Artist Discography from that date. The hope is that this producer discography is error-free. Be forewarned, the sites mentioned above and Wikipedia are helpful but sprinkled with inaccuracies. For an accurate, concise accounting of artists and guest artists I've produced, see the alphabetized list (executive production is excluded).

Selected Discography

ARTIST RECORDINGS: VOCAL AND INSTRUMENTAL

1982	"No Magazines" b/w "What They Like"* *(as Charlie Peacock Group)*	VAVAVA	Single
1984	*Lie Down in the Grass*	Exit	Album
1985	*Lie Down in the Grass*	A&M Records	Album

Reissue released by A&M Records, contains the songs "Young in Heart" and "Love Doesn't Get Better," replacing "Watching Eternity" and "Human Condition" from the 1984 release.

1986	*Charlie Peacock***	Island Records	Album
1988	*West Coast Diaries, Vol. I*	Jamz Ltd.	Album
1988	*West Coast Diaries, Vol. II*	Jamz Ltd.	Album
1989	*West Coast Diaries, Vol. III*	Jamz Ltd.	Album
1990	*The Secret of Time****	Sparrow Records	Album
1990	*West Coast Diaries, Vol. I, II, & III*	Sparrow Records	Album

Reissues released by Sparrow on CD. Later compiled as a deluxe box set with thirty-two-page liner notes for release in 1992. A remixed/remastered version by engineer Richie Biggs of volume II was released by Runway Network in 2008. Limited edition vinyl of volume II was released by Allender Creative in 2019.

1990	*FRONT ROW: Charlie Peacock—an Acoustic Concert Experience*	Sparrow Records	Video

Filmed at Caravan of Dreams, Fort Worth, Texas, fete. CP, Jimmy Abegg, and Vince Ebo.

1991	*Love Life*	Sparrow Records	Album
1994	*Everything That's on My Mind*	Sparrow Records	Album
1996	*. . . In the Light: The Very Best of Charlie Peacock*	re:think/EMI	Album
1996	*strangelanguage*	re:think/EMI	Album
1999	*Live in the Netherlands*	CP Collector Series	Album

1999	*Last Vestiges of Honor******	CP Collector Series	Album

"No Magazines" and "What the Like" from the 1982 single were combined with five other unreleased recordings from The Charlie Peacock Group (1981–1982) featuring Mark Herzig (guitar), Erik Kleven (bass), Jim Caselli (drums), and Darius Babazadeh (sax). Engineered, coproduced, and cowritten by Stephen Holsapple. Remastered fortieth-anniversary edition released in 2022.

1999	*Kingdom Come*	re:think/EMI	Album

2005	*Love Press Ex-Curio*	Runway Network	Album
		Emergent/ RED	

Featuring: bassists James Genus, Craig Nelson, and Victor Wooten; guitarists Myles Boisen, Jerry McPherson, Henry Robinett, and Kurt Rosenwinkel; saxophonists Jeff Coffin, Ravi Coltrane, and Kirk Whalum; drummers Joey Baron, Gino Robair, and Jim White; synthesists Tony Miracle and Kip Kubin; trumpeter Ralph Alessi; and organist Roger Smith.

2008	*Arc of the Circle* w/Jeff Coffin	Runway Network	Album

Featuring: Marc Ribot (guitar); Derrek Phillips (drums, glockenspiel); Tony Miracle (laptop synths); Joe Murphy (tuba); and Chad Howat (keyboards and ambient treatments); woodwind arrangements by Jeff Coffin.

2012	*No Man's Land*	Twenty Ten Music	Album

2013	Various, *College Radio Day: The Album, Vol. 2*	College Radio Day	Album

Along with Wilco and My Morning Jacket, CP's "Death Trap" from No Man's Land *was included at No. 4.*

2014	*Lemonade: Collected Solo Piano Improvisations*	Twenty Ten Music	Album

2016	"That's the Way They Came to Us"	Twenty Ten Music	Single

2016	"White Bikini"	Twenty Ten Music	Single

2017	"In the Light"	Twenty Ten Music	Single

Featuring: Andy Leftwich (mandolin) and Bryan Sutton (acoustic guitar).
Recorded live at the Art House, Nashville, 2012, video at https://www.youtube
.com/@CharliePeacock.

2018	*When Light Flashes Help Is on the Way*	Twenty Ten Music	Album

Featuring: Scott Mulvahill, Felix Pastorius, and Matt Wigton (bassists); Jordan Perlson and Ben Perowsky (drummers); Hilmar Jensson and Jerry McPherson (guitarists); Jeff Coffin (woodwinds); Andy Leftwich (fiddle and mandolin); Tony Miracle (synthesizer); Jeff Taylor (accordion, pump organ); and Matthew White (trumpet).

2018	"Automatt"	Twenty Ten Music	Single

Featuring: Vicente Archer (bass), Jeff Coffin (tenor sax), Jerry McPherson (guitar), and Derrek Phillips (drums). Filmed and recorded live at the Silent Planet, Nashville, video at https://www.youtube.com/@CharliePeacock.

2019	*Epic Dream Day*	Meta, Inc.	EP
2019	*Memories like Diamonds: Piano & Orchestration*	Meta, Inc.	EP
2019	*Lil' Willie*	Meta, Inc.	Album
2019	*Family Fiddle*	Meta, Inc.	EP
2020	*Dance Magnificat: Piano & Orchestration*	Meta, Inc.	EP
2020	*East Village 3AM*	Meta, Inc.	Album
2020	*Music for Film: Composer Series, Volume One*	Meta, Inc.	Album
2020	"With God Everything Is Possible" w/ Ladysmith Black Mambazo	Squint Entertainment	Single

Remastered single from Roaring Lambs (2000 release on Squint), featuring CP (piano), Don Alias (percussion), James Genus (bass), and Tony Miracle (programming). Composition by Joseph Shabalala.

2020	"After All These Years" w/Steve Swallow	Meta, Inc.	Single
2020	"One Together" w/Scott Mulvahill	Meta, Inc.	Single

Written and produced by CP for bassist and vocalist Scott Mulvahill, summer of 2020.

2020	"Freedom Come Tonight" w/Brandon Heath	Meta, Inc.	Single

Featuring vocal performance from Ruby Amanfu. Cowritten by CP and Brandon Heath.

2020	"Surprised Me Too"	Meta, Inc.	Single

Featuring instrumental performances from CJ Camerieri (trumpet) and Gabriel Cabezas (cello), members of yMusic Ensemble, and Jeff Coffin (woodwinds).

2020	*See for Miles*	Meta, Inc.	Album

Featuring Jeff Coffin (saxophones), Philip Lassiter (trumpet), and Matthew White (trumpet).

2020	*Your Stardust Kiss*	Meta, Inc.	Album

Featuring Andy Leftwich (fiddle, mandolin) and Bryan Sutton (acoustic guitar) on "The One I Love the Most."

2020	"Holding On and Letting Go" w/Sarah Masen	Meta, Inc.	Single

Written and produced by CP for Sarah Masen in the summer of 2020.

2020	"When You Move Me" w/Tony Miracle	Meta, Inc.	Single

Included in designer Michael Kors's fortieth-anniversary film.

2021	*Skin and Wind*	Meta, Inc.	Album

Featuring instrumental performances from CJ Camerieri (trumpet) and Gabriel Cabezas (cello), members of yMusic Ensemble, and Jeff Coffin (woodwinds).

2021	*Paisley Crusader*	Meta, Inc.	Album
2021	*Trout Creek Ranch (Remixed & Remastered)*	Meta, Inc.	Album

This album of solo piano performances was recorded in Studio C at Sear Sound, NYC, September 29, 2017, then picked up by Meta, Inc. for 2021 release.

2021	*Eye on the Spy*	Meta, Inc.	EP

Featuring Peter Bernstein (guitar) and Eric Harland (drums) on "This Time."

2021	*Lake Charles Two-Step*	Meta, Inc.	EP

Featuring Tom Ashworth (trombone) and Andy Leftwich (fiddle, mandolin).

2021	"Brooklyn Brother Bond" w/ John Patitucci	Meta, Inc.	Single
2021	*Go Light, Go Free w/Turtle Island String Quartet*	Meta, Inc.	Single

(2) song single of CP compositions "Go Light, Go Free" and "My Bonny Red-head," performed by CP (piano) and The Turtle Island String Quartet.

| 2021 | *São Paulo Silhouette* w/Jeff Coffin & WonderTwins | Meta, Inc. | Single |

(2) song single of CP compositions "São Paulo Silhouette" and "Istanbul, Gate to Prosperity."

| 2021 | *That Kind of Girl* | Meta, Inc. | EP |

Includes "Straight from the Heart," featuring Al Perkins (dobro), "Lullaby, Little Boat to Bethlehem," with Sarah Masen (vocal).

| 2021 | Charlie Peacock, "Veuillez Choisir L'amour" | Meta, Inc. | Single |

Featuring Jeff Coffin (woodwinds), Mike Clark (drums), and Mioune (cowrite and vocal).

| 2022 | *Blue for You* | Meta, Inc. | EP |

(3) CP compositions featuring Eric Harland (drums), John Patitucci (upright bass), Chris Potter (saxophone), and Marcus Printup (trumpet).

| 2022 | *Swingin' Mack Daddy* w/Bill Ashworth Big Band | Meta, Inc. | EP |

(3) '40s-style big-band compositions written in honor of CP's father, Bill Ashworth.

| 2022 | *Sketches of Noir* | Meta, Inc. | EP |

(3) CP compositions featuring CP (piano, vibes, bass), Chris Brown (drums), Jeff Coffin (saxophone), and Matthew White (trumpet).

| 2022 | *Two We Will One Day Meet* w/Nashville Recording Orchestra | Meta, Inc. | Single |

(2) song single of CP compositions "Two We Will One Day Know" and "My One Unchanging Love." Arranged by David Davidson.

| 2022 | *Bolingo Ya Lelo* | Meta, Inc. | EP |

Compositional collaboration with World Music Method (UK), featuring Edd Bateman, King Fire, Tony Essamay, Felix Ngindu. Also featuring Jeff Coffin (saxophones/flutes), Eric Harland (drums), and Matthew White (trumpet).

| 2022 | *Keep Movin'* w/Eddie Henderson | Meta, Inc. | EP |

Featuring Mike Clark (drums "I Didn't Did It"), Jeff Coffin (woodwinds, horn section, sax/flute soloist), Eddie Henderson (trumpet soloist), Matthew White (trumpet, horn section), and Dangerboy (rap). "I Didn't Did It" and "Nothin' to It (Take U Back to '94)," cowritten by CP and Dangerboy.

2023	"Come On (Klay on a 3 Point Streak)"	Meta, Inc.	Single
2023	"Dance 4 Me All Night (Afrobeat '23)"	Meta, Inc.	Single
2023	"Eyes on You" w/Sam Ashworth	Meta, Inc.	Single
2023	"Number One" w/Big B & Lil' B	Meta, Inc.	Single
2023	"Passion Action Playbook"	Meta, Inc.	Single
2023	"Breath of Beauty, Light of Love" w/ Nashville Recording Orchestra	Meta, Inc.	Single
2023	"Brasil Dançando Na Rua" w/Jeff Coffin	Meta, Inc.	Single
2024	"Sound of the Room" w/ John Patitucci	It's Time to Art	Single
2024	*Every Kind of Uh-Oh******	It's Time to Art/ Universal	Album

All projects produced by Charlie Peacock except as noted:

* Stephen Holsapple and Charlie Peacock
** Nigel Gray, coproduced by Brent Bourgeois and Charlie Peacock
*** Brown Bannister
**** Stephen Holsapple and Charlie Peacock
***** Charlie Peacock and Sam Ashworth
FRONT ROW: Charlie Peacock—an Acoustic Concert Experience, directed by Jim Rowley, produced by David Benware, Bill Hearn, and Peter York.
All compositions by Charlie Peacock except where noted.

COLLABORATIONS: VOCAL AND INSTRUMENTAL

2004	*Full Circle (A Celebration of Songs & Friends)**	Sparrow Records	Album
	Featuring: Jimmy Abegg, Sam Ashworth, Avalon, Margaret Becker, Brent Bourgeois, Christine Denté, Béla Fleck, Sara Groves, Darwin Hobbs, Phil Keaggy, Sarah Masen, Kevin Max, Bart Millard, Michael Roe, Sixpence None the Richer, Aaron Smith, Switchfoot, Tait, Steve Taylor, and Toby-Mac; produced by CP and various producers.		
2019	Charlie Peacock, *Jazz Composer, Vol. One*	Meta, Inc.	EP

CP compositions performed by Chris Brown (drums), Jeff Coffin (saxophone), Matt Endahl and Chris Walters (piano), Matthew White (trumpet), and Matt Wigton (upright bass).

2019	Charlie Peacock, *Souled-Out Fellowship of Friends & Funk*	Meta, Inc.	EP

Rhythm section of Alphonza Kee (bass), Jerry McPherson (guitar), Aaron Smith (drums), and Roger Smith (Rhodes, clavinet, and B3). Featuring vocal performances from CP, Ruby Amanfu, Sam Ashworth, Brinsley Ashworth, Jason Eskridge, and Jonathan Winstead.

2019	Charlie Peacock and Marc Martel, "The Finish Line"	Meta, Inc.	Single

CP composition performed by vocalist
Marc Martel.

2019	Charlie Peacock and Abigail Flowers, *Flower in Bloom*	Meta, Inc.	Single

(2) song single performed by ukelele/vocal artist, Abigail Flowers.

Compositions "Flower in Bloom" and "My Kind of Night" by CP and Jac Thompson.

2019	Charlie Peacock, *Three for Alice*	Meta, Inc.	EP

(3) CP compositions performed by Matt Endahl (piano) and Jody Nardone (vocals).

Written in honor of CP's mother, Alice Ashworth.

2019	Charlie Peacock, *Drinking from the Wordless Well*	Meta, Inc.	EP

(5) CP compositions with vocal performances by Ruby Amanfu, Sam Ashworth, Sandra McCracken, and Ellie Schmidly.

2019	Charlie Peacock and Les Chanteuses, *She Sang for Me, Vol. 1*	Meta, Inc.	Album

(20) CP compositions performed by female artists Ruby Amanfu, Bridget Ashworth, Baylie Brown, Erika Daves, Lenachka, Lex Kuhl, Rachael Lampa, Femme Mystere, and Emily West. VeNTUR BRV$$ guests on Lex Kuhl's "Happy & Free."

2019	Charlie Peacock and Sam Ashworth, "Top of the Beautiful"	Meta, Inc.	Single

CP composition performed by vocalist Sam Ashworth.

2019	Charlie Peacock and VeNTUR BRV$$, *Young & Free*	Meta, Inc.	EP

Selected Discography

(4) compositions cowritten with VeNTUR BRV$$ (vocal performer).

2020	Charlie Peacock, *Behind the Board: Volume One*	Meta, Inc.	Album

Featuring vocal performances from Ruby Amanfu, Sam Ashworth, Erika Daves, Jason Eskridge, Rachael Lampa, Lucm, David Monsta Lynch, Denver M, Ben Van Maarth, YungLad NYC, Swagg R'Celious, LeeBerk the Student.

2020	Charlie Peacock, *Behind the Board: Volume Two*	Meta, Inc.	Album

Featuring vocal performances from Sam Ashworth, Andy Davis, Jeremy Lister, Nate Gott, and Dain Ussery.

2020	Charlie Peacock, "Beauregard Breakdown Blues"	Meta, Inc.	Single

CP composition performed by Andy Leftwich (fiddle, mandolin) and Bryan Sutton (acoustic guitar).

2020	Charlie Peacock, *Lyricus Minimus Voxology*	Meta, Inc.	Album

Featuring vocal performances by CP, Ruby Amanfu, Sam Ashworth, Bridget Ashworth, Lenachka, and Grant Parker.

2020	Charlie Peacock, "Whole Lot Different Whole Lot the Same"	Charlie Peacock	Single

Featuring vocal and instrumental performances by CP (piano); Jimmy Abegg (guitar); Sam Ashworth, Brent Bourgeois, and Eric Heilman (bass); Michael Roe (guitar); Aaron Smith (drums); Bongo Bob Smith (percussion); and Roger Smith (B3 organ).

A one-off, pandemic reinvention of the song from Lie Down in the Grass (1984), video at https://www.youtube.com/@CharliePeacock.

2020	Charlie Peacock, "Sunny Everywhere We Go"	Meta, Inc.	Single

CP composition performed by vocalists Sam Ashworth and Sydney Layne.

2021	Charlie Peacock, *Way That You Move*	Meta, Inc.	EP

Featuring vocal performances by Ruby Amanfu, VeNTUR BRV$$, and Swagg R'Celious.

2021	Charlie Peacock, "Bailando en la Arena"	Meta, Inc.	Single

CP composition performed and cowritten by vocalist Natta.

2023	Charlie Peacock, "No Stoppin' (We Never Quit)"	Meta, Inc.	Single
	CP composition performed by True Dat Collective.		
2023	Charlie Peacock, "Downtown Magic Memory"	Meta, Inc.	Single
	CP composition performed by Karis.		
2023	Charlie Peacock, "Ready to Live My Life"	Meta, Inc.	Single
	CP composition performed by Sam Ashworth.		
2023	Charlie Peacock, "Big Hope, Big Love, Big Everything"	Meta, Inc.	Single
	CP composition performed by Sam Ashworth.		
2023	Charlie Peacock, "Come On (Gimme That Smile)"	Meta, Inc.	Single
	CP composition performed by Sam Ashworth.		

All projects produced by Charlie Peacock except as noted:

* Produced by CP, Sam Ashworth, Richie Biggs, Brent Bourgeois, Todd Collins, Scott Denté, Taylor Harris, Mark Heimermann, Tony Miracle, Dan Muckala, and Jon Foreman. Executive producers: Richie Biggs, Scott Denté, and Brad O'Donnell. A Runway Network Production.

All compositions by Charlie Peacock except where noted. *Full Circle* (2004) includes the song "The Way of Love," cowritten by CP and Bongo Bob Smith.

GUEST ARTIST/VOCALIST APPEARANCES

1983	Vector, *Mannequin Virtue*	Exit Records	Album
	CP joined the band created by Steve Griffith and Jimmy Abegg for their debut recording.		
	He played Memorymoog synthesizer, sang background vocals, and made one lead vocal appearance on the song "Running from the Light," which he cowrote with Abegg and Griffith. He also cowrote "Mannequin Virtue," "Substitute," and "The Hunger and the Thirst."		

1997	Various, *At the Foot of the Cross (Vol. Two)*	Word	Album

CP sang "Beloved Ones" written by Derald Daugherty and Steve Hindalong.

1999	Various, *Listen to Our Hearts (Vol. Two)*	Sparrow	Album

CP sang the hymn "Take My Life and Let It Be."

2001	Various, *Make Me Your Voice: Worship Leaders Unite for the Voiceless of Sudan*	Spring Hill	Album

CP sang his composition "Stand Up."

2018	Philthy, *Philip Lassiter Presents Party Crashers*	Ropeadope	Album

CP contributes lead vocals (along with Tommy Sims and PL), background vocals, and Fender Rhodes on "Life Success."

SESSION MUSICIAN/VOCALIST APPEARANCES (*Separate from Productions*)

1988	Russ Taff, *Russ Taff*	A&M/Myrrh	Album

CP sang background vocals on his own composition, "Down in the Lowlands," and on "Higher." The first, joined by Clarice Devisschu (Jones), Rebecca Sparks, and Vince Ebo.

The second, Annie Stocking and Vince Ebo.

1988	Scott Stewart, *Scott Stewart & the Other Side*	SGA/ Allegiance	Album

CP contributed keyboards. Produced by Phil Sillas.

1990	Twila Paris, *Cry for the Desert*	Star Song	Album

CP created track arrangements, played keyboards, and sang on (3) songs, "Cry for the Desert," "Celebration/Kingdom of God," and "Fix Your Eyes."

1990	Phil Keaggy, *Find Me in These Fields*	A&M/Myrrh	Album

CP sang background vocals on "Be in My Heart."

1991	Amy Grant, *Heart in Motion*	A&M Records	Album

On "Every Heartbeat," CP created the track and horn arrangements (w/ Chris McDonald) and played keyboards. Same credit for "Hats." On "How Can We See That Far" he programmed drums; on "You're Not Alone," played keyboards. Produced by Brown Bannister.

Selected Discography

1991	Jimmy A, *Entertaining Angels*	Sparrow	Album

CP sang lead vocals on "I'll Meet You in Heaven," played Fender Rhodes, contributed background vocals, and programmed beats.

1993	Various, *The New Young Messiah*	Sparrow	Album

CP arranged and played keyboards on "O Thou That Tellest Good Tidings to Zion," featuring vocalists Susan Ashton, Christine Denté, and Cindy Morgan.

1994	Julie Miller, *Invisible Girl*	Street Level Records	Album

CP and Valerie Carter sang background vocals on "I Will Be with You."

1995	dc Talk, *Jesus Freak*	Forefront/ Virgin	Album

CP sings a guest vocal on the ending of his song "In the Light."

1997	Say-So, *Say-So*	Organic/ Pamplin	Album

CP played cornet on "Wonderful World" along with Steve Taylor on trombone.

1997	Switchfoot, *The Legend of Chin*	re:think/EMI	Album

CP played Fender Rhodes electric piano and trumpet.

2000	Newsong, *Sheltering Trees*	Benson	Album

CP sang on "Sheltering Trees."

2002	Sixpence None the Richer, "Christmastime Is Here"	Word/EMI/ Provident	Album

CP played the role of pianist Vince Guaraldi in this classic cover recorded at Fantasy Studios in Berkeley, CA, released on WOW, Christmas, 2002.

2003	Christine Denté, *Becoming*	Rocketown	Album

CP played piano on a song he cowrote with Scott and Chris Denté, "Bigger Story."

2003	Michael W. Smith, *Healing Rain*	Reunion/ Provident	Album

CP is the string arranger on "I Am Love," produced by his son, Sam Ashworth.

2008	Jon Foreman, *Spring, Summer, Fall, Winter*	lowercase people	Album

CP played Wurli 200A electric piano, B3 and Astro Organs, piano, and Pro One bass.

| 2015 | Switchfoot, *Oh! Gravity* | Columbia Records | Album |

CP played chimes on "Let Your Love Be Strong."

| 2023 | Bob Cheevers, "Easy Chair" | Independent | Single |

A song cowritten by Bob and Stephen Holsapple. CP played drums, bass, piano, and sang background vocals. From the album Legends and Kings.

SELECTED PRODUCER DISCOGRAPHY

| 1979 | Labial Fricative, "Chumps" b/w "Auto/ Erotica" | Esoteric Records | 7-inch Single |

Coproduced with Steve Holsapple.

| 1984 | The 77s, *All Fall Down* | Exit/A&M | Album |

Including 7-inch vinyl single (Exit/A&M), "Mercy Mercy" b/w "Something's Holding On."

| 1986 | The Choir, *Diamonds and Rain* | LA Myrrh | Album |

Including 7-inch vinyl single (LA Myrrh), "Kingston Road" b/w "Render Love."

A-side written by CP. B-side cowritten by CP and Steve Hindalong.

| 1987 | Various, *Wired for Sound* | A&M/ Horizon | Album |

Includes "Render Love" by The Choir, produced and cowritten by CP.

| 1987 | I Love Ethyl, *I Love Ethyl* | Mad Rover Records | Album |

CP produced the B-side of this album (four songs).

| 1988 | Steve Scott, *Lost Horizon* | Exit/ Alternative | Album |

CP produced (7) songs on this indie compilation, previously meant to be released via Exit's distribution deal with A&M Records.

| 1989 | Margaret Becker, *Immigrant's Daughter* | Sparrow Records | Album |

| 1990 | Steve Scott, *Magnificent Obsession* | Alternative | Album |

Coproduced with Steve Scott, Michael Roe, and Randy Layton.

Selected Discography

| 1990 | Various, *Our Christmas* | Reunion Records | Album |

A coproduction with Brown Bannister on Al Green's "The First Noel" and a Phil Keaggy and Kim Hill duet of "God Rest Ye Merry, Gentlemen."

1990	The Swoon, *Neverland / Ben Son Ben Son Beatrice*	Narrowpath Records	Album
1991	Out of the Grey, *Out of the Grey*	Sparrow Records	Album
1991	Margaret Becker, *Simple House*	Sparrow Records	Album

Including UK release of 7-inch vinyl single (Sparrow), "Talk about Love" b/w "All I Ever Wanted." A-side cowritten by CP and Margaret Becker.

| 1992 | Rich Lang, *Big Dream* | Wonderland/ Word | Album |
| 1992 | Various, *Coram Deo: In the Presence of God* | Sparrow Records | Album |

(10) compositions written by CP with vocal performances from CP, Susan Ashton, Michael Card, Michael English, and Out of the Grey. A Spanish-language version featuring Enrique & Lucia and guests, e.g., Crystal Lewis, was also released in 1992.

| 1992 | Various, *No Compromise (Remembering the Music of Keith Green)* | Sparrow Records | Album |

CP produced Margaret Becker, "Oh Lord, You're Beautiful"; Rich Mullins, "You Are the One"; and himself, "I Can't Believe It."

| 1992 | Vince Ebo, *Love Is the Better Way* | Warner Brothers | Album |

CP produced "Long Time Comin'" and "These Are the Questions."

| 1992 | Out of the Grey, *Shape of Grace* | Sparrow Records | Album |
| 1992 | Margaret Becker, "This Love" | Sparrow Records | Single |

CP produced this single for a best-of compilation, Steps of Faith, 1987–1991.

| 1993 | Margaret Becker, *Soul* | Sparrow Records | Album |

| 1993 | Various, *Coram Deo II: People of Praise* | Sparrow Records | Album |

Vocal performances from CP, Margaret Becker, Bob Carlisle, Steven Curtis Chapman, Steve Green, Out of the Grey, and CeCe Winans.

| 1993 | Bob Carlisle, *Bob Carlisle* | Sparrow Records | Album |

CP produced "Bridge between Two Hearts," "Giving You the Rest of My Life," and "Goin' Home."

| 1994 | Cheri Keaggy, *Child of the Father* | Sparrow Records | Album |

| 1994 | Lisa Bevill, *All Because of You* | Sparrow Records | Album |

CP produced "Fall into Your Arms," "No Condemnation," and "Trouble the Waters."

| 1994 | Out of the Grey, *Diamond Days* | Sparrow Records | Album |

| 1994 | Brent Bourgeois, *Come Join the Living World* | Reunion Records | Album |

CP produced the first (6) songs.

| 1995 | Margaret Becker, *Grace* | Sparrow Records | Album |

CP produced (7) songs.

| 1995 | Out of the Grey, *Gravity* | Sparrow Records | Album |

| 1995 | Scott Krippayne, *Wild Imagination* | Word Records | Album |

| 1995 | Tony Vincent, *Tony Vincent* | Star Song | Album |

Coproduced with Brent Bourgeois.

| 1996 | Avalon, *Avalon* | Sparrow Records | Album |

| 1996 | Eric Champion, *Transformation* | Essential Records | Album |

Produced by CP, coproduced by Rick Will.

| 1996 | Cheri Keaggy, *My Faith Will Stay* | Sparrow Records | Album |

Selected Discography

1996	Various, *One Point Oh*	re:think/EMI	Album

Vocal and instrumental performances from CP, Diana Beach, Karen Bradley, Ensemblepossible, Sarah Hart, Sarah Masen, Brent Milligan, Joey Richey, Aaron Smith, and Richard Thomas.

1996	Sarah Masen, *Sarah Masen*	re:think/EMI	Album
1997	Various, *God with Us: A Celebration of Christmas Carols & Classics*	Sparrow Records	Album

CP produced Avalon, "Angels We Have Heard on High"; Cheri Keaggy, "What Child Is This"; and Out of the Grey, "O Holy Night."

1997	Scott Krippayne, *More*	Word Records	Album
1997	Avalon, *A Maze of Grace*	Sparrow Records	Album

Produced by CP, coproduced by Chris Harris.

1998	Sarah Masen, *Carry Us Through*	re:think/EMI	Album
1998	Out of the Grey, *Remember This (The Out of the Grey Collection)*	Sparrow Records	Album

A best-of collection with (2) new songs produced by CP and Out of the Grey: "This Is What It Is" and "Walk by Faith." Including a remix, "Wishes '98," produced by CP, Richie Biggs, and Gil Gowing. Also includes the unreleased instrumental "Way Late" produced by CP in 1993.

1998	Various, *Happy Christmas: A BEC Holiday Collection*	BEC Recordings	Album

CP produced Sarah Masen, "Heaven's Got a Baby."

1998	Michelle Tumes, *Listen*	Sparrow Records	Album
1998	Michelle Tumes, *Feel*	EMI Records	Single

A (3)-song CD single released by EMI Records in Japan only. Includes "Feel," "Listen," and a previously unreleased track titled "That's How a Father Loves."

1998	Samuel Brinsley Ashworth, *Sauté*	CP Productions	Album
1999	Various, *Listen/Louder*	Sparrow Records	Album

CP produced Sarah Masen, "Psalm 139," and Switchfoot, "Spirit."

1999	Twila Paris, *True North*	Sparrow Records	Album

Selected Discography

1999	Audio Adrenaline, *Underdog*	Forefront Records	Album

CP produced and cowrote "Good Life" and "Hands & Feet."

1999	Switchfoot, *New Way to Be Human*	re:think/EMI	Album

2000	Various, *Roaring Lambs*	Squint Entertainment	Album

CP produced and appeared as coartist with Ladysmith Black Mambazo, "'Akehlulek' Ubaba (With God Everything Is Possible)."

2000	Switchfoot, *Learning to Breathe*	re:think/EMI	Album

CP produced tracks 1, 2, 4, 5, and 9, including "I Dare You to Move" and "Learning to Breathe."

2002	Various, *A Walk to Remember (Sound Track)*	Epic Records/ Sony	Album

CP produced tracks for Switchfoot: "Dare You to Move," "Learning to Breathe," "You," and "Only Hope." Soundtrack includes Mandy Moore's version of "Only Hope."

2002	Various, *Left Behind Worship (God Is with Us)*	ForeFront Records	Album

CP produced tracks for his vocal duet with Tait, "The Only Light We Need," and Jill Phillips, "Forever and Ever."

2002	Nichole Nordeman, *Woven & Spun*	Sparrow Records	Album

CP produced (7) songs.

2002	Aaron Spiro, *Sing*	Sparrow Records	Album

Produced by CP and Jacquire King.

2002	Stacie Orrico, *Bounce Back*	ForeFront Records	Maxi-Single

CP produced "Genuine: Very Real Remix." Original production by Tedd T.

2003	Audio Adrenaline, *Worldwide*	ForeFront Records	Album

CP produced (5) songs.

2003	David Crowder Band, *Illuminate*	Sparrow/ sixsteps	Album

CP produced "O Praise Him (All This for the King)" and "Open Skies."

2003	Various, *The Message/Remix (Eugene Peterson)*	Audible/Oasis	Album

CP produced various artists reading from The Message.

2004	Switchfoot, *The Beautiful Letdown*	Columbia Records	Album

CP received coproduction credit on "Dare You to Move," with John Fields, once it was discovered that elements of CP's version of the song in 2000 were used in the new version. This album went through several iterations beginning in 2003 with Sparrow- and RED-distributed versions before Columbia took over the distribution and promotion, and corrected the producer attribution.

2004	Avalon, *The Creed*	Sparrow Records	Album

CP produced "Far Away from Here" and "Renew Me."

2004	Sara Groves, *The Other Side of Something*	INO Records/Sponge	Album

CP produced (4) songs.

2004	Various, *Gloria: A Christmas Celebration*	Rocketown/SonyBMG	Album

Produced by CP and Scott Denté. Vocal performances by CP, Alathea, Christine Denté, Amy Grant, Shaun Groves, Wayne Kirkpatrick, Cindy Morgan, Christy Nockels, Ginny Owens, George Rowe, Michael W. Smith, and Taylor Sorenson.

2004	Various, *For Christ Alone*	Fuseic Music	Album

Produced by CP and Scott Denté. Vocal performances by CP, Margaret Becker, Christine Denté, Nirva Dorsaint, Sara Groves, Cindy Morgan, Chris Rice, and Taylor Sorenson.

2005	Various, *Elektra: The Album (Soundtrack)*	Wind-Up/Epic	Album

CP produced the Switchfoot song "Sooner or Later." Additional production by John Fields.

2005	Nathan Tasker, *Must Be More*	Cross-Word Music	Album

Produced by CP and Scott Denté.

2006	Karl Denson's Tiny Universe, *Once You're There*	Tibetan Prawn Shop	EP

Selected Discography

2007	Miriam Jones, *Being Here*	Independent	Album
2008	Isaac and Anna Slade, "O Love That Will Not Let Me Go"	Hymns Project	Single
2008	Maeve, *And the World Became Kind*	Simple & Wonderful	Album
2008	Warren Barfield, *Worth Fighting For*	Essential Records	Album
	CP produced (7) songs.		
2008	Anna Gilbert, *Your Love My Medicine*	Runway Network	Album
2008	Various, *Sony/ATV Nashville Classic Covers, Volume One*	Sony/ATV	Album
	Classic songs in the Sony/ATV Nashville catalog reimagined by CP with guest artists, including Leigh Nash, Paper Route, Joe Tex, Roger Miller, Jon Foreman, and more.		
2009	Adjoa Skinner, "The Drum Song"	Art House America	Video
	Video at https://www.youtube.com/@AdjoaSkinner.		
2009	Sara Groves, *Fireflies and Songs*	INO Records/ Sponge	Album
2009	Daves Highway, *Just for You*	Twenty Ten Music	EP
2009	Newsong, *Give Yourself Away*	HHM Records	Album
2009	Kendall Payne, *Wounds to Scars*	KPW Inc.	Album
2009	The Civil Wars, *Poison & Wine*	Sensibility	EP
	All TCW indie recordings produced by CP were rereleased by Columbia Records, including the original Poison & Wine *EP.*		
2009	Ten out of Tenn, *Any Day Now*	Ten out of Tenn	Video
	CP (Executive Producer of film), along w/Richie Biggs, mixed and produced the music captured from live performances while on tour. Featuring Butterfly Boucher, Trent Dabbs, Andy Davis, Katie Herzig, Griffin House, Tyler James, Matthew Perryman Jones, Jeremy Lister, Erin McCarley, and k.s. Rhoads.		

2009	Switchfoot, *Hello Hurricane (Box Set)*	Atlantic Records	Album

Bonus CD contains "Mess of Me" (Charlie Peacock Sessions, August 2007), previously unreleased.

2010	Various, *The Jensen Project (Soundtrack)*	NBC/ Walmart/ P&G	Album

TV movie soundtrack coproduced with Randy Jackson, featuring artists Warren Barfield, Justin York, and Jillian Edwards. CP produced songs on two subsequent soundtracks with RJ, A Walk in My Shoes (2010) and Change of Plans (2011) with various artists, including Anna Gilbert, Daves Highway, and Tanner Azzinaro.

2010	Brooke Waggoner, *And the World Opened Up*	Swoon Moon/ TTM	Album

Released with a film of the same title, produced and directed by CP.

2010	*The Legend Hank Cochran*	Sony/ATV & BMI	Video

CP directed and produced the music for this tribute film to legendary song-writer Hank Cochran, featuring performances from Merle Haggard, Lee Ann Womack, and more. Cameos: Cowboy Jack Clement, Elvis Costello, and Willie Nelson.

2011	Attwater, "Never Gonna Happen"	Twenty Ten Music	Single
2011	Attwater, *Christmas*	Twenty Ten Music	EP
2011	Nathan Tasker, *Home*	Luxtone	Album
2011	The Civil Wars, *Barton Hollow*	Columbia/ Sensibility	Album
2012	Keith and Kristyn Getty, *Hymns for the Christian Life*	Getty Music	Album

CP produced (10) of twelve songs. Featuring guest artists Moya Brennan, Alison Krauss, and Ricky Skaggs.

2012	Ruby Amanfu, *The Simple Sessions*	Twenty Ten Music	EP
2013	The Lone Bellow, *The Lone Bellow*	Descendant/ Sony	Album

| 2013 | Ben Rector, *The Walking in Between* | Aptly Named Recs. | Album |

"Beautiful," produced by CP. "Sailboat," produced by CP and Jamie Kenney.

| 2013 | Al Lewis, *Battles* | Twenty Ten Music | Album |

CP produced (7) songs.

| 2013 | Andrew Ripp, *Won't Let Go* | Be Music Ent. | Album |

Featuring guest vocalist Vince Gill on "Rescue Me."

| 2013 | Holly Williams, *The Highway* | Georgiana Records | Album |

Produced by CP. Coproduced by Holly Williams. "Let You Go," produced by Chris Coleman. Featuring guest artists Dierks Bentley, Jackson Browne, Jakob Dylan, and Gwyneth Paltrow.

| 2013 | The Civil Wars, *The Civil Wars* | Columbia/ Sensibility | Album |

Produced by CP, except "I Had Me a Girl," instrumentation and mix produced by CP, TCW performance produced by Rick Rubin.

| 2013 | Various, *12 Years a Slave (Music from and Inspired By)* | Columbia Records | Album |

CP produced Chris Cornell featuring Joy Williams on "Misery Chain."

| 2013 | The Civil Wars, *To Be Determined* | Columbia/ Sensibility | EP |

10-inch vinyl EP featuring "I Want You Back," "Dance Me to the End of Love," "Goodbye Girl," and "Marionette."

| 2013 | Brett Dennen, *Smoke and Mirrors* | F-Stop/ Atlantic | Album |

| 2014 | The Civil Wars, *Between the Bars* | Columbia/ Sensibility | EP |

10-inch vinyl EP featuring "Sour Times" and "Talking in Your Sleep," produced by CP, with "Between the Bars" and "Billie Jean," produced by Rick Rubin.

| 2014 | Joy Williams and Matt Berninger, "Hush" | Universal/ Republic | Single |

| 2014 | Various, *AMC's Turn: Washington's Spies (Soundtrack)* | Universal/ Republic | Album |

Selected Discography

CP produced and cowrote the title theme "Hush," featuring vocals Joy Williams and Matt Berninger (The National).

2014	Kris Allen, *Horizons*	Dog Bear Records	Album
2014	Kris Allen, "Baby It Ain't Christmas without You"	Dog Bear Records	Single
2014	Lenachka, *Lenachka*	Twenty Ten Music	EP

CP produced "Breaking Down," "Good Luck," and "I Want to Love You."

2014	Brent Bourgeois, *Don't Look Back*	Donahue Ent.	Album

CP coproduced "All She Ever Wanted" with BB.

2015	Zeke Duhon, *Zeke Duhon*	Music of Big Deal	EP
2015	Jon Foreman, *The Wonderlands: Shadows*	lowercase people	Album

CP coproduced "Good for Me" with Andrew Messon.

2015	Joy Williams, *Venus*	Columbia/ Sensibility	Album

CP coproduced with Matt Morris and Daniel James. "You Loved Me" produced by Michael Einziger.

2016	Gracie Schram, *I Am Me*	Full Ride Records	Album
2016	Joy Williams, *Venus Acoustic*	Sensibility	Album

Produced by CP, except "You Loved Me," produced by Michael Einziger.

2016	Angelica Garcia, *Medicine for Birds*	Warner Brothers	Album
2016	Castro, *Diamond Dreams*	Curb Records	Album
2017	Selah, *Unbreakable*	Curb Records	Album

(1) song, "People of the Cross," produced by CP.

2018	Scott Mulvahill, *Himalayas*	West Sterling Music	Album

CP coproduced with Scott Mulvahill and Gary Paczosa.

2018	Sarah Masen, "Three Strangers"	Twenty Ten Music	Single

2018	Chris Cornell, *Chris Cornell*	Universal Music	Album
	Career-spanning retrospective, including CP-produced "Misery Chain."		
2019	Sam Ashworth, *Songs of My Father*	Meta, Inc.	EP
	Includes the single, "Love Is Like a Compass," with Ellie Schmidly.		
2019	Sarah Masen, "Like Lightning"	Twenty Ten Music	Single
2021	*Rainbow Motherfunk Demo Factory*	Meta, Inc.	Album
2021	*Homegrown Honey*	Meta, Inc.	Album
2021	Keith and Kristyn Getty, *Confessio: Irish American Roots*	Getty Music	Album
	CP produced (1) song, "In Christ Alone," featuring Alison Krauss.		

EXECUTIVE PRODUCER, A&R, AND MISCELLANEOUS

1991	Jimmy A, *Entertaining Angels* (Exec. Producer)	Sparrow	Album
1997	Switchfoot, *The Legend of Chin* (A&R, Exec. Producer)	re:think/EMI	Album
	Produced by Jimmie Lee Sloas, engineered by Shane D. Wilson.		
1999	Darwin Hobbs, *Mercy* (Exec. Producer)	re:think/EMI Gospel	Album
2003	TobyMac, *Re:Mix Momentum* (A&R)	Forefront/ EMI	Album
2003	Tait, *Lose This Life* (A&R)	Forefront/ EMI	Album
2003	Various, *Mixdown* (Exec. Producer)	Forefront/ EMI	Album
2005	Sam Ashworth, *Gonna Get It Wrong Before I Get It Right* (A&R)	Runway Network Emergent/ RED	Album
2002	The Benjamin Gate, *Contact* (A&R/Exec. Producer)	Forefront/ EMI	Album

2002	The O.C. Supertones, *Hi-Fi Revival* (Exec. Producer)	Forefront/ EMI	Album
2002	Various, *Left Behind Worship (God Is with Us)* (Exec. Producer)	ForeFront Records	Album
2008	Jon Foreman, *Spring, Summer, Fall, Winter* (Exec. Producer)	lowercase people	Album
2008	Jon Foreman, *Limbs & Branches* (Exec. Producer)	Credential	Album
2009	*To Save a Life* (Music Supervisor)	Affirm/Sony	Film
2010	Brooke Waggoner, *And the World Opened Up* (Producer/Director)	TTM/Art House	Film
2010	The Daylights, "Oh Oh," *Rabbit Hole* (A&R)	Twenty Ten Music	Film
2011	Joseph Lemay, *Precursor to Earthtones* (Exec. Producer)	Independent	EP

LIST OF ARTISTS AND GUEST ARTISTS PRODUCED BY CHARLIE PEACOCK

Aaron Smith
Aaron Spiro
Abigail Flowers
Alathea
Al Green
Alison Krauss
Al Lewis
Al Perkins
Amy Grant
Andrew Ripp
Andy Davis
Andy Leftwich
Angelica Garcia
Anna Gilbert
Ashley Cleveland
Audio Adrenaline
Avalon
Bart Millard
Baylie Brown

Béla Fleck
Ben Rector
Ben Van Maarth
Bobby Bare **
Bob Carlisle
Bongo Bob Smith
Brandon Heath
Brent Bourgeois
Brent Milligan
Brett Dennen
Bridget Ashworth
Brooke Waggoner
Bryan Sutton
Butterfly Boucher *
Canon Blue
Castro
CeCe Winans
Cheri Keaggy
Chris Brown

Chris Cornell
Chris Potter
Chris Rice
Christine Denté
Christy Nockels
Chris Walters
Cindy Morgan
CJ Camerieri (yMusic)
Dain Ussery
Dangerboy
Dan Haseltine
Danielle Young
   (Caedmon's Call) ***
Darwin Hobbs
Daves Highway
David Crowder Band
David Monsta Lynch
Dean Dillon **
Derrek Phillips

Selected Discography

Diana Beach
Dierks Bentley
Don Alias
Edd Bateman
Eddie Henderson
Ellie Schmidly
Emily West
Ensemblepossible
Eric Champion
Eric Harland
Erika Daves
Erin McCarley *
Felix Ngindu
Felix Pastorius
Gabriel Cabezas
  (yMusic)
Gene Watson **
George Rowe
Ginny Owens
Gino Robair
Gracie Schram
Grant Parker
Griffin House *
Gwyneth Paltrow
Henry Robinett
Hilmar Jensson
Holly Williams
I Love Ethyl
Jackson Browne
Jakob Dylan
James Genus
Jamey Johnson **
Janna Long
Jason Eskridge
Jeff Coffin
Jeff Taylor
Jeremy Lister
Jerry Douglas
Jill Phillips
Jillian Edwards
Jimmy Abegg
Jody Nardone

Joe Tex, with Edie ****
Joey Baron
Joey Richey
John Patitucci
Jonathan Winstead
Jon Foreman
Joy Williams
Justin York
Karen Bradley
Karl Denson's Tiny
  Universe
Katie Herzig *
Keith and Kristyn Getty
Kendall Payne
Kevin Max
Kim Hill
King Fire
Kirk Whalum
Kris Allen
k.s. Rhoads *
Kurt Rosenwinkel
Labial Fricative
Ladysmith Black
  Mambazo
Lee Ann Womack **
Leigh Nash
Lenachka
Lex Kuhl
Linda Good
Lisa Bevill
Mac Powell
  (Third Day) ***
Marc Martel
Marc Ribot
Marcus Printup
Margaret Becker
Mark Stuart (Audio
  Adrenaline) ***
Matt Berninger (The
  National)
Matt Endahl

Matthew Perryman
  Jones
Matthew White
Matt Wigton
Melissa Brock
  (Superchic[k])
Merle Haggard **
Michael Card
Michael English
Michael Roe
Michael W. Smith
Michelle Tumes
Miriam Jones
Myles Boisen
Nashville Recording
  Orchestra
Nate Gott
Nathan Tasker
Newsong
Nichole Nordeman
Nirva Dorsaint
Out of the Grey
Paper Route
Peter Bernstein
Philip Lassiter
Phil Keaggy
Rachael Lampa
Ralph Alessi
Ravi Coltrane
Rebecca St. James ***
Red Lane **
Rich Lang
Rich Mullins
Ricky Skaggs
Rico Thomas
Roger Miller ****
Roger Smith
Ruby Amanfu
Sam Ashworth
Sam and Ruby,
  feat. Flynn
Sandra McCracken

Selected Discography

Sara Groves
Sarah Hart
Sarah Masen
Savanah Packard
Scott Krippayne
Scott Mulvahill
Selah
Shaun Groves
Sixpence None the
Richer
Stacie Orrico
Steve Green
Steven Curtis Chapman
Steve Scott
Steve Swallow
Steve Taylor
Susan Ashton

Swagg R'Celious
Switchfoot
Sydney Layne
Tait
Tanner Azzinaro
Taylor Sorenson
The Choir
The Civil Wars
The Lone Bellow
The 77s
The Swoon
Tim Keegan
TobyMac
Tommy and the Whale
Tommy Hans
Tony Essamay
Tony Miracle

Tony Vincent
Trent Dabbs *
Turtle Island String
Quartet
Twila Paris
Tyler James *
VeNTUR BRV$$
Vicente Archer
Victor Wooten
Vince Ebo
Vince Gill
Warren Barfield
Wayne Kirkpatrick
Whitey Shafer **
WonderTwins
Zeke Duhon

* *Ten out of Tenn* (film)
** *The Legend Hank Cochran* (film)
*** *The Message/Remix* (audiobook)
**** Sony/ATV gave CP access to the original lead vocals of Roger Miller ("King of the Road") and Joe Tex ("I Gotcha") for the reinventions.

SELECTED LIST OF ARTISTS WHO HAVE RECORDED SONGS WRITTEN OR COWRITTEN BY CHARLIE PEACOCK

Aaron Spiro
Abigail Flowers
Al Perkins
Amy Grant
Andy Davis
Andy Leftwich
Anna Gilbert
Anthem Lights
Audio Adrenaline
Avalon
Bart Millard
Béla Fleck
Beth Williams
Bourgeois Tagg

Brandon Heath
Brent Bourgeois
Bryan Sutton
Castro
CeCe Winans
Cheri Keaggy
Chris Potter
Chris Rice
Christine Denté
Cindy Morgan
CJ Camerieri
Clare Bowen
Crystal Lewis
Dain Ussery

Darwin Hobbs
Daves Highway
David Monsta Lynch
dc Talk
Eddie Henderson
Elle King
Ellie Schmidly
Emily West
Enrique & Lucia
Eric Champion
Eric Harland
Gabriel Cabezas
Geoff Moore
Gracie Schram

Selected Discography

Jason Eskridge
Jason Gray
Jeff Coffin
Jeremy Lister
Jill Phillips
Jimmy A
Jody Nardone
Joey Richey
Joseph Solomon
Joy Williams
Keith and Kristyn Getty
Kevin Max
Kris Allen
Larry Tagg
Lenachka
Lisa Bevill
Marc Martel
Margaret Becker
Matt Berninger
Matt Endahl
Matthew White
Michael Card
Michael English
Michael Roe
Nashville Recording
    Orchestra

Nate Gott
Nathan Tasker
Newsong
Nia Peeples (*Fame*)
Nichole Nordeman
Nirva Dorsaint
Out of the Grey
Peter Bernstein
Philip Bailey
Philip Lassiter
Rachael Lampa
Ruby Amanfu
Russ Taff
Sal Valentino
Sam Ashworth
Sam Palladio
Sandra McCracken
Sara Groves
Sarah Masen
Scott Krippayne
Scott Mulvahill
Shane & Shane
Sixpence None
    the Richer
Steve Green
Steven Curtis Chapman

Steve Swallow
Steve Taylor
StorySide:B
Susan Ashton
Swagg R'Celious
Switchfoot
Tait
Taylor Sorenson
The Choir
The Civil Wars
The Damnwells
The Lone Bellow
The Wayside
TobyMac
Tony Miracle
Tony Vincent
Turtle Island String
    Quartet
Vector
VeNTUR BRV$$
Vince Ebo
Warren Barfield

NOTES

PRELUDE

1. Quotes in succession from: Wendell Berry, *Home Economics: Fourteen Essays* (New York: North Point, 1987), 56–57.

CHAPTER ONE

1. Adam Gold, "Civil Wars' Joy Williams: 'We Haven't Been on Speaking Terms,'" *Rolling Stone*, August 5, 2013, https://www.rollingstone.com/music/music-news/civil-wars-joy-williams-we-havent-been-on-speaking-terms-65989/.
2. Dave Itzkoff, "Citing 'Irreconcilable Differences,' The Civil Wars Cancels Tour Dates," *New York Times*, November 7, 2012, https://archive.nytimes.com/artsbeat.blogs.nytimes.com/2012/11/07/citing-irreconcilable-differences-the-civil-wars-cancels-tour-dates/.
3. Will Hermes, "The Civil Wars," *Rolling Stone*, August 1, 2013, https://www.rollingstone.com/music/music-album-reviews/the-civil-wars-109375/.

CHAPTER TWO

1. Frederick Law Olmsted, *Journey through Texas: A Saddle Trip on the Southwestern Frontier* (Lincoln: University of Nebraska Press, 2004), 386–87. Originally published (New York: Dix, Edwards, 1857).
2. Gonzaga University law professor and author Jason Gillmer is arguably the most academically stringent Ashworth researcher. His book, *Slavery and Freedom*

in Texas: Stories from the Courtroom, 1821–1871 (Athens: University of Georgia Press, 2017), is invaluable and the best source for detailed footnoting.

3. Bruce A. Glasrud and Michael N. Searles, eds., *Black Cowboys in the American West: On the Range, on the Stage, behind the Badge* (Norman: University of Oklahoma Press, 2016).

4. Quintard Taylor, *In Search of the Racial Frontier: African Americans in the American West, 1528–1990* (New York: Norton, 1998).

5. Tim Hashaw, *The Birth of Black America: The First African Americans and the Pursuit of Freedom at Jamestown* (New York: Basic Books, 2007).

6. Isabel Wilkerson, "How Did the Great Migration Change the Course of Human History?" *TED Radio Hour/NPR*, April 30, 2021, https://www.npr.org/2021/04/30/992040563/isabel-wilkerson-how-did-the-great-migration-change-the-course-of-human-history.

7. Details of the story in quotations are compiled from two Lake Charles newspaper clippings without masthead: (1) September 27, 1897 (courtesy of Verna Thompson, Ancestry.com) and (2) *Southern Items of Interest: Gleaned by the Picayune's Corps of Special Correspondents*, dated July 3, 1897 (courtesy of Ancestry.com), and the following full-page excerpts from Newspapers.com: *Times-Picayune* (New Orleans), July 3, 1897, p. 8; *Times-Democrat* (New Orleans), July 4, 1897, p. 9; *True Democrat* (St. Francisville, LA), July 10, 1897, p. 1; *Semi-Weekly Times-Democrat* (New Orleans), July 6, 1897, p. 3.

8. Detailed descriptions of the Ashworth brothers' sentencing, appearance, and subsequent deaths are found in *Register of the Louisiana State Penitentiary (Angola) No. 61*. Archie, prisoner No. 13600; Dempsey, 13599; and Owen, 13601. Transcript courtesy of Ancestry.com—photocopies of register in author's collection.

CHAPTER THREE

1. Charlie Peacock, "The Secret of Time," Sparrow Song admin. by capitol cmgpublishing.com/EMI Blackwood Music, Inc./Sony Music Publishing ©1990. All rights reserved. Used by permission.

2. Peacock, "The Secret of Time."

CHAPTER FOUR

1. Rainer Maria Rilke, *Letters to a Young Poet*, trans. M. D. Herter Norton, rev. ed. (New York: Norton, 2004), 27.

2. Quotes in succession from Steve Turner, *Jack Kerouac: Angelheaded Hipster* (New York: Viking Penguin, 1996), 23.

3. Turner, *Jack Kerouac*, 187.

4. Lewis Porter, *John Coltrane: His Life and Music* (Ann Arbor: University of Michigan Press, 2000), 96.

5. "The Five Pillars," Pluralism Project, Harvard University, accessed March 15, 2024, https://hwpi.harvard.edu/files/pluralism/files/the_five_pillars_1.pdf.

6. Jiddu Krishnamurti, "Banaras 1st Public Talk," January 9, 1955, https://www.jkrishnamurti.org/content/banaras-1st-public-talk-9th-january-1955/1955.

7. Unless otherwise indicated, biblical quotations in this book come from the New International Version (2011).

8. Chris DeVito, ed., *Coltrane on Coltrane: The John Coltrane Interviews* (Chicago: Chicago Review Press, 2010), 263.

9. Porter, *John Coltrane*, 258.

CHAPTER FIVE

1. Kimberly J. Bright, "'The Lord Works in 'Mysterious Ways' (or the Church That Nearly Destroyed U2)," *Dangerous Minds*, July 30, 2013, https://dangerous minds.net/comments/the_lord_works_in_mysterious_ways_or_the_church _that_nearly_destroyed_u2/.

2. Steve Beard, "U2 Observes the Passing of Its 'North Star': Pastor Jack Heaslip, RIP," *Thunderstruck: A Truckstop for the Soul*, February 26, 2015, https://thunder struck.org/u2-observes-the-passing-of-its-north-star-pastor-jack-heaslip-rip/.

3. The assertion is that the Christian rock artist was born out of the West Coast Jesus Movement. A movement made up of nondenominational, charismatic churches almost exclusively composed of white people. Black artists such as André Crouch and Jessy Dixon did play a role. However, one could argue that Sister Rosetta Tharpe was the first Christian rock artist of the twentieth century, not Larry Norman.

4. Duane Pederson, "Somebody Lied," *Hollywood Free Paper* 2, no. 15 (August 4, 1970).

5. Larry Norman, "Larry Norman: The Growth of the Christian Music Industry," *Cross Rhythms*, October 11, 2006, http://www.crossrhythms.co.uk/articles/music /Larry_Norman__The_Growth_Of_The_Christian_Music_Industry/24341/p3/.

6. Interview with Karen Hughes, *The Dominion* (Wellington, New Zealand), May 21, 1980, as collected in *Bob Dylan: The Essential Interviews*, ed. Jonathan Cott (New York: Simon & Schuster, 2017), 293.

7. Clinton Heylin, *Bob Dylan: Behind the Shades Revisited* (New York: HarperCollins, 2003), 491–502.

8. Bob Sylva, "Despite Lows, Rock Music Is Here to Stay," *Sacramento Bee*, June 20, 1983, 13.

9. David Barton, "Rock 'n' Roll Is Born Again," *Sacramento Bee*, November 25, 1983, 33.

10. For a deeper dive, see Charlie Peacock and Molly Nicholas, "Of Baptists and Folk Musicals," in *At the Crossroads* (Colorado Springs: Shaw/Random House, 2004), 55–63, and Leah Payne, *God Gave Rock and Roll to You: A History of Contemporary Christian Music* (New York: Oxford University Press, 2024).

11. The complete Exit Records roster was The 77s, Thomas Goodlunas and Panacea, Vector, Steve Scott, First Strike, Robert Vaughn and the Shadows, and CP.

12. See *Rolling Thunder Revue: A Bob Dylan Story*, Martin Scorsese's Netflix documentary.

13. I have written on this topic in full here: Charlie Peacock and Andi Ashworth, "The (Christian) Name Game: To Musicians and Music Lovers," in *Why Everything That Doesn't Matter, Matters So Much* (Nashville: HarperCollins, 2024).

14. David W. Stowe, "How Kennedy Center Honoree Amy Grant Has Walked the Line between 'Christian' and 'Secular' Music," *Salon*, November 26, 2022, https://www.salon.com/2022/11/26/how-kennedy-center-honoree-amy-grant-has-walked-the-line-between-christian-and-secular-music_partner/.

15. Ken Tucker, "Bob Dylan Redeems a Frequently Scorned Period of His Career on 'Trouble No More,'" *NPR Music*, November 1, 2017, https://www.npr.org/2017/11/01/561341675/bob-dylan-redeems-a-frequently-scorned-period-of-his-career-on-trouble-no-more/.

CHAPTER SIX

1. Bud Scoppa, "Jackson Browne," *Rolling Stone*, March 2, 1972, https://www.rollingstone.com/music/music-album-reviews/jackson-browne-98920/.

2. Bud Scoppa, *Music Connection*, March 21–April 3, 1988.

3. Fabio Testa, "Atlantic on the Pacific—Big Noise from the End of the Hallway," *Music Connection*, March 21–April 3, 1988.

CHAPTER SEVEN

1. Stephen Thompson, "The Lone Bellow, Live in Concert: Newport Folk 2013," *NPR Music*, July 28, 2013, https://www.npr.org/2013/07/28/204516999/the-lone-bellow-live-in-concert-newport-folk-2013.

2. Grady Smith, "The Ten Best Country Albums of 2013," *Entertainment Weekly*, December 18, 2013, https://ew.com/article/2013/12/18/best-country-albums-of-2013/.

3. Holly Gleason, "The Lone Bellow: *The Lone Bellow*," *Paste*, January 29, 2013, https://www.pastemagazine.com/article/the-lone-bellow-the-lone-bellow.

4. Eric R. Danton, "Holly Williams Follows Family's Americana Tradition on 'The Highway,'" *Rolling Stone*, January 28, 2013, https://www.rollingstone.com/music/music-news/holly-williams-follows-familys-americana-tradition-on-the-highway-243977/.

5. Gayle Forman, *Where She Went* (New York: Penguin Books, 2011), 37.

Notes

CHAPTER EIGHT

1. "The Pilgrim: Chapter 33." Words and Music by Kris Kristofferson. Copyright © 1970 Resaca Music Publishing Co. Copyright Renewed. All Rights Administered by Sony Music Publishing (US) LLC, 424 Church Street, Suite 1200, Nashville, TN 37219. International Copyright Secured All Rights Reserved. Reprinted by Permission of Hal Leonard LLC.
2. D. T. Suzuki, *Essays in Zen Buddhism (Second Series)* (London: Rider & Co., 1950), 5.
3. Paul Simon, *Seven Psalms*, 2023.

CHAPTER TEN

1. John Paul II, "Angelus," Adelaide, Australia, November 30, 1986, https://www.vatican.va/content/john-paul-ii/en/angelus/1986/documents/hf_jp-ii_ang_19861130.html.
2. David Dark, *Life's Too Short to Pretend You're Not Religious* (Downers Grove, IL: InterVarsity Press, 2016), 189.

CHAPTER TWELVE

1. Ann Powers, "The Civil Wars: Marching into the Unknown," Pop & Hiss, *Los Angeles Times*, February 17, 2011.
2. Used with permission of Capitol Christian Music Group Publishing.

CHAPTER THIRTEEN

1. Jack Kerouac, *On the Road* (New York: Penguin Books, 1976), 5.
2. Kerouac, *On the Road*, 181.
3. Chris Heath, "The Epic Life of Carlos Santana," *Rolling Stone*, March 16, 2000.
4. Charlie Peacock, "Climb a Tree," Sparrow Song, admin. by capitolcmgpublishing.com ©1994. All rights reserved. Used by permission.
5. Charlie Peacock, "Deep Inside a Word," Patron & Profit Publishing ©2012. All rights reserved. Used by permission.
6. Wendell Berry, excerpt from "The Peace of Wild Things" from *New Collected Poems*. Copyright © 2012 by Wendell Berry. Reprinted with permission of the Permissions Company, LLC, on behalf of Counterpoint Press, counterpointpress.com.

CHAPTER FOURTEEN

1. John A. Sutter, "The Discovery of Gold in California," originally published in *Hutchings' California Magazine*, November 1857, http://www.sfmuseum.org /hist2/gold.html.

2. Mike Andrelczyk, "General Sutter Inn in Lititz Removes Statue of John Sutter," *LancasterOnline*, June, 19, 2020, https://lancasteronline.com/news /general-sutter-inn-in-lititz-removes-statue-of-john-sutter/article_a0f881a2-b16d -11ea-aa88-8b85f6cfe229.html.

CHAPTER FIFTEEN

1. Augustine, *The City of God* (London: Catholic Way Publishing, 2015), 903.

2. Chris Gray, "Gatemouth Brown's Grave Intact . . . Sort Of," *Houston Press*, September 25, 2008, https://www.houstonpress.com/music/gatemouth-browns -grave-intact-sort-of-6755687.

3. Nolan Thompson, "Ashworth Act," *Handbook of Texas Online*, accessed March 20, 2024, https://www.tshaonline.org/handbook/entries/ashworth-act.

4. Jack Kerouac, *Mexico City Blues: 242 Choruses* (New York: Grove Atlantic, 2007), 211.

5. Peter Scholtes, "They'll Know We Are Christians," © 1966, F.E.L. Publications. Assigned 1991 Lorenz Publishing Company (Administered by Music Services). All Rights Reserved. Used by permission.

6. Bono, "Keynote Address at the 54th National Prayer Breakfast," delivered February 2, 2006, Hilton Washington Hotel, Washington, DC, https://www .americanrhetoric.com/speeches/bononationalprayerbreakfast.htm.

7. Robert Bellah, "Civil Religion in America," *Dædalus: Journal of the American Academy of Arts and Sciences* 96, no. 1 (Winter 1967): 1–21, http://hirr.hart sem.edu/Bellah/articles_5.htm.

8. Bellah, "Civil Religion in America."

9. George W. Bush, "President Sworn-In to Second Term," White House, Office of the Press Secretary, January 20, 2005, https://georgewbush-whitehouse .archives.gov/news/releases/2005/01/20050120-1.html.

10. Michael Gerson, "Opinion: Trump Should Fill Christians with Rage. How Come He Doesn't?," *Washington Post*, September 1, 2022, https://www.washing tonpost.com/opinions/2022/09/01/michael-gerson-evangelical-christian-maga -democracy/.

11. Reprinted by permission of Jay's widow, Jamie Swartzendruber.

CHAPTER SIXTEEN

1. Christopher Wilson, "The Moment When Four Students Sat Down to Take a Stand," *Smithsonian*, January 31, 2020, https://www.smithsonianmag.com

/smithsonian-institution/lessons-worth-learning-moment-greensboro-four-sat
-down-lunch-counter-180974087/.

2. Wendell Berry, "It All Turns on Affection," Jefferson Lecture in the Human-
ities, 2012, https://www.neh.gov/article/wendell-berry-library-america.

3. For Art House information, see "Resources," in Peacock and Ashworth,
Why Everything That Doesn't Matter, Matters So Much.

4. Erin Clements, "My Brightest Diamond: The 5 Things I Can't Live Without," *Huffington Post*, October 6, 2011, https://www.huffpost.com/entry/my
-brightest-diamond_n_996580.

CHAPTER SEVENTEEN

1. Leah Payne, *God Gave Rock and Roll to You: A History of Contemporary
Christian Music* (New York: Oxford University Press, 2024), 71.

2. Mark F. Turner, "Charlie Peacock: Love Press Ex-Curio," album review,
All about Jazz, September 19, 2005, https://www.allaboutjazz.com/love-press-ex
-curio-charlie-peacock-runway-network-review-by-mark-f-turner.

3. See Charlie Peacock and Andi Ashworth: "Dangling over the Cliff and
Other Dangers: To the Sick and Suffering," in *Why Everything That Doesn't Matter, Matters So Much.*

4. See Peacock and Ashworth, chapters 12 and 13, *Why Everything That Doesn't
Matter, Matters So Much.*

CHAPTER EIGHTEEN

1. Charlie Peacock, "Experience," Sparrow Song admin. by capitolcmgpub
lishing.com/EMI Blackwood Music, Inc./Sony Music Publishing ©1990. All
rights reserved. Used by permission.

2. Peacock, "The Secret of Time."

3. Peacock, "The Secret of Time."

POSTLUDE

1. Production credits for *Stage Left* are omitted from the Selected Discography
since the project was not complete before publishing *Roots & Rhythm.*

2. Charlie Peacock, "Welcome," ©2024.